Managers in European Law

Bulletin of Comparative Labour Relations

VOLUME 118

Founding Editor

The series started in 1970 under the dynamic editorship of Professor Roger Blanpain (Belgium), former President of the International Industrial Relations Association. Professor Blanpain, Professor Emeritus of Labour Law, Universities of Leuven and Tilburg, was also General Editor of the International Encyclopedia of Laws (with more than 1,600 collaborators worldwide) and President of the Association of Educative and Scientific Authors Authors. He passed away in October 2016.

General Editor

In 2015 Frank Hendrickx, Professor of labour law at the Faculty of Law of the University of Leuven (Belgium) joined as a co-Editor. Frank Hendrickx has published numerous articles and books and regularly advises governments, international institutions and private organisations in the area of labour law as well as in sports law. He is the Editor-in-Chief of the European Labour Law Journal and General Editor of the International Encyclopaedia of Laws.

Introduction

The Bulletins constitute a unique source of information and thought-provoking discussion, laying the groundwork for studies of employment relations in the 21st century, involving among much else the effects of globalization, new technologies, migration, and the greying of the population.

Contents/Subjects

Amongst other subjects the Bulletins frequently include the proceedings of international or regional conferences; reports from comparative projects devoted to salient issues in industrial relations, human resources management, and/or labour law; and specific issues underlying the multicultural aspects of our industrial societies.

Objective

The Bulletins offer a platform of expression and discussion on labour relations to scholars and practitioners worldwide, often featuring special guest editors.

The titles published in this series are listed at the end of this volume.

Managers in European Law

Rights and Duties of Executive and Non-executive Managers in a European Perspective

Edited by

Natalie Videbæk Munkholm
Vincenzo Pietrogiovanni
Karsten Engsig Sørensen

Contributors

Peter Ahlberg
Charlotte Bruynseraede
Ana Cristina Ribeiro Costa
Sjur Swensen Ellingsæter
Gerard Everaet
Mette Søsted Hemme
Andrea Iossa
Pernille Wegener Jessen
Line Herman Langkjær
Natalie Videbæk Munkholm
Fieke van Overbeeke
Vincenzo Pietrogiovanni
Paul Schoukens
Achim Seifert
Gitte Søgaard
Karsten Engsig Sørensen
Christoph Teichmann

General Editor
Frank Hendrickx

Founding Editor
Roger Blanpain

Wolters Kluwer

Published by:
Kluwer Law International B.V.
PO Box 316
2400 AH Alphen aan den Rijn
The Netherlands
E-mail: lrs-sales@wolterskluwer.com
Website: www.wolterskluwer.com/en/solutions/kluwerlawinternational

Sold and distributed by:
Wolters Kluwer Legal & Regulatory U.S.
920 Links Avenue
Landisville, PA 17538
United States of America
E-mail: customer.service@wolterskluwer.com

ISBN 978-94-035-3286-8

e-Book: ISBN 978-94-035-3316-2
web-PDF: ISBN 978-94-035-3326-1

Printed in the Netherlands.

Notes on Contributors

Peter Ahlberg is an attorney with the law firm Poul Schmith/Kammeradvokaten where he specializes in EU law in a broad sense, including EU anti-discrimination law, fundamental rights, general principles of EU law, Member State liability and state aid and market regulation. He has represented the Danish State and public institutions in various court cases concerning EU law before the national courts and the Court of Justice of the EU. He is also an external lecturer at Aarhus University.

Charlotte Bruynseraede is a doctoral researcher at the Institute for Social Law at the Catholic University of Leuven, Belgium. In her research, she focuses on recalibrating the financing method for the social protection of self-employed workers in Belgium. Based on an evaluation of the Belgian system against predefined EU criteria and a comparative law study, her research formulates concrete proposals to optimize the Belgian system in order to provide a more adequate social protection for self-employed workers without jeopardizing the financial sustainability of the system.

Ana Cristina Ribeiro Costa holds a Ph.D. from Universidade Católica Portuguesa, Faculdade de Direito, Escola do Porto, Portugal. She is Associate Professor at the same institution and affiliated to the Católica Research Centre for the Future of Law. Her research has focused on international labour law, particularly occupational health and safety law. She is a scholar of the United States of America Department of State, designated by the Fulbright Commission for the program Study of the United States Institutes on Youth, Workplace Development, and Closing the Skills Gap. Ana also works as a lawyer, serving currently as a managing counsel – Employment at Remote.

Sjur Swensen Ellingsæter is since 2020 Associate Professor at the Department of Law and Governance at BI Norwegian Business School. In 2019, he obtained a Ph.D. from the University of Oslo, Norway, having written a doctoral thesis on creditor priority in EU bank insolvency law. His research primarily concerns bank insolvency law, general insolvency law and financial regulation. He chairs the research group on Supervision and Enforcement of EU/EEA Law Economic Regulation (SupER) hosted at BI and is a member of the Younger Academics Network of Insolvency Law (YANIL) of INSOL Europe.

Gerard Everaet is a doctoral researcher and teaching assistant at the Catholic University of Leuven's Institute for Social Law, Belgium. His research focuses on the *lex loci laboris* principle in the context of social security coordination within the European Union. More concretely, he examines whether the choice for the *lex loci laboris* principle as the main connecting factor for social security coordination is still justified and if solutions could be proposed to deal with the difficulties encountered with this connecting factor.

Mette Søsted Hemme is Assistant Professor at the Department of Law, Aarhus University, specialized in labour and employment law, European labour law and public employment law. She holds a Ph.D. in Danish dismissal law. She has published journal articles in esteemed national and international journals, and she has contributed to several books on labour law-related topics such as the right to strike, the EU Directive on adequate minimum wages and platform work. Since 2019, she has been National Expert (Denmark) for the European Labour Law Network (ELLN), and she is member of the research group ARROW – Aarhus Research on Regulation of Work. In her current research, she focuses on public employment, and she is the co-author of a textbook on the administrative law aspects of employment in the public sector.

Andrea Iossa is Senior Lecturer in Labour Law at Kristianstad University, Sweden. He holds a Ph.D. in Labour Law from Lund University, Sweden, and has been Postdoctoral Fellow at the Faculty of Law of Lund University. He has been Visiting Fellow at the Global College of Law at the UC Louvain, Belgium, and Visiting Scholar at the Centre for Sociological Research at KU Leueven, Belgium. He is in the organizing and scientific committee of the Moving Labour Collective – an international network of progressive labour lawyers. His research interests cover European and comparative labour law and industrial relations, EU internal market law, labour migration, and legal geography.

Pernille Wegener Jessen, Ph.D., is Professor at the Department of Law, Aarhus University, Denmark, specialized in competition and state aid law. She is the author and co-author of multiple national and international publications and has participated in a variety of national and international research projects. She is appointed Deputy Chairman of the Telecommunications Board of Appeal; appointed substitute member of the Danish Rail Regulatory Body; former appointed member of the Danish Competition Council; board member of the Danish State Aid Law Association and board member of the Danish Competition Law Society; further, she is a member of the research group ARROW – Aarhus Research on Regulation of Work.

Line Herman Langkjær, Ph.D., is since 2021 Associate Professor at the Department of Law, Aarhus University, Denmark. She specializes in insolvency and civil procedural law. She is the author and co-author of publications internationally and in Denmark, addressing different matters on national and international insolvency and civil procedural law. Line is a member of multiple international and European insolvency law organizations, such as the International Insolvency Institute and CERIL. She participates in several European and Global research projects. She is a board member of

INSOL Europe, and since 2018 Line has been advising and representing the Danish Government in UNCITRAL Working Group V (insolvency).

Natalie Videbæk Munkholm, is Associate Professor at the Department of Law, Aarhus University, Denmark. She holds a Danish cand.jur. law degree, an LLM (University of New South Wales, Australia), and a Ph.D. in Labour and Employment Law. She specializes in labour and employment law, European labour law, non-discrimination and fundamental rights at work. She is the author and co-author of multiple publications addressing all matters relating to the regulation of the workplace and industrial relations. Natalie is National Expert (Denmark) to the European Labour Law Network (ELLN) which advises the European Commission. She participates in several Danish, Nordic, European and Global research projects, as well as advises social partners and the Ministry of Employment. She is a board member of the Danish Association of Labour Law and the Danish representative to the International Society of Labour and Social Security Law (ISLSSL); appointed member of the Danish Board of Equal Treatment; chairman of the board of the Danish Research Foundation for Labour Law; and co-founder of the research group ARROW - Aarhus Research on Regulation of Work affiliated with the Labour Law Research Network (LLRN).

Fieke van Overbeeke is CEO and legal counsel for private international law and foreign law at The Hague-based non-profit 'Internationaal Juridisch Instituut' (IJI). Fieke is also a research fellow in private international law at the University of Antwerp, Belgium, and Guest Lecturer in private international law at various universities, such as the University of Amsterdam, the Netherlands, and the University of Aruba, Aruba. Her primary consulting, teaching and research expertise covers commercial law, cross-border litigation and conflict of laws. Fieke holds a Doctorate in Law from the University of Antwerp, Belgium, regarding social competition and conflict of laws in the European road transport sector. Fieke has published many private international law-oriented articles and is often invited to speak and lecture about this topic in places all over the world.

Vincenzo Pietrogiovanni holds a Ph.D. from the University of Bari, Italy. Currently serving as Associate Professor at the Law Department of the University of Southern Denmark, his academic journey has been marked by a dedication to international, European and comparative aspects of labour law. His research portfolio encompasses a wide spectrum, with a primary focus on global, international, European, and comparative labour law, along with a keen interest in industrial relations and human rights at work. He is currently investigating the implications of artificial intelligence and climate change on labour law, as well as the far-reaching impact of the recently enacted Directive on Adequate Minimum Wages in Europe. Beyond his research endeavours, he is an esteemed member of the Editorial Board of the *Italian Labour Law e-Journal* and the co-founder of the research group ARROW - Aarhus Research on Regulation of Work. His contributions extend internationally, as he has also been a member of the Advisory Committee of the Labour Law Research Network (LLRN) and a founder member of the Moving Labour Collective, in which he takes part in the Organising Committee of the Summer Camp 'Working on The Future of Labour Law'.

Paul Schoukens is Full Professor of Social Security Law at the KU Leuven (Faculty of Law), Belgium. At Tilburg University, the Netherlands, he holds the *Chair International and European Social Security Law*, endowed by the *Instituut Gak*. He became in 2013 Secretary-General of the European Institute of Social Security, an international scientific network of persons professionally active in the fields of social security and social protection. He is Academic Director of the specialized Master's programme Social Security in Europe. He earned his doctorate with research on the impact of European Union law on the social protection of self-employed people and specialized further in the domain of atypical work in social security. He is the author of a high number of academic articles and is often invited to speak at international meetings and conferences. In his capacity as researcher, he is involved in a number of international projects, some of them specifically related to the development of social security regulations and models in Central and Eastern Europe. He was the head of the Erasmus+ project *Efese*, developing virtual exchange modules for hybrid distance education and is currently running the student exchange office of the Faculty of Law (KU Leuven, Belgium).

Achim Seifert is Professor of Private Law, German and European Labour Law and Comparative Law at the Friedrich-Schiller-University Jena, Germany. He previously taught European and International Labour Law at the University of Luxembourg and Private Law as well as Labour Law at the University of Trier, Germany, and the Johann-Wolfgang Goethe-University Frankfurt/Main, Germany. His main fields of interest are European and international labour law as well as comparative labour law including in particular employee participation in the board and employee data protection. He serves as a member of the Editorial Board of the *European Labour Law Journal* (ELLJ), the *Comparative Labor Law & Policy Journal* (CLLPJ) and of the *Revue de droit comparé du travail et de la sécurité sociale*. He has been Visiting Professor at the Universities of Bordeaux, Leuven, Nantes, Paris 1 (Panthéon-Sorbonne) and at the University Luigi Bocconi in Milan and Visiting Fellow at the Centre for Business Research of the University of Cambridge.

Gitte Søgaard, Ph.D., is Associate Professor at the Department of Law, Aalborg University, Denmark. Her research is within the scope of Danish and international company law and group law. She is the author and co-author of national and international books and articles. Gitte Søgaard is also a lawyer.

Karsten Engsig Sørensen is Professor at the Department of Law, Aarhus University, Denmark. He holds a Danish law degree, an LLM (from Exeter), a Ph.D. (on EU Company Law), and a Danish Dr. Jur. (on joint ventures). His research is mainly focused on company law and EU law and in particular the regulation of the internal market. Within these areas, he has published several books and articles in both Danish and English. He is the co-author of a comprehensive textbook on EU law (EU-Retten) which is now in its 8th edition, and he has recently co-edited a book marking the fifty-year anniversary of the Danish EU membership.

Christoph Teichmann is Professor at the University of Wuerzburg, Germany, where he teaches Civil Law, German and European Commercial and Company Law. He graduated from the University of Heidelberg, Germany, where he also obtained his doctoral degree. He then worked for two years as a lawyer for a law firm in Frankfurt, Germany. In 1998, he returned to the University of Heidelberg, Germany, where he wrote his habilitation thesis (Binnenmarktkonformes Gesellschaftsrecht). He worked as a lecturer at the universities of Heidelberg and Bielefeld. In 2007, he accepted a chair (tenure track) at the University of Wuerzburg, Germany. His research focuses on German, comparative and European company law. He is a co-editor of *ZGR* (*Zeitschrift für Unternehmens- und Gesellschaftsrecht*) and ECFR (*European Company and Financial Law Review*) and a member of several international working groups on company law, including the EMCA group (European Model Company Act) and the ICLEG (Informal Company Law Expert Group).

Summary of Contents

Table of Contents

PART I Overall Framework

CHAPTER 1

Introduction

Natalie Videbæk Munkholm, Vincenzo Pietrogiovanni & Karsten Engsig Sørensen

§1.01 INTRODUCTION

All forms of business organizations depend on having one or more persons[1] who can legitimately make strategic business decisions in the ongoing activities of running the businesses. Managers have an important role to play in ensuring economic growth as well as high levels of social and environmental sustainability. The more complex and diverse a business organization gets, the more compound become the levels of managerial tasks and activities. But what are the legal entitlements of such key professionals? They are imposed special duties by different kinds of legislation and do not usually enjoy all labour law rights and protections. This raises the question of how managers' rights and duties are determined. Often, it will be a question of differentiating managers from employees, but other problems may arise, for instance, when differentiating managers from owners.

Despite the importance of these topics, however, the legal research on the status of managers has been limited. The legal entitlements of managers have often been neglected in labour law scholarship, and the comparable topic of their rights and duties is often also under-researched in other areas of law. Furthermore, there has not yet been any attempt to take a broader comparative look at how the delimitation of rights and duties of executive and non-executive managers is done in different areas of law.

This book aims to contribute with a broader investigation of this topic and provide structural insights into the topic of the legal status of managers in European law. Moreover, the broad approach of the book will allow us to pinpoint similarities and differences across the different fields of European law.

---

1. Some countries allow for corporate directors, whereby legal persons are appointed to manage the company. Corporate directors raise a number of different questions and will therefore not be the focus of this book.

The need to deepen our knowledge on the legal dimensions of executive and non-executive managers stems from a potential flaw in the current legislation: despite being at the forefront in the transition towards a new economic and business model, this group of workers may not enjoy consistent protections. An analysis of the current legislations in Europe – i.e., domestic rules as well as EU rules – will enable ascertaining more specifically if and from where any discrepancies in their legal framework originate.

A number of recent legal developments may affect how managers operate and, thus, affect their rights and duties. These developments make the focus of the book even more topical.

First, the fact that the corporate form is sometimes used for abusive practices may have as a consequence that those registered as managers may not be those who are in fact managing the companies. Such uses of front directors make it more difficult to determine the rights and duties of both the front directors and those who act as de facto managers.

Second, there is an ongoing discussion on how employees (and to some degree even other stakeholders) may be more involved in the management of the companies, *inter alia*, to enhance a more sustainable business model. This raises the question of which rights and duties should be provided to such stakeholder representatives, given they are involved in the management of companies. This issue becomes even more complicated when employees are invited to participate in the ownership of the company.

Third, there are several trends in current EU law that increase the need to protect managers, such as interpretations of the Court of Justice of the European Union (CJEU) in recent case law, for instance, in Case C-101/21, *HJ*;[2] Case C-587/20, *HK Danmark*;[3] and Case C-232/09, *Danosa*[4] as well as trends that increase the need to hold managers liable: for instance, the new Directive (EU) 2022/2555 on cyber security[5] which underlines that the management bodies of essential and important entities must approve and oversee cybersecurity risk-management measures and can be held liable for infringements, cf. Article 20(1).

Fourth, one of the reasons for the lack of research on the status of managers in labour law is definitely the idea that managers usually are powerful professionals who, first, have considerable strength vis-à-vis the company as employer when negotiating terms and conditions of their work, and, second, within the company, they usually act as bosses, representing the company's interests as employer and using their managerial prerogatives on their behalf: For these reasons, they have often been excluded from general employment protections provided by labour laws. The position of managers,

2. Case C-101/21, *HJ v. Ministerstvo práce a sociálních věcí*, 5.5.2022, ECLI:EU:C:2022:356.
3. Case C-587/20, *Ligebehandlingsnævnet acting on behalf of A v. HK/Danmark and HK/Privat*, 2.6.2022, ECLI:EU:C:2022:419.
4. Case C-232/09, *Dita Danosa v. LKB Līzings SIA*, 11.11.2010, ECLI:EU:C:2010:674.
5. Directive (EU) 2022/2555 of the European Parliament and of the Council of 14 December 2022 on measures for a high common level of cybersecurity across the Union, amending Regulation (EU) No. 910/2014 and Directive (EU) 2018/1972, and repealing Directive (EU) 2016/1148 (NIS 2 Directive) (Text with EEA relevance).

nowadays, is however no longer as marginal or elevated as it used to be. According to EU statistics in 2019, nearly 9.4 million persons held a managerial position across the EU's Member States. The new reality of business models, with increased numbers of managerial positions even at lower levels of the hierarchal structures of decision-making, means that many managers currently can no longer inherently be considered unworthy of employment protection. Often, they lack substantial strength vis-à-vis the company as the employer, being under strict scrutiny of top managers, and they are not automatically placed in a position to fully exercise any managerial prerogatives over other employees.

The aim of the book therefore is to further investigate in a comparative and interdisciplinary way the concrete allocation of rights and duties for natural persons performing work as executive and non-executive managers.

§1.02 STRUCTURE AND METHODOLOGY

In order to reconstruct a clear and comprehensive legal framework on managers in Europe, the authors will analyse the position of managers under different areas of law and across different jurisdictions (namely, EU and national law).

The book is divided into three parts. Part I introduces the overarching theme and addresses the main definitions and methodologies of the book. Part II provides discipline-based reflections, with the aim to briefly outline either the main rights or duties of managers in the field and how it is delimited or defined which managers are subject to such rights or duties, in domestic legal systems as well as at EU level. The chapters cover a diverse range of rights and duties such as managers' right to exercise their freedom of movement within the EU, the consequences of their disqualifications, how managers may be the target of sanctioning for infringements of competition law, the applicable private international law rules for the regulation of managers, the right to information and consultation for managers, the status of employees appointed to company boards and taking a seat as non-executive management, as well as the protection of managers in relation to occupational health and safety, non-discrimination in access to management positions, and their rights in the event of insolvency of the company. Part III builds on all previous contributions, analysing cross-cutting themes related to indicators, convergences, problems and possible solutions across the different fields of EU law.

The prevailing method of each contribution is the legal dogmatic method. But the overall approach of the book is interdisciplinary, understood as the same issue of rights and duties addressed in different legal fields, and comparative, understood as investigating similarities and differences among domestic legislations as well as between domestic and EU levels.

This interdisciplinary approach allows similarities and differences to surface as well as to question if there are any incoherencies or deficits in the existing European legal framework. Incoherencies and deficits are understood as apparent contradictions, conflicting overlaps, or clear gaps in the rights and duties of managers. And it allows us to investigate whether such potential flaws can be traced back to variations in the method for delimiting the concept of managers (vis-à-vis worker) in the different fields of law.

The functional starting point of the analysis is the situation of the natural person performing work as a manager for a company. The idea is that if the status of the person fluctuates substantially across different aspects of European law, and this fluctuating status does not follow an underlying rationale or purpose of the different fields of law, this uncertainty of status would lead to uncertainty about rights and duties for the person performing work as a manager, as well as for the companies employing the managers. And – in the very broad picture – uncertainties or legal conflicts in the rights and duties of managers could give room for speculations as to how and where to organize and structure companies in the European markets.

§1.03 CONCEPTS AND DEFINITIONS

Another methodological challenge is that the subjects of the book are 'managers'. For a book with the legal status of 'managers' as the main theme, an immediate point of attention is that different Member States have different corporate systems, a variety of structures and mandates for decision-making bodies, and also various legal terms for the members of the decision-making bodies and managers in general.

In order to facilitate the consistency, the cross-referencing, and the comparative conclusions and perspectives aimed for with the book, all chapters in the book refer to a common cross-cutting terminology, when possible. In addition, Chapters 2 and 3 of the book are dedicated to mapping out differences in structure and terminology with a view to give a shared baseline for the rest of the chapters.

The terms 'executive managers' and 'non-executive managers' are used throughout the book.

An 'executive manager' is someone who is involved in the day-to-day running of the company, and who has a senior position where he or she refers to a board, or to the shareholders' general meetings. The term is used for the general references and descriptions.

A 'non-executive manager' is a person who is not involved in the day-to-day management but has a – normally part-time – position in the company where he or she takes on a supervisory role vis-à-vis executive management, and sometimes are also involved in taking certain important decisions.

When discussing members of management in a specific jurisdiction, authors use the more appropriate terms applicable, i.e., director, member of supervisory board, etc., and include the national expression in brackets, e.g., managing director (*administrerende direktør*).

Managers, in particular non-executive managers, will normally be part of a company's management organ(s). A company's management organs may be a board of directors, a supervisory board, or similar. If a specific jurisdiction is discussed, the more precise terms for the decision-making organ are used. But, if the reference is to such organs in mere general terms, the terms 'board of executive and non-executive managers' or similar are used.

The term 'company' refers to all corporate forms. If a particular type of company is discussed, i.e., private limited company, cooperatives, etc., that term is used.

§1.04 OVERVIEW OF THE BOOK

[A] Part I, Chapters 1-3

In *Part I, Chapter 1* is the introduction.

In *Chapter 2 on governance structures*, the author describes and discusses the great variety of governance structures in Europe, as corporate governance structures have not been harmonized by EU law. On top of the complexity of having different structures with different organs of different names and functions, there are also different names for the actors being members of these organs. Governance roles can be seen as split between persons who have either 'executive' or 'non-executive' roles, but these functions are not necessarily allocated to different company organs. Day-to-day management of the business organization is related to executive roles, while matters of strategic importance and/or supervisory functions, which are not involved in the day-to-day management of business, are taken care of by persons with non-executive roles.

Chapter 3 on executive and non-executive directors in EU provides a further overview and analysis of the roles of executive and non-executive directors in the EU Member States. National company law provides the framework for mechanisms for attributing tasks and duties to the directors and/or the shareholders. Among the rights and duties allocated to directors is the right to represent the company vis-à-vis third parties, the duty to manage the internal affairs of the company, and ensuring the company complies with duties in the public interest. The chapter discusses the definitions of de jure, de facto, and shadow directors and potential liabilities. Most often, liabilities apply to the de jure director, as well as to others with comparable managing power, which is assessed by the courts on a case-by-case basis.

[B] Part II, Chapters 4-14

Part II analyses the status of managers in EU law and how to delineate the natural persons who may be affected by specific liabilities and who are entitled to specific rights. Chapters 4-5 investigate potential sanctions and liabilities imposed on executive and non-executive managers and whether this applies equally to de jure, de facto and shadow managers, as well as employee representatives on boards; Chapters 6-13 investigate rights or protections given to employees under EU law and analyse to what extent these benefits are extended to managers.

Chapter 4 on disqualification investigates which persons may be disqualified from being part of management organs. EU law requires that Member States have national rules on disqualification, and the chapter analyses the disqualification rules in Norway, Denmark and the UK. The three jurisdictions take a functional approach and equate de facto and de jure participation in management organs. The public interest in ensuring qualified management of companies applies to both de jure and de facto management. For a disqualification order to be effective, it is necessary to counteract circumvention by the use of formally appointed 'straw men' or front directors taking orders from shadow managers.

Chapter 5 on individual sanctioning of managers for complicity in competition law infringements discusses the significance of managerial status in relation to the Member States' sanctioning for competition law infringements under Article 101 TFEU. When a national authority enforces Article 101, the sanctioning of undertakings must comply with the EU *acquis* and be effective, proportionate and dissuasive. Conversely, sanctions against natural persons in the EU Member States are not harmonized in this area, and the legal position of non-executive and executive managers will depend on which national jurisdiction(s) undertake(s) the enforcement of a particular competition law infringement. When an EU Member State enables sanctioning of natural persons, it is often directed at individuals in managerial positions that may influence the conduct of the undertaking, e.g., exercise de facto leadership in relation to the company's infringement of competition law.

Chapter 6 on free movement of managers explains that companies and managers can challenge national rules that may hinder the free movement of managers. In this, managers may invoke free movement of workers (Article 45 TFEU), or free movement as self-employed under freedom of establishment (Article 49) and freedom to provide services (Article 56). The concept of 'worker' in Article 45 is an autonomous uniform concept at EU level. When deciding whether a manager is a worker or is self-employed, the CJEU uses a functional approach where it becomes decisive whether the managers according to national company law may be instructed and dismissed by another corporate body. For executive managers who are employed and supervised by either a supervisory board or a board of directors consisting of both executive and non-executive directors, it is likely that there is the necessary level of subordination to grant worker status. For non-executive and executive managers elected by the shareholders at the general meeting, a worker status seems less likely. The rules protecting the free movement of managers between the EU and third countries are however considerably more formalistic.

Chapter 7 on managers as employees in private international law analyses whether managers in cross-border situations are covered by private international law rules aiming to protect 'employees'. EU Private International Law rules on choice of jurisdiction,[6] choice of law,[7] and recognition and enforcement of judgments,[8] recognize that employees should receive special protection. If managers are qualified as employees, the Private International Law provisions could prevent a company from choosing a jurisdiction and labour law system with little protection for managers. The

6. Regulation (EU) No. 1215/2012 of the European Parliament and of the Council of 12 December 2012 on jurisdiction and the recognition and enforcement of judgments in civil and commercial matters, OJ L 351, 20.12.2012 (Brussels 1a).
7. Regulation (EC) No. 593/2008 of the European Parliament and of the Council of 17 June 2008 on the law applicable to contractual obligations (Rome I), OJ L 177, 4.7.2008.
8. Brussels 1a, Arts 36-39.

term 'employee' in Brussels 1a on jurisdiction is interpreted in light of the concept of 'worker' in Article 45 TFEU, where subordination between the manager and the company is key. The assessment is based on all factors and circumstances characterizing the relationship between the parties rather than the formalities in the contractual relationship. The conflict-of-law rules of Rome I have not yet been interpreted in the context of managers. Further incoherencies can occur if Rome I is applied in conjunction with the Posting of Workers Directive,[9] as here the temporary working state (host state) determines the status of the worker. Combined with a variety of legislation in the Member States on the topic of managers and employee protection, this could have negative implications for the legal certainty and foreseeability of the application of these Private International Law instruments.

Chapter 8 analyses the *coordination of social security for managers* in cross-border work situations. The Member States define the content and scope of their social security systems as social security is outside the competency of the EU as stated in Article 153(3) TFEU. For managers working in cross-border situations, the coordination between the Member States' social security systems is regulated by EU Regulation 883/2004 on the coordination of social security systems, and its implementing Regulation 987/2009.[10] The EU Regulations give precedence to wage-earner activities over self-employed activities when indicating which state is the competent state for social security purposes. This is particularly interesting when the competent state must assess the nature of activities in another Member State when work is performed simultaneously in several Member States. Under national law, a manager may fall under either an employee social security scheme, a self-employed social security scheme or a special social security scheme, which is illustrated in the chapter's analysis and comparison of five selected national social security systems. The national variety in scope and content of social security systems for managers leads to a number of questions for managers performing work in another Member State, in particular when performing work simultaneously in several Member States. This is further complicated by the current lack of an option under EU law for the competent state to requalify the status given by another Member State, as well as the emergence of new forms of work, such as telework and managing from a distance, where the current rules for designating the competent state are far from clear.

---

9. Directive 96/71/EC of the European Parliament and of the Council of 16 December 1996 concerning the posting of workers in the framework of the provision of services, OJ L 18, 21.1.1997; Directive 2014/67 of the European Parliament and of the Council of 15 May 2014 on the enforcement of Directive 96/71/EC concerning the posting of workers in the framework of the provision of services and amending Regulation 1024/2012 on administrative cooperation through the Internal Market Information System (Enforcement Directive), OJ L 159, 28.5.2014; Directive (EU) 2018/957 of the European Parliament and of the Council of 28 June 2018 amending Directive 96/71/EC concerning the posting of workers in the framework of the provision of services (Revision Directive), OJ L 173, 9.7.2018.
10. Regulation (EC) No. 883/2004 of the European Parliament and of the Council of 29 April 2004 on the coordination of social security systems (Regulation 883/2004), 29.04.2004, and implementing Regulation (EC) No. 987/2009 of the European Parliament and of the Council of 16 September 2009 laying down the procedure for implementing Regulation (EC) No. 883/2004 on the coordination of social security systems (Regulation 987/2009), 16.09.2009.

Chapter 9 on the right to information and consultation investigates managers' access to the fundamental right to information and consultation as 'workers'. A right to information and consultation is expressed in Article 27 of the Charter of Fundamental Rights in the EU as well as in several secondary EU law sources, including the Information and Consultation Directive,[11] the European Works Council Directive,[12] the Collective Redundancies Directive,[13] the Transfer of Undertakings Directive,[14] the Insolvency Directive[15] and the new Directives on Restructuring and Insolvency and on Cross-Border Conversions, Mergers and Divisions.[16] The scope of 'workers' is deferred to the Member States in all these Directives. EU law determines managers' duties to ensure that employees at company level are properly informed and consulted. The question of holdership, i.e., the personal entitlement to exercise the right to information and consultation for managers, is more complicated. The nature of a right to information and consultation is that it is an individual right that can be exercised collectively. A group of managers may receive information and provide opinions through company organs, where they often sit. Exercising their right collectively through representatives at company level may seem meaningless, as per the position of managers at the same time representing and performing the tasks of the company as employer. Exercising their right to information and consultation collectively through a managers' trade union, of which many examples exist at national as well as at EU level, may seem more feasible.

Chapter 10 on the status of employee representatives on boards focuses on the scheme in many Member States, where employees can elect representatives to the strategic decision-making organ of the company, i.e., the supervisory board or the board of directors. In most Member States with a board-level representation scheme in the board of directors, the employee representatives normally become *non-executive* directors as the rest of the board members and are in general deemed to have the same

11. Directive 2002/14/EC of the European Parliament and of the Council of 11 March 2002 establishing a general framework for informing and consulting employees in the European Community – Joint declaration of the European Parliament, the Council and the Commission on employee representation, OJ L 080, 23.3.2002.
12. Directive 2009/38/EC of the European Parliament and of the Council of 6 May 2009 on the establishment of a European Works Council or a procedure in Community-scale undertakings and Community-scale groups of undertakings for the purposes of informing and consulting employees (Recast), OJ L 122, 16.5.2009.
13. Council Directive 98/59/EC of 20 July 1998 on the approximation of the laws of the Member States relating to collective redundancies, OJ L 225, 12.8.1998.
14. Council Directive 2001/23/EC of 12 March 2001 on the approximation of the laws of the Member States relating to the safeguarding of employees' rights in the event of transfers of undertakings, businesses or parts of undertakings or businesses, OJ L 082, 22.3.2001.
15. Directive 2008/94/EC of the European Parliament and of the Council of 22 October 2008 on the protection of employees in the event of the insolvency of their employer (codified version), OJ L 283, 28.10.2008.
16. Directive (EU) 2019/1023 of the European Parliament and of the Council of 20 June 2019 on preventive restructuring frameworks, on discharge of debt and disqualifications, and on measures to increase the efficiency of procedures concerning restructuring, insolvency and discharge of debt, and amending Directive (EU) 2017/1132, OJ L 172, 26.6.2019; and Directive (EU) 2019/2121 of the European Parliament and of the Council of 27 November 2019 amending Directive (EU) 2017/1132 as regards cross-border conversions, mergers and divisions, OJ L 321, 12.12.2019.

rights and duties as board members representing shareholders, including potential liabilities. At the same time, many Member States determine that employee representatives must be appointed/elected among the employees of the company, and as such have status as an employee. The chapter discusses complicated topics of independence of the employee representatives including conflicts of interests due to their employment relationship, the duties of care and of skill of directors including a recommendation of adequate training of employee representatives, the confidentiality duty of employee representatives, and aspects of remuneration of employee representatives on boards. The rights, duties and liabilities of employee representatives are regulated by both labour law and company law, which creates conflicts and tensions between the competing purposes, which needs to be reconciled. There is no general rule in Member States deciding whether one or the other area of law shall prevail in case of a conflict, which leaves the matter to be solved by national law.

Chapter 11 on Occupational Health and Safety (OSH) addresses the challenges of protecting managers against occupational hazards. Managers perform their work and share the same working environment as the employees, and in addition, a range of factors specific to the management position may pose specific risks, particularly to the psychosocial health and safety of managers. The chapter outlines the legal framework for OSH protection in international law instruments as well as in EU law. The scope of the OSH Framework Directive 89/391[17] is defined as *employment by an employer*. The demarcation of the scope of the individual directives enacted within the meaning of Article 16(1) of the OSH Framework Directive is less clear. The most clear is the interpretation of the OSH Pregnancy Directive 92/85[18] that was given a wide scope by the CJEU in Case C-232/09, *Danosa*,[19] in light of the Directive's social purpose. Other Directives under the OSH Framework Directive, such as Directive 2003/88 on the organization of working time,[20] however specifically exempts persons in management positions. The author concludes that recent developments in EU law and international law may lead to improved access to OSH protections for executive managers.

Chapter 12 on non-discrimination of persons in management positions investigates the protection of managers against discrimination on the grounds protected by EU law, i.e., age, disability, sexual orientation, religion or faith, as well as race and ethnic origin. In many sources of labour and employment rights under EU law, the status of managers as a 'worker' as defined in Article 45 TFEU or in national law is decisive. However, in the area of non-discrimination, the CJEU has recently clarified that the scope of application of Directive 78/2000 on non-discrimination[21] includes all persons

17. Council Directive 89/391/EEC of 12 June 1989 on the introduction of measures to encourage improvements in the safety and health of workers at work, OJ L 183, 29.6.1989, p. 1-8.
18. Council Directive 92/85/EEC of 19 October 1992 on the introduction of measures to encourage improvements in the safety and health at work of pregnant workers and workers who have recently given birth or are breastfeeding (tenth individual Directive within the meaning of Article 16 (1) of Directive 89/391/EEC).
19. Case C-232/09, *Dita Danosa v. LKB Līzings SIA*, 11.11.2010, ECLI:EU:C:2010:674.
20. Directive 2003/88/EC of the European Parliament and of the Council of 4 November 2003 concerning certain aspects of the organization of working time, OJ L 299, 18.11.2003, p. 9-19.
21. Council Directive 2000/78/EC of 27 November 2000 establishing a general framework for equal treatment in employment and occupation, OJ L 303, 2.12.2000, p. 16-22.

who perform their services as an 'occupation', without being in a subordinate position as 'employees'. Managers and others are entitled to be protected against discrimination regardless of whether they are classified as 'workers' according to Article 45 TFEU; decisive for directives enacted with a legal basis in Article 19 TFEU is whether the activity performed is professional, real and genuine. The chapter discusses the implications of the ruling and suggests a broad interpretation. Executive as well as most non-executive managers would have a right to non-discrimination, as they perform an activity which is professional, real and genuine, even if the remuneration is minor. Managers in both executive and non-executive positions are thus protected against direct and indirect discrimination, harassment and victimization on the protected grounds. This includes discriminatory rules for access to management positions or board positions outlined in a company or association's bylaws.

Chapter 13 on protection in the event of employer insolvency analyses the protection of managers' claims for outstanding remuneration in this situation. The Insolvency Directive 2008/94[22] obligates Member States to establish a body which guarantees payments of outstanding claims to employees in the event of employer insolvency. As such, the Insolvency Directive pursues a social objective. The definition of 'employee' is left to the Member States, but the scope of application may not be hindered by national requirements of seniority, by national exclusion of persons in fixed-term, part-time and temporary employment relationships, by arbitrary exclusions from the national concept of 'employee', and may not otherwise be limited in a manner, that undermines the social objective. The CJEU essentially deploys the principle of *effet utile* in the interpretation of the Insolvency Directive similarly to its interpretation of other EU labour law directives. The Insolvency Directive allows for certain exclusions of employees from the scope of protection. The authors discuss whether managers can be considered employees under national concepts of employee and, thus, covered by the Directive. It is also discussed whether a manager, who is an employee under national law, could be excluded from the Directive due to one of the mentioned exclusions. The authors conclude that 'managers' cannot be excluded *en bloc*, but a manager may nonetheless specifically be excluded due to his or her special position and responsibilities in the company. In so far as national law operates with a presumption rule that excludes top management, the CJEU has recently held that such presumption must be rebuttable.

[C] Part III, Chapter 14

Finally, this last chapter provides some systemic insights stemming from the interdisciplinarity of its structure – namely on definitions, rights, duties and sanctions – as well as a few overall conclusions.

22. Directive 2008/94/EC of the European Parliament and of the Council of 22 October 2008 on the protection of employees in the event of the insolvency of their employer, amended by Directive 2015/1794/EU.

CHAPTER 2

Governance Structures in European Companies

Gitte Søgaard

§2.01 INTRODUCTION

All forms of business organizations depend on having one or more (natural) persons who can legitimately make decisions and monitor business and, thereby, navigate in the shark-filled waters of delicately balancing various conflicting interests in the internal and external environment of the business organization – for instance, shareholders and other types of owners, board members, officers, customers, suppliers, employees, etc.

Some business organizations are characterized by being some sort of a fictional phenomenon with merely a legal (and no natural) personality. Therefore, an internal framework, a governance structure, must be set up so that decision-making and supervisory rights and duties can be allocated and those parties having such rights and duties can monitor business and the other governance organs, decisions can be made according to existing decision-making procedures and instructions, and proper sanctions can be activated when procedures and agreed precautions are violated.

In a European context, four archetypes of business organizations (plus several hybrids) are common.

The sole trader organization is a one-person operation with no formal separation between personal and business assets as far as creditors are concerned, and personal savings and/or loans form the financial basis for all business activities. With only one person involved in owning and managing the business, no formal governance structures are needed, and usually no codified rules or registration requirements apply.

Various forms of general partnerships exist in Europe. A common feature of general partnerships is that they are, in essence, personal relationships and of a contractual nature. Partners have no limited liability. No formal governance structures are required: in some forms, each individual partner has the power to manage the partnership's business, but no authority to bind other partners by contracting with third parties, while in other forms of general partnerships, partners can do both.[1]

Limited partnerships are in many ways like general partnerships and yet also different in some respects. Most European countries have limited partnership forms called, for instance, *société en commandite simple*, SCS (France), *Kommanditgesellschaft*, KG (Germany), *commanditaire vennootschap*, CV (Netherlands), and *kommanditselskab*, K/S (Denmark). Limited partnerships have two different types of partners: general partners and limited partners. Limited partners have limited liability, but only few or no executive rights at all, while decision-making rights are vested with the general partners ('executive partners').

Private and public companies are well-known business forms in all European jurisdictions and have common features such as: (1) separate legal personality, (2) limited liability for shareholders, (3) transferable shares, (4) shared ownership, and (5) governance structures with delegated powers to a board structure.[2]

Such features are codified in national company acts, and all European jurisdictions have at least two forms of companies: private limited liability companies and public limited liability companies.[3]

The regulatory framework for private limited liability companies is more liberal than for public limited liability companies. This is due to the fact that private limited liability company law is designed to meet the requirements of smaller business operations with few members and no access to public funding from public capital markets.

In this chapter, there is a particular focus on governance structures in public limited liability companies since this is where fundamental differences in company law regimes are illustrated the best. The less complex governance structures in private limited liability companies are, though, also described briefly later in §2.03[A] of this chapter.

Governance structures vary widely in Europe. From a historical perspective, they reflect the many different approaches to markets and organizing and financing business in Europe. When studying European governance structures, it becomes clear that such differences exist on all levels of the governance infrastructure.

On the shareholder level, issues such as share ownership patterns and the approaches when it comes to shareholder engagement practices differ from jurisdiction to jurisdiction, *see also* §2.03[C]) below. Recent EU harmonization has focused on enhancing long-term active ownership in public companies traded on a regulated market,[4] but even before that, active ownership had already bloomed in some Member States as an integrated part of governance traditions well codified also in company law provisions.

1. *See also* Adriaan F.M Dorresteijn et al., *European Corporate Law*, 15 (Kluwer Law International 3d ed. 2017).
2. *See also* Reinier Kraakman et al., *The Anatomy of Corporate Law*, 5-15 (Oxford University Press 3d ed. 2017), and Gitte Søgaard et al., *Business Law, Europe*, 185-189 (Ex Tuto Publishing A/S 2d ed. 2021).
3. For example, Directive (EU) 2017/1132 of the European Parliament and of the Council of 14 June 2017 relating to certain aspects of company law, OJ L 169, 30.6.2017, Annex II with a list of comparable forms of companies in EU Member States (and the UK).
4. Directive (EU) 2017/828 of the European Parliament and of the Council of 17 May 2017 amending Directive 2007/36/EC as regards the encouragement of long-term shareholder engagement, OJ L 132, 20.5.2017.

Stakeholders play an increasingly important role, and both EU law and national law have different built-in levels of co-determination and protection of such parties. Some jurisdictions have a long tradition of employees being represented in formal organs, while others have less formal or no rules for the employees being represented in governance organs, *see also* §2.03[D] below. In recent years, there have also been ongoing discussions in the EU about broadening the influence of other types of stakeholders. How this may or may not influence future governance structures has yet to be seen.[5]

Also, cultural footprints can be seen in governance values and traditions: in some jurisdictions, concepts of collaboration and consensus are imprinted in governance structures, whereas other governance structures are oriented towards markets, competition, and solving conflicts of interests between various parties.

For those members of governance organs involved in governance activities in foreign (and maybe even cross-border based) companies, understanding the nature of this diversity is a come-hell-or-high-waters precondition since much is at stake for the company and possibly also for the members of governance organs in person in order to maintain limited liability between the various companies in a group of companies and/or between the individual company and its shareholders, and furthermore in order to prevent claims against companies and members of governance organs for breach of company law governance rules.

Definitions and terminology are a major challenge when analysing governance structures in Europe. In §2.02, important key concepts are defined and explained in a comparative context. Then, in §2.03, three typological and one hybrid category of governance models are introduced, illustrating different paths in European company law regimes. Also, in §2.03, the roles of the shareholders and the employees are described from a governance perspective. In §2.04, there is a separate focus on governance structures from an EU company law perspective, and in §2.05, specific aspects related to governance structures in groups of companies are discussed. In §2.06, a few cross-border aspects related to governance structure issues are discussed. Finally, in §2.07, a brief conclusion completes this chapter.

§2.02 DEFINITIONS AND TERMINOLOGY

Getting lost in terminology happens quite easily when studying the various corporate actors involved in governance structures.

In §2.01 above, it was described how natural persons have certain roles that are defined by their functions in the governance structures of business organizations.

From a generic perspective, such roles can be seen as split between persons who have either 'executive' or 'non-executive' roles. Day-to-day management of the business organization is related to executive roles, while matters of strategic importance and/or supervisory functions are taken care of by persons with non-executive roles.[6]

---

5. Proposal for a Directive of the European Parliament and of the Council on Corporate Sustainability Due Diligence and amending Directive (EU) 2019/1937, COM(2022) 71 final, 23.2.2022.
6. Carsten Gerner-Beuerle & Michael Schillig, *Comparative Company Law*, 284 et seq. (Oxford University Press 2019).

Beyond this apparent simplicity lies the fact that, according to the various governance structures of European company law regimes, these executive and non-executive functions are defined in different ways, the number and nature of governance organs differ, and our terminology related to governance subjects is far from being similar.

Especially, the term 'director' causes some confusion and misunderstanding since the various jurisdictions use this word for different meanings. In some jurisdictions, a 'director' is a member of the board of directors or of a supervisory board. In others, a 'direktør' is a member of the executive board (in other jurisdictions, called a 'manager' or 'officer').

In some jurisdictions, only a natural person may be a 'director', while in other jurisdictions, 'directors' may also be so-called corporate directors, i.e., companies acting as directors.

Directors in the meaning of a member of the board of directors can, in some jurisdictions, be either 'executive' or 'non-executive' directors. Executive directors are often also referred to as 'inside directors', and non-executive directors are often referred to as 'external directors'.

Non-executive directors may also be 'independent' and, thus, be referred to as 'independent non-executive directors'. The status of being 'independent' is defined differently across jurisdictions. The underlying assumption is that independent non-executive directors would be inclined to efficiently supervise the members of other governance organs ('management'). In some jurisdictions, non-executive directors merely have a supervisory role (*see* §2.03[B] below).

In other jurisdictions, a 'director' is a manager or an officer, which means that he or she is a salaried employee appointed by the board of directors or a supervisory board. A 'director' ('general manager', 'directeur général', 'Vorstandsvorsitzender', 'direktør') could, for instance, in business life (but not in a company law terminology), be known as the chief executive officer (CEO). Other kinds of 'directors' could be the chief financial officer (CFO), the chief operating officer (COO), or the chief accounting officer (CAO).

Directors (here, in the understanding of a member of the board of directors) can be de jure directors, meaning that they have been validly appointed according to company law rules and the company's articles of associations, and meaning that they exercise their rights and duties as prescribed in company law provisions, case law, articles of association, etc. However, persons who are not properly appointed (and/or registered) according to company law rules or the company's articles of association may instead act as de facto directors. If a de facto director short-circuits the formal governance structure of a company by undertaking roles that legitimately belong to a de jure director, such a person may possibly be held accountable as a director and thus be liable for losses inflicted on, for instance, the company, shareholders, or creditors. Some jurisdictions have both codified provisions and case law about de facto directors, and others do not.[7]

---

7. Reinier Kraakman et al., *The Anatomy of Corporate Law*, 128 et seq. (Kluwer Law International 3d ed. 2017).

There will also be examples of so-called shadow directors issuing directions or instructions which are followed by an elected director, who will then act like a 'puppet' or just as a front person ('strawman director'). European company law regimes handle such phenomena in different ways. In some jurisdictions, such concepts are integrated into statutory law[8] and/or case law.[9] In other jurisdictions, these concepts are unknown or not a part of the case law.[10]

EU terminology is not always consistent either. However, in the SE Regulation[11] what is usually called the 'board of directors' in a one-tier system is called an 'administrative organ', and in the two-tier structure of a SE company, there must be a 'supervisory organ' plus a 'management organ'. One or more 'managing directors' shall, in both structures, be responsible for the day-to-day management. The 'members' of the 'administrative organ' shall be appointed by the general meeting. The supervisory board is called the 'supervisory organ', and its members are called 'members'. Rather similar definitions are used in other EU company law directives and regulations.

§2.03 GOVERNANCE STRUCTURES: COMMON GROUND AND DIFFERENCES

In a broad European context, the functions of directing and supervising companies are embedded in diverse structures with organs such as the general meeting (the shareholders), boards of directors (non-executive and/or executive directors), supervisory boards, and executive boards. (Among European jurisdictions, it is highly disputed whether the general meeting can be defined as an organ at all, which is not such a great surprise since the view of the shareholders' governance roles differs from jurisdiction to jurisdiction, *see also* §2.03[C] below.) The way in which rights and duties are attributed to these organs and their members in national company law reflects the different history and cultures of company law. Irrespective of jurisdiction, the choice of board structure has an immense impact on the weight and character of directors' duties and liabilities.

Governance structures are designed to deal with numerous general governance issues, which are often analysed by using an economist's theory about 'agency problems' or 'principal-agent problems'.[12] According to such theories, three generic conflicts prevail: (1) conflicts between managers and shareholders, (2) conflicts between controlling and non-controlling shareholders, and (3) conflicts between

8. For example, Cyprus, the Czech Republic, Hungary, and referred to statutory law in Belgium, Italy (by analogy to criminal law), the Netherlands (insolvency rules), Portugal (insolvency rules), Spain, and the UK, *see* Carsten Gerner-Beuerle et al., *Study on Directors' Duties and Liability*, Department of Law, London School of Economics, 45-54 (2013).
9. *Ibid., e.g.*, Austria, Belgium, Denmark, Estonia (criminal law), (probably) Finland, France, Germany, Greece, Ireland, Luxembourg, Malta, Romania, Sweden.
10. *Ibid., e.g.*, Croatia, Latvia, Slovakia, and Slovenia.
11. Council Regulation (EU) No. 2157/2001 of 8 October 2001 on the Statute for a European company (SE), OJ L 294/1, 10.11.2001, Title III.
12. *See also* Reinier Kraakman et al., *The Anatomy of Corporate Law*, Chapter 2 (Oxford University Press 3d ed. 2017).

shareholders and the company's other contractual counterparties, for instance, creditors and employees. For each of the governance structures mentioned in §2.03[B] below it is described how a specific legal solution is embedded in the structure to solve these conflicts, which are not equally dominant and have different shapes in the various European jurisdictions. Important parameters, such as the fact that different companies have different requirements, when it comes to governance structures (*see* §2.03[A]), the different roles of shareholders (*see* §2.03[C]), and the different roles of employees (*see* §2.03[D]) have, among other parameters, contributed to the development of these different legal governance structures.

[A] Different Companies: Different Requirements

Although the focus of this chapter is primarily on governance structures in public limited liability companies, it is worth mentioning that most European jurisdictions have more flexible and less complicated governance structures for private limited liability companies[13] and numerous other forms of business organizations.

For private limited liability companies, most jurisdictions have minimum requirements for just one executive director, provided this person is a natural person. Often, these companies are managed by those who have a controlling interest, are the founders of the company, and/or have more than an investor's interest (for instance, their job) at stake.[14]

Often, there will be no specific supervisory mechanism since the shareholders' right to intervene in the executive directors' decision-making and/or to remove a director is generally accepted – sometimes even at any time with or without cause. In other cases, private limited liability companies, which are large in terms of capital or number of employees, are required to also have a supervisory organ.

[B] Governance Structures: An Overview

In a European context, it is common to see governance structures described as two basic models: a one-tier structure and a two-tier structure.[15] However, it would seem proper to add a third one too since a Nordic model also has its distinct characteristics (although EU company law seems to put a strain on the Nordic perception of governance structures since EU gathers inspiration from the Anglo-American law tradition on the one hand and the German company law tradition on the other hand).[16] Furthermore, a fourth group of miscellaneous hybrids should be mentioned briefly. In Table 2.1 is a guiding overview of board structures in some European jurisdictions.

13. For a comparative perspective, *see also* Adriaan F.M. Dorresteijn et al., *European Corporate Law*, 185-243 (Kluwer Law International 3d ed. 2017).
14. *See also* Hanne S. Birkmose et al., *Shareholders' Duties*, §1.03[C] (Kluwer Law International 2017).
15. *See also* Paul L. Davies & Klaus J. Hopt, *Boards in Europe – Accountability and Convergence*, ECGI – Law Working Paper No. 205/2013, 10 et seq. (2013).
16. Jesper Lau Hansen, *Udfordringerne fra EU-retten til den nordiske ledelsesmodel*, 4 NTS, 13 et seq. (2019).

Table 2.1 Board Structures in Public Limited Liability Companies in a Selection of European Countries

One-Tier Structure	*Two-Tier Structure*	*The Nordic Structure*	*Optional One-Tier and Two-Tier Structure*	*Hybrid Systems*
Cyprus[17]	Austria	Denmark[18]	Bulgaria	Belgium[19]
Greece	Estonia	Finland[20]	Croatia	Italy[21]
Ireland[22]	Germany	Iceland	The Czech Republic	Portugal[23]
Malta	Latvia	Norway	France[24]	
Spain	Poland	Sweden	Hungary	
United Kingdom[25]			Lithuania	
			Luxembourg	
			The Netherlands[26]	
			Romania	
			The Slovak Republic	
			Slovenia	
			Switzerland	
			EU SE company	

Source: Adapted from the OECD-Corporate Governance Factbook 2021 and Carsten Gerner-Beuerle et al., *Study on Directors' Duties and Liabilities,* Department of Law, London School of Economics (2013).

17. No mandatory rules exist.
18. There is a legal option between the Nordic model and the two-tier board structure. The two-tier structure is only rarely used.
19. There is an option between a one-tier board structure or a mixed structure (some powers may be transferred from the board of directors to a 'direction committee' ('comité de direction')).
20. There is a legal option between the Nordic model and the two-tier board structure. Two-tier structures are rarely used.
21. There are three optional structures: (1) board of directors + board of statutory auditors, (2) one-tier, (3) two-tier.
22. No mandatory rules exist.
23. There are three optional structures: (1) board of directors + board of statutory auditors, (2) one-tier, (3) two-tier.
24. If the one-tier structure is chosen, the company may use a PDG-model ('président-directeur général'): the CEO and the chair of the board is the same office.
25. No mandatory rules exist.
26. Large companies must have a two-tier structure.

A (much too) simplified way to illustrate the three basic governance structures could be as shown in Figure 2.1.

Figure 2.1 Governance Structure

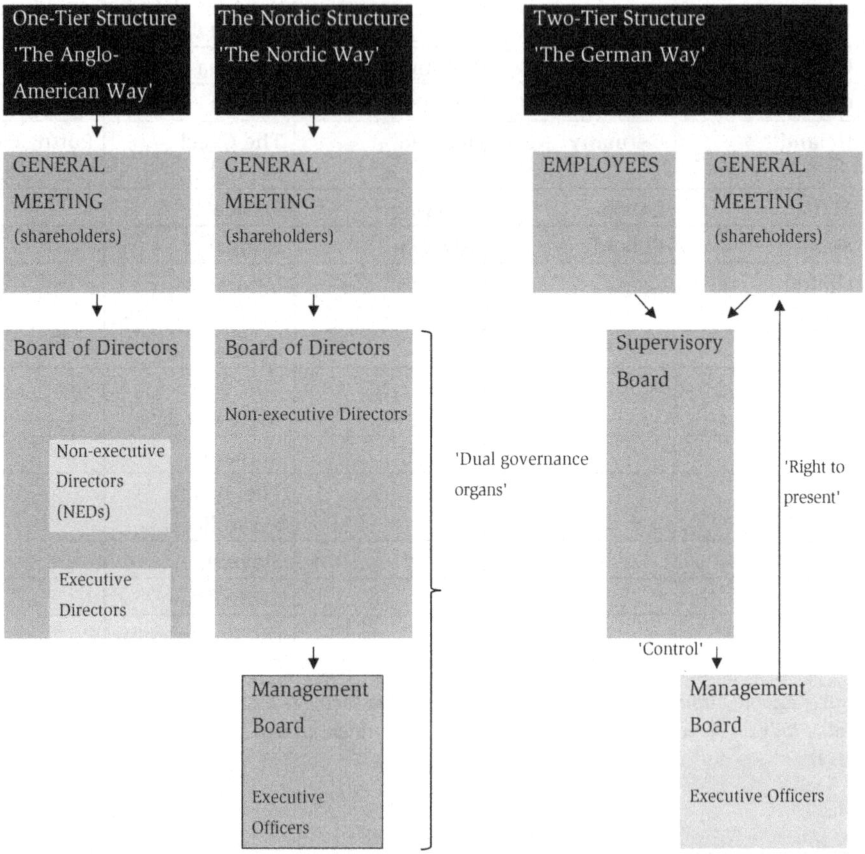

Source: The author partly with inspiration from Jesper Lau Hansen in *Introduktion til selskabsretten og kapitalmarkedsretten*, 2nd ed. 2018, 299 et seq.

[1] The One-Tier Governance Structure

The one-tier governance structure has its origin in the Anglo-American company law tradition, where ownership patterns are rather dispersed. In general, there is no strong tradition for shareholder engagement or activism, although the so-called shareholder primacy doctrine is inherited in the limited liability company form. Consequently, the governance organs only depend scarcely on the shareholders.

In the one-tier governance structure, all management and supervisory functions are vested in a single and very powerful board of directors.[27,28] On the board, there are both executive and non-executive directors.[29] In public companies, the directors of the board are elected by the shareholders at the annual general meeting.[30]

However, the board of directors is often divided into subdivisions, each having either non-executive (supervisory) or executive directors, respectively. Often, the division between the supervisory and the executive functions is not very institutionalized and not strictly observed. Now and then, directors delegate management powers to executive officers, and the one-tier governance structure is, therefore, predominantly described as a quite pragmatic approach with a high degree of self-management.

In listed companies, at least half of the directors must be independent, meaning that they may not represent any large shareholder. In practical life, this means that these directors would have a supervisory function and that day-to-day management is rather separated from the supervisory function.

The board has a 'chair', which is usually independent of both the company and of majority shareholders. The chairman and the managing director may not be the same person.

In the one-tier structure, the members of the board of directors are elected by the general meeting. Usually, shareholders hold only a modest influence over the company, although most jurisdictions with one-tier structures have a quite liberal legal approach allowing shareholders to intervene in the executive directors' decision-making and/or removing executive directors, often at any time with or without cause.[31]

Among the pros of choosing a one-tier structure, it is often mentioned that non-executive directors are more closely involved in decision-making processes in the company and that decision-making is faster in a one-tier structure. Generally, administrative burdens are assumed to be less with only one board or organ. Furthermore, access to information is shorter for non-executive directors since all information is produced and presented in just one organ.

[2] The Two-Tier Governance Structure

The two-tier governance structure has its origin in German Public Company Law (*Aktiengesetz*). It has a very distinct and institutionalized separation of non-executive

27. The UK Companies Act 2006 of the Parliament of the United Kingdom has no prescriptions as far as the structure and functions of the board of directors as an organ are concerned. Instead, the UK CA 2006 has provisions related to the company's directors.
28. A UK private company must have at least one director, and a public company must have at least two directors (*see* The UK Companies Act 2006, 154). A company must have at least one director who is a natural person (155(1)), which means that both natural and corporate directors are legitimate in UK company law.
29. The UK Companies Act 2006 does not categorize directors into executive and non-executive directors. This division is based on modern corporate practice. *See also* Alan Dignam & John Lowry, *Company Law*, 284 et seq. (Oxford University Press 11th ed. 2021).
30. The UK Companies Act 2006, 160.
31. *See also* Carsten Gerner-Beuerle & Michael Schillig, *Comparative Company Law*, 307 et seq. (Oxford University Press 2019).

supervision in the *Aufsichtsrat*-organ[32] and executive management in the *Vorstand*-organ,[33] and no double duty is allowed.

A formal reporting duty (written report) lies with the executive board, and the supervisory board may require additional information from the executive board.[34] However, the supervisory function of the supervisory board has changed over time so that supervision is no longer based merely on retrospective but also 'preventive' control. Established case law (and business practice) now requires current discussions (*ständige Diskussion*) and advice (*laufende Beratung*) to ensure that the supervisory board performs such adequate (retrospective and preventive) control with the executive board.[35]

If the supervisory board detects issues that may endanger the interests of the company (*das Wohl der Gesellschaft*), it may call in the general meeting (the shareholders). Only a very few specific executive decisions can be made by the supervisory board, and if the supervisory board does not support the executive board on such occasions, the executive board has a sort of short-circuit mechanism, as it has a right to present the case for the general meeting for its decision. The general meeting itself cannot, however, initiate an interference with decisions made by the executive board.

The influence of the general meeting (*Hauptversammlung*) on the company is basically restricted to investor-related issues such as capital issues, distribution issues, approving financial reports, and electing members to the supervisory organ.

As a rule, the members of the supervisory board are elected by the shareholders at the general meeting. However, if the company has more than five hundred employees, the employees elect one-third of the members of the supervisory board. If the company has more than two thousand employees, the employees elect half of the members of the supervisory board.

The two-tier governance structure is rooted deeply in a company law tradition with a focus on stakeholder interests, which is unlike the Anglo-American tradition, where the so-called shareholder primacy doctrine applies.

The members of the executive board are hired and fired by the supervisory board. Removing an executive member of the management board does, however, require a cause (*ein wichtiger Grund*).[36] Hiring an executive board member can be for a period of maximum five years, although the period can be longer in practice since consecutive periods can be decided.[37]

Among the pros of the two-tier structure is often mentioned the fact that there is a clear distinction of responsibilities between members of the supervisory and the executive organs, and that there is a clear separation of the roles of chairman of the supervisory board and the executive board. The cons are primarily described as reduced flexibility and a significant concentration of power and autonomy within the

32. Aktiengesetz (AktG), § 111
33. *Ibid.*, § 76.
34. *Ibid.*, § 90.
35. *See* Bundesgerichtshof (BGH), Aktiengesellschaft (AG) 1991, 312, and AG 1997, 377.
36. AktG, § 84 (4).
37. *Ibid.*, § 84.

executive management organ. In a German context, the high priority for employee co-determination (*Mitbestimmung*) in the supervisory organ is also mentioned as a reason for reduced flexibility, *see* more in §2.03[D] below.

[3] The Nordic Governance Structure

The Nordic governance structure[38] is usually described as a highly flexible and shareholder-friendly governance framework, which enhances active and long-term-oriented shareholder engagement. A majority shareholder, or a coalition of shareholders in a dispersed ownership situation, may ultimately and effectively control the company.[39]

The Nordic approach is also based on enhancing cooperation between governance organs, and dialogue between organs on all levels (including the general meeting) goes along with a formal division of powers and duties in a hierarchic order.

The hierarchic nature of this governance model implies that the general meeting may decide on any theme that is not placed with other organs by statutory law or the articles of association. There is an underlying premise that, ultimately, shareholders exercise 'active ownership' by monitoring and disciplining the board.

However, a wide range of decisions are formally allocated to the various organs, and micro-management from the shareholders within the general meeting is a rare phenomenon. Instead, focus is on themes of an exclusive duty nature (approving financial reports, the allocation of profits or loss, appointing members of the board of directors and the auditor of the company, equity issues, mergers, etc.).

The directors of the board are elected by the shareholders within the general meeting, but they may also be dismissed by the general meeting without any stated cause and at any time. Even though the board of directors is accountable to the general meeting, it also has extensive powers to run the business of the company for as long as it all happens in the best interest of the company.

The directors of the board are mainly non-executive members, even though certain executive decisions may be made by the board of directors and even though a member of the executive board may also be a member of the board of directors. The focus of the board of directors is on monitoring the business and the executive level, but the board is also responsible for the overall strategic aspects of the company's business, whereas the executive level is responsible for all day-to-day running of the business.

The board of directors hires and fires members of the executive organ.[40] A member of the executive board may also be a member of the board of directors, but never the chairman, since double duties in these positions are not allowed.

---

38. *See* comparative analysis in George Ringe, *German Versus Nordic Board Models: Form, Function, and Convergence*, 65 NJB 1, 27 et seq. (2016).
39. *The Nordic Governance Model*, 52 et seq. (Per Lekvall ed., SNS Förlag 2014).
40. In Sweden, the executive role lies with one single person (The Swedish Companies Act (SFS. 2005:551), Chapter 8, s. 27), whereas in Denmark, the executive role may also be placed with an executive board with more than one member (Danish Company Law (*Selskabsloven* § 111)). In Finland, it is an option, but not mandatory, to have an executive director (Finnish Public Company Law – Aktiebolagslag 21.7.2006/624, Chapter 6, § 1). In Norway, it is an option, but not mandatory, to have an executive director (*daglig leder*), and if decided in the articles of the

What is extraordinary is the fact that the board of directors together with the executive board form a dual governance structure which enhances flexibility and cooperation – while still maintaining, at least in formality, a separation of rights and responsibilities due to explicit statutory company law provisions lining up both roles and liabilities.

In the Nordic governance structure regimes, employee co-determination on the board of directors is mandatory even in quite small companies, but only when the employees require this kind of co-determination.[41] Those members of the board of directors who are also employees have the same legal rights and duties as any other member of the board. This category of members of the board of directors must be employed by the company, and no 'external' representatives or professional board members can be appointed by the employees in their place, *see also* in §2.03[D] below.

Executive board members are normally appointed and/or dismissed by the board of directors, and shifting members of the executive board requires only the lack of confidence of the board of directors.[42] In that sense, the members of the executive board have the same status as other employees, although members of the executive board often have special agreements on severance pay or long notice periods upon dismissal.

The members of the executive board are responsible for all day-to-day management of the company according to the strategic decisions and the supervision of the board of directors. Members of the executive board may normally represent the company in external affairs and sign on behalf of the company.

The chief managing director of the executive board has the right to attend general meetings in his or her capacity as such irrespective of whether he or she is, in formality, a board member.

[4] Hybrid Systems

Numerous hybrid governance structures exist in Europe.

In some jurisdictions, regular boards of statutory auditors exist. For instance, Italian and Portuguese company law allows for a choice of three governance structures:

---

company, there may be more than one executive director who may act as a collective organ (executive board) (Norwegian Public Company Law – Aksjeloven § 6-2(1)).

41. In Norway, companies with more than two hundred employees are required to have a corporate assembly organ (*bedriftsforsamling*), unless the company and the employees agree otherwise. This corporate assembly organ must have at least twelve members, or a higher number which can be divided by three. Two-thirds of the members are elected by the general meeting, while one-third are elected by and among the company's employees. This organ is mainly active in relation to board elections and matters related to important changes in the company's workforce (*Lov om Aksjeselskaper (aksjeloven)*, § 6-35).
42. In some Nordic company law regimes, it is possible to have a supervisory board instead of a board of directors, and in such cases, the supervisory board is entitled to appoint and/or dismiss the board of directors. Such supervisory boards are, however, a rare phenomenon in Nordic companies. In Finland, a special arrangement is possible since it is an option to have a supervisory board (*förvaltningsråd*) placed in the hierarchy between the general meeting and the board. The main role of such a supervisory board is to supervise the governance practices of the company since it cannot itself represent the company in any external context (*Aktiebolagslag* 21.7.2006/624, Chapter 6, § 21). This structure is also only rarely used.

a one-tier structure, a two-tier structure, and a structure including both a board of directors and a board of statutory auditors.

In Belgium, it is possible to choose a mixed structure with some powers transferred from the board of directors to a 'direction committee' (*comité de direction*).

However, the most prevalent governance structures are those described above (the one-tier structure, the two-tier structure, and the Nordic structure).

[C] The Role of the Shareholders

Company law traditions and regulations across Europe have rather different approaches when it comes to shareholder influence on governance topics. In some jurisdictions, shareholders are seen as inherently powerful, while others see shareholders as vulnerable to the power of the board of directors.[43]

Such different approaches can partly be explained by the fact that various European jurisdictions have a different history when it comes to ownership patterns.[44] In some European countries, shares are often held by one or only a limited number of major shareholders, and due to this concentration of shares, such shareholders are capable of monitoring and controlling any governance organ, whereas minority shareholders may find it difficult to monitor a controlling shareholder, and both executive and non-executive board members may see their power shrink. Also, the existence of a controlling shareholder may reduce the focus on transparency and disclosure.

When, on the contrary, share ownership is dispersed, more power is vested with the organs of the governance structure (boards of directors and executive boards), and there is more scope for both the executive and non-executive members of these organs to pursue their own agendas (both their own personal ones, such as remuneration, and the agenda of the business).

If a company has dispersed ownership, shareholders may act in concert with other shareholders (whenever permitted according to national company law) to pool their engagement. Some European countries have company laws that allow for so-called control-enhancing mechanisms (CEMs) so that shareholders can gain power over the company by law or by provisions in their articles of association. Examples of such CEMs are multiple voting rights on shares, non-voting preference shares, priority shares, voting-right ceilings, ownership ceilings, golden shares, and shareholder agreements.

According to the European Commission, shareholder engagement is generally seen as positive since an active and constructive relationship between shareholders and the board will, according to the Commission, effectively benefit both the shareholders and the companies, and thus, ultimately, also the societal economy.[45]

---

43. Hanne S. Birkmose, *Shareholders' Duties*, §1.04 (Kluwer Law International 2017).
44. *See also* Paul L. Davies & Klaus J. Hopt, *Boards in Europe – Accountability and Convergence*, ECGI – Law Working Paper No. 205/2013, 4 (2013).
45. European Commission, *Green Paper – Corporate governance in financial institutions and remuneration policies*, COM(2010) 285 final, and European Commission, *GREEN PAPER The EU corporate governance framework*, COM(2011) 164 final.

[D] The Co-determination of the Employees

The employees may, as already mentioned in §2.03[B] above, be represented on the board in some jurisdictions but not in all. In company law regimes with a 'shareholder primacy' focus, there is a tradition of having no or only some co-determination by employees on the board, while in other jurisdictions with a stakeholder focus, co-determination and representation in governance organs play an important role, as, for instance, in Germany.[46]

Directive (EU) 2009/38/EC has rules about European Works Councils and other procedures for informing and consulting employees. However, no harmonization of genuine company law co-determination on a board level has yet been adopted, although specific provisions about employees' rights in case of cross-border transactions such as mergers, divisions, and conversions are now included in company law Directive (EU) 2017/1132 as amended by Directive (EU) 2019/2121. Also, separate directives about the rights of the employees were issued along with the SE Regulation[47] and the SCE Regulation (European Cooperative Society).[48]

This diversity of a company law approach to employee co-determination on the board is illustrated in Table 2.2. In some jurisdictions, company law provisions allow for employee co-determination on the board in small companies; in others, only in large companies; and in some jurisdictions, a relatively small proportion of board members can be employees; in others, a relatively larger proportion of the board members can be employees.

Table 2.2 Employees' Representation on Boards in Public Limited Liability Companies

Jurisdiction	*Minimum Number of Employees*	*Minimum Requirement*	*Maximum Allowance*
Austria	300	33%	–
Belgium	–		
The Czech Republic	500	33%	50%
Denmark	35	2 members	Less than 50%
Estonia	–		

46. *See also* Adriaan F.M. Dorresteijn et al., *European Corporate Law*, 184 & Chapter 7 (Kluwer Law International 3d ed. 2017).
47. Council Regulation No. 2157/2001 on the Statute for a European company (SE) and Directive 2001/86 supplementing the Statute for a European company with regard to the involvement of employees.
48. Council Regulation no. 1435/2003 of 22 July 2003 on the Statute for a European Cooperative Society (SCE) and Council Directive 2003/72 of 22 July 2003 supplementing the Statute for a European Cooperative Society with regard to the involvement of employees.

Jurisdiction	*Minimum Number of Employees*	*Minimum Requirement*	*Maximum Allowance*
Finland	Special arrangement based on agreements. If board representation, min. number of 150 employees is required, minimum number is one member and maximum is four members or 25%.		
France	1,000 (in France)	1 member if the board has 12 or less members, otherwise 2 members.	33% or 5 members
	5,000 (worldwide)		
Germany	501-2,000	33%	–
	2,001 and above	50%	50%
Greece	–		
Hungary	200	33%	–
Iceland	–		
Ireland	–		
Italy	–		
Latvia	–		
Lithuania	–		
Luxembourg	1,000	33%	33%
The Netherlands	100	–	33%
Norway	31-50	1 member	–
	32-51	33% min. 2 members	
	52-201	33% min. 3 members	
Poland	–		
Portugal	–		
The Slovak Republic	50	33%	–
Slovenia	–	33%	–
Spain	–		
Sweden (right to appoint representatives, not necessarily employees)	25-999	2 members	50%
	1,000	3 members	50%
Switzerland	–		
United Kingdom	–		

Source: Adapted with inspiration from OECD (2021), 'OECD Corporate Governance Factbook 2021', https://www.oecd.org/corporate/corporategovernance-factbook.htm, Table 4.8.

§2.04 GOVERNANCE STRUCTURES IN EU COMPANY LAW

Strong efforts have indeed been made by the EU to harmonize governance structures in limited liability companies (particularly public limited liability companies), but the path has been long and cumbersome, and so far with no (or only little) success:[49]

> The first Draft Fifth Company Law Directive was adopted by the Mansholt Commission in September 1972.[50] It prescribed a so-called two-tier structure quite similar to the principles for German public limited-liability companies. Under the Thorn Commission, the draft was altered so that both one-tier and two-tier structures could be used, and then in 1990 and 1991, the Delors Commission added further changes to the draft. Both under the Thorn and the Delors Commissions, employee representation on the board was a challenging issue. Then, in 2001, the Prodi Commission withdrew the draft proposals as 'no longer topical' and thereby exposed the profound disagreements and difficulties between Member States in finding a common path forward in harmonizing governance structures.

Since the failure of the Draft Fifth Company Law Directive, several important initiatives have been taken on an EU level:

> After the so-called Winter Report (2002), the Commission published an EU Action Plan (2003) focusing on four important governance themes: (1) Modernizing boards of directors (balance of executive and non-executive directors, separate roles for the chair of the board and the CEO, independent directors, disclosure regarding directors' remuneration); (2) Enhancing governance disclosure (all listed companies are now required to include a corporate governance statement based on a 'comply or explain' principle in their annual report); and (3) strengthening shareholders' rights.[51]

Then, in 2012, the EU Action Plan was published with a focus on increasing long-term growth-orientated investments which were aimed at obtaining more competitive and sustainable companies. One important statement was the Commission's recognition of different board models in the legal systems of all Member States, and also a clear message to Member States that no further harmonization of board structures would be attempted.[52]

---

49. *See also* EUR-Lex: Procedure 1972/0003/SYN, https://eur-lex.europa.eu/procedure/EN/1972_3.
50. Vorschlag einer fünften Richtlinie zur Koordinierung der Schutzbestimmungen, die in den Mitgliedstaaten den Gesellschaften im Sinne des Artikels 58 Absatz 2 des Vertrages im Interesse der Gesellschafter sowie Dritter hinsichtlich der Struktur der Aktiengesellschaft sowie der Befugnisse und Verpflichtungen ihrer Organe vorgeschrieben sind, ABl. nr. C 131/49, 13.12.72, https://eur-lex.europa.eu/legal-content/DE/TXT/PDF/?uri = CELEX:51972PC0887&from = EN.
51. Communication from the Commission to the Council and the European Parliament. Modernizing Company Law and Enhancing Corporate Governance in the European Union – A Plan to Move Forward, COM(2003) 284 final, 21.5.2003, https://eur-lex.europa.eu/LexUriServ/LexUriServ.do?uri = COM:2003:0284:FIN:EN:PDF.
52. Communication from the Commission to the European Parliament, The council, the European Economic and Social Committee and the Committee of the Regions, COM(2012) 740 final, 12.12.2012, 5, *See also* about EU-initiatives Klaus J. Hopt & Patrick C. Leyens, *Board Models in Europe – Recent Developments of Internal Corporate Governance Structures in Germany, the United Kingdom, France, and Italy*, ECGI Law Working Paper No. 17/2004, 23-24 (2004).

When it comes to the SE company, there is a free choice between a one-tier and a two-tier structure, and the statutes of the company decide the choice.[53] All Member States, and as such also those only accepting one of the structures in their national company law, must allow for an SE registered in their jurisdiction to choose between these two structures. However, certain national rules may modify this rule to create some alignment with national public limited liability companies.

§2.05 GOVERNANCE STRUCTURES IN GROUPS OF COMPANIES

A group of companies has no legal entity of its own, and it has no de jure governance structure of its own. In a company law context, a group of companies consists of a parent company and one or more subsidiaries, and each of these individual companies has its own autonomous governance structure with governance organs which are responsible for enhancing the best interests of each company.

The relationship between such group-related companies can be purely based on ownership, with a majority shareholder controlling the group, and/or the link can be based on a business model where the business activities of the companies are highly integrated as if they were one entity (de facto economic entity). However, in a company law context, the distinction between legal and economic entity is crucial since a group of companies may very well act as an economic entity, but there is no legal entity.

Company group law is not harmonized, and the approach of European jurisdictions to groups of companies is as diverse as has also been seen when discussing above the harmonization of governance structures.

When it comes to the various European group law regimes, the group governance theme arouses enthusiasm in some jurisdictions and considerable resistance in others. Since the group is no legal entity of its own, no company law regime has rules about group governance structures.

In the German-inspired *Konzernrecht*, however, so-called *Beherrschungsverträge* can be made so that a parent may on a contractual basis make certain governance-related decisions on behalf of also a subsidiary.[54]

Basically, group management mechanisms conflict with the 'corporate benefit doctrine', which applies in most company law regimes. According to the corporate benefit doctrine, any member of any company organ is required to pursue whatever is in the best interest of the individual company.

In the real business world, however, group management structures exist, group management is exercised, and nobody would probably question the legitimacy of some sort of group-based coordination of business activities within the group, despite the obvious issues with traditional and codified company law principles.

53. Council Regulation (EU) No. 2157/2001 of 8 October 2001 on the Statute for a European company (SE), OJ L 294/1, 10.11.2001, Title III.
54. AktG, § 291.

In an EU context, efforts are made to agree on a 'recommendation' in Article 288 TFEU sense for the Member States to recognize the concept of 'group interest'. In some specific legal contexts, group management is, nowadays, even mandatory.[55]

The status quo on the theme of group governance and group management is, especially in a cross-border context, thus characterized by significant legal uncertainty since, in most jurisdictions, judges must shape applicable law.

Engaging in intra-group governance as a member of a governance organ in a parent company or a subsidiary company may, in some respects, be a decision that calls for profound company law insights and vigilance.[56] Much is at stake: first, a director or an officer may risk compromising the limited liability feature of having a company structure with separate companies with each their own separate legal personalities.

Next, for the members of the board of directors and the executive board in a subsidiary, there may be a risk of personal liability for not having followed statutory provisions and/or case law about directors' (and officers') duties. A passive approach to allowing persons from other group-related companies to act as de facto directors, shadow directors, dirigeants de fait, etc., might very well lead to claims.

Finally, those persons who have acted on behalf of the group parent or other group-related entities as de facto directors, shadow directors, and/or dirigeants de fait may also face liability and, in some jurisdictions, even criminal law sanctions.

§2.06 CROSS-BORDER ISSUES

In the above sections of this chapter, the diversity of governance structures within Europe has played a major role. This, of course, raises numerous questions and creates challenges when companies operate in a cross-border context.[57]

Jurisprudence from the Court of Justice of the European Union makes it possible for a company to be incorporated in one Member State and to have its headquarters, directors' residence, central management and/or principal establishment in another Member State.[58] This is seen as a core element of the freedom of establishment

---

55. *See also* Karsten Engsig Sørensen, *The Legal Position of Parent Companies: A Top-Down Focus on Group Governance*, Nordic and European Company Law Working Paper No. 19-05, 433-474 (2021).
56. *See also* Gitte Søgaard, *Aspects of Structural Risk Management in Groups*, 367-369 (Ex Tuto Publishing A/S 2d ed. 2021).
57. *See also* Stephan Rammeloo, *Companies & Firms in a Cross-Border EU Context: The Hybrid Legal Status of Managers in Cross-Border Civil Procedural Law … and Further …*, 16 ECL 4, 104-105 (2019), and Stephan Rammeloo, *CJEU C-603/18 (Bosworth & Hurley v. Arcadia & Others): The Status of Company Officers (or Employees?) in Cross-Border Civil Proceedings & Jurisdictions of Courts under the 2007 'Lugano II' Convention*, 17 ECL 2, 53-63 (2020).
58. *See, e.g.*, Case C-212/97, *Centros Ltd v. Erhvervs- og Selskabsstyrelsen*, 9.3.1999, ECLI:EU:C:1999:126, Case C-208/00, *Überseering BV v. Nordic Construction Company Baumanagement* GmbH, 5.11.2002, ECLI:EU:C:2002:632, Case C-167/01, *Kamer van Koophandel en Fabrieken voor Amsterdam v. Inspire Art Ltd.*, 30.9.2003, ECLI:EU:C:2003:57, and Case C-106/16, *Polbud - Wykonawstwo sp. z o.o*, 25.10.2017, ECLI:EU:C:2017:804.

guaranteed by the Treaty on the Functioning of the European Union (TFEU). Consequently, when choosing a jurisdiction for the incorporation of the company, a choice of governance structure (and what must apply concerning directors' duties and liability) has been made as well. However, when operating on a cross-border basis within Europe, the large diversity of governance structures now and then creates legal uncertainty.

In some jurisdictions, company law provisions exclusively apply to general civil liability issues in a directors' duties context, whereas in other jurisdictions, other provisions function as substitutes for company law liability provisions and thus may function in a different way than specialized company law provisions. In cross-border scenarios, where a company operates outside the jurisdiction of its incorporation, a director may thus become liable both according to company law provisions in one jurisdiction, the general civil law provisions in another jurisdiction, and/or according to insolvency rules.[59]

One example would be cases about directors' duties in the vicinity of insolvency. In some jurisdictions, such duties are described in company law provisions alone, in others in insolvency law alone, in others again in criminal law alone, and finally, some jurisdictions may have a mixed approach to solving the issue.[60] Legal uncertainty may arise due to the different scope of the private international law rules and different criteria for classification of provisions on directors' duties in the vicinity of insolvency.

Another important issue is deciding the relationship between company law rules and employment law rules when determining the liability of directors. Basically, the liability of a director must be decided according to the company law rules of the jurisdiction where the company is incorporated. However, some European jurisdictions permit in their company law provisions that, under certain circumstances, less stringent employment legislation can apply to mitigate the liability of directors. The applicable employment rules are, though, determined by applying common private international law rules.[61]

§2.07 CONCLUSIONS

This chapter shows that a great variety of governance structures exist in Europe. No EU harmonization of governance structures has been adopted except for those forms of companies that are genuine EU forms of companies, such as, for instance, the SE company. Differences can be explained partly by the fact that business organizations differ and thus call for different solutions. Besides, as this chapter has had its primary focus on public limited liability companies, it has shown that even within one specific group of quite similar business organizations, quite profound differences prevail. Some of these differences can be explained by differences in ownership patterns. Others can

59. *See, e.g.*, Case C-594/14, *Simona Kornhaas v. Thomas Dithmar als Insolvenzverwalter über das Vermögen der Kornhaas Montage und Dienstleistung Ltd.*, 10.12.2015, ECLI:EU:C:2015:806.
60. *See also* Carsten Gerner-Beuerle et al., *Study on Directors' Duties and Liability*, Department of Law, London School of Economics, Table 5.2.3.a, 233-234 (2013).
61. *Ibid.*, 232 et seq.

be explained by different traditions and approaches in balancing shareholders' interests versus stakeholders' interests.

When studying governance structures in a comparative or cross-border context, terminology may be a challenge. On top of the complexity of having different structures with different organs with different names and functions, there are also different names for the actors being members of these organs and similar denominations, such as 'director', may be used for different actors with different roles in the governance structure.

Previously, when analysing governance structures in Europe, common ground has been the assumption that two models exist: the one-tier structure and the two-tier structure. It could be argued, however, that a Nordic structure can also be defined as a model governance structure. Finally, as always, when using models as an analytical tool, it should be remembered that numerous hybrid models exist.

Beyond the discussion of allocating executive and non-executive functions to the actors of various governance structures and types of organs, this chapter has also focused on the relationship between shareholders and employees on the one hand and the governance organs on the other hand. History has shown that the rights and duties of shareholders and employees have been rather defining for how jurisdictions have basically designed governance mechanisms in companies.

Another important issue in European company law is governance in a group of companies' context. The fundamental question is whether, and in the affirmative, how and to what degree, group management is legitimate in European jurisdictions. In a few jurisdictions, this question has been firmly settled in codified company law provisions or case law, but in most, it has not.

In cross-border business operations, a keen eye must be kept on the great variety of national governance structures and on the opportunity to choose between national governance structures within the EU area due to the rules and principles of free establishment in the TFEU. However, some legal uncertainty still exists due to the fact that national labour law, insolvency law, and criminal law may interact in diverse ways with national company law and common private international law.

CHAPTER 3

Executive and Non-executive Directors under EU Company Law

Christoph Teichmann

§3.01 INTRODUCTION

Within the framework of EU company law, the governance of companies is still mainly governed by national law. As a point of comparison, it seems useful to start with the functions a director has to fulfil in any company law system (*see* §3.02 below). The company needs one or more directors to manage its affairs and to represent it. In addition, company law tries to support the functioning of the company by offering a framework for internal corporate governance, which includes mechanisms for attributing tasks and duties to the directors and/or the shareholders.

Attempts by the European Commission to harmonise the internal structure of public companies, be it as part of the regulation on the European Company or in the so-called fifth directive, have failed in the last decades of the twentieth century (*see* §3.03 below). Due to this lack of harmonisation in corporate governance, we see a variety of governance systems in today's national laws of the Member States (*see* §3.04 below). The two most visible counterparts are the German two-tier system and the Anglo-Saxon one-tier system, but there are many intermediary forms, particularly in Scandinavia.[1] While modern comparative research seems to suggest that the diversity is more in form than in substance, there are still differences that are probably more important than acknowledged by the convergence theory.

Nowadays, when adopting company law directives (CLDs), the European Commission usually takes the viewpoint that the diversity of national corporate governance

1. *See also* Carsten Gerner-Beuerle et al., *Study on Directors' Duties and Liabilities* 7 (London School of Economics 2013). Board structures in a number of Member States cannot easily be classified according to the 'monistic' and 'dualistic' divide.

systems should be respected and not be overturned by secondary law.[2] The overall impression that European secondary law is somewhat 'corporate governance neutral' may not be completely adequate though. It is true that the EU has given up any attempts to unify the national corporate governance models. But the harmonisation of company law quite often touches issues that cannot be regulated without taking into account the national corporate governance system. As a consequence, even those proposals that do not aim at regulating corporate governance as such are influenced by and influence the corporate governance systems of the Member States (*see* §3.05 below). This chapter therefore finally pleads for more awareness in the legislative process regarding the corporate governance framework within which a particular proposal will have to be implemented (*see* conclusions §3.06 below).

§3.02 THE FUNCTIONS OF A DIRECTOR UNDER COMPANY LAW

The analysis of the importance of European company law regarding the functions and duties of executive and/or non-executive directors starts with a general assessment of the functions that are attributed to directors in the national legal systems: Usually, directors represent the company vis-à-vis third parties (*see* [A] below), they assume the management function within the internal corporate governance framework (*see* [B] below) and they are held responsible for the fulfilment of numerous duties in the public interest (*see* [C] below). Sometimes de facto directors act as if they had been nominated as directors, or, the other way round, nominee directors who have been appointed do not actively assume the functions of a director. Both cases raise the question as to who should, for the application of a particular legal provision, be considered to be the director of the company (*see* [D] below).

Our further analysis will show that provisions of European company law have an impact on the functions attributed to directors by national law. This is particularly true for the first directive on disclosure (adopted 1968) insofar as it deals with the legal representation of a company vis-à-vis third parties. In the years to follow, the European Commission first tried to harmonise the corporate governance systems of the Member States and then, due to the failure of this approach, decided not to interfere with the national corporate governance systems any longer. In 2017, the main achievements of harmonisation in company law – including the first directive – have been consolidated in the directive relating to certain aspects of company law, hereinafter referred to as 'CLD' or 'Company law Directive'.[3]

2. Recital 28 of Directive 2007/36/EC of the European Parliament and of the Council of 11 July 2007 on the exercise of certain rights of shareholders in listed companies, OJ L 184, 14.7.2007: 'It is therefore important to respect the diversity of corporate governance systems within the Union, which reflect the Member States' views about the roles of companies and of bodies responsible for the determination of the remuneration policy and of the remuneration of individual directors.'
3. Directive (EU) 2017/1132 of the European Parliament and of the Council of 14 June 2017 relating to certain aspects of company law, OJ L 169/46, 30.5.2017.

[A] Representation of the Company Vis-à-Vis Third Parties

The reason why a company needs a director lies in the legal nature of the company. In the famous wording of the *Daily Mail* case, 'unlike natural persons, companies are creatures of the law'.[4] When duly incorporated a company acquires legal personality separate from the personality of its members. As a separate legal entity, the company is to be treated like any other person with rights and liabilities of its own.[5] As opposed to natural persons, however, the company as a legal person cannot interact with other persons in the real word unless there are natural persons acting on behalf of it. 'Companies, being artificial persons, of necessity have to be run by and act through individuals.'[6]

Regarding the representation of a company, two theories had evolved in different European jurisdictions:[7] The German *Organtheorie* assumes that company law has to provide the company with legal organs whose function consists in taking the decisions and expressing the will of the company. The word 'organ' indicates the similarity to human beings where the acts of their hands or the words of their mouth are directly attributed to the individual – ensuing legal consequences such as tort liability or contractual obligations. The director, in this concept, is the organ whose function is to act as the mouth of the company. Consequently, declarations expressed by the director are to be treated as declarations expressed by the company. This function of representing the company is based on company law and not on the will of the shareholders. The shareholders can pick the person whom they wish to be the director. But, they cannot change his or her legal status of being the representative of the company.

As opposed to this, the *mandate theory* is based on the relationship between an agent and the principal. In general civil law, individuals may appoint agents to act on their behalf. The power of the agent to act on behalf of the principal is limited by the authority the principal has voluntarily granted to the agent. If the principal asks the agent to buy a car for a maximum price of EUR 40,000, the principal has no legal authority to conclude a contract for a price of EUR 60,000. Applied to company law, this concept results in the director being an agent of the company. His or her power of representation is not simply based on the legal status of being a director; instead, it is derived from the authority granted by the shareholders. As a consequence, the ultra vires doctrine limits the authority to represent the company to the object of the

4. Case 81/87, *The Queen v. H. M. Treasury and Commissioners of Inland Revenue, ex parte Daily Mail and General Trust plc*, 27.9.1988, ECLI:EU:C:1988:456, para. 19.
5. In England, this principle has been confirmed in the *Salomon v. Salomon case* (*see* Brenda Hannigan, Company Law 42 (Oxford University Press 4th ed. 2016)). In Germany, the creation of a separate legal entity can be derived from §11 and §13 GmbH-Gesetz (private companies) and §1 (1) AktienG (public companies).
6. Vanessa Edwards, *EC Company Law* 34 (Oxford University Press 1999).
7. For an account of the two theories, *see* Stefan Grundmann, *European Company Law* 143 (De Gruyter 2007); *Supra* n. 6, 43 et seq. (1999); Alexander Schall & David Günther, *Article 9 Acts of the Organs of a Company and Its Representation*, 1, 98 (Peter Kindler & Jan Lieder eds 2021); Christoph Teichmann, *Binnenmarktkonformes Gesellschaftsrecht* 204 et seq. (De Gruyter 2006).

company.[8] The object of the company reflects the will of the shareholders and must be respected by the director. Hence, the director of a company, the object clause of which limits its activities to acquiring and selling cars has no legal authority to buy and sell fruit and vegetables. The *Organtheorie*, however, would argue that such activities are legally binding for the company, even if they exceeded the object clause of the company because the director is the 'organ' of the company, and an action of the director equates an action of the company.

The first CLD (1968) has opted in favour of the *Organtheorie*, stating that 'acts done by the organs of the company shall be binding upon it even if those acts are not within the objects of the company, unless such acts exceed the power that the law confers or allows to be conferred on those organs'. The same provision can nowadays be found in Article 9 CLD. It is worth mentioning that this article reflects the German approach even though all the other Member States at the time of the adoption of the first directive – with the UK not having joined the Community yet – followed the ultra vires doctrine.[9] It might be surprising that a directive did not adopt the majority rule in this respect. It could be argued, however, that a rule protecting third parties and dispensing them from enquiring the internal delegation rules of the company was more appropriate for being applied in a cross-border environment.[10]

[B] Management of the Company and Relationship to the Shareholders

The second reason why a company needs a director is related to the internal organisation of the company. Depending on the size of the business, shareholders usually are not in a position to personally run the daily affairs of the company. They delegate this task to the management. This does not exclude shareholders from assuming a management position, but for the sake of clarity, the functions of ownership and management are legally separated.[11] As the relationship between the shareholders and the management does not directly affect third parties, the details of the internal structure are generally left to the articles and are subject to the resolutions of the shareholders.[12]

It follows that shareholders are free to nominate one director or a board of directors with several members. They may attribute functions and titles, such as chief executive officer, chief finance officer, etc., as they wish. This freedom granted for the internal organisation of the company is a core feature of English company law.[13] In other jurisdictions, such as Germany, it may be restricted to private companies

8. *See* Mihir Naniwadekar, *The Law of Agency as Applied in Company Transactions* 5 ECFR 280, 286 (2008).
9. Edwards, *supra* n. 6, at 33 et seq.
10. Grundmann, *supra* n. 7, at 143, Teichmann, *supra* n. 7, at 232.
11. *See* Gregor Bachmann et al., *Regulating the Closed Corporation* Special Volume 4 ECFR 92 (2014).
12. Instead of mandatory rules, legislators offer either default rules or enabling rules concerning the internal affairs of the company, *see* Bachmann, *supra* n. 11, 18 et seq.
13. *See* Jonathan Rickford, *Fundamentals, Developments and Trends in British Company Law – Some Wider Reflections* ECFR 391, 405 (2004): 'There is in principle an infinite range of

(*Gesellschaft mit beschränkter Haftung*), while the internal structure of a public company (*Aktiengesellschaft*) is regulated by mandatory law.[14] Other jurisdictions may have found different solutions to the same problem that companies need flexibility for their internal affairs. In France, for instance, the legislative invention of the '*société par actions simplifiée (SAS)*' was a response to the needs of businesses asking for a more flexible corporate structure.[15]

Notwithstanding the differences of the national corporate governance framework, academic debates usually focus on the same problems that need to be solved inside a company: The directors owe a duty of loyalty to the company, they have to apply professional standards of care when managing the company and they have to avoid conflicts of interest, just to name a few. The different national systems with regard to duties and liabilities of directors have been thoroughly analysed by a comparative study in 2013.[16] In their study, Gerner-Beuerle, Paech and Schuster point out differences in the regulatory approach (legal rules versus case law, general clause versus detailed list of duties), in the addressees of directors' duties (validly appointed board members and de facto directors), in the understanding of the duty of loyalty (as the duty to avoid conflicts of interest), the nature of liability (collective or individual) and the limitations of liability (ratification by the board or the shareholders, D&O insurance, etc.).[17]

Any harmonisation of this area of company law seems an impossible task since the duties and liabilities are deeply rooted in the national legal systems and strongly connected to other areas of the law. 'All legal systems', Gerner-Beuerle, Paech & Schuster conclude, 'draw on principles of general contract law, tort law, or fiduciary principles to supplement the company law-specific rules where necessary'.[18] In Germany, for instance, directors owe damages to the company if they do not apply professional standards of care; the burden of proof as to whether the management applied reasonable care and diligence lies on the director.[19] Some Member States follow the same approach; others put the burden of proof on the applicant.[20] What makes comparison even more difficult is the fact that functionally comparable liability rules may be found in company law, tort law or insolvency law. Even on the national level,

relationships which can be set by and under the articles between the company in general meeting and the board, and between the board and its parts, or indeed other agents and employees.'

14. The flexibility of a German GmbH is expressed indirectly by § 46 (2) GmbH-Gesetz stating that the following provisions on internal organisation are default rules. The rigidity of the German Aktiengesellschaft is rooted in § 23 (5) Aktiengesetz stating that provisions in this act are mandatory while default rules are the exception (a principle also known as 'Satzungsstrenge').
15. Pierre-Henri Conac, *La société par actions simplifiée: une revolution démocratique*, 9 (Pierre-Henri Conac & Isabelle Urbain-Parleani eds, 2016).
16. Gerner-Beuerle et al., *supra* n. 1, at 240.
17. *Ibid.*, at 240, the conclusions.
18. *Ibid.*, introduction, viii.
19. *See* §93(2) Aktiengesetz: 'Vorstandsmitglieder, die ihre Pflichten verletzen, sind der Gesellschaft zum Ersatz des daraus entstehenden Schadens als Gesamtschuldner verpflichtet. Ist streitig, ob sie die Sorgfalt eines ordentlichen und gewissenhaften Geschäftsleiters angewandt haben, so tritt sie die Beweislast. ...'.
20. Gerner-Beuerle, *supra* n. 1, 98 et seq.

it is not always clear in legal literature and in case law whether an instrument should be classified as company law, insolvency law or tort law.[21]

[C] Attributing Duties in the Public Interest

Finally, the legal status of a director is not exclusively governed by legal rules that are concerned with the functioning of the company. In many areas of the law, the director of a company is mentioned as the person responsible for the fulfilment of particular duties in the public interest. For instance, it is the directors who are responsible for setting up the annual accounts and for filing them with the competent register.[22] It is the directors who may be prosecuted if the environment is polluted or if taxes or social security contributions are not paid when they are due. Such rules also may be explained by the fact that the company is an artificial legal entity. The legal entity cannot really be impressed by sanctions that are traditionally designed to address the behaviour of human beings. For these reasons, the directors are personally held accountable in cases where duties are violated which are regulated in the public interest. An example from German law is the duty to file for insolvency (§ 15a *Insolvenzordnung*) which is addressed to the organ representing the company vis-à-vis third parties (*Vertretungsorgan*). Directors who are failing to comply with this duty are committing a tort and will be liable to the creditors for any deterioration of their position caused thereby.

In cases where European law creates a duty in the public interest, it usually follows the above-mentioned 'corporate governance neutrality' approach (*see* §3.01) and does not attribute these duties to a particular organ of the company. The directive on annual fiscal statements[23], for example, creates duties that are attributed to the undertaking as such. In this sense, Article 4(1) of the directive states that the annual financial statements 'shall *for all undertakings* comprise, as a minimum, the balance sheet, the profit and loss account and the notes to the financial statements'.[24] The directive itself does not specify the persons who shall be responsible for drawing up the financial statements. Instead, Article 33 of the directive requires the Member States to point out the addressees of such duties:

> Member States shall ensure that the members of the administrative, management and supervisory bodies of an undertaking, *acting within the competences assigned to them by national law*, have collective responsibility for ensuring that: the annual financial statement, the management report and, when provided separately, the

21. *Ibid.*, introduction, viii et seq.
22. At least this is the situation in Germany, *see* §325(1) Handelsgesetzbuch: 'Die Mitglieder des vertretungsberechtigten Organs einer Kapitalgesellschaft haben für die Gesellschaft folgende Unterlagen, sofern sie aufzustellen oder zu erstellen sind, in deutscher Sprache offenzulegen: …'.
23. Directive 2013/34/EU of 26 June 2013 on the annual financial statements, consolidated financial statements and related reports of certain types of undertakings, OJ L 182/19, 29.6.2013.
24. Emphasis added by the author.

corporate governance statement ... are drawn up and published in accordance with the requirements of this Directive ... .[25]

Applied to a German *GmbH*, which regularly does not have to establish a supervisory board, this means that only the directors are responsible for drawing up the annual financial statement (cf. §325(1) *Handelsgesetzbuch*); in a public company (*AG*), the management board will draw up the financial statement and the supervisory board will approve it (cf. §§170 et seq. *Aktiengesetz*).

[D] Nominee and De Facto Directors

Life would be easy if it were always clear who is really addressed by the duties imposed on the 'director' of a company. Reality knows different shades of grey when it comes to determine the person who is really managing the company and/or the person who should be responsible for managing the company. In the above-mentioned study, a helpful classification of such cases can be found:[26] The main addressees of directors' duties are the persons who are validly appointed to be a director or a member of the body managing the company ('de jure director'). Most Member States, however, also discuss the duties of persons who influence the management of the company as if they were de jure directors or who act on behalf of the company as if they were de jure directors. Such persons may be addressed by classifications such as '*shadow director*', '*dirigeant de fait*' or '*faktischer Geschäftsführer*'.

The reverse problem arises where de jure directors do not effectively manage the company. As mere 'front' or 'nominee directors' they are shielding those persons who really manage the company from the liability attached to the function of a de jure director.[27] The obvious and widespread reaction seems to be holding the de jure director accountable.[28] It seems that Member States insofar agree. The vast majority also agrees that the duties of the de jure director should be applied to other persons with a comparable managing power.[29] But, it is usually left to the courts to determine what factual elements are required to apply the duties of a de jure director to persons who have not been officially nominated as directors.

It seems that European company law has not a lot to offer to solve the problem.[30] The issue of 'shadow directors' who exercise a certain power over the de jure directors and may even give instructions regarding the management of the company is closely linked to corporate groups,[31] just another area where the EU until now has failed to find

25. Emphasis added by the author.
26. Gerner-Beuerle, *supra* n. 1, at ix.
27. For a deeper analysis of the problem, *see* Karsten Engsig Sørensen, *'Front' or 'Straw men' Directors: A Missing Element in the Effort to Prevent Abuse of Companies?* ECFR 749 et seq. (2021).
28. Sørensen *supra* n. 27, at 761.
29. Gerner-Beuerle, *supra* n. 1, at ix.
30. Sørensen *supra* n. 27, at 771 sees a strong case for further regulation in this field.
31. For a comparative analysis of the liability of shadow directors in a group context, *see* Forum Europaeum Corporate Group Law, *Corporate Group Law for Europe* 1 EBOR 165, 192, 248 et seq. (2000) DOI: 10.1017/s1566752900000148.

a common approach.[32] In other cases, it is not company law but other areas of the law which make sure that specific duties are imposed on those persons who are really running the business.[33] Germany may be referred to as a country which has introduced provisions in insolvency law regarding the directors' duty to file for insolvency: In a company where no management exists ('*führungslose Gesellschaft*'), the shareholders are personally accountable for the fulfilment of this duty (§15a(3) Insolvenzordnung).

The above-mentioned provisions of the CLD that go back to the first CLD clearly focus on de jure directors. This is confirmed by Article 8 CLD, referring to irregularities in the appointment of the director. Such irregularities shall be barred by the formalities of disclosure. A third party, in other words, can rely on the formalities of disclosure and can assume that the person who is disclosed as director of the company has the power to represent the company. Such a provision would be useless if the directive was addressing de facto directors who, by definition, have never been appointed at all. The focus on de jure directors is in line with the overall motivation of the directive to protect third parties against a situation where the obligations entered into in the name of the company are not valid.[34] In the interest of third parties, it is sufficient to clarify that the person who is appointed and disclosed as being the director of the company has the authority to enter into agreements on behalf of the company.

Finally, the problem of de facto directors may be connected with European secondary law insofar as the '*effet utile*' principle is concerned. If European law creates a particular duty in the public interest, Member States have to make sure that such a duty is effectively enforced in their national system. As a consequence, it might be a matter of effectively transposing a directive to ensure that those persons who are de facto managing the company are held accountable for compliance with such duties.

§3.03 FAILED ATTEMPTS TO DEVELOP A EUROPEAN CORPORATE GOVERNANCE MODEL

In the early days of the European Community, the diversity of national company law was considered an obstacle for the Common Market. The ambitious harmonisation programme of the European Commission aimed at creating a true 'European company law' starting with the formation of the company and ending with its liquidation. It also included an attempt to harmonise the corporate governance of large companies. In 1970, the Commission published a proposal for a regulation on the statute of European

32. *See* Christoph Teichmann, *Towards a European Framework for Cross-Border Group Management* 13 ECL 5, 150 et seq. (2016) DOI: 10.54648/eucl2016022.
33. Sørensen *supra* n. 27, at 765 mentions Regulation (EC) 1071/2009 regarding road transport operators as an example.
34. Cf. Recital 5 Directive (EU) 2017/1132 of the European Parliament and of the Council of 14 June 2017 relating to certain aspects of company law (codification) Text with EEA relevance, OJ L 169, 30.6.2017: 'The protection of third parties should be ensured by provisions which restrict to the greatest possible extent the grounds on which obligations entered into in the name of companies limited by shares or otherwise having limited liability are not valid.'

stock corporations[35] two years later, accompanied by the proposal for a fifth directive on the internal structure of public companies.[36] These proposals regulated a corporate governance system which was inspired by the German two-tier model.[37] The most striking feature of these early attempts to find a European corporate governance system was the mandatory rule that employees should have a right to nominate one-third of the supervisory board members.[38] The accession of new Member States who did neither apply a two-tier structure nor co-determination on the board level led to criticism and fostered a less intrusive way of regulating the European Company Statute.[39] Finally, the European Company Regulation as adopted in 2001 offers to companies the choice between the one-tier and the two-tier structure,[40] while the proposal for a fifth directive was officially withdrawn by the Commission in 2001.[41]

While the European Company was still negotiated, the European Commission, in 1999, announced an initiative to evaluate national corporate governance codes with a view to developing a European code. The purpose of the study was to further the understanding of commonalities and differences in corporate governance practices among EU Member States.[42] It turned out that, at the time of the study, every Member State except Austria and Luxembourg had at least one code; some of them even had several codes.[43] The study found that most - if not all - of the codes placed significant emphasis on the need to establish a supervisory body that is distinct from management to ensure accountability and provide strategic guidance.[44] It was also widely acknowledged by codes that supervisory functions might be delegated to board committees.[45] This applied particularly to areas where the interests of management and the interests of the company might come into conflict, such as audit, remuneration and nomination.

The study concluded: 'For the most part, the code recommendations are remarkable in their similarity and serve as a converging force.'[46] For these reasons, the study did not strongly advocate a EU-wide corporate governance code. The authors saw the risk that such a code would be more likely to result in a lowest common denominator

35. Proposal for a council regulation embodying a statute for the European Company, COM/70/600 FINAL, OJ EC, 10.10.1970, C 124/1.
36. Proposal for a fifth directive on the coordination of safeguards which for the protection of the interests of members and outsiders are required by Member States of companies within the meaning of Art. 59, second paragraph, with respect to company structure and to the power and responsibilities of company boards, OJ 1972, COM (1972) 887.
37. *See* Arts 62 et seq. of the proposal for the Statute of European stock corporations.
38. *See* Art. 137 of the proposal for the Statute of European stock corporations. *See also* the European Commission 'green paper' on Employee Participation and Company Structure, COM(75) 570 final, Bulletin of the EC, Supplement 8/75, in particular of 'Sociétés Anonymes'.
39. *See, e.g.*, Edwards, *supra* n. 6, at 388.
40. Article 38 of the Statute for a European Company Council Regulation (EC) No. 2157/2001, OJ L 294/1, 10.11.2001.
41. *Withdrawal of the Commission Proposals which are no longer topical*, COM(2001) 763 final.
42. Holly J. Gregory & Robert T. Simmelkjaer II, *Comparative Study of Corporate Governance Codes Relevant to the European Union and Its Member States* 1 (2002).
43. *Ibid.*, 2.
44. *Ibid.*, 5.
45. *Ibid.*, 5.
46. *Ibid.*, 6.

rather than 'best practice'.[47] Instead, the study recommended focusing legislative efforts on the reduction of legal and regulatory barriers to shareholder engagement and cross-border voting.[48] The Commission in its Plan to Move Forward agreed with these conclusions and assumed that a European corporate governance code would not contribute significantly to the improvement of corporate governance in the EU.[49]

§3.04 THE EUROPEAN LANDSCAPE OF CORPORATE GOVERNANCE

[A] Convergence of National Corporate Governance Systems

The above-mentioned study comparing national corporate governance codes understood 'corporate governance' as involving the mechanisms by which a business enterprise, organised in a limited liability corporate form, is directed and controlled; this includes, in particular, mechanisms by which corporate managers are held accountable for corporate conduct and performance.[50] The study concludes that while codes tend to express a relatively common view of what good governance means, the greatest distinctions result from differences in law.[51] In 2013, the study on directors' duties and liabilities found out that despite recent trends of convergence, one can still find a significant degree of variation between the company laws of the EU Member States.[52]

Academic authors came to similar conclusions,[53] and, based on comparative work of the last decades, it can be assumed that the conclusion is still justified.[54] The concept of a unitary board where all directors would be in the same position to manage the company is no longer valid in large and particularly in listed companies. Here, the functions of *managing* the company and of *supervising* the management's activities are separated.[55] It is worth mentioning that *representing* the company in relation to third parties sometimes is regarded as a third function to be distinguished from the first two

47. *Ibid.*, 7.
48. *Ibid.*
49. European Commission Communication, *Modernising Company Law and Enhancing Corporate Governance in the European Union – A Plan to Move Forward* 11, COM(2003) 284 final.
50. Gregory, *supra* n. 42, at 1.
51. *Ibid.*, 3.
52. Gerner-Beuerle, *supra* n. 1, at 3.
53. For example, Eddy Wymeersch, *A Status Report on Corporate Governance Rules and Practices in Some Continental European States* 1045 et seq. (Klaus Hopt et al. eds, European Corporate Governance Institute 1998).
54. *See* for instance: Klaus J. Hopt, *Der Aufsichtsrat – Bedeutungswandel, Konvergenz, unternehmerische Mitverantwortung, Pflichten- und Haftungszuwachs, Zeitschrift für Unternehmens und Gesellschaftsrecht*, Zeit. Unt. Ges. Recht po. 507 et seq. (2019) DOI: 10.1515/zgr-2019-0016; for a comparative analysis of Germany, the UK and the US, *see* Klaus J. Hopt & Patrick C. Leyens, *The Structure of the Board of Directors: Boards and Governance Strategies in the US, the UK and Germany* 116 et seq. (Afra Afsharipour & Martin Gelter eds, European Corporate Governance Institute 2021); Adriaan Dorresteijn & Cornelis de Groot, *Corporate Governance Codes: Origins and Perspectives* 31 et seq. (Steef M. Bartman ed. 2006).
55. Wymeersch, *supra* n. 53, at 1045.

functions.[56] Taking a management decision does not necessarily imply carrying out this decision by way of contracting with third parties. And supervision of management does not necessarily involve power of representation vis-à-vis third parties.

The comparative study of corporate governance codes found the trend towards convergence to be more numerous and more powerful than any trend towards differentiation: 'For the most part, the code recommendations are remarkable in their similarity and serve as a converging force.'[57] This was even true for the structural difference between the one-tier and the two-tier board. Both systems recognise a supervisory function and a managerial function, although the distinction is more formalised in the two-tier structure.[58] The one-tier system may result in a closer cooperation and better information flow within the board, while the two-tier system offers a clearer, formal separation of management and control.[59]

[B] Divergence of National Corporate Governance Systems

At first sight, the one-tier and the two-tier system may be clearly distinguished: In the one-tier system, management and monitoring powers are conferred to the unitary board of directors; in the two-tier system, the functions of management and control are delegated to two different organs. While British law, even after Brexit, can be referred to as the role model for a one-tier system within Europe, it should also be kept in mind that many EU Member States with a one-tier system - such as France and Spain - belong to the continental law family and therefore cannot easily be put into the same basket as the British system.

A striking difference between the French and the British corporate governance system emerges when comparing the regulatory approaches of the two countries: The UK *Companies Act* is completely silent regarding the tasks of directors and the functioning of the board; it does not even mention the board.[60] The sophisticated division of functions between executive and non-executive directors can only be found in the UK Corporate Governance Code. This Code only addresses listed companies and is not even legally binding; instead, it relies on the 'comply or explain' mechanism.[61] From a continental law perspective, it is also a difficult task to understand the legal

56. *Ibid.* (1095/1096).
57. Gregory, *supra* n. 42, at 6.
58. *Ibid.*, 4.
59. *Ibid.*
60. *See* the scarce provision of Art. 154 Companies Act: '(1) A private company must have at least one director. (2) A public company must have at least two directors.' In practice, most companies apply the Model Articles attached to the Companies Act. But the Model Articles do not mention the board either, instead they only speak about 'director' or 'directors'. Cf. Art. 7 of the Model Articles for public companies: 'Decisions of the directors may be taken - (1) at a directors' meeting, or (2) in the form of a directors' written resolution.'
61. UK Code (p. 3): 'The Code is applicable to all companies with a premium listing, whether incorporated in the UK or elsewhere', p. 1: 'The Code does not set out a rigid set of rules; instead, it offers flexibility through the application of Principles and through "comply or explain" Provisions and supporting guidance.' The regulatory technique of corporate governance codes is analysed in a comparative way by Adriaan Dorresteijn & Cornelis de Groot *supra* n. 54, 31, 40/41.

provision regarding the power of the directors to bind the company. Article 40 of the Companies Act stipulates that 'the power of the directors to bind the company ... is deemed to be free of any limitation under the companies constitution'. It remains unclear whether this power refers to any individual director or to the board (which is not mentioned expressly) as a whole;[62] the complex relationship between company law and the common law principles of agency remains quite opaque for continental readers.[63]

The British approach may be contrasted with the French *Code de Commerce* regulating in much detail by mandatory law the structure of management and control. The traditional one-tier board (*conseil d'administration*) is established by Article L. 225-17 Code de Commerce.[64] The law also regulates the nomination and functions of the chairman ('*président du conseil d'administration*').[65] The members of the unitary board, however, have no management functions.[66] Instead, the law provides for an additional management position, called '*directeur général*', nominated by the board.[67] This person is managing the company and representing it in relation to third parties.[68] The two functions may be combined - resulting in the prestigious title of '*Président Directeur Général*' (PDG).[69] If more managers are needed, the board may appoint one or more persons as '*directeur général délégué*'.[70]

Looking at the dichotomy of 'comply or explain' versus mandatory law, the French unitary system is much closer to the German model than to the British approach. This can be explained by the assumption that the comply or explain model is relying on market forces. It is up to the investors to assess the quality of the corporate governance system of each individual company. In this respect, the UK Code speaks for itself: 'It is the responsibility of boards to use this flexibility wisely and of investors and their advisors to assess differing company approaches thoughtfully.'[71] From a German perspective, it can be confirmed that the legislature does not believe in the wisdom of boards designing their own corporate governance system, nor in investors to force them to do so.[72] The same may be assumed for France.

62. For a discussion of this issue, *see* Alexander Schall, *Power to Directors to Bind the Company* 97 et seq. (Alexander Schall et al. ed. 2014). In this respect, the German rule arguably offers more legal clarity. Compare §78(2) German AktG: The members of the management board represent the company collectively, unless otherwise stipulated in the articles.
63. For a detailed account, *see* Naniwadekar, *supra* n. 8, at 280.
64. 'La société anonyme est administrée par un conseil d'administration composé de trois membres au moins.'
65. Cf. Art. L. 225-47 and Art. L. 225-51 Code de Commerce.
66. Maurice Cozian, Alain Viandier & Florence Deboissy, *Droit des Sociétés* 345 (no. 861) (LexisNexis 33d ed. 2020).
67. Article L. 225-51-1 Code de Commerce.
68. Cozian, *supra* n. 66, at 368 (no. 920).
69. *Ibid.*, 353, The French Code of Corporate Governance, however, recommends separating the two functions.
70. Article L. 225-53 Code de Commerce.
71. UK Corporate Governance Code, 1.
72. The history of the German two-tier system is a history of rectifying deficiencies of public companies' board organisation, *see* Christoph Teichmann, *Binnenmarktkonformes Gesellschaftsrecht* 545-558 (De Gruyter 2006).

Economic research indicates that the different approaches on the continent compared to the UK and, arguably, even more in comparison to the US[73] are due to a different ownership pattern.[74] In a liquid market with dispersed ownership, the market for corporate control will punish those boards which establish a poor corporate governance system. Since takeovers usually result in dismissing the managers, management has a strong incentive to increase the share price and thereby protect themselves against hostile takeovers. As long as investors are rewarding good corporate governance, there is an incentive to strive for an efficient corporate governance system. It has been pointed out by numerous authors that this system of 'outsider control' does not function the same way in continental Europe which contributed to the development of internal checks and balances imposed on companies by mandatory law.[75]

[C] Employee Co-determination

The greatest difference identified by the comparative study in 2002 related to employee representation in the board.[76] This has been confirmed by the 2013 study on directors' duties and liabilities.[77] Co-determination means that the shareholders are not free to elect all members of the board which results in a fundamental difference in the strength of shareholder influence in the company.[78] It also plays an important role with regard to the practical effect of rules on directors' duties and liabilities.[79] Almost half of the Member States (12 out of 27) grant employees some form of influence over the composition of the board.[80] In principle, members of the board elected by employees have the same duties and obligations as members who are nominated by the shareholders.[81] This is also a European rule to be found in the Directive on the European Company: Every member who has been elected, appointed or recommended by employees 'shall be a full member with the same rights and obligations as the members representing the shareholders, including the right to vote'.[82] Having regard to the harmonisation of European company law, employee co-determination always was and still is the main stumbling block that prevents uniform EU rules on corporate governance.

73. *See* Hopt, *supra* n. 54, at 116 et seq.
74. *See* Fabrizio Barca & Marco Becht, *Introduction*, 37 (Fabrizio Barca & Marco Bech eds, 2010), who conclude that in most Continental European countries, there is a fairly uniform distribution of the largest voting block, whereas in the UK and in the US, there is a strong 'market/management bias' towards dispersed control.
75. In this sense, Dorresteijn, *supra* n. 54, at 31, 35.
76. Gregory, *supra* n. 42, at 3.
77. Gerner-Beuerle, *supra* n. 1, at 12.
78. Gregory, *supra* n. 42, at 3.
79. Gerner-Beuerle, *supra* n. 1, at 12.
80. *Ibid.*
81. *Ibid.*
82. Council Directive 2001/86/EC of 8.10.2001, OJ 10.11.2001, L 294/22, Annex, Standard rules, part 3.

§3.05 EUROPEAN DIRECTIVES: ARE THEY REALLY CORPORATE GOVERNANCE NEUTRAL?

The European Commission nowadays takes the viewpoint that the diversity of national corporate governance systems should be respected and not be overturned by secondary law. This regulatory approach could be classified as 'corporate governance neutral' and has been clearly stated in Recital 28 of the Shareholder Rights Directive:[83] 'It is therefore important to respect the diversity of corporate governance systems within the Union, which reflect the Member States' views about the roles of companies and of bodies responsible for the determination of the remuneration policy and of the remuneration of individual directors.' A closer look at those provisions which have an inherent connection to corporate governance, however, leads to the conclusion that it is not always possible to regulate in a 'corporate governance neutral' way. Illustrations can be found in the directive relating to certain aspects of company law (*see* §3.05[A] below) as well as in the reformed shareholder rights directive (*see* §3.05[B] below).

[A] The Directive Relating to Certain Aspects of Company Law ('CLD')

In 2017, most of the existing CLDs have been consolidated in the directive relating to certain aspects of company law (CLD).[84] A quick search of the word 'director' in the CLD results in zero hits. It therefore seems that EU company law is completely ignorant about the fact that a company needs a director. But this is only half the truth. The function of directors is addressed at several occasions throughout the directive, even though the word 'director' is missing in the text.

In some provisions, the CLD, in more or less similar wording, refers to the bodies of management and control of a company ('bodies responsible for representing the company vis-à-vis third parties, administration, management, supervision or control of the company'[85]). It thereby addresses the basic functions of executive and non-executive directors: They manage the company (executive directors), they supervise or control the company (non-executive directors) and they – or at least some of them – represent the company vis-à-vis third parties.

The rules dealing with the bodies of management and control date back to the first CLD of 1968.[86] The objective of this directive was the coordination of national rules concerning disclosure, the validity of obligations entered into by a company and the nullity of companies.[87] As far as disclosure and validity of obligations were concerned,

83. *Supra* n. 2.
84. *Supra* n. 3, relating to certain aspects of company law, OJ L 169/46, 30.5.2017.
85. *See*, for instance, Art. 3(e) CLD regarding the information provided in the statutes or instrument of incorporation. Similar wording can be found in Article 8 regarding the effects of disclosure and Art. 9 regarding acts of the organs of a company.
86. First Council Directive of 9 March 1968 on co-ordination of safeguards which, for the protection and in the interests of members and others, are required by Member States of companies within the meaning of the second paragraph of Art. 58 of the Treaty, with a view to making such safeguards equivalent throughout the Community, OJ L 65/8, 14.3.1968.
87. *See* second recital of the first CLD of 1968.

the directive inevitably touches the particular functions of directors in company law. Insofar as directors represent the company when entering into obligations vis-à-vis third parties, third parties can rely on the validity of such an obligation. Moreover, third parties shall have the possibility to inform themselves about the persons who are representing the company.

The importance of this directive cannot be overestimated.[88] Third parties interact with companies every day, and in cross-border circumstances, it is extremely helpful to know who can enter into legally binding obligations on behalf of the company. The directive meets the needs of cross-border business in two ways: It offers information about those who act on behalf of the company, and it regulates a protection of third parties who interact in good faith with persons who have been disclosed as being representatives of the company.

Member States shall establish a register in which a file shall be opened for each company (Article 16(1) CLD). The information stated in the register should be reliable for third parties. To this end, Member States should provide for 'preventive administrative or judicial control' of the instrument of constitution, the company's statutes and any amendments to those statutes. If there is no preventive administrative or judicial control, those documents shall be drawn up and certified in due legal form (Article 10 CLD). The latest amendment to the CLD in 2019 has even increased the standard of preventive control by rules providing for procedures to ensure verification, among other things, of the legality of the object of the company, the legality of the name of the company and the appointment of directors.[89] The latter provision has been introduced for the online formation of companies. But, it can be argued that the same level of verification should apply to traditional paper-based formations.[90]

The disclosure shall protect third parties who rely on the information in good faith. Even an irregular appointment will be irrelevant if the person concerned has been disclosed as being a member of an organ authorised to represent the company (Article 8 CLD). Once more, the focus is on those who represent the company in relation to third parties and whose power to represent the company is based on company law ('persons who, as an organ of the company, are authorized to represent it').

As already mentioned above (*see* §3.02[A] above), persons who are acting on behalf of the company may derive this authority from either civil law or company law: In most Member States, national company law provides for an organ which is entitled to represent the company vis-à-vis third parties. In German private companies, this would be the person which is nominated as '*Geschäftsführer*', and in public companies, the members of the management board ('*Vorstand*') collectively. A person who is appointed to such a position has unlimited authority to represent the company. Those who are not appointed to be part of an organ of the company may acquire delegated

88. Stefan Grundmann, *European Company Law* 132 (Intersentia 2007), rightly classifies the first directive as a 'cornerstone for European Company Law'.
89. Article 13g (3) Directive (EU) 2019/1151 of 20 June 2019 amending Directive (EU) 2017/1132, OJ L 196/80, 11.07.2019.
90. Christoph Teichmann, *Die digitale GmbH-Gründung: Ein Entwicklungssprung für die vorsorgende Rechtspflege*, GmbH-Rundschau 1237, 1243 (2021).

power of attorney, based on the civil code. This delegation does not automatically come with a certain position; it has to be accorded by the organ of the company to the particular person.

These provisions build upon the '*Organtheorie*' of German company law, and they tried to abolish the 'ultra vires' doctrine which was predominant in other Member States (*see* §3.2[B] above). This attempt to regulate against the company law tradition of Member States without changing the basic concepts of company law did not fully succeed. It has been pointed out by British authors that their system did not really live up to the expectation of the directive that the ultra vires doctrine would be abolished.[91] The traditions of company law proved to be more resistant than the European Commission expected. This led to the result that German courts did never accept the British register as valid proof for the power of representation of a director, even though this was the very intention of the first directive to facilitate such task and notwithstanding the fact that German courts would have no problem to accept an extract issued by Member States which belong to the continental legal family.[92]

[B] Remuneration of Directors (Shareholder Rights Directive 2017)

Another example of the short-sighted regulatory approach of a corporate governance neutrality is the directive on shareholder rights. The original version of this directive did not address the functions of executive or non-executive directors. The revision of this directive in 2017, however, introduced a provision whereby shareholders should have an effective say on the remuneration policy for directors.[93] This obviously raises the question of what the directive means by the term 'director'. Being aware of the different corporate governance systems in the Member State, the European Commission proposed a catch-all definition: 'director means any member of the administration, management or supervisory bodies of a company'.[94]

At first sight, it looks like a Salomonic solution to apply the rules on directors' remuneration to all kinds of directors in the different corporate governance systems. From a functional perspective, however, a corporate governance-neutral solution seems to be erroneous in this matter. In law and economics literature, remuneration of directors is an essential tool to realign the interests of shareholders and management. Based on the theory of the principal/agent conflict, the academic debate argues that there is a separation of management and ownership in large companies which creates adverse incentives for management to act in their own interests and not in the interest of shareholders. One solution to overcome this divide between management and

91. Edwards, *supra* n. 6, at 42 et seq.
92. *See* Oberlandesgericht Düsseldorf, NZG 1385 (2019).
93. Recital 29 of Directive (EU) 2017/828 amending Directive 2007/36/EC as regards the encouragement of long-term shareholder engagement.
94. Insertion to Art. 2 of the Directive, *see* Proposal for a Directive of the European Parliament and the Council amending Directive 2007/36/EC as regards the encouragement of long-term shareholder engagement and Directive 2013/34/EU as regards certain elements of the corporate governance statement, COM(2014) 213 final.

ownership consists in creating checks and balances within the corporate structure that enable the shareholders to monitor the performance of the management. Another solution consists in linking the remuneration scheme to the stock price which results in a realignment of shareholders' and managers' interests.

Member States have chosen different varieties of these two solutions. Since shareholders usually do not have the time and the capacity to effectively monitor the management, non-executive directors should do the job. In such a system, the non-executive directors should also determine the remuneration of the executive directors. Usually, this task is delegated to a remuneration committee that should consist of independent non-executive directors. Legally, however, in a one-tier system, they may be members of the same board as the executive directors. In the above-mentioned definition created by the Commission's proposal, they would all be covered as being 'members of the administration body'. This treatment ignores the basically different functions of executive and non-executive directors.

The academic debate concerns remuneration instruments that are linked to the price of the shares as an important element in fighting the negative effects of the so-called principal-agent conflict. The major agency problem in large companies lies in assuring that managers are responsive to the owners' interests rather than pursuing their own personal interests.[95] In order to solve this problem, 'governance strategies' may be applied which seek to facilitate the principals' control over their agents' behaviour.[96] As a consequence, any initiative to regulate the procedures and competences for the determination of directors' remuneration goes to the heart of the corporate governance debate in each Member State. The Commission realised this when it proposed the shareholder vote on remuneration without taking into account that in the two-tier system, the supervisory board is competent for the remuneration policy. It does not come as a surprise that such a proposal faced some criticism in the German debate. It is a rare occasion that trade unions and corporate law professors concur in their opinions. Academic scholars argued that the shareholder meeting with its dispersed ownership structure is not the appropriate organ to determine the details of a remuneration policy.[97] Trade unions criticised that the shift of competence from the supervisory board, where co-determination applies, to the shareholder meeting would reduce the importance of co-determination.[98] As a consequence, the final wording of the directive gives Member States the choice to opt for either a competence of the shareholder meeting or of the supervisory board. It does not come as a surprise that Germany opted for the second solution. The ideal of a unified system in Europe, however, was not achieved.

---

95. Reinier Kraakmann et al., *The Anatomy of Corporate Law* 36 (Oxford University Press 2d ed. 2009).
96. *Ibid.*, 38
97. Peter Hommelhoff, *Aktuelle Impulse aus dem europäischen Unternehmensrecht: Eine Herausforderung für Deutschland*, NZG 1329 (1333) (2015).
98. Deutscher Gewerkschaftsbund, *Stellungnahme zum Entwurf eines Gesetzes zur Umsetzung der zweiten Aktionärsrechterichtlinie (ARUG II)*, 13 May 2019, 4.

§3.06 CONCLUSIONS

Notwithstanding an impressive body of EU secondary law regarding the creation and the functioning of companies, EU law has not really to offer a lot when it comes to determining the division of functions between executive and non-executive directors. The European rules on disclosure focus on the power of the persons nominated to the board to represent the company vis-à-vis third parties. Most of the other European company law rules try to adopt a corporate governance-neutral approach, respecting the diversity of corporate governance systems in the Member States.

To some extent, diversity may be regarded rather as a theoretical problem than a practical issue, as most company law systems have to solve the same problems of management and control within a company. But important differences remain, in particular those related to the involvement of employees in the management or supervisory organ. European legislation in some cases did not achieve its full unifying impact due to the fact that it neglected the differences between the national corporate governance systems. Consequently, future harmonisation in company law should take into account the fact that there is still a considerable degree of divergence among EU Member States.

PART II Liabilities and Rights

CHAPTER 4

Disqualification of Directors

Sjur Swensen Ellingsæter

§4.01 INTRODUCTION

This chapter discusses and compares which persons under Danish, Norwegian and UK law may be disqualified from being part of management organs or holding other positions in private and public limited liability companies.

Disqualification of directors is a field that so far has been subject to little EU law harmonization. Following the insertion of a new Article 13i in Directive (EU) 2017/1132 in 2019,[1] EU law now requires Member States to have rules on the disqualification of directors. This provision requires the Member States to apply such rules to persons mentioned in point (i) of Article 14(d), that is, persons that either as a body constituted by law or as members of such a body are authorized to represent the company in dealings with third parties and in legal proceedings.[2] However, the Directive leaves for each Member State to determine other key issues of any disqualification regime, such as whether persons other than those mentioned in point (i) of Article 14(d) should also be liable to disqualification, as well as the effects of disqualification.[3]

Disqualification is generally not viewed as punishment for past misbehaviour. Rather, the rationale is to protect the public from future improper conduct. Nonetheless,

1. Directive (EU) 2019/1151 of the European Parliament and of the Council of 20 June 2019 amending Directive (EU) 2017/1132 as regards the use of digital tools and processes in company law [2019] OJ L 186.
2. Moreover, the Directive specifies that the disqualification rules shall make it possible to take into account the fact that a person is disqualified in another Member State or other relevant information from another Member State. The Directive does not set out requirements regarding on what grounds such persons may be disqualified.
3. *See also* Council Regulation (EC) No. 2157/2001 of 8 October 2001 on the Statute for a European company (SE) Art. 47, which provides that persons that are subject to certain restrictions under national disqualification regimes may not be part of a European public limited liability company's organs.

a disqualification is onerous for the person concerned. She could face restrictions on her freedom to serve on a company's management organs or take up senior employment positions. Moreover, a disqualified person may in practice be barred from using an 'owner-manager company' – i.e., a company where the sole shareholder and only member of the management organs is the same person – to conduct business under limited liability.

The scope of disqualification regimes is typically – although not always – at the outset restricted to persons that have held positions in the management organs of a company that has become subject to insolvency proceedings. Conversely, neither shareholders nor (other) employees are usually at risk of being disqualified for any misbehaviour they may have displayed. Accordingly, director disqualification regimes differentiate between members of management organs and other persons connected to companies. However, this may merely be a starting point. A disqualification regime that only extends to persons that have formally held positions in management organs may easily be circumvented by appointing 'straw men' that act on the instructions of the real decision-makers. A measure that potentially could mitigate this issue is to extend the disqualification regimes to persons that – notwithstanding not being formally appointed to a company's management organs – are considered as de facto having acted in such positions by virtue of their influence over the management organs' decision-making. This necessitates drawing up criteria for identifying the persons who on account of such influence should be included in the personal scope of the disqualification powers. If the criteria employed are vague, the result would be to blur the distinction between managers and other persons such as (other) employees and shareholders. This would in turn decrease legal certainty for persons involved in decision-making in companies.

Against this background, this chapter seeks to investigate three questions: First, which formal positions at limited liability companies render a person susceptible to being disqualified under the Danish, Norwegian and UK disqualification regimes? Second, when may persons be disqualified on account of having de facto functioned as a member of a management organ? Third, what restrictions does disqualification entail?

National disqualification regimes are chosen as the objects of analysis due to the low degree of harmonization under current EU and European Economic Area (EEA) law. Norwegian and UK law are chosen on account of being jurisdictions that for several decades have had in place disqualification regimes. Danish law is included as an example of a jurisdiction whose disqualification rules are of a relatively recent vintage.

The chapter predominantly focuses on the disqualification of persons who de jure or de facto have been part of the management organs of private and public limited liability companies. We will only consider the extent to which persons may be disqualified due to a disregard for interests typically protected under company law. Accordingly, our enquiry will not concern whether persons may be disqualified following personal insolvency proceedings or due to breaches of competition law.[4]

4. *See, e.g.*, Company Directors Disqualification Act (CDDA) section 9A.

§4.02 WHICH PERSONS MAY BE DISQUALIFIED: DE JURE ROLES

[A] Introduction

This section discusses the extent to which persons come within the scope of the disqualification regimes due to having held certain positions at a company. We will term appointments to such positions as de jure roles. This contrasts with the subject of §4.03 below, which is the extent to which a person who has not held de jure roles at a company may be disqualified for having de facto acted as a member of its management organs.

For each national regime, the following sections describe the management organs of national limited liability companies, the extent to which persons are susceptible to disqualification due to having been appointed to these organs, and whether the personal scope of the disqualification regime extends to other formal roles.

[B] Danish Law

The Danish Insolvency Act § 157 sets out the power for Danish courts to disqualify persons who have participated in the management of businesses that have entered insolvency proceedings.

Which formal roles equate participating in the management of a private or public limited liability company's business?[5] The answer depends on what management structure the company has chosen. Danish company law offers two avenues in this regard.[6]

Under the first approach, a company's general meeting elects the board of directors (*bestyrelsen*).[7] As a main rule, the board, in turn, appoints the executive board (*direktionen*). The board of directors is responsible for the overall and strategic management of the company and is generally authorized to make any decision that is not reserved for another company organ. The executive board is by virtue of its appointment authorized to make decisions concerning the day-to-day management of the company, i.e., decisions that are neither of great importance nor of an unusual nature.[8] The board of directors is under an obligation to ensure that the company's bookkeeping and financial reporting are satisfactory and that there are satisfactory procedures for risk management and internal controls. Moreover, the board of directors must ensure that it receives information about the financial affairs of the company and that the executive board properly discharges its obligations.

5. In Danish company law, an *anpartsselskab* is a private limited liability company, while an *aktieselskab* is a public limited liability company.
6. *See* the Danish Companies Act § 111.
7. In certain cases, the employees may have the right to appoint board members, *see* the Danish Companies Act § 140, and the articles of association may provide that other persons shall have the right to appoint board members, *see* §120.
8. The Danish Companies Act § 117.

For the purposes of the Insolvency Act § 157, the view in the preparatory works and the literature is that persons that are either appointed to the board of directors or the executive board of a company and registered as such with the Danish Business Authority will be considered as participating in the management of the company's business.[9]

Under the second approach, the executive board is responsible for the overall and strategic management of the company.[10] If the company is either a private limited liability company with employees that have exercised a right to representation in the company's management or a public limited liability company, the company must have a supervisory board (*tilsynsråd*) that supervises the executive board. As a main rule, the company's general meeting appoints the supervisory board. The duties of the supervisory board correspond to those of the board under the first approach, except that the supervisory board does not have overall responsibility for managing the company and ensuring that it is soundly organized, as this is the responsibility of the executive board.[11] If the company does not have a supervisory board, the general meeting elects the executive board.

For the purposes of the Insolvency Act § 157, the view expressed in the preparatory works and the literature is that persons that sit on a supervisory board or the executive board and are registered as such with the Danish Business Authority will be considered as participating in the management of the company's business.[12]

The power of Danish courts to disqualify persons necessitates the opening of insolvency proceedings against a body corporate or a natural person (the 'debtor').[13] A person who has been involved in the management of the debtor's business may be disqualified if he/she is deemed unfit to partake in the management of a business due to grossly irresponsible business conduct. Such conduct must have taken place later than the date falling one year before the relevant date (*fristdagen*), which usually is the date on which the court received the petition to place the company in insolvency proceedings.[14] Before making a disqualification decision, the court must consider whether the person's actions and other circumstances make it reasonable to disqualify him/her.[15] The courts will often consider the questions of unfitness and reasonableness together.[16]

[C] Norwegian Law

The Norwegian Insolvency Act § 142 sets out the powers of Norwegian courts to disqualify persons. Among those who fall within the personal scope of these powers

9. Bet. 2011:1525 135; Ulrik Rammeskow Bang-Pedersen et al., *Konkurs* 658 (Jurist- og Økonomforbundets Forlag 2d ed. 2020); Karsten Engsig Sørensen, *Konkurskarantæne* 175–176 (Mette Neville & Karsten Engsig Sørensen eds, Jurist- og Økonomforbundets Forlag 2013).
10. The Danish Companies Act § 111.
11. The Danish Companies Act §§ 116 and 118.
12. Bet. 2011:1525 135; Bang-Pedersen et al., *supra* n. 9; Engsig Sørensen, *supra* n. 9.
13. The Danish Insolvency Act § 157.
14. The Danish Insolvency Act § 1.
15. The Danish Insolvency Act § 157, 2.
16. Eva Staal & Jens Røn, *Konkurskarantæne – en status*, UfRB 25, 30 (2020).

are persons who have served as board members (*styremedlem*), alternate board members or executive managers (*daglig leder*) of a 'company'[17] that has entered insolvency proceedings.

Board members and alternate board members of private and public limited liability companies (*aksjeselskaper* and *allmennaksjeselskaper*, respectively) are generally appointed by the company's general meeting.[18] The board has the overall responsibility for managing the company's business. While the board may delegate tasks to the company's employees, it retains an obligation to ensure that the company is properly organized and must ensure that the company's business, accounts and the management of its assets are subject to sufficient control.

A public company must appoint an executive manager, while this is optional for private companies. By virtue of his/her appointment, the executive manager is authorized to make decisions concerning the day-to-day management of the company's business.[19] Conversely, the executive manager is not authorized to make decisions on matters that are unusual or of significant importance to the company. The executive manager has an obligation to ensure that the company's accounts satisfy statutory requirements and that its assets are managed in a sound manner.

The disqualification of a company's board members, deputy board members or executive manager necessitates the company having entered insolvency proceedings and such persons having held such positions during the twelve months preceding the proceedings.

The Norwegian Insolvency Act § 142 sets out two grounds for disqualifying a person falling within its personal scope. First that there is probable cause for suspecting him/her of a criminal offence in connection with the insolvency proceedings or the business that caused the insolvency. Second, that he/she has displayed inappropriate business conduct that gives reason to believe that he/she is unfit to form a new company or be a board member or executive manager of such a company. In addition to at least one ground for disqualification being met, the court must be satisfied that it is reasonable to disqualify the person concerned.

[D] UK Law

The UK disqualification regime consists of several provisions set out across the provisions of the Company Directors Disqualification Act (CDDA) that empower the courts to disqualify persons on different grounds. The powers differ in terms of the scope of persons potentially liable to be disqualified.

---

17. The Insolvency Act § 142 states that the following bodies corporate are considered companies for the purposes of the disqualification rules: private limited liability companies, public limited liability companies, branches of foreign companies, foundations, housing cooperatives, general cooperatives, mutual insurance companies and state enterprises.
18. Private Limited Liability Companies Act § 6-3; Public Limited Liability Companies Act § 6-3. Norwegian company law gives the employees of companies with more than thirty employees a right of representation, which, in turn, may require that employees appoint representatives to the board.
19. Private Limited Liability Companies Act § 6-14; Public Limited Liability Companies Act § 6-14.

CDDA section 6 empowers the courts to disqualify persons deemed 'unfit to be concerned in the management of a company'. Unfitness is the disqualification ground most frequently invoked.[20] The personal scope of CDDA section 6 comprises any 'director of a company' that has become subject to insolvency proceedings or dissolved without entering insolvency proceedings. The reference to companies includes companies registered under the Companies Act 2006 – i.e., both limited and unlimited companies – and a company that may be wound up under Part 5 of the Insolvency Act 1986, i.e., 'any association and any company, with the exception of a company registered under the Companies Act 2006'.[21] Moreover, the provisions of CDDA also extend to directors of foreign companies (which may not necessarily be subject to the insolvency jurisdiction of UK courts),[22] as well as certain other forms of bodies corporate, e.g., building societies.[23]

All companies must have at least one director, while public companies must have at least two.[24] The directors form the board of directors. UK law leaves for the company's articles of association to determine both the process of electing directors to the board and the powers of the board.[25] Insofar as the applicable articles are the current model articles developed by the UK government, the general meeting will have the power to appoint directors to the board.[26] The model articles moreover provide that the directors as a main rule 'are responsible for the management of the company's business, for which purpose they may exercise all the powers of the company'.[27] Unlike shareholders and the board, the company's senior employees do not have a formal place in a UK company's legal structure.[28] While a company's articles of association may permit the board to delegate substantial decision-making powers to senior employees, such delegation does not per se make the relevant employee a director and hence liable to disqualification for unfitness.[29]

The personal scope of the powers to disqualify persons on other grounds than unfitness is for the most part not limited to directors. CDDA sections 2–5A and 10 empower the courts to disqualify persons on account of other and more serious forms of business-related misconduct: their conviction for certain criminal offences, fraud in

20. *See* The Insolvency Service, *Insolvency Service Enforcement Outcomes: 2020/21*, https://www.gov.uk/government/statistics/insolvency-service-enforcement-outcomes-202021. *See also* Kristin van Zwieten, *Goode on Principles of Corporate Insolvency Law* para. 14-59 (Sweet & Maxwell 5th ed. 2018).
21. Insolvency Act 1986 section 220.
22. *See* CDDA section 22(2A).
23. *See* CDDA sections 22A–22H.
24. *See* Companies Act 2006 section 154.
25. Paul L. Davies et al., *Gower's Principles of Modern Company Law* paras 9-001 and 9-008 (Sweet & Maxwell 11th ed. 2021).
26. With respect to private companies limited by shares, *see* The Companies (Model Articles) Regulations 2008, Sch. 1, Art. 17.
27. With respect to private companies limited by shares, *see* The Companies (Model Articles) Regulations 2008, Sch. 1, Art. 3.
28. Paul L. Davies & Sarah Worthington, *Gower's Principles of Modern Company Law* para. 14-9 (Sweet & Maxwell 10th ed. 2016).
29. However, as we shall discuss in §4.03, persons that are not de jure directors could come into the personal scope of CDDA section 6 insofar as they are de facto or shadow directors.

relation to the company, breaches of reporting requirements under companies' legislation, and fraudulent and wrongful trading. For instance, section 2 makes a person liable to disqualification insofar as he/she is convicted of 'an indictable offence (whether on indictment or summarily) in connection with the promotion, formation, management, liquidation or striking off of a company with the receivership of a company's property or with his being an administrative receiver of a company'. These are activities that may be undertaken by persons that are not directors.

Likewise, section 4(1)(b), which concerns disqualification for fraud or other breaches of duty, is not restricted to directors; the provision's personal scope comprises, among other persons, 'officers', which include 'managers' and 'secretaries' in addition to directors.[30] A person can thus be an officer, who can be disqualified, without being a director. While it appears difficult to pin down exactly when a person is a 'manager' and therefore is within the personal scope of section 4(1)(b), this category seemingly comprises not only persons who are appointed to the board but also persons who partake in the central management in other positions, thereby distinguishing such persons from rank-and-file employees.[31]

[E] Discussion

The scope of the Norwegian and Danish disqualification provisions, as well as the power of UK courts to disqualify for unfitness under the CDDA section 6, is at the outset restricted to persons that have held formal positions in the management organs recognized by the company law of the respective jurisdictions.[32] This could perhaps be interpreted as a logical consequence of such persons having special responsibilities under company law that other persons connected to the company do not have. Employees that are not part of a management organ generally do not risk disqualification under these provisions, notwithstanding that they may have important roles in the corporate hierarchy. This is particularly relevant for larger companies where the sheer size of the company's business makes delegation to other personnel a necessity. For instance, a chief financial officer who is not appointed to the board would not per se fall within the ambit of the powers to disqualify for unfitness in any of the jurisdictions.

In some instances, a person may agree to be appointed to hold a formal position in a management organ as a 'straw man' or 'nominee director'. The straw man ('A') exercises this position in accordance with the instruction of another person ('B'). While A in this case is a member of the management organ in name only, it is the case in all jurisdictions concerned that this does not remove him/her from the scope of the disqualification powers. Under Danish law, a person agreeing to be appointed as a straw man is generally deemed to constitute grossly irresponsible business conduct and

30. CDDA section 22(6).
31. Adrian Walters & Malcolm Davis-White QC, *Directors' Disqualification & Insolvency Restrictions* paras 14-39 et seq. (Sweet & Maxwell 3d ed. 2010).
32. This does not follow explicitly from the text of the Danish Insolvency Act § 157, but the preparatory works indicate that this is how the provision is to be understood, *see* Bet. 2011:1525 135.

that the person concerned is thus at high risk of being disqualified.[33] Likewise, under UK law, a nominee director is liable to disqualification for unfitness under CDDA section 6. In one case, the court held that 'the fact that [a person] has been willing, systematically and deliberately, to hold himself out as a director of ... many companies, but on a nominee basis, abrogating his responsibility for those companies, is of itself, ... an extremely serious matter deserving of a substantial period of disqualification'.[34] Norwegian law operates in a similar fashion, as the fact that a person has agreed to be appointed to the board or as executive in name only does not remove him/her from the scope of the Norwegian Insolvency Act § 142[35] and may easily lead to the conclusion that the person concerned should be disqualified for unfitness.[36]

As we shall return to in §4.03 below, the person – B in the above example – instructing the straw man is also within the personal scope of the disqualification powers, notwithstanding that he/she is not formally appointed to the relevant company's management organs.

Another relevant issue is that it is not uncommon for companies to operate across borders. It may, for example, be the case that a private limited liability company incorporated under Danish company law conducts business in Norway. The 'host state' – in this example, Norway – may wish to apply its disqualification provisions to persons holding management positions in companies incorporated under the laws of another state but operating in the host state; it would otherwise be easy to circumvent the disqualification regime of the host state. Indeed, the Danish, Norwegian and UK regimes all empower courts to disqualify persons involved in managing foreign companies or their branches. An issue that arises when drawing up disqualification powers that extend to managers of foreign companies is how to identify what management positions in a foreign company that are to be regarded as equivalent to the positions in a domestic company that renders a person liable to disqualification. This difficulty stems from the fact that the foreign company could have a management system that, in significant respects, differs from that of the host state. The three jurisdictions have taken different approaches to this issue.

At first glance, the Danish disqualification regime appears to skirt the issue by delineating its scope of the Insolvency Act § 157 by reference to whether a person has participated in the management of the business of a company or person who has entered insolvency proceedings. By employing such a criterion, the provision does not delineate its scope by reference to formal concepts specific to Danish company law but instead takes a functional approach. However, some comparison between Danish company law and the laws of the foreign company's home state seems inevitable: As discussed above, the starting point is that when the Danish Insolvency Act § 157 is applied following the insolvency of a limited liability company, only persons appointed to the company's management organs are considered as having participated in the management of its business. I am not aware of court cases or statements in the

33. *See* Bet. 2011:1525 98, 135 and Staal & Røn, *supra* n. 16, at 27.
34. *Official Receiver v. Vass* [1999] BCC 516.
35. Kristian Huser, *Gjeldsforhandling og konkurs*, vol. 2, 426 (Juristinformasjon 1988).
36. Decision of the Borgarting Court of Appeals LB-2017-140114.

preparatory works to the Danish Insolvency Act that provide guidance on this issue. It is thus not entirely clear how this question is to be approached. One possibility is to compare the functions of the position at the foreign company with those of the management organs of Danish companies and consider whether they are sufficiently similar.

An alternative legislative approach is to specify the positions a person must have held at a foreign company for him/her to be within the ambit of the host state's disqualification regime. This is the approach of UK law. Following recent reform, the power to disqualify for unfitness under CDDA now extends to the directors of an 'overseas company' – that is, any company 'incorporated or formed outside of Great Britain'.[37] A court assessing an application to disqualify a person on account of his/her connection to an insolvent foreign company must determine whether he/she was a director of the relevant company. This in turn gives rise to the need for some abstract notion of when a given role in a foreign company is to count as being a director for the purposes of the CDDA section 6. This seems to be a difficult task as the only guidance provided by CDDA on the concept of a director is that it 'includes any person occupying the position of director, by whatever name called'.[38]

A somewhat different issue arises in connection with the Norwegian disqualification regime, which extends to persons who have been appointed as a board member, alternate board member or executive manager of *a Norwegian branch* of a foreign company. Neither the Insolvency Act nor its preparatory works provide much guidance as to the criteria to be employed for determining whether a person falls within these categories. Some guidance can be found in the preparatory works to the Norwegian Business Enterprise Register Act (*foretaksregisterloven*) § 3-8, which employs the same terms. These state that an executive manager of a branch is a person who is responsible for the branch's day-to-day operations and is authorized to act on the company's behalf towards counterparties and public authorities in matters related to those operations.[39] More uncertainty attaches to the criteria for determining whether a person is a board member of a Norwegian branch as no corresponding guidance exists for this question.

§4.03 WHICH PERSONS MAY BE DISQUALIFIED: DE FACTO ROLES

[A] Introduction

As discussed in §4.02 above, the scope of the Danish, Norwegian and UK disqualification powers is often confined to persons who have had certain roles at a company. For the Danish and Norwegian regimes as well as the UK power to disqualify for unfitness, these are appointments to the management organs recognized under national company law. As touched upon in §4.01 above, appointment to a company's management organ(s) is not the only route towards influencing a company's high-level

37. CDDA section 22(2A).
38. CDDA section 22(4).
39. *See* the Ministry of Trade and Shipping's explanatory notes to its proposal of 1985 for a new business enterprise register act, Ot.prp. nr. 50 (1984–1985) 47-48.

decision-making, however. A person may – by virtue of legal rights or other means of persuasion – be able to control how the management organs exercise their powers. Moreover, high-ranking personnel may have delegated to them – whether explicitly or tacitly – authority to decide matters normally handled by management organs. A policy of preventing persons who have contributed to the mismanagement of a company from managing businesses in the future could suggest that such persons are also included in the scope of the disqualification provisions. This section considers the extent to which this is the case under Danish, Norwegian and UK law.

[B] Danish Law

As discussed above, the Danish disqualification regime takes aim at persons that have been involved in the management of an insolvent debtor's business. A person may be deemed to have been involved in the management of a limited liability company despite him/her not holding a formal position in the company's management organs.

This conclusion could, for instance, be reached if he/she performs all management functions while the persons appointed to the management organ are managers in name only.[40] The same conclusion will also likely be reached if a person has sufficient influence over the company's managers to instruct them as to the exercise of their roles.[41] Conversely, the mere ownership of shares in a company is not considered as management of its business.[42]

The disqualification provisions could also be applicable to persons who have not instructed the members of a company's management organs but nonetheless been involved in their decision-making. It is difficult to pinpoint exactly when such involvement brings a person within the ambit of the regime. This is because the merits provided in the relevant court rulings are quite short. In one case, two persons (C and J), who had successively been the sole member of the company's executive board, had explained that they together with P – who was never appointed to this board – had jointly managed the company. This, in combination with the fact that P was part of the executive board of a company that owned shares in the insolvent company, led the Holstebro Court of First Instance to conclude that he had participated in its management.[43] The court's reference to the statements of C and J is not particularly informative with respect to how the court understood the legal concept of 'participating in the management of the company's business' in this context: Taken at face value, the court's reasoning is that P participated in the management of the company's business – and thereby was within the personal scope of the disqualification rules – because witnesses stated that he had managed the company together with them. However, the court's account of J's testimony could provide more insight into its legal reasoning: J had explained that C, J and P jointly made significant decisions. It is *possible*, but not

40. Decision of the Western High Court U 2018.3318V; Decision of the Western High Court U 2018.2472V; Decision of the Eastern High Court FM 2019.168.
41. Decisions of the Supreme Court U 2019.2000H; U 2019.2012H.
42. Bet. 2011:1525 99.
43. The conclusion was upheld by the Western High Court U 2017.1591V.

certain, that this circumstance is what motivated the court's conclusion. This would in turn mean that the underlying rationale is that if a management organ will only make significant decisions after reaching agreement with a person that is not part of that organ, then that person is considered as participating in the management of the company's business and thus within the scope of the disqualification provision.

In another case, the Eastern High Court found that the fact that a person – who was not part of the company's management organs – had executed certain tasks concerning accounting and bookkeeping and was involved in activities connected to a company did not warrant the conclusion that he was de facto part of that company's management.[44] Again, the merits are quite brief. It is perhaps of interest to note the court's account of the legal arguments of the person against whom the order was sought: He pleaded that he was outside the scope of the disqualification provisions as he was not in charge of the overall and strategic management of the company, which, under the governance model chosen by the relevant company, was a responsibility of the executive board.[45] Implicit in this argument is the view that a person cannot be considered as participating in the management of a company unless he exercises the tasks of one of its management organs. It is possible that the Eastern District Court followed this reasoning, but the short merits do not warrant a firm conclusion in this respect.

[C] Norwegian Law

The disqualification power under the Norwegian Insolvency Act § 142 extends not only to persons that have formally been appointed as board members, alternate board members or an executive manager but also persons that de facto have acted as such.

The Norwegian Insolvency Act does not provide any guidance as to the determination of whether someone has de facto acted as a board member or executive manager. The preparatory works indicate that the wording of § 142 was intended to empower the courts to disqualify persons that have procured the appointment of 'straw men' to the management organs.[46] It thus seems clear that a person who on a continuous basis provides instructions to the appointed board members or executive manager de facto exercises the functions of the management organs. However, the preparatory works leave unanswered when a person shall be deemed as de facto part of the company's management organs on account of lesser degrees of influence or less frequent instructions. The preparatory works reveal that the provision was intentionally couched in vague language as it was not considered possible to provide detailed prescriptions for the assessment of when a person de facto exercises the said positions.[47] To my knowledge, there are no Supreme Court decisions that deal with this question.

---

44. Decision of the Eastern High Court U 2016.2123Ø.
45. The Danish Companies Act § 117, 2.
46. *See* the Ministry of Justice's explanatory notes to its proposal of 1981 for a new insolvency act, Ot.prp. nr. 50 (1980–1981) 125.
47. *Ibid.*

Relevant decisions made by the Norwegian courts of appeal do not elaborate at length upon what de facto being a board member or executive manager involves.[48] However, it is possible to identify certain arguments that the courts have employed for justifying the conclusion that a person de facto acted in such positions: control over the business operations,[49] the person describing himself/herself as the executive manager,[50] and the handling of communications and contact with the company's auditor, counterparties, and public authorities.[51] In one case, a person being authorized to access the company's bank account was not by itself considered as sufficient.[52]

[D] UK Law

As discussed in §4.02 above, the power to disqualify persons for unfitness under CDDA s. 6 is restricted to company directors. For the purposes of that provision, a 'director' includes not only persons appointed as directors in accordance with the company's articles of association. First, pursuant to the courts' interpretation of the term 'director', this also includes 'de facto directors'. Second, CDDA section 6(3C) states that references to directors in that provision includes 'shadow directors', which is a term defined in section 22(5).

When is a person considered a de facto director? In the UK Supreme Court case *Commissioners of HM Revenue and Customs v. Holland*,[53] Lord Collins summarized this case law. He highlighted that for determining whether a person is a de facto director, the following tests 'are the most relevant'. *First*, 'whether the person was the sole person directing the affairs of the company (or acting with others equally lacking in a valid appointment), or if there were others who were true directors, whether he was acting on an equal footing with the others in directing its affairs'. The implication seems to be that a person cannot be considered a de facto director if his influence over the management of the company is not at least equal to that of an individual de jure director. *Second*, 'whether there was a holding out by the company of the individual as a director, and whether the individual used the title'. Accordingly, a person that repeatedly purports to enter into agreements on behalf of the company as a director could potentially be classified as a de facto director.[54] *Third*, whether the person was part of 'the corporate governing structure' of the company. A ruling from 2021 treats the company's governance structure as 'an important starting point' for the assessment

48. *See* decisions of the Borgarting Court of Appeals LB-1999-1548; LB-2012-174098; LB-2017-140114; LB-2021-69027.
49. Decisions of the Borgarting Court of Appeals LB-1999-1548; LB-2017-140114; LB-2021-69027.
50. Decision of the Borgarting Court of Appeals LB-1999-1548.
51. Decisions of the Borgarting Court of Appeals LB-1999-1548; LB-2004-44021; LB-2017-140114; decision of the Gulating Court of Appeals LG-2018-142488; LB-2021-69027. *See, however*, the Borgarting Court of Appeal's decision in LB-2012-174098, where the Court found a person's contact with a company's customers, accountant, and auditor while the formally appointed executive manager was ill as insufficient for establishing that he/she de facto was the company's executive manager.
52. Decision of the Borgarting Court of Appeals LB-2002-3602.
53. *Commissioners of HM Revenue and Customs v. Holland* [2010] UKSC 51.
54. Walters & Davis-White, *supra* n. 31, at para. 3-24.

of whether a person acted as a de facto director; '[t]hose who assume and exercise powers and functions that can only properly be exercised or discharged at that highest level of management will, consistent with the purpose of the disqualification legislation, be within its scope as de facto directors'.[55]

We now turn to the criteria for a person being a shadow director. CDDA section 22(5) defines a shadow director as 'a person in accordance with whose directions or instructions the directors of the company are accustomed to act'.[56] Several questions arise from the requirement that the directors of the company must be 'accustomed to act' in accordance with the directions or instructions of a person. *First*, to what degree must a person wield power over the appointed directors? In the Court of Appeals case *Secretary of State for Trade and Industry v. Deverell*,[57] Morritt LJ addressed this question by explaining that while it is sufficient that the de jure directors 'cast themselves in a subservient role or surrendered their respective discretions', it is not necessary that they always did so upon receiving the alleged shadow director's direction or instructions. *Second*, must the person have the requisite degree of influence over all matters related to the management of the company? The courts have answered this question in the negative.[58]

There could be cases where a person only exerts influence over a minority of the company's de jure directors. That person would then not satisfy the definition of a shadow director. To remedy this gap, CDDA section 8ZA empowers courts to make a disqualification order against persons that have provided directions or instructions to one or more directors.[59] A condition for making a disqualification order under this provision is that the de jure directors who have taken instructions or directions themselves have been disqualified under CDDA section 6 (or have agreed to a so-called disqualification undertaking to the same effect) as a result of acting in accordance with such directions or instructions. A corresponding requirement does not apply for disqualifying a shadow director under CDDA section 6: A shadow director may be disqualified notwithstanding that none of the de jure directors has been disqualified.

[E] Discussion

Section 4.02 above noted that the scope of the Norwegian and Danish disqualification provisions, as well as the power to disqualify persons for unfitness under CDDA section 6, at the outset is restricted to persons that have held positions in the management organs recognized by the company law of the respective jurisdictions. This starting point seems natural, as persons appointed to management organs have accepted to assume the special obligations that are attached to the decision-making powers of such organs.

55. *The Official Receiver v. Atkinson & Ors* [2021] EWHC 175 (Ch) [167].
56. The provision goes on to state that certain acts – e.g., 'advice given by that person in a professional capacity' – shall not by themselves cause a person to be deemed a shadow director.
57. *Secretary of State for Trade and Industry v. Deverell* [2001] Ch. 340.
58. *Ibid.*
59. Davies et al., *supra* n. 25, at para. 20-006.

The preceding subsections have showed that the relevant disqualification provisions also extend to persons that de facto partake in the management of the company on par with its management organs or otherwise exercise influence over such organs. The rationale for such extensions is likely to ensure that companies are not managed by persons who previously have caused a company to be seriously mismanaged, regardless of whether the person was appointed to that company's management organ.[60]

The UK regime delineates several different categories of persons who may be disqualified for unfitness, notwithstanding not having formally been a director. Two of these categories – shadow directors and de facto directors – serve as a useful point of reference for analysis of similarities and differences in the national approaches to extending the scope of the disqualification provisions to persons not formally appointed to management organs.

As defined by statute, a shadow director is a person in 'accordance with whose directions or instructions the directors of the company are accustomed to act'.[61] The assessment of whether a person is a shadow director can give rise to difficult questions – e.g., with exactly what frequency must de jure directors comply with the alleged shadow director's directions or instructions? Nonetheless, this category remains conceptually clear. It makes perfect sense to speak of a person (the shadow director) having influence over how persons (the member(s) of a management organ) exercise certain legal powers (the powers of the management organ). While the relevant Danish nor Norwegian statutory provisions do not explicitly state that a shadow director may be disqualified, the above sections show that a person being both able and willing to give instructions to the management organs will likely be considered as 'participating in the management of the company' and 'de facto exercising a role as a member of the company's board', respectively. Accordingly, the personal scope of the Danish and Norwegian disqualification powers includes such shadow directors.

UK law also renders a de facto director susceptible to being disqualified for unfitness. As discussed in §4.03[D] above, the UK Supreme Court stated in *Commissioners of HM Revenue and Customs v. Holland* that there is not a single test for determining whether a person is a de facto director. Rather, several tests are taken into account. The implication is likely that it is not possible to give a single definition of a de facto director. This in turn means that it is more difficult to ascertain the circumstances in which a person will be deemed a de facto director than what is the case for a shadow director. For instance, it is not entirely clear when a high-ranking employee who is not a director could be considered as a de facto director.

Drawing such distinctions is also an issue under the Danish and Norwegian regimes. The discussion in §4.03[B] above indicates that it is possible under the Danish regime for persons who informally take part in the decision-making of a company's management organs to be considered as having participated in the management of the company's business, and hence within the personal scope of the disqualification powers. The discussion in §4.03[C] above of Norwegian law shows that also behaviour

60. *See, e.g.*, for Danish law, Bet. 2011:1525 84.
61. CDDA section 22(5).

other than akin to a shadow director may lead to a person being considered de facto having acted as a company's board member or executive. An issue common to the relevant Danish and Norwegian decisions is that the courts do not make their assessments against any explicitly stated notion of what it entails to de facto act as board member or executive. This in turn makes it difficult to ascertain exactly what it is that brings persons within the scope of the disqualification provisions by virtue of having been involved in the decision-making of the management organs.

A question of practical relevance is to what extent the disqualification powers extend to the managers or employees of a subsidiary company's parent company, notwithstanding that they were not appointed to the subsidiary's management organs.

Under UK law, the power to disqualify for unfitness extends to both de facto directors and shadow directors. An important starting point for the assessment of whether a person has acted as a company's de facto director is the governance structure of the company. When considering the involvement of a director of a parent company with the management of a subsidiary, it is of relevance whether he acted in the capacity as director of the parent or as director of the subsidiary.[62] Conduct connected to a person being a director or employee of a parent company does not automatically entail that the person is also a de facto director of a subsidiary company. The test applied by the UK courts is whether such conduct is consistent with what may be expected from a director of the parent company.[63] If that is the case, the courts may be inclined to hold that the director did not act as a de facto director of the subsidiary.

It follows from the statutory definition of a shadow director that, in order for the parent company's directors to be considered as shadow directors of a subsidiary company, the directors of the subsidiary must be 'accustomed to act' in accordance with their directions or instructions. One implication is that it would be sufficient to conclude that a parent company's directors have acted as shadow directors of a subsidiary insofar as they provide detailed instructions to the subsidiary's board that are invariably rubber-stamped.

In Danish law, the question of whether a person connected to a parent company could be disqualified on account of its involvement in a subsidiary company's business is one of whether the person participated in the management of the subsidiary's business. Danish cases show that a shareholder instructing the management organs may easily be deemed as satisfying this criterion. In line with this, the preparatory works to the disqualification provisions state that the parent company's management in principle could be deemed as having participated in the management of the subsidiary company's business.[64] The fact that Danish company law in many cases enables shareholders to instruct the management organs through the general meeting[65] raises the question of when a parent company's voting at the general meeting results in

62. *Smithton Ltd v. Naggar* [2014] EWCA Civ 939 at [36].
63. *Smithton Ltd v. Naggar* [2014] EWCA Civ 939 at [65].
64. Bet. 2011:1525 136; L 131 Forslag til lov om ændring af konkursloven, retsplejeloven og retsafgiftsloven (konkurskarantæne), legislative proposal presented by the Danish Minister of Justice on 30 January 2013, 28.
65. Troels Michael Lilja, *Konkurskarantene og kapitalselskaber*, 16 NTS 29, 37 (2014).

those in charge of deciding how votes are cast being considered as participating in the management of the subsidiary company's business. The preparatory works go on to provide the following answer: The parent company's exercise of its rights in its capacity as shareholder, e.g., at the subsidiary's general meeting, does not constitute management of the subsidiary. It is possible that a line must be drawn between behaviour attributable to the exercise of shareholder rights and that which goes beyond this and therefore constitutes the management of the company's business. As I have not found published court cases dealing with this question, it is not possible to infer exactly where Danish courts will draw this line. It seems possible to adopt an approach like that of UK courts, e.g., to deem the parent company's employees as having participated in the management of the subsidiary company only to the extent that their conduct goes beyond what may be expected from the parent company.

Under Norwegian law, the answer to the question of whether a parent company's managers or employees may be disqualified following a subsidiary's insolvency hinges on whether such persons are considered as de facto having acted as board members or executive manager of the subsidiary. On the one hand, it is generally accepted that the parent company's mere exercise of its shareholder rights will not by itself cause its managers or employees to be deemed as de facto managers of the subsidiary.[66] On the other, the wording of the provision suggests that de facto management would likely be found where a parent company over time uses the power that the general meeting under Norwegian law has to give instructions to the subsidiary's board with a level of detail and frequency that would involve micromanaging its business. As there does not appear to be published court decisions that deal with this issue, it is difficult to identify where the line is to be drawn. The lack of authoritative sources means that the courts could adopt an approach along the lines of that taken by UK courts, as discussed above.

§4.04 WHAT DOES DISQUALIFICATION ENTAIL?

[A] Introduction

Having discussed the personal scope of the national disqualification regimes, we now turn to what disqualification entails. This is of importance for the purposes of this chapter, as the practical significance of the delineation of the personal scope of the disqualification provisions depends on what it means to be disqualified.

[B] Danish Law

A Danish disqualification will normally last for three years, but the court may decide upon a shorter term in special circumstances.[67] A disqualified person is prohibited from participating in the management of any business unless he/she has personal and

66. Kjetil Schonhowd, *Konkurskarantene* 26 (Juristforbundets Forlag 2001); Knut Ro & Håvard Wiker, *Konkursloven: Kommentarutgave* 535 (Universitetsforlaget 2003).
67. The Danish Insolvency Act § 158.

unlimited liability for all debts incurred by the business. Importantly, this means that a disqualified person cannot have positions – whether formal or de facto – in a limited liability company's management organs. If a person holds positions at the management organs of other companies when a disqualification enters into force, she is thus to be removed from that position.[68] On the other hand, a disqualified person may trade in her own name. Moreover, a disqualification does not prevent a person from taking high-ranking employment at companies (other than as executive manager).

The mere ownership of shares in a company is not considered management of its business.[69] Accordingly, disqualified persons are free to retain or acquire shares in companies, notwithstanding that such holdings may give them a decisive majority at the company's general meeting. Moreover, they may be employed by limited liability companies.

A person that participates in the management of a company in breach of a disqualification decision may under certain circumstances set out in the Danish Insolvency Act § 167 become personally liable for the company's debts should it enter insolvency proceedings.

A person's failure to observe a disqualification decision is also a criminal offence.[70]

[C] Norwegian Law

The Norwegian regime provides for two forms of disqualification orders. The first form is forward-looking: Pursuant to the Insolvency Act § 142, third paragraph, the court may prohibit that the person *forms* a company or *assumes* a position as a board member, alternate board member or executive manager. The prohibition is aimed at both de jure and de facto assumption of such positions. The prohibition lasts for two years.

This form of disqualification does not impose restrictions on the taking up of high-ranking employment positions at companies (other than as executive manager). Nor is a disqualified person prohibited from trading in his/her own name. While the prohibition comprises the formation of a company, a disqualified person is not prohibited from acquiring shares in an existing company through the purchase of outstanding shares or subscribing for shares issued in connection with a capital increase.[71]

The second form of disqualification results in the person both becoming subject to the forward-looking restrictions discussed above and being removed from any positions as a board member, alternate board member or executive manager that he/she holds at the time the decision is made. This form of disqualification may only be made where a person is disqualified for criminal conduct (*see* §4.02[C]). Unlike a purely forward-looking disqualification, this second form of disqualification interferes with the status quo.

68. Engsig Sørensen, *supra* n. 9, at 183.
69. Lilja, *supra* n. 65, at 42.
70. The Danish Criminal Act § 131.
71. *See* Jan Skåre, *Lov om aksjeselskaper med kommentarer* 273 (Tanum-Norli 1980).

Unlike under the Danish and UK regime, Norwegian law does not contain any rules that make a person managing a company in contravention of a disqualification order per se liable for the debts of the company concerned.

A disqualified person's failure to observe a disqualification decision is a criminal offence.[72]

[D] UK Law

If the conditions for disqualification for unfitness under CDDA section 6 are satisfied, the court shall make a disqualification order for a period between two and fifteen years.

In cases where the conditions for disqualification on grounds other than unfitness are satisfied, the court has discretion as to whether to make a disqualification order and the length of the disqualification. The maximum term varies according to the ground for disqualification. For instance, a disqualification order for certain convictions and fraud has a maximum term of fifteen years, while the maximum period of disqualification for 'persistent breaches of companies legislation' is five years.[73]

According to the CDDA section 1, a disqualified person is not only prohibited from being appointed as director but also prohibited from being 'concerned or [taking] part in the promotion, formation or management of a company'. It follows that a disqualification order will prohibit a disqualified person from being a de jure director of a company. If a person holds directorships at other companies when a disqualification enters into force, she is thus required to resign. Moreover, the prohibition also extends to being a de facto or shadow director.[74] As CDDA s.1 makes clear, a disqualification order prohibits activities beyond that of being a director. The language is far-reaching and may, among other things, mean that a disqualified person that takes up high-ranking employment positions in companies would be at risk of breaching the disqualification order, as he/she could be considered to take part in the 'management of a company'.[75]

The courts can grant a disqualified person leave to be a director of a company.[76] The court's discretion in this regard has been described as 'largely unfettered'.[77] The court may attach conditions to the granting of leave and will usually only grant leave if the application relates to specific companies.[78]

A person that is involved in the management of a company in breach of a disqualification order will be personally liable for the debts that the company incurs while he is so involved.[79]

72. The Norwegian Insolvency Act § 143a.
73. CDDA sections 4(3) and 3(5), respectively.
74. Walters & Davis-White, *supra* n. 31, at para. 14-25.
75. *See* the discussion in Walters & Davis-White, *supra* n. 31, at paras 14-39 et seq.
76. CDDA section 1(1)(a).
77. van Zwieten, *supra* n. 20, at para. 14-82.
78. Walters & Davis-White, *supra* n. 31, at para. 15-03.
79. CDDA section 15.

An individual that contravenes a disqualification order is also liable to criminal penalties.[80]

[E] Discussion

The above analysis shows that there are differences as to what disqualification entails. One apparent difference is that the maximum term of the disqualification is much longer in UK law (fifteen years) than in Danish and Norwegian law (three and two years, respectively). The UK Insolvency Service reports that the average length of disqualification orders made in the period 2020–2021 was five years and nine months.[81]

There are also differences as regards the restrictions that apply during the disqualification. In Danish law, there is a clear link between the activities that bring a person within the personal scope of the disqualification regime – i.e., the participation in the management of a business – and what a person is prohibited from doing while disqualified. The link is less clear in Norwegian law, as the disqualification of a board member or executive manager results not only in restrictions on his/her ability to hold such appointments but also in the formation of companies. The same is all the truer for UK law, where a disqualified person – including directors disqualified for unfitness – may not 'in any way, whether directly or indirectly, be concerned or take part in the promotion, formation or management of a company'.

The Norwegian regime stands out in that the scope of what a disqualification may entail depends on the grounds for disqualification. Where a person is disqualified for unfitness, the person must not assume new appointments as a board member, alternate board member or executive manager. Conversely, the person may retain existing appointments. If a person is disqualified for criminal conduct, the court making the disqualification decision may decide that the person is also to be removed from any current positions at company management organs.

A feature common to all jurisdictions is that disqualification will interfere with not only appointments as a manager of a company formed under the laws of that jurisdiction but also the taking up of certain positions with foreign companies: Disqualified persons are not permitted to take appointments to the management organs of foreign companies. In Danish law, the restrictions on participation in the management of a business are taken to include any such activities with respect to any foreign company.[82] Likewise, the restrictions on being a board member, alternate board member or executive manager under a Norwegian disqualification order also apply in respect of Norwegian branches of foreign companies. In a similar vein, the restrictions that a UK law disqualification order imposes on the taking up of a position as director

80. CDDA section 13.
81. The Insolvency Service, *supra* n. 20.
82. L 131, *supra* n. 64, at 32. However, due to the geographical scope of the Danish Criminal Act, the prohibition will in practice only be enforced insofar as either the foreign company has a Danish branch or the disqualified person conducts the management from Denmark, *see* Engsig Sørensen, *supra* n. 9, at 186.

and certain other activities apply with respect to not only UK companies but also any foreign company that may be wound up under Part 5 of the Insolvency Act 1986. This includes foreign companies with a sufficient connection to the UK.[83]

Section 4.02 above discussed the difficulties that attach to applying disqualification provisions that reference national concepts to cases where a person has held a position at a foreign company. These challenges could also be present when determining whether a disqualification order given in the jurisdictions examined will prevent a person from taking up a given position in a company that is incorporated in another jurisdiction but conducts business in the jurisdiction where the order was given. Extending the effects of a disqualification to the prohibition of holding positions at foreign companies is beneficial for the effectiveness of the disqualification; the disqualified person is not able to use a foreign company to circumvent the restrictions. The difficulties attached to determining what positions a disqualified person is prohibited from holding at a foreign company means that this benefit comes at the expense of legal certainty as to what is, and what is not, prohibited.

§4.05 CONCLUSIONS

This chapter set out to consider three questions: First, which formal positions at limited liability companies render a person susceptible to being disqualified under the Danish, Norwegian and UK disqualification regimes? Second, when may persons be disqualified on account of having de facto functioned as a member of a management organ? Third, what restrictions does disqualification entail?

As regards the scope of the disqualification regimes, the chapter shows that disqualification powers are generally restricted to persons who have been appointed to the management organs recognized under the company law of the jurisdiction concerned. While the UK regime empowers the courts to disqualify other persons connected to the company, this is reserved for instances of specific types of misbehaviour or where the person concerned has been convicted of a criminal offence.

The regimes aim at not only those that formally have been appointed as managers but also those that in practice have exercised such functions. Among other things, this means that both shareholders and employees not appointed to management organs may be susceptible to disqualification. Such persons could find themselves within the scope of the disqualification provisions if they exercise behaviour akin to that of a 'shadow director' under UK law, i.e., making use of their influence over the company's management organs by issuing instructions as to how such organs are to exercise their powers. The same is the case for persons who have been delegated decision-making on matters normally decided by the management organs or who act as the company's representative towards counterparties and public authorities. The line may here sometimes be blurry, as it does not seem that the jurisdictions examined have drawn up a single definition of when high-ranking employees or other persons connected to the company conduct decision-making at such a high level as to bring him/her into the

83. Walters & Davis-White, *supra* n. 31, at para. 16-25.

personal scope of the disqualification regime on par with a member of the management organ. What seems to happen in practice is that courts make their conclusions following an overall assessment.

Turning to the consequences of disqualification, some variation persists in terms of what a person is prohibited from doing while disqualified. In all cases, the person may neither formally nor de facto be part of a company's management organs. In some instances, the prohibition extends to other activities. To take one example, a person subject to a UK disqualification order is also prohibited from being 'concerned or [taking] part in the promotion, formation or management of a company'.[84] However, the starting point remains that a disqualification does not restrict a person's ability to take up employment or positions at a company other than as member of its management organs. As a disqualification prohibits the person concerned from de facto being a member of a company's management organ, disqualified persons should nonetheless exercise caution when taking on high-level tasks delegated from management organs in order to avoid the risk of breaching the disqualification order. There is also variation as to the term of the disqualification: A UK disqualification order can last for up to fifteen years, while the maximum in Danish and Norwegian law is three and two years, respectively.

By equating de facto and formal participation in management organs, Danish, Norwegian and UK law all take a functional approach to delineate both the personal scope of the disqualification provisions relating to unfitness and the roles a disqualified person is prohibited from taking on. This makes sense from a policy perspective: If a person has been involved in decision-making on par with what one would expect of a member properly appointed to the management organs, then there is no reason for that person being exempt per se from the disqualification regime. The public interest in preventing persons who have shown themselves unfit to manage companies from continuing to do so is no less strong if the person concerned was never formally appointed to a management organ. Likewise, a functional approach is also necessary to ensure that a disqualification order is effective: the order could easily be circumvented if disqualified persons are free to give 'straw men' appointed to management organs instructions as to how they are to exercise their powers.

Future reform – whether through national initiatives or further harmonization at EU/EEA level – would ideally involve further specification of when persons not appointed to management organs are to be treated as equal to persons holding such appointments. The UK example of distinguishing between 'shadow' and 'de facto' directors should be followed and refined to increase legal certainty. Such reform should be accompanied by a principled discussion of what activities should equate a person not being part of a management organ with persons holding such positions, and hence render that person susceptible to disqualification. This policy issue has, up to now, not been fully addressed in the jurisdictions examined and hence implicitly left for the courts to decide. For instance, the fact that a person has purported to be part of a company's management organs when communicating with its counterparties and

84. CDDA section 1.

public authorities is of relevance for ascertaining whether a person is a 'de facto director' or a 'de facto board member/executive' under the UK and Norwegian regimes, respectively. Although it is lamentable to describe oneself as holding a position that one does not hold, this circumstance does not necessarily imply that the person has been involved in making decisions normally made by the relevant management organs. It is therefore not apparent why this circumstance should be able to result in a person being equated with a person appointed to a company's management organ(s).

CHAPTER 5

Non-executive and Executive Managers: Individual Liability and Sanctions for Complicity in Competition Law Infringements

Pernille Wegener Jessen

§5.01 INTRODUCTION

On 11 February 2022, the City Court of Copenhagen acquitted three natural persons – all holding a managerial position[1] – from the public prosecutor's charges with individual fines and imprisonment for complicity in a competition law infringement committed by the companies to which they were associated.[2]

The infringement of Article 101 TFEU[3] and the Danish Competition Act (DCA) section 6[4] by the two companies involved had been established by the Danish Supreme Court in a preceding case decided in November 2019.[5] The subsequent criminal proceedings in the City Court of Copenhagen concerned the question of whether the companies and the three natural persons fulfilled the conditions for being met with sanctions due to the infringement. Since the parties were not found to have acted with

1. The status of the natural persons is not disclosed in the published ruling, but it appears from the news that the individuals seem to include the overall manager ('direktør') of one of the companies and two executive managers ('ledende medarbejdere') from the other company: *Berlingske: To firmaer er tiltalt for kartelaftale på vejstribe-opgaver*, Ritzau (25 November 2021), https://www.berlingske.dk/samfund/to-firmaer-er-tiltalt-for-kartelaftale-paa-vejstribe-opgaver.
2. Ruling of Municipal Court of Copenhagen, 11 February 2022, Case No. SS 3-3526/2020.
3. Consolidated version of the Treaty on the Functioning of the European Union (TFEU), OJ C 326/47, 26.10.2012.
4. The DCA, Consolidated Act No. 360 of 4 March 2021.
5. The Danish Supreme Court, ruling of 27 November 2019 in case 191/2018, *Danish Road Marking Consortium*, https://domstol.fe1.tangora.com/media/-300016/files/191-18.pdf.

intent or gross negligence, the City Court acquitted both the companies and the individuals from the charges.

The case mentioned above is one of a few Danish court proceedings in which natural persons have been charged with both fines and imprisonment due to a competition law infringement committed by the company with which the individuals are associated.[6] So far, no individual has been sentenced with imprisonment in a competition law enforcement context in Denmark, but the case represents very well the severe circumstances in which non-executive and executive managers potentially risk finding themselves, not only in Denmark but also – to a varying degree – in most of the other EU Member States[7] and also in other parts of the world.[8] This risk does not only concern the possibility of being met with personal liability and sanctions but also the considerable extent of time it may take to handle a case in the administrative and judicial system, which individuals risk having to endure before the case is finally closed in respect to public enforcement[9] – not to mention the potential follow-on private enforcement, like compensation for damage, that in a broader perspective might involve company non-executives and executive managers due to their responsibility for the company's participation in a competition law infringement. The case mentioned originally started in 2014 and was initiated on the basis of a complaint and subsequent investigations (including dawn raids at the companies' premises conducted by the Danish Competition and Consumer Authority). Even though the final conclusions regarding the companies' infringements of competition law were established by the Danish Supreme Court in 2019, the criminal proceedings regarding possible subsequent sanctions imposed on the companies and the individuals at a managerial level have not yet been finally settled as

6. In some cases, the prosecutor's charges explicitly refer to fines and imprisonment; in other cases, the charges are just stating that the individual should be sanctioned and left to the court to decide the appropriate sanction. An overview of the most recent national judgments is available at: *Danish Competition and Consumer Authority: National judgements,* https://www.en.kfst.dk/competition/national-judgements/.
7. *See, e.g.*, regarding Poland: Dariusz Aziewics, *Antitrust Penalties for Individuals in Poland*, Kluwer Competition Law Blog (14 January 2022), http://competitionlawblog.kluwercompetitionlaw.com/2022/01/14/antitrust-penalties-for-individuals-in-poland/.
8. *See, e.g.*, regarding USA, Canada and Australia: *US Department of Justice Antitrust Division: The US District Court for the Eastern District of North Carolina sentences a former engineering executive for rigging bids and defrauding the North Carolina Department of Transportation (Brent Brewbaker)*, e-Competitions September 2022, Art. no. 108585 (8 September 2022), https://www.concurrences.com/en/bulletin/news-issues/september-2022/the-us-district-court-for-the-eastern-district-of-north-carolina-sentences; *Canadian Competition Bureau, The Canadian Competition Authority secures a fifth guilty plea and $25,000 from an engineering executive implicated in the Gatineau bid rigging scandal (Francois Paulhus / Genivar)*, e-Competitions October 2022, Art. no. 109129 (14 October 2022), https://www.concurrences.com/en/bulletin/news-issues/october-2022/the-canadian-competition-authority-secures-a-fifth-guilty-plea-and-25-000-from; *Australian Competition Authority, The Australian Competition Authority secures a guilty plea from the former CEO of a waste management company for price fixing (Daniel Tartak)*, e-Competitions October 2022, Art. no. 109173 (20 October 2022), https://www.concurrences.com/en/bulletin/news-issues/october-2022/the-australian-competition-authority-secures-a-guilty-plea-from-the-former-ceo.
9. In Denmark, a case may be initiated in the administrative system by the Danish Competition and Consumer Authority and subsequently – if not settled – be subject to judicial proceedings (civil proceedings towards companies and criminal proceedings towards natural persons).

the 2022 judgment of the City Court has been appealed to the High Court, thus placing the individuals under continuous personal stress.

In the context of potential liabilities for non-executive and executive managers, the purpose of this contribution is to provide an overview of the *importance of managerial status in relation to the sanctioning of natural persons for a competition law infringement* under Article 101 TFEU. This will especially involve exploring the *role or position of the natural persons* that may risk being subject to liability and individual sanctions in the form of a fine and/or imprisonment in the case of complicity in an infringement committed by a company to which the individual is or has been affiliated with at the point of time of the infringement.

Since the EU Commission – when enforcing Article 101 TFEU – only has the possibility of imposing fines on *undertakings* and not on *natural persons*, the analysis will focus on the enforcement of Article 101 TFEU by a national competition authority.[10] In contrast to the powers of the EU Commission, the EU Member States' national competition law to a varying degree contains the options of, e.g., fining, imprisoning or disqualifying natural persons when national competition authorities enforce Article 101 TFEU. More specifically, the starting point of the analysis will be Article 101 TFEU infringements enforced by Danish authorities applying national law in regard to the sanctioning of individuals under Danish competition (and criminal) law.[11] Individual liability under Danish law includes fines and imprisonment as possible sanctions, however, with the possibility to apply for leniency as harmonized in national law by the ECN + Directive.[12] Under Danish law, as well as under the law of other EU Member States, individuals risking personal liability will – as an overall starting point – have a managerial position in the offending companies.

§5.02 OVERVIEW AND CONTEXT

The conduct of companies engaged in economic activities, i.e., the offering of goods or services on a given market (normally for a profit),[13] is subject to legal constraints under EU competition law. This implies that a company is not necessarily free to pursue just any business strategy that a company may find profitable or strategically appropriate.

10. Council Regulation (EC) No. 1/2003 of 16 December 2002 on the implementation of the rules on competition laid down in Arts 81 and 82 of the Treaty, OJ L 1/1, 4.1.2003, Art. 23.
11. In cases where an anti-competitive agreement affects trade between Member States, Art. 101 TFEU is applied in parallel with DCA section 6 or alone, *see* DCA section 2(6). The obligation for national authorities to apply Art. 101 TFEU in such cases follows from Council Regulation (EC) 1/2003, *supra* 10. 9, Art. 3(1).
12. Directive (EU) 2019/1 of the European Parliament and of the Council of 11 December 2018 to empower the competition authorities of the Member States to be more effective enforcers and to ensure the proper functioning of the internal market (ECN + Directive), OJ L 11/3, 14.1.2019. As a starting point, the ECN + Directive provides a minimum harmonization of the relevant law of the EU Member States. However, regarding the leniency rules, the Directive provides a total harmonization of the leniency systems in the EU Member States, *see* Recitals 10 and 11 of the Directive.
13. Case C-74/16, *Congregación de Escuelas Pias Provincia Betania v. Ayuntamiento de Getafe*, 27.6.2017, ECLI:EU:C:2017:496, paras 41 and 45; Case C-138/11, *Compass-Datenbank GmbH v. Republik Österreich*, 12.7.2012, ECLI:EU:C:2012:449, paras 35-39.

On this background, Article 101 TFEU prohibits *anti-competitive agreements*, whereas Article 102 TFEU prohibits *abuse of a dominant market position*. These rules in the Treaty are complemented by the control of *concentrations* with an EU-dimension provided by the Merger Regulation,[14] and also by the obligation applicable to core digital platform services nominated as *gatekeepers*, not to carry out *unfair practices* as stated by the EU Digital Markets Act,[15] and the Platform-to-Business Regulation promoting fairness and transparency for business on online platforms.[16]

The overall purpose of the EU competition rules is to support the enabling of the proper functioning of the EU internal market. Thus, rules promoting effective competition provide a level playing field for the companies carrying out economic activities and confer benefits to the consumers and society, in the form of wider choices of better-quality products and services at more competitive prices due to the competitive pressure companies acting independently within the same relevant market puts on each other.

The relevant competition provision in the framework of this contribution is Article 101 TFEU regarding anti-competitive agreements. According to the rule: '... all agreements between undertakings, decisions by associations of undertakings and concerted practices which may affect trade between Member States and which have as their object or effect the prevention, restriction or distortion of competition within the internal market', are prohibited as incompatible with the internal market.

In this context, *cartel agreements* where competitors agree to, e.g., fix prices, or divide markets or customers,[17] are considered as severe infringements due to their direct purpose of restricting competition. If an agreement between undertakings, a decision by an association of undertakings or a concerted practice is prohibited pursuant to Article 101 TFEU, it shall automatically be deemed void.[18]

Article 101 TFEU is enforced jointly by the EU Commission and the EU Member States. Infringement decisions based on Article 101 TFEU may thus be taken by: (1) the EU Commission,[19] and (2) national authorities, including the national competition

14. Council Regulation (EC) No. 139/2004 of 20 January 2004 on the control of concentration between undertakings (Merger Regulation), OJ L 24/1, 29.01.2004.
15. Regulation (EU) 2022/1925 of the European Parliament and of the Council of 14 September 2022 on contestable and fair markets in the digital sector and amending Directives (EU) 2019/1937 and (EU) 2020/1828 (Digital Markets Act), OJ L 265/1, 12.10.2022. The competition rules in the Treaty also include the prohibition on State aid in Art. 107 TFEU, constraining the conduct of the EU Member States (and not the conduct of undertakings).
16. Regulation (EU) 2019/1150 of the European Parliament and of the Council of 20 June 2019 on promoting fairness and transparency for business users of online intermediation services (P2B Regulation), OJ L 186/57, 11.7.2019.
17. *See, e.g.*, the definition stated in the ECN + Directive Art. 2, 1.(11): '"cartel" means an agreement or concerted practice between two or more competitors aimed at coordinating their competitive behavior on the market or influencing the relevant parameters of competition through practices such as, but not limited to, the fixing or coordination of purchase or selling prices or other trading conditions, including in relation to intellectual property rights, the allocation of production or sales quotas, the sharing of markets and customers, including bid-rigging, restrictions of imports or exports or anti-competitive actions against other competitors'.
18. Article 101(2) TFEU.
19. The decisions of the Commission are subject to judicial review by the European Courts. For applying Art. 101(1) TFEU, the Commission has the powers provided for by Council Regulation (EC) 1/2003, *supra* n. 10, cf. Art. 4.

authorities (in individual cases) and national courts.[20] The joint application ensures that similar rules apply to all companies operating within the internal market engaged in cross-border activities, regardless of whether an infringement of Article 101 TFEU is scrutinized by the EU Commission or by a national authority.

The provision is only applicable if trade between Member States is affected,[21] delineating the jurisdiction of EU competition law from the jurisdiction of the national competition law of the EU Member States. However, even though an infringement is within the scope of EU competition law, national competition law may be applied in parallel when national authorities enforce Article 101 TFEU.[22] Further, to promote a coherent and effective application of the EU competition rules, the Commission and the EU Member States cooperate within the framework of the European Competition Network (ECN).[23]

When finding that a company has infringed Article 101 TFEU, the sanctions applicable to the company and possible natural persons depend on whether the infringement decision is made by the EU Commission or by a national authority. As mentioned, under EU competition law, in relation to an infringement decision made by the EU Commission, the Commission only has the possibility of imposing fines on *undertakings*, but not on natural persons.[24]

When a national authority enforces Article 101, the possible imposition of sanctions is decided by national law, however subject to EU harmonization in regard to the fining of *undertakings*; i.e., the EU Member States shall ensure the possibility of imposing *effective, proportionate and dissuasive* fines on undertakings and association of undertakings acting *intentionally or negligently*,[25] whereas EU law does not interfere with the possible sanctioning of *natural persons*. As a result, the law of the EU Member States may to a varying degree contain the options to, e.g., fine, imprison or disqualify natural persons.

Thus, the fining of undertakings on the basis of national law rests upon a similar legal fundament, whereas regarding individuals, the rules of the EU Member States are *not harmonized*, but differ, making it less predictable for non-executive and executive

20. Council Regulation (EC) 1/2003, *supra* n. 10, Arts 5 and 6.
21. Article 101(1) TFEU.
22. Council Regulation (EC) 1/2003, *supra* n. 10, Art. 3(1).
23. *European Commission: European Competition Network (ECN)*, https://competition-policy.ec.europa.eu/european-competition-network_en. *See also* Council Regulation (EC) 1/2003, *supra* n. 10, Arts 11 and 15. Further, in accordance with Art. 16(1) and (2), national authorities cannot take decisions running counter to a decision adopted by the EU Commission, and national courts may avoid giving decisions which would conflict with a decision contemplated by the EU Commission in proceedings it has initiated.
24. Council Regulation (EC) 1/2003, *supra* n. 10, Art. 23.
25. ECN+ Directive Art. 14(1): 'Member States shall ensure that national administrative competition authorities may either impose by decision in their own enforcement proceedings, or request in non-criminal judicial proceedings, the imposition of effective, proportionate and dissuasive fines on undertakings and associations of undertakings where, intentionally or negligently, they infringe Article 101 or 102 TFEU', *see also* Art. 14(3). 'This Article is without prejudice to national laws allowing for the imposition of sanctions in criminal judicial proceedings provided that the application of such laws does not affect the effective and uniform enforcement of Articles 101 and 102 TFEU', cf. Art. 14(2).

managers to foresee their legal position since their legal position will depend on which national jurisdiction(s) that undertake(s) the enforcement of a particular cross-border competition law infringement.[26]

Several EU Member States have chosen to provide the legal basis for sanctioning natural persons in relation to a company competition law infringement,[27] and as it appears, a managerial (or supervising) role is of importance when appointing possible liable natural persons. For example, in Portugal:

> Article 73(1) of the Portuguese Competition Act allows liability for antitrust infringements to be attributed to members of the board of directors, as well as to those who are responsible for managing or supervising the areas of activity where the infringement occurred. Such persons may be fined when (i) the infringement was committed in their name and in the collective interest of the company *or* (ii) when they knew or should have known about the infringement but did not adopt the adequate measures to cease it immediately.[28]

And in Poland:

> The possibility to impose financial fines on individuals in case of undertaking anti-competitive agreements by companies was introduced into the Polish competition law in 2015. It is a responsibility of a subsidiary nature – firstly, an undertaking must be in breach of Polish or EU prohibitions of anti-competitive agreements. Subsequently, the President of the Office of Competition and Consumers Protection ('PCA') may impose a fine on a 'managing person' that may amount up to PLN 2 000 000 000 (i.e., approx. EUR 500 000). The fine is a risk when the managing person intentionally allowed the infringement of antitrust rules. Just to be clear – other fines may be imposed on individuals for breach of competition law provisions in Poland. These are: (i) bid-rigging cases – where criminal charges may be pressed, and a person may be convicted with imprisonment sentence – up to 3 years, (ii) dawn-raids obstructions, (iii) lack of merger filings, when such action is required.[29]

---

26. As part of the ECN, the national competition authorities inform each other of new cases and envisaged enforcement decisions, so, e.g., a cartel case is less likely to be subject to simultaneous enforcement proceedings by national competition authorities. Normally, the competition authority receiving a complaint or starting an ex officio procedure will remain in charge of the case, but a case may be reallocated to another 'well placed to act' competition authority, or – where appropriate – subject to parallel action by two or more national competition authorities, *see* Commission Notice on cooperation within the Network of Competition Authorities, OJ C 101/43, 27.4.2004, points 6 and 12.
27. In an overview from 2013, it appears that: 'In nineteen of the twenty-seven Member States of the EU, individuals can currently be sanctioned for infringements of competition law. Fourteen Member States have introduced criminal penalties for competition law infringements, sometimes parallel to a system of administrative fines', *see* Marco Slotboom, *Individual Liability for Cartel Infringement in the EU: An Increasingly Dangerous Minefield*, Kluwer Competition Law Blog (25 April 2013), http://competitionlawblog.kluwercompetitionlaw.com/2013/04/25/individual-liability-for-cartel-infringements-in-the-eu-an-increasingly-dangerous-minefield/.
28. Joaquim Vieira Peres & Catarina Vieira Peres de Fraipont, *Non-compete Clauses and Fines on Natural Persons: The Blueotter and EGEO Case (Portugal)*, 13 Journal Eur. Comp. L. P. 4, 285 (2022), referring to *Lei da Concorrência*, no. 19/2012, Diário da República no. 89/2012, I of 2012-05-08.
29. Aziewics, *supra* n. 7.

And the Netherlands:

> In the Netherlands, the NCA may impose a fine on undertakings as well as natural persons pursuant to Article 56 Dutch Competition Law Act in conjunction with Article 5:1, under 2 and 3, of the Dutch General Administrative Law Act.[30]

In some EU Member States, the possible sanctioning of a natural person seems to include both the situation where: (1) a national authority has applied Article 101 TFEU itself and (2) as a follow-on national (criminal) case imposing sanctions on an individual on the basis of an EU Commission company infringement decision.[31] Further, international non-executive and executive managers are not likely to escape the imposition of sanctions just because they are not citizens of the enforcing EU Member State or do not speak the language.[32]

However, in cartel cases within the scope of EU competition law, the offending companies may try to invoke the EU Commission's *leniency programme* in relation to enforcement cases undertaken by the EU Commission,[33] or a national leniency programme in relation to national enforcement cases,[34] in order to obtain either total immunity from the fine or a reduction of the fine that would otherwise be imposed on the company. These national leniency programmes applied in relation to Article 101 TFEU infringements are not alone subject to total harmonization by the ECN+ Directive,[35] but the *interplay* between applications for immunity from fines and sanctions on *natural persons* is also subject to harmonization.[36] Thus, the ECN+ Directive does not harmonize the sanctions on natural persons as such, but it requires that if national law contains the possibility of such sanctions, then natural persons should be fully protected from sanctions imposed in national administrative proceedings, as well as national criminal and non-criminal judicial proceedings, in relation to their involvement in a secret cartel covered by a leniency application.[37] Accordingly, the national harmonized leniency rules for companies will also protect non-executive and executive managers covered by a company leniency application, but it will depend

30. Mariska van de Sanden & Tialda Beetstra, *Dutch Court Holds Former Director Personally Liable for North Sea Shrimps Cartel Fine*, Kluwer Competition Law Blog (13 October 2020), http://competitionlawblog.kluwercompetitionlaw.com/2020/10/13/dutch-court-holds-former-director-personally-liable-for-north-sea-shrimps-cartel-fine/.
31. Slotboom, *supra* n. 27: 'In some Member States, like the Netherlands, the national competition authority might even impose fines on individuals in cross-border cartel cases while the European Commission punishes the companies in question.'
32. *See* regarding Poland: Aziewics, *supra* n. 7.
33. Commission Notice on Immunity from fines and reduction of fines in cartel cases, OJ C 298/17, 8.12.2006.
34. *See, e.g.*, DCA section 23d-23i, implementing the ECN+ Directive Arts 17-23.
35. ECN+ Directive Arts 17-23.
36. Article 23 of the ECN+ Directive. As regards the protection of leniency statements and settlement submissions the Directive is applicable even when national law is applied on a stand-alone basis, cf. ECN+ Directive Recital 4, and Art. 1(2): 'This Directive covers the application of Articles 101 and 102 TFEU and the parallel application of national competition law to the same case. As regards Article 31(3) and (4) of this Directive, this Directive also covers the application of national competition law on a stand-alone basis.'
37. Article 23 (1) and (2) of the ECN+ Directive.

on the individual national law of the EU Member States whether there are any sanctions to be protected from.

Next to the public enforcement of competition law, as a further follow-on *private enforcement* tool, anyone who has suffered harm due to the infringement of competition law may claim *compensation for damages* from the undertaking or association of undertakings that has caused the harm.[38] Provided that national rules addressing corporate executives and non-executive managers' liability offer the opportunity, non-executive and executive managers may also risk being subject to follow-on damage claims.[39] This may include not only competitor or consumer claims for compensation for damages but also, e.g., the offending company's civil claim to recover a cartel fine from a former executive manager, who was involved in the competition law infringement:

On 23 September 2020, a former director of one of the North Sea shrimp cartelists was held personally liable for damage of over EUR 13 million by the Dutch District Court of Noord-Nederland. According to the Court, the director's personal involvement in the cartel qualified as improperly fulfilling his duties as a director. This justifies his personal liability to pay damages to the bankruptcy estate based on Dutch corporate directors' liability rules.[40]

The Damage Directive harmonizes certain rules necessary to ensure the effective exercise of the right to claim full compensation for damages from the harming *companies* infringing competition law.[41] However, the Damage Directive only to a very limited extent addresses the link between the granting of leniency in relation to a cartel infringement and company civil liability in relation to compensation for damages.[42] Thus, the granting of leniency does not as such result in immunity from damage claims, but leniency may have an impact when considering joint and several liability if more companies are involved in the infringement.

According to the Damage Directive Article 11(1), in joint infringement cases, each of the undertakings involved is bound to compensate for the harm in full, and the

38. Access to compensation for damage from the harming *companies* is subject to harmonization by Directive 2014//104/EU of the European Parliament and of the Council of 26 November 2014 on certain rules governing actions for damages under national law for infringements of the competition law provisions of the Member States and the European Union, OJ L 349/1, 5.12.2014 (Damage Directive).
39. *See, e.g.*, Van de Sanden & Beetstra, *supra* n. 30:

    The central questions of law before the Court were:

    - whether the defendant acted wrongfully (whether a personal serious blame can be made) towards the joint creditors based on which he is liable pursuant to Article 6:162 of the Dutch Civil Code (tort) for the deficit related to bankruptcy, and/or
    - whether improper management (improper performance of duties) can be established based on which he is liable pursuant to Article 2:9 of the Dutch Civil Code (corporate directors' liability) for the fine imposed on Heiploeg by the European Commission.

    Only the second claim was successful.
40. Van de Sanden & Beetstra, *supra* n. 30.
41. Damage Directive Art. 1.
42. Damage Directive Art. 11(4).

injured party has the right to require full compensation from any of the companies until the injured party has been fully compensated. However, an immunity recipient is only jointly and severally liable as follows:

> (a) to its direct or indirect purchasers or providers; and (b) to other injured parties only where full compensation cannot be obtained from the other undertakings that were involved in the same infringement of competition law.

This does not address the civil liability of natural persons, but since only full compensation (i.e., no over-compensation) may be granted to the natural or legal person who has suffered harm, the question is whether the rules of the Damage Directive will also have a side-effect on the liability of non-executive or executive managers covered by a leniency application facing civil damage claims. On the other hand – as a reflection based on the Dutch Schrimps case – it may also be questioned whether a fined company may try to (partly) pass on follow-on damage claims by third parties to a (former) director based on the potential corporate director's liability rules.[43]

Altogether, the prohibition in Article 101 TFEU on anti-competitive agreements; the risk of detection of cartels as a consequence of the leniency rules (bringing game theory and prisoner's dilemma into play); the risk of fines imposed on *undertakings* and fines, imprisonment, etc., imposed on *natural persons*; and the risk of having to pay compensation for damages all form part of the purpose of deterring companies from entering into anti-competitive agreements and cartels and the purpose of destabilizing already existing cartels, the achievement of which depends on the quality of every single element and the overall combination of the elements.

§5.03 WHICH NATURAL PERSONS MAY RISK BEING LIABLE AND SANCTIONED UNDER DANISH LAW?

To appoint and further characterize which natural persons may be considered liable for complicity and potentially subject to sanctions under the DCA in relation to a company's breach of Article 101 TFEU, it is relevant to consider both the Danish rules on *personal fines*, *imprisonment* as well as the Danish – EU-harmonized – *leniency rules* applicable in (secret) cartel cases, as these provisions as indicated above are interlinked[44] and collectively provide guidance as to the delimitation of 'who'.

[A] Fines and Imprisonment

The legal basis for imposing sanctions (i.e., fines and imprisonment) on individuals is found in the DCA section 23(4).[45] This provision implies that a *natural person* ('en fysisk person') may be punished with a *fine* if the person *intentionally or with gross*

43. *See* reflection by Van de Sanden & Beetstra, *supra* n. 30.
44. The provisions are interlinked in the sense that individuals that may be considered liable may escape the sanctions based on the leniency rules.
45. Supplemented by relevant provisions in the Danish Criminal Code, Consolidated Act of 20 September 2021, no. 1851.

negligence[46] is complicit in an infringement of Article 101 TFEU committed by an undertaking or an association of undertakings (e.g., an industry association).[47] The fine is calculated on the basis of an assessment of the *gravity and duration* of the infringement, distinguishing between *less serious* infringements (the fine should be at least DKK 50,000[48]), *serious infringements* (the fine should be at least DKK 100,000[49]) and *very serious infringements* (the fine should be at least DKK 200,000[50]), and further distinguishing between infringements of a *shorter duration* (less than one year), of *medium duration* (1-5 years, resulting in a surcharge of up to 50% of the amount established in respect to the gravity of the infringement) and of *longer duration* (over 5 years, resulting in a surcharge of 10% of the amount established in respect to the gravity of the infringement).[51]

Further, the punishment may increase to *imprisonment* 'for up to one year and six months' if the natural person is complicit in an infringement of Article 101 TFEU in relation to an undertaking or an association of undertakings entering into a *cartel agreement*[52] and if 'the breach is intentional and of a grave nature, especially due to the extent of the infringement or its potentially damaging effects'.[53] The sanction of imprisonment is intended to be restricted to infringement with close similarities to severe economic crime. This is further underlined by the Danish Criminal Code, implying that a liable natural person under particularly aggravating circumstances risks imprisonment for up to six years for complicity in a company's participation in a cartel agreement.[54]

As a starting point, the concept of a *natural person* is widely understood and may without any further denominators in principle include any natural person. However, the delimitation of potentially liable natural person in relation to competition law infringement is – both regarding fines and imprisonment – closely linked to the concept

46. The responsibility norm for natural persons in Danish law (intention or gross negligence) is tightened compared to the responsibility norm for companies provided by the ECN+ Directive Art. 14(1) as implemented by the DCA section 23(1) (intention or negligence).
47. DCA section 23(4), 1st sentence.
48. Approximately EUR 6,700.
49. Approximately EUR 13,300.
50. Approximately EUR 26,700.
51. Proposal for a legal act amending the Danish Competition Law and the Danish Criminal Code, L 116 of 9 December 2020, preparatory work – Remarks to the proposal, 47.
52. A 'cartel agreement' under this sentence shall mean: an agreement, concerted practice, or decision between undertakings, operating at the same level of trade, on: (i) prices, profits, etc., for the sale or resale of goods or services; (ii) restrictions on production or sales; (iii) sharing of markets or customers; or (iv) coordination of bid, cf. DCA section 23(4), 3rd sentence. This definition in the DCA seems to have a more limited scope than the definition of a cartel agreement stated in the ECN+ Directive Art. 2, 1.(11), thus reserving the risk of imprisonment to particular cartel agreements (the general definition of a cartel agreement stated in the ECN+ Directive is implemented in the DCA section 5b, 6).
53. DCA section 23(4), 2nd sentence.
54. The Danish Criminal Code, Part 28: Offences against property, section 299 c: '1) Imprisonment for a term not exceeding six years is imposed on any person who is complicit, in particularly aggravating circumstances, in the conclusion by an enterprise or a business combination of a cartel agreement falling within the second sentence of section 23(4) of the Competition Act. Especially extensive violations, or violations likely to entail serious harm, are considered particularly aggravating circumstances. (2) Subsection (1) only applies to natural persons.'

of complicity, and therefore closely linked to the possibility for a natural person affiliated with a company to behave in a way that affects the company's conduct towards a competition law infringement. In the context of the DCA, the *concept of complicity* shall be understood in accordance with the Danish Criminal Code,[55] implying that the penalty provided for an offence applies to natural persons who are complicit in the act by *incitement, aiding or abetting*.[56] Thus, the natural person subject to liability must at least be related to the company in a way where it is possible to incite, aid or abet the company in the act of infringing competition law, e.g., by actively participating in the crime or by knowingly advise or encourage the act in some way before or when it is committed.

In cartel cases having imprisonment as a possible sanction,[57] it is stated in the preparatory work of the DCA that the *subject to punishment* will be natural persons which on behalf of an undertaking are complicit in the undertaking's entering into a cartel agreement with undertakings operating at the same level of trade, i.e. competitors, and it is further elaborated that this may include, e.g., the *chairman or director* ('formanden eller direktøren') of an association of undertakings.[58]

Accordingly, it is indicated that there is a link between the position or role which the affiliated natural person has in relation to the company or association of companies and the assessment of complicity of the natural person. Logically, behind any company decision, there is a natural individual making a decision, and to narrow down potentially complicit natural persons, it is therefore relevant to consider the role or position of the natural individual in question towards the company.

This link is especially apparent in a departmental note by the Director of Public Prosecutions[59] addressing the prosecutor's choice of *liability subject* ('ansvarssubjekt') in cases concerning company liability. From the departmental note, it appears that the prosecuting authority may prosecute a natural person if the management of a company ('selskabets ledelse') or a superior employee ('overordnet ansat'), including the director ('direktøren'), has acted intentionally or with gross negligence. However, in the case of a subordinate employee ('underordnet ansat') being involved, the employee will only be prosecuted under exceptional circumstances.[60]

Thus, even though DCA section 23(4) by its wording to a wide extent includes natural persons within its scope, in practice only the management of a company and

---

55. The Danish Criminal Code, section 23: '(1) The penalty provided for an offence applies to everybody who is complicit in the act by incitement, aiding or abetting. The punishment may be reduced where a person intended only to provide minor assistance or support an intent already formed, and where the offence has not been completed or intentional complicity failed.'
56. Proposal for a legal act amending the Danish Competition Law and the Danish Criminal Code, *supra* n. 51, 109.
57. As defined by DCA section 23(4), 3rd sentence.
58. Proposal for a legal act amending the Danish Competition Law and the Danish Criminal Code, *supra* n. 51, 109. An association of undertakings includes all kinds of industry associations and other kinds of organized cooperation between undertakings (FT 1996-97, A, p. 3658).
59. Criminal liability for legal persons, RM 5/1999 – revised 17 April 2015. The Director of Public Prosecutions (Rigsadvokaten) manages the prosecution service as regards criminal law, administration, and development.
60. Criminal liability for legal persons, *supra* n. 59, section 3.1.2. and the Proposal for a legal act amending the Danish Competition Law and the Danish Criminal Code, *supra* n. 51, 111.

superior employees are likely to be prosecuted. From a general perspective, this overall approach involves the question of differentiating *the management of the company* and *superior employees* (including the director) from *subordinate employees*.

Before elaborating further on this point and to complete the picture, it is interesting first to address the leniency rules.

[B] Leniency

As mentioned, while there is no criminal liability under EU competition law making it possible to punish natural persons and no harmonization of the EU Member States' (criminal) sanctioning of natural persons in these cases,[61] the ECN+ Directive as a starting point provides a full harmonization[62] of the national leniency programmes to the benefit of companies participating in secret cartels, and further provides a harmonization of the rules governing the *interplay* between applications for immunity from fines and sanctions on natural persons.[63] The harmonization of the interplay will be of relevance to the extent that the law of the enforcing Member State contains one or more options for punishing natural persons.

For the purposes of the ECN+ Directive, *leniency* means 'both immunity from fines and reduction of fines', and a *leniency programme* means:

> a programme concerning the application of Article 101 TFEU or a corresponding provision under national competition law on the basis of which a participant in a secret cartel, independently of the other undertakings involved in the cartel, cooperates with an investigation of the competition authority, by voluntarily providing presentations regarding the participant's knowledge of, and role in, the cartel in return for which the participant receives, by decision of by discontinuation of proceedings, immunity for, or a reduction of, fines for its involvement in the cartel.[64]

National leniency programmes are a key tool for the prevention, detection, and destabilization of secret cartels – and consequently for the effective enforcement of competition law – and a common approach is needed to ensure the effectiveness of the leniency system at EU-wide and national levels. Thus, harmonization promotes legal

61. Recital 12 of the ECN+ Directive states that the Directive does not apply to national laws insofar as they provide for the imposition of criminal sanctions on natural persons, except for the rules governing the interplay of leniency programmes with the imposition of sanctions on natural persons.
62. Recitals 10 and 11 of the ECN+ Directive and Chapter VI, Leniency programmes for secret cartels, Arts 17-23 of the ECN+ Directive. Immunity from fines is harmonized by Art. 17, whereas reduction of fines is harmonized by Art. 18.
63. Article 23 of the ECN+ Directive.
64. Article 2(15) and (16) of the ECN+ Directive. *Immunity from fines* means 'an exemption from fines that would otherwise be imposed on an undertaking for its participation in a secret cartel in order to reward it for its cooperation with a competition authority in the framework of a leniency programme', Art. 2(13) of the ECN+ Directive. *Reduction of fines* means 'a reduction in the amount of the fine that would otherwise be imposed on an undertaking for its participation in a secret cartel, in order to reward it for its cooperation with a competition authority in the framework of a leniency programme', Art. 2(14) of the ECN+ Directive.

certainty for natural persons affiliated with companies applying for immunity, making it more likely that a cartel member will apply for leniency if the involved individuals know that they are shielded from individual sanctions such as fines, disqualification or imprisonment imposed by the enforcing EU Member States.[65]

As a consequence of the harmonization provided by the ECN+ Directive, the leniency programmes are applicable in all the EU Member States, enabling the granting of immunity from or reduction of fines to companies disclosing their participation in secret cartels infringing Article 101 TFEU.[66] As mentioned, the ECN+ Directive harmonizes the interplay in the national law of the EU Member States between applications for immunity from fines and sanctions on natural persons. In this context, the Directive also provides a starting point for how widely the group of natural persons that an EU Member State may decide to benefit from a leniency programme could be defined.

Thus, natural persons protected by Article 23 of the ECN+ Directive are: *current and former directors, managers and other members of staff of applicants* for immunity from fines. The Directive requires that this group of natural persons should be fully protected from sanctions imposed in national administrative proceedings, as well as national criminal and non-criminal judicial proceedings, in relation to their involvement in a secret cartel covered by a leniency application.[67] Under Danish law, this application may be submitted by the undertakings participating in a cartel automatically covering the relevant natural persons[68] or it may be submitted by the natural persons themselves.[69] The legal consequence for the natural person is either the dismissal of charges[70] (both in relation to fines and imprisonment)[71] or a reduction of

65. *See* Recitals 11 and 64 of the ECN+ Directive. The leniency programme applied by the EU Commission (when enforcing EU competition law against companies) is communicated in Commission Notice on Immunity from fines and reduction of fines in cartel cases, *supra* n. 33. While this programme is stated in a notice (soft law), the leniency programmes of the EU Member States are subject to harmonization by means of a Directive.
66. *Immunity from fines* means 'an exemption from fines that would otherwise be imposed on an undertaking for its participation in a secret cartel, in order to reward it for its cooperation with a competition authority in the framework of a leniency programme', *see* Art. 2(13) of the ECN+ Directive. For the purposes of the ECN+ Directive, a *cartel* is defined as 'an agreement or concerted practice between two or more competitors aimed at coordinating their competitive behaviour on the market or influencing the relevant parameters of competition through practices such as, but not limited to, the fixing or coordination of purchase or selling prices or other trading conditions, including in relation to intellectual property rights, the allocation of production or sales quotas, the sharing of markets and customers, including bid-rigging, restrictions of imports or exports or anti-competitive actions against other competitors', and a secret cartel means 'a cartel, the existence of which is partially or wholly concealed', *see* Art. 2(11) and (12) of the ECN+ Directive.
67. Article 23 (1) and (2) of the ECN+ Directive.
68. DCA section 23i(1). *See, e.g.*, The State Prosecutor for Special Crime and International Crimes, decision of 29 November in case SØK-91250-00004-10, https://www.kfst.dk/afgorelser-ruling/konkurrenceomraadet/straffedomme-og-boedevedtagelser/horisontale-aftaler/storkoebenhavnske-byggekarteller/20161129-julius-nielsen-soen-as/.
69. DCA section 23i(4).
70. As mentioned, under the ECN+ Directive, leniency encompasses immunity from fines and reductions of fines, cf. Art. 2(15). This does not entirely correspond to the leniency provided for a natural person under Danish competition law encompassing dismissal of charges and reduction of fines.

the fine,[72] whereas a possible reduction of a prison sentence is decided by the court under the Danish Criminal Code.[73]

As the ECN + Directive does not harmonize the potential liability or sanctioning of natural persons but only the interplay with the leniency rules, it is a matter for the individual EU Member States to decide whether there is in fact *any sanctions* a natural person could apply for immunity from in national administrative and judicial proceedings. It is also a matter for the individual EU Member State to decide the possible *kind of sanctions* a natural person might risk, i.e., fines, imprisonment, disqualification, confiscation or other personal sanctions.

However, to ensure the interplay, the group of natural persons that should logically be able to benefit from the leniency programmes of a particular EU Member State must be at least the same group of natural persons that could risk being liable and met with sanctions in national enforcement proceedings. In accordance with the ECN + Directive, this could consequently involve *current and former directors, managers, and other members of staff.*

Accordingly, to comply with the intention of the Directive, it is likely to expect that if an EU Member State chooses to prosecute and sanction natural persons in competition law cases, there should be a definitional correspondence between the natural subjects that risks sanctions and the potential beneficiaries of the leniency programme in the sense that all natural persons appointed as potential (liable and) sanctionable subjects should be within the scope of the national leniency programme. Whether this group of individuals is in fact widely or narrowly defined in the specific EU Member State will depend on the national rules respectively, as the sanctioning of natural persons for company infringements of competition law relies upon national law. Thus, the appointed group of natural persons in a particular Member State may in practice be defined more narrowly than what the wording of the ECN + Directive implies.

The group of natural persons appointed in the ECN + Directive seems to include any natural persons that could meaningfully have the required impact on the business of the company. Since it is only meaningful to include natural persons which somehow have the possibility to influence the conduct of a company towards a competition law infringement, it is hardly likely that an EU Member State would go even further and extend liability to natural persons which are not somehow affiliated with (or has been affiliated with) the business of the infringing company at the point of time of the infringement. In this respect, it is important to note that the conduct of an independent service provider cannot be imputed to a company, apparently making it unlikely that a natural person affiliated with an independent service provider on the other hand may

71. DCA section 23i(2).
72. DCA section 23i(3). Dismissal of charges for natural persons are granted by the State Prosecutor, DCA section 23i(6).
73. Danish Criminal Code section 82(9) or (10), considering (9) 'that the offender voluntarily reported himself to the authorities and made a full confession'; and (10) 'that the offender has provided information crucial to solving criminal acts committed by others', a mitigating circumstance when determining a sentence.

be able to act as a complicit in relation to a company's infringement of Article 101 TFEU.[74]

The Danish text of the ECN+ Directive is directly translated from the English edition: 'current and former directors, managers and other staff' i.e.: 'nuværende og tidligere direktører, ledere og andre ansatte', or translated back into English: current and former executive directors, managers, and other staff,[75] seemingly leaving non-executives outside the scope of the rule. However, it is noteworthy that in Danish: 'director' may be translated as both executive director ('direktør') and non-executive director ('bestyrelsesmedlem').

In contrast, the wording chosen in the leniency rules of the DCA is slightly different from the Danish text of the ECN+Directive, reflecting the broader understanding of a 'director'. Thus, DCA section 23i(1) states that an application of leniency from a company automatically covers *current and former directors, managing employees and other staff* ('nuværende og tidligere bestyrelsesmedlemmer, ledende medarbejdere og andre ansatte').[76] From the Danish translation, it follows that this includes executive and non-executive directors.

Recalling that the provisions of fines and imprisonment in DCA section 23(4) have *natural persons* within its scope, a definitional correspondence between the scope of the leniency rules in the DCA section 23i(1) and the rules on fines and imprisonment in the DCA section 23(4) implies that a *natural person* may be further qualified as encompassing *current and former directors* (including executive and non-executive directors), *managing employees and other staff*. This interpretation is also in compliance with the aim of the ECN+ Directive's harmonization of the interplay between applications for immunity from fines and sanctions on natural persons.[77]

[C] Can We Come Any Closer?

So, on the basis of the above, under Danish competition law, sanctions may be imposed on *natural persons*[78] encompassing *current and former executive and non-executive directors, managers and other members of staff*[79] of the offending company. However, in practice, only *the management of the company* and *superior employees* will be prosecuted, whereas *subordinate employees* will merely be prosecuted under exceptional circumstances.[80]

---

74. Case C-542/14, *SIA 'VM Remonts' (formerly SIA 'DIV un KO') and Others v. Konkurences padome*, 21.7.2016, ECLI:EU:C:2016:578, para. 25: '... where a service provider offers, in return for payment, services on a given market on an independent basis, that provider must be regarded, for the purpose of applying rules aimed at penalising anti-competitive conduct, as a separate undertaking from those to which it provides services and the acts of such a provider cannot automatically be attributed to one of those undertakings'.
75. Article 23(1) of the ECN+ Directive (Danish version).
76. DCA section 23i(1).
77. Article 23 of the ECN+ Directive.
78. DCA section 23(4).
79. DCA section 23(i)(1) and Art. 23 of the ECN+ Directive.
80. Criminal liability for legal persons, *supra* n. 59, section 3.1.2. and the Proposal for a legal act amending the Danish Competition Law and the Danish Criminal Code, *supra* n. 51, at 111.

As mentioned, this overall approach seems to involve the question of differentiating *the management of the company* and *superior employees* (including the director) from *subordinate employees.*

It is not clear whether this distinction corresponds to differentiating *executive and non-executive managers* from *other members of staff* since there is not necessarily a parallel between the different notions. However, as a starting point, the question is raised: When is a natural person to be considered as part of the managerial or superior employee level and when is a natural person to be considered as part of the subordinate/other member of staff level?

Under Danish competition law, there is no exhaustive list of managerial functions held by natural persons in a company that automatically qualifies for personal liability and sanctions for complicity in a competition law infringement. In fact, the distinction does not seem to have been tested in legal practice. An explanation may be that the distinction rests upon an administrative note by the Director of Public Prosecutions, and further that strong evidence for complicity in criminal cases is required, making it likely for the prosecutor to only choose to prosecute individuals where there is a certain probability for conviction, thus staying well above the subordinate 'threshold'. Hence, there does not seem to be Danish legal cases where a subordinate/other member of staff has been neither charged, found liable, nor sanctioned as complicit in a competition law infringement.

Further, the position of the individuals in the infringing company is sometimes disclosed in public newspapers, but rarely disclosed in the public records of neither settlements of fines[81] nor relevant court rulings, but some examples may be found: director of an industry association;[82] executive director and vice-executive director of, e.g., an industry association;[83] chairman of the board and executive director of an industry association;[84] managing employees.[85] Also, some further qualifications of the position of an individual may be found in guidance from the Danish Competition and Consumer Authority, stating that in practice charges have been raised against employees at a managerial level, i.e., employees having the function as executive directors

81. DCA section 23j. In the context of companies, a 'settlement submission' is defined in the ECN + Directive Art. 2(1) (18) as 'a voluntary presentation by, or on behalf of, an undertaking to a competition authority, describing the undertaking's acknowledgement of, or its renunciation to dispute, its participation in an infringement of Article 101 or 102 TFEU or national competition law and its responsibility for that infringement, which was drawn up specifically to enable the competition authority to apply a simplified or expedited procedure'.
82. The Danish Supreme Court, ruling of 30 August 2010 in case 319/2009 (UfR 2010.2980 H), personal fine: DKK 25,000 (issued for a violation conducted before the increased level of fines entering into force in Denmark in March 2013).
83. The Danish Supreme Court, ruling of 30 Aug. 2010 in case 320/2009 (UfR 2010.2986/1 H), personal fines amounting to DKK 25,000 each (before increased level of fines entered into force in Denmark in March 2013).
84. Municipal Court of Horsens, ruling of 4 October 2007, Case No. SS 785/2007, personal fines amounting to DKK 10,000 each (before increased level of fines entered into force in Denmark in March 2013).
85. Municipal Court of Glostrup, ruling of 21 April 2022, case CL-13554/2019 (SØK-91250-00021-17), *HMN Naturgas*, personal fines amounting to DKK 100,000, DKK 75,000, DKK 100,000 and DKK 50,000.

('direktører'), or head of sales ('chef for salg') or head of offering ('chef for tilbudsgivning').[86]

Next to this, legal practice does not seem to provide further nuances as to decisive factors in specific cases. However, even though the professional title of an individual may indicate a managerial position, it is likely to assume that the actual title will remain an indication, whereas the actual exercise of managerial powers will be decisive, regardless of the title of the natural person.

As previously mentioned, fining a natural person requires that the person *intentionally or with gross negligence* is found to be complicit in an infringement of Article 101 TFEU committed by an undertaking or an association of undertakings.[87] It is noteworthy that a proactive attempt to avoid violations of competition law may serve as an indication that the natural person in question neither acted intentionally nor with gross negligence. Thus, the existence of a compliance programme in the offending company or the seeking of professional legal advice seems to be able to have an impact when deciding personal (prosecution and) liability[88] and may also serve as a mitigating factor when deciding the level of the fine imposed on the infringing company. However, the existence of a compliance programme or the seeking of professional legal advice[89] does not eliminate the infringement of competition law by the company as such, but may affect the assessment of personal liability and may also serve as a mitigating factor when deciding the level of the fine imposed on the infringing company.

Also, it is noteworthy that if an individual is found to be liable for a fine, in practice, the level of the individual's managerial responsibility may be considered as a mitigating circumstance when determining the level of the fine. Hence, in the *HMN Naturgas* ruling, the court found that in relation to an individual, who did not have a managerial responsibility to the same extent as some of the other individuals charged, the level of the fine should be sentenced to a lower amount.[90] This reasoning is not further elaborated on in the court ruling, but it implies that the capability of affecting the company's conduct towards a competition law infringement following from the managerial responsibility of an individual may have an impact on the level of the fine.

§5.04 CONCLUDING REMARKS

Behind every business decision made by a company or an association of companies, there is a natural person. To be able to affect the business decisions, these natural persons must possess - or have possessed - a certain position in the company, making it possible to, e.g., order or exercise de facto leadership in relation to the company's infringement of competition law.

86. The Danish Competition and Consumer Authority, *Guidance on the obligation to provide information and the protection against self-incrimination* (October 2021).
87. DCA section 23(4), 1st sentence.
88. *See* case SS 3-3526/2020, *supra* n. 2, at 90 (under appeal).
89. *See* case 191/2018, *supra* n. 5, at 10.
90. *Supra* n. 85, fines amounting to DKK 100,000, DKK 75,000, DKK 100,000 and DKK 50,000.

Since such behaviour is prohibited under Article 101(1) TFEU, it is the responsibility of the managerial level of the company, both not personally to engage in anti-competitive behaviour and to prevent the company from doing so, and further to detect when infringements happen and finally to put an end to such infringement. Depending on the managerial position of the individual, the expectations may vary in practice: a non-executive director may not be expected to have thorough insight into the daily activities of the company but may be expected to ensure appropriate compliance tools, whereas an executive director may be expected to have a more detailed insight into the daily business of the company. Managers within areas with a higher exposure to competition law risks like marketing, sales, or brand management may be expected to have a special awareness not to infringe competition law, whereas a compliance manager may very well have a deep insight into competition law issues, but may not be expected to have any special insight in the possible infringements of the company than any other director of the company.[91]

Company awareness and compliance programmes are key tools to try to prevent infringements. If the responsibility not to engage in and further prevent, detect and stop competition law infringements of the company is not undertaken, non-executive and executive managers which are or have been affiliated to a company with cross-border activities within the scope of Article 101(1) TFEU risk being subject to personal sanctions depending on the individual law of the EU Member State that undertakes to enforce Article 101(1) TFEU.

If the law of an EU Member State provides the possibility of sanctioning natural persons, it is likely that this is directed at individuals possessing a managerial position, i.e., individuals that have the possibility of influencing the conduct of the undertaking. Under the ECN+ Directive and in the context of the harmonization of the leniency programmes of the EU Member States and the interplay with national rules on sanctions on natural persons, a broadly defined group of individuals, including *current and former directors, managers and other members of staff of applicants* for immunity from fines,[92] should be able to benefit from the granting of leniency to a company. However, the exact scope of natural persons will depend on the individual Member State. Under Danish law, it is difficult to appoint exactly which title, actual managerial functions or maybe even de facto exercise of leadership that may put an individual at risk, but in practice, it seems to involve the question of differentiating *the management of the company* and *superior employees* (including the director) from *subordinate employees*.[93]

The personal sanctions at risk as a consequence of a competition law infringement may include fines, imprisonment, or disqualification, and implies severe personal consequences for the individual. Further, follow-on compensation for damages may be at risk.

91. *See Pinsent Masons: Individual liability for UK competition law infringements*, OUT-LAW GUIDE (1 December 2020), https://www.pinsentmasons.com/out-law/guides/individuals-liability-uk-competition-law-infringements.
92. Article 23 of the ECN+ Directive.
93. Criminal liability for legal persons, *supra* n. 59, section 3.1.2., DCA section 23i(1) and DCA section 23(4).

The harmonization of the leniency programmes of the EU Member States ensures that former and present non-executives and executive managers may also benefit from the immunity from/lower fines that the applying company obtains, including immunity from other sanctions or less invasive sanctions as a consequence of the ECN+ Directives rules on the interplay between the leniency rules and individual administrative or criminal sanctions in the EU Member States. Also, the leniency rules are related to the Damage Directive, which may also be to the benefit of individuals.

Altogether, the prohibition on anti-competitive agreements in Article 101(1) TFEU and the subsequent sanctions for the companies and natural persons, combined with the leniency rules and the risk of having to pay compensation for damages, forms part of the aim of deterring companies – and the company decision-makers – from engaging in anti-competitive behaviour and further to destabilize and detect already existing cartels. The consequences may be severe for the individual manager.

The joint application of Article 101(1) and the ECN+ Directives' harmonization of company fines ensure that similar rules apply to all companies operating within the internal market. However, except for the interplay between the leniency rules and the sanctioning of individuals, the rules regarding sanctions of natural persons in the EU Member States are *not harmonized*, providing less legal certainty for non-executive and executive managers as to their legal position. Therefore, non-executive and executive managers must pay attention to and be aware of the competition rules to avoid ending up in a personally difficult situation.

CHAPTER 6

Free Movement of Members of Corporate Management

Karsten Engsig Sørensen

§6.01 INTRODUCTION

When members of corporate management exercise free movement within the EU, they may experience different types of discriminating or restricting rules that hinder such movement. This may be, for instance, the situation if there is a residence or nationality requirement, but it may also be a non-discriminating condition such as requirements for shareholdings or specific qualifications. In some cases, such requirements may also be a restriction to the free movement of companies, as the companies may, for instance, find it difficult to set up a branch in a different Member State.

This chapter will analyse how managers and the companies that engage them may directly or indirectly benefit from the different free movement rights, in particular the free movement of workers, the freedom of establishments and the freedom to provide services.[1] This is addressed first in §6.02 below by briefly discussing which types of cases raise this issue. Then, in §6.03, it is examined how the line is drawn between managers that are workers and those that are self-employed, as only those

1. The harmonisation of company law hardly addresses the issue discussed here, and therefore it will not be discussed further. New rules on disqualified directors are, however, found in Directive 2019/1132 amending the Consolidated Company Law Directive, Directive 2017/1132. For European company forms such as the European Company (SE Company), European Interest Groupings (EEIG) and European Cooperation, there are some general requirements for the management structure, but the regulation does normally not extend to the requirement that each individual manager must fulfil. However, again there are rules that ensure the enforcement of a disqualification order, *see* SE Statute, Regulation 2157/2001, Art. 47(2). In the following, reference will only be made to EU and EU law, but the reader should be aware that the same will normally apply to the EEA area. Thus, the EEA agreements contain rules on free movement similar to those found in the Treaty of the Functioning of the European Union (hereinafter 'TFEU').

that have the status of workers benefit from the rights of free movement of workers. In §6.04 below, it is discussed how those managers that have the status as self-employed may benefit from EU law. Next, in §6.05, the protection given to managers will be outlined, and in particular, it will be discussed whether it matters what status we grant managers under EU law. Finally, in §6.06 below, there is a brief discussion of the free movement of managers under the new trade and cooperation agreement between the UK and the EU. Section §6.07 concludes.

§6.02 WHICH CASES RAISE THE ISSUE OF THE STATUS OF MANAGERS AS EITHER WORKER OR SELF-EMPLOYED?

There are many cases on free movement involving rules that directly or indirectly affect managers, but not all of these cases need to focus on the question whether the managers are workers or self-employed. However, managers who find that they are discriminated or restricted in accessing the position as manager need to figure out which freedom they may invoke. If they have the status as a worker, they are protected by Article 45 TFEU, but if self-employed, they may invoke either the freedom of establishment, Article 49 TFEU, or the freedom to provide services, Article 56 TFEU. If the manager has the status of a self-employed service provider, it may also be relevant for him/her to invoke the Service Directive (Directive 2006/123/EC).[2]

Many cases, however, involve companies that invoke free movement rights to protect against a discriminating or restrictive requirement imposed on the management. Most of these cases are concerned with situations where the company argues that it is prevented or hindered from making an establishment in another Member State or that the company is restricted in its effort to provide services in another Member State.[3] The first situation occurs when a company setting up a branch or subsidiary cannot freely choose who should manage the branch/subsidiary.[4] The second situation may surface where a company is not allowed to provide services in another Member State, unless it adapts its management so as to comply with requirements in the state where the services are to be provided.[5] For those companies providing services that are covered by the Service Directive, this directive should be invoked instead of Articles 49 and 56 TFEU, both when a service provider is providing service in another Member

2. Performing management is a service covered by the Directive, but if the management is conducted for one of the type of activities excluded from the Directive, it may also mean that the manager cannot invoke the Directive.
3. To invoke Art. 49 or 56, the company needs to be covered by those corporate forms defined in Art. 54. However, it is a very generous definition that mainly excludes companies that do not work for profit.
4. *See e.g.*, Case C-221/89, *The Queen v. Secretary of State for Transport, ex parte Factortame Ltd and others*, 25.7.1991, ECLI:EU:C:1991:320.
5. *See*, for instance, the legislation in Case C-114/97, *Commission of the European Communities v. Kingdom of Spain*, 29.10.1998, ECLI:EU:C:1998:519. In theory, a company supplying goods to another Member State could also be hindered from doing so by national requirements addressing how the management of the company should look, and in this case Arts 34 and 35 TFEU could be applicable. However, regulation of trade in goods seems unlikely to address how the management of the producer should be.

State and where a service provider is establishing itself in a Member State. In all the cases mentioned above, it will not matter what status the managers have, as it is the company that invokes the free movement rights on its own behalf.[6] Therefore, these cases will not be relevant for the analysis in the next two sections.

But, the Court of Justice of the European Union (CJEU) has held that an employer (in our case, the company) may also invoke Article 45 TFEU in order to be able to employ the manager.[7] It must be a prerequisite that there is a cross-border link, for instance, that the manager the company likes to employ is from a different Member State. If the recruited manager is self-employed, it may be possible to argue that there is a restriction on the freedom to provide services, as the company as a receiver of a service (from the self-employed manager) is restricted from contracting with the service provider (manager) they want due to the national requirement imposed on the manager. Therefore, in these cases where the company aims to enforce the rights of their managers, the question whether the manager has status as a worker or self-employed will surface.

Finally, the shareholders of the company may invoke the free movement rights if their freedom to compose the composition of the management in the company is affected by national requirements. In most cases, the shareholders may rely on the right for free movement of capital according to Article 63 TFEU which has been the case in the so-called 'Golden-Share' cases.[8] The Golden-Share cases have also addressed national requirements for the composition of the management in privatised companies.[9] But in Case C-566/15, *Erzberger*,[10] the CJEU accepted that a shareholder may invoke Article 45. In this case, a shareholder challenged the composition of the German parent company in the TUI-group based on the argument that the workers employed by a foreign subsidiary in the TUI-group should have participated in the election of workers' representatives in the board of the parent company. The case would indicate

6. It may be considered whether the manager can invoke Art. 49 or 56 TFEU on behalf of the company that employs him/her. This may be relevant when the manager does not himself/herself qualify to rely on free movement rights, for instance, because he/she is a national of the Member State where the company is employing him/her (and the situation therefore is purely internal), or the manager is not an EU/EEA national. The judgment in Case 79/85, *D. H. M. Segers v. Bestuur van de Bedrijfsvereniging voor Bank- en Verzekeringswezen, Groothandel en Vrije Beroepen*, 10.7.1986, ECLI:EU:C:1986:308, may indicate that it is possible for the director to do that, as the director in the case (*Segers*) was allowed to invoke the freedom of establishment even though he himself had not exercised any free movement, as only the company employing him had.
7. *See* Case C-350/96, *Clean Car Autoservice GesmbH v. Landeshauptmann von Wien*, 7.5.1998, ECLI:EU:C:1998:205, para. 25.
8. If the shareholder owns or controls enough shares to exercise control, the shareholder may invoke freedom of establishment, as further addressed below.
9. *See*, for instance, Case C-112/05, *Commission of the European Communities v. Federal Republic of Germany*, 23.10.2007, ECLI:EU:C:2007:623, where the Federal Republic of Germany and the Land of Lower Saxony each had the right to appoint two members of the supervisory board of Volkswagen. *See also* Joined cases C-463/04 and C-464/04, *Federconsumatori and Others (C-463/04) and Associazione Azionariato Diffuso dell'AEM SpA and Others (C-464/04) v. Comune di Milano*, 6.12.2007, ECLI:EU:C:2007:752, where the articles of association of a privatised company conferred the right to appoint a number of directors that was disproportionate to the shareholding of that authority.
10. Case C-566/15, *Konrad Erzberger v. TUI AG*, 18.7.2017, ECLI:EU:C:2017:562.

that a shareholder may also be in a position to invoke either the free movement of workers or one of the rights protecting self-employed managers on behalf of the managers. It does, however, seem less likely that a shareholder would have an interest in doing so.

Finally, requirements for managers can be challenged by the Commission or the EFTA Surveillance Authority (ESA), of which there are plenty of examples. The Commission will be free to choose whether they will invoke the free movement to protect the company or the managers, but in the latter case, the issue of status will again surface.

§6.03 ARE MANAGERS WORKERS OR SELF-EMPLOYED?

There are a number of cases addressing the question whether managers are workers or self-employed, and these cases will be analysed in §6.03[A], and in §6.03[B], the factors relevant for determining the status will be discussed in more detail.

[A] The Case Law

Looking at the case law of the CJEU, we see that the Court has accepted that managers in relation to free movement rights may have a status both as a worker and as a self-employed person. It should be recalled that the concept of workers and the group of self-employed protected by Articles 49 and 56 (and the Service Directive) are autonomous concepts developed in EU law, and not concepts that are left to the Member State to flesh out.

The clearest cases seem to be those where the manager is also the main or only shareholder of the company. Thus, in Case C-107/94, *Asscher*,[11] a director, who was also the only shareholder in the company, was regarded as being self-employed, and was therefore entitled to invoke the freedom of establishment. The Court, with reference to the test for worker status in the *Lawrie-Blum* case,[12] stressed that as the sole shareholder his activities as a director was not carried out in the context of a relationship of subordination and, consequently, he could not have the status of a 'worker'.[13]

If the director is not the controlling shareholder, the question is more open. In Case C-350/96, *Clean Car*, the CJEU assumed that the manager who is appointed by a legal person, a commercial law partnership or a civil partnership is a worker. However, there was no discussion of the question as the referring national court assumed that the

11. Case C-107/94, *P. H. Asscher v. Staatssecretaris van Financiën*, 27.6.1996, ECLI:EU:C:1996:251.
12. *Ibid.*, para. 25. In Case 66/85, *Deborah Lawrie-Blum v. Land Baden-Württemberg*, 3.7.1986, ECLI:EU:C:1986:284, the Court established that in relation to the concept of 'worker' under Art. 45 (then 48) of the Treaty, the essential characteristics of the employment relationship are that for a certain period of time, a person performs services for and under the direction of another person in return for which he/she receives remuneration, cf. para. 17.
13. *See* para. 26 of Case C-107/94, *P. H. Asscher*.

manager had that status, and this was not challenged by the CJEU. Thus, the case tells us very little about the status of managers.

A more interesting case is Case C-270/13, *Iraklis Haralambidis*,[14] where the CJEU had to decide the status of the president of the Port Authority of Brindisi. The president was appointed by the Italian Minister of Infrastructure and Transport after a range of public authorities and chambers of commerce had nominated each their candidate. The president was entrusted with a wide range of tasks, and he was therefore an executive manager.[15] To determine whether that person was a 'worker' according to Article 45 TFEU, the CJEU first recalled that the concept of worker has an autonomous meaning specific to EU law and must not be interpreted narrowly.[16] The essential feature of an employment relationship '...is that for a certain period of time a person performs services for and under the direction of another person in return for which he receives remuneration (see judgment in *Lawrie-Blum*, 66/85[...])'. The Court then concentrated on the condition of subordination, which was closely examined. The president was appointed for four years by the minister, and that appointment was renewable once. Furthermore, the minister was able to remove the president in certain situations, for instance, when there was a balance sheet deficit or important irregularities in the management. Additionally, the minister supervised the president and even had to approve certain decisions, for instance, the budget. The CJEU pointed out that the president of the Port Authority '...lacks the features which are typically associated with the functions of an independent services provider, namely, more leeway in the terms of choice of the type of work and tasks to be executed, of the manner in which that work or those tasks are to be performed, and of the time and place of work, and more freedom in the recruitment of his own staff'.[17] Based on these observations, the CJEU concluded that the president performed his task under the management and supervision of the minister and was therefore in a relationship of subordination. As he was also remunerated for the position, he was a worker and thus protected by Article 45 TFEU.

Interestingly, the CJEU in Case C-270/13, *Iraklis Haralambidis* also made an extensive reference to the judgment in Case C-232/09, *Danosa*.[18] This case concerned the protection provided for pregnant workers according to Directive 92/85/EEC. One of the questions the Court addressed in the case C-232/09, *Danosa*, judgment was whether the members of the board of directors of a capital company could be regarded as workers within the meaning of the Directive. The CJEU started by pointing out the main features of the concept of a 'worker' and, *inter alia*, referred to Case 66/85, *Lawrie-Blum*, thus indicating that the Court used the concept of worker as found in Article 45 TFEU as the starting point.[19] Ms Danosa was a director of a Latvian company. The Latvian company as well as the Latvian government made the point that a member

14. Case C-270/13, *Iraklis Haralambidis v. Calogero Casilli*, 10.9.2014, ECLI:EU:C:2014:2185.
15. *See also* AG Wahl in his opinion, para. 29.
16. Case C-270/13, *Iraklis Haralambidis*, para. 27.
17. *Ibid.*, para. 33..
18. *Ibid.*, para. 41; Case C-232/09, *Dita Danosa v. LKB Līzings SIA*, 11.11.2010, ECLI:EU:C:2010:674.
19. Case C-232/09, *Danosa*, para. 39.

of the board is not under the instruction of anyone but is supposed to work independently. Therefore, they argued that there was no subordination. The CJEU, nevertheless, came to the opposite conclusion. It insisted that each individual case must be assessed based '...on all the factors and circumstances characterising the relationship between the parties'.[20] For a member of a board of directors, it '...is necessary to consider the circumstances in which the board member was recruited; the nature of the duties entrusted to that person; the context in which those duties are performed; the scope of the person's powers and the extent to which he or she was supervised within the company; the circumstances under which the person could be removed'.[21] When the specific case was examined, it turned out that Ms Danosa was the sole member of the board of directors, being elected for three years to manage the company. Even though she had a margin of discretion in the performance of her duties, she had to report to the supervisory board and cooperate with that board. The supervisory board could also suspend her from her position, and the general meeting of shareholders could remove her from the position. Therefore, the Court concluded in paragraph 51:

> While it cannot be ruled out that the members of a directorial body of a company, such as a board of directors, are not covered by the concept of 'worker' as defined in paragraph 39 above, in view of the specific duties entrusted to them, as well as the context in which those duties are performed and the manner in which they are performed, the fact remains that board members who, in return for remuneration, provide services to the company which has appointed them and of which they are an integral part, who carry out their activities under the direction or control of another body of that company and who can, at any time, be removed from their duties without such removal being subject to any restriction, satisfy prima facie the criteria for being treated as workers within the meaning of the case-law of the Court, as referred to above.

The CJEU relied extensively on its judgment in Case C-232/09, *Danosa*, when subsequently deciding Case C-229/14, *Balkaya*.[22] The case concerned Directive 98/56/EC on collective redundancies, and one of the issues addressed was whether a director in a German GmbH should be counted as a 'worker' in the sense this concept was used in the Directive. The judgment does not establish that the concept of workers in the Directive should be interpreted as the concept of worker in Article 45, but the judgment uses a very similar definition[23] and furthermore seems to assume that Case C-232/09, *Danosa*, can be used by analogy.[24] This would indicate that the case may also be relevant for the question discussed here. However, in the subsequent part of the judgment, there is a discussion of whether it would serve the purpose of the Directive to award such a director 'worker'-status, and this indicates that the Court is using a concept of workers that is at least partly adjusted to the Directive, and therefore may not be fully aligned with the concept in Article 45.[25] But at least for the part of the

20. *Ibid.*, para. 46.
21. *Ibid.*, para. 47.
22. Case C-229/14, *Ender Balkaya v. Kiesel Abbruch*, 9.7.2015, ECLI:EU:C:2015:455.
23. *Ibid.*, para. 34.
24. Thus, the *Danosa* judgment is referred to in *inter alia* paras 34, 36-39 and 41.
25. Case C-229/14, *Balkaya*, paras 44-46.

judgment where the Court uses an analogy of Case C-232/09, *Danosa*, it may be possible to tease out some input for the issue discussed here.

The case again turned around the issue of whether there was the necessary subordination for the director to be a worker. Here, contrary to the case C-232/09, *Danosa*, the director was appointed by the general meeting, and the shareholder could also at any time revoke the director mandate, even against the will of the director. Furthermore, the director was, in the exercise of his functions, subject to the direction and supervision of the general meeting. The CJEU then added: "Moreover, although it is not by itself a decisive factor in that context, it must be observed that a director, such as the one in the main proceedings, does not hold any shares in the company for which he carries out his functions."[26] The Court thus concluded that the required subordination was present, and as the director was remunerated, he had the status as a worker according to the Directive.

The judgment not only seems to confirm Case C-232/09, *Danosa*, but also adds a few additional elements to that judgment. First, whereas in Case C-232/09, *Danosa*, the director was subordinated to primarily a supervisory board, Case C-229/14, *Balkaya*, shows that also subordination under the general meeting may suffice to fulfil the requirement of subordination if the general meeting may remove the director and may supervise and instruct the director. Also, the CJEU seems to indicate that the fact that a director does not own any shares in the company may indicate that he/she has the status as a worker. However, the judgment makes a reservation that makes it difficult to put much weight on this part of the judgment. We know from *Asscher* that if a manager has a controlling shareholding, then this makes it unlikely that this person is a worker. However, a small shareholding that does not allow the manager to affect the decisions in the company substantially should probably not exclude worker status, and the comment made by the CJEU in Case C-229/14, *Balkaya* (*see* above), may just indicate that since there is no shareholding, there is no need to consider whether there is a shareholding that may affect the status of the director.

Thus, the judgment in Case C-270/13, *Iraklis Haralambidis*, Case C-232/09, *Danosa*, and Case C-229/14, *Balkaya*, indicates that the determination of whether a member of management is a worker or self-employed requires a close examination of the position of that manager. In both cases, the judgment revolves around the question whether the manager is working under the direction of another body. That was the case in Case C-270/13, *Iraklis Haralambidis*, as the minister could remove the president given certain irregularities and, furthermore, needed to approve certain decisions. The same was the case in Case C-232/09, *Danosa*, where the manager acted under the supervision of the supervisory board and needed to cooperate with that body and, furthermore, could be suspended or removed by the supervisory board and the general meeting, respectively. In Case C-229/14, *Balkaya*, the general meeting had the power to remove, supervise and instruct the directors.

26. Paragraph 40.

Even though the CJEU in Case C-232/09, *Danosa*, paragraph 51, acknowledges that managers need not be workers, it seems that the Court is inclined to assign worker status to managers.

The judgment in Case C-603/17, *Bosworth*,[27] in comparison seems more reluctant to assign this status to managers. The case concerned the question whether two directors should be allowed to benefit from the favourable rules on jurisdiction that are awarded to persons subject to an individual contract of employment under the Lugano II Convention.[28] The CJEU did not find that the directors were covered by this provision, as there was no required relationship of subordination between the company and the directors.[29] The directors had either drafted their own contract of employment or had it drafted at their direction. Thus, the two directors '...exercised control over by whom, where and on what terms they were employed'.[30] The fact that the shareholders may give the directors general directives and may revoke the directorship was not enough to establish that they were in a position of subordination to the general meeting of shareholders.[31] Thus, the case points towards giving managers the status as self-employed since it seems that being under the general instruction of another corporate body, which may also dismiss the manager, may not suffice to grant worker status.

However, one should remember that the two directors held a very powerful position that will not be typical in most companies – it is after all not the norm that directors determine their own terms of employment, unless they are also the majority shareholder. The CJEU also stresses that being under the general directives of another corporate body may not suffice. Even if a general meeting may give instructions to a manager, such instructions may be of a general nature, leaving the manager free to decide how and when to implement them. A right to give such general instructions may not amount to subordination as required for worker status.[32] Furthermore, it should be noted that it is not clear that the CJEU in Case C-603/17, *Bosworth*, uses the same concept of worker as that used under Article 45 TFEU. Thus, there is no reference in the judgment to TFEU Article 45 or the jurisprudence connected to it. Furthermore, Advocate General Øe in his opinion suggested[33] that the CJEU should not automatically apply the same concept of worker in different fields of EU law, as the scope of application of each provision should be interpreted in light of the purposes and aims of

27. Case C-603/17 *Peter Bosworth and Colin Hurley v. Arcadia Petroleum Limited and Others*, 11.4.2019, ECLI:EU:C:2019:310.
28. Convention on jurisdiction and the recognition and enforcement of judgments in civil and commercial matters, OJ L 339, 21.12.2007.
29. In fact, the case concerned a group of companies, where the two directors seem to have acted as directors of all companies, despite only being formally appointed in two of the companies.
30. Case C-603/17, *Bosworth*, para. 30.
31. *Ibid.*, para. 33.
32. *See also* the discussion by Thomas Garber, *Zur Arbeitnehmereigenschaft von Organpersonen einer Gesellschaft*, GPR, 229-232 (2019).
33. Opinion of AG Øe in Case C-603/17, *Bosworth*, para. 49.

the relevant legal instrument.[34] The fact that the CJEU did not refer to the concept of workers under Article 45 may be seen as an acceptance of the suggestion made by AG Øe.

The issue of the status of management in relation to free movement was addressed again in the recent judgment from the EFTA Court in Case E-9/20, *EFTA Surveillance Authority v. Norway*.[35] The EFTA Surveillance Authority (ESA) challenged different requirements in Norwegian law. Most importantly, for private and public limited companies (*aksjeselskaper* and *allmenaksjeselskaper*), it was required that the general manager and at least half of the members of the board should reside in Norway. This, however, did not apply to EU nationals or national of a member of the European Economic Area (EEA) as long as they lived in an EU/EEA state.[36] ESA argued that the EU/EEA residence requirement in Norwegian law infringed the provisions ensuring the free movement of workers. ESA argued that in particular the general manager would be a worker.[37] The Norwegian government on the other hand disagreed since, in its opinion, executive managers do not work under the direction of another person as they are responsible for the day-to-day management of the company, and they may be held personally liable for damages caused.[38] The Commission intervened in the case and argued that the question must be answered on a case-by-case basis, but that the notion of worker is sufficiently broad to cover executive managers as well as non-executive managers.[39] Unfortunately, for our purpose, the EFTA Court refrained from ruling on the issue, as they concluded that the rules on free movement of workers did not apply because it does not apply to rules that hinder free movement between third countries and the EU/EEA area.

[B] The Relevant Factors in Determining the Status of Managers as Workers or Self-Employed

Thus, it is clear that the status of managers as workers or self-employed persons will have to be decided based on a case-by-case evaluation of the position of the managers. Most important is the question whether the managers work under the instruction of another corporate body, for instance, because the managers need that body's approval for a certain decision, and whether the managers may be dismissed by another corporate body. Both of these indicate subordination that may grant worker status, but

34. However, the CJEU in Case C-603/17, *Bosworth*, makes several references to Case C-47/14, *Holterman Ferho Exploitatie BV and Others v. F.L.F. Spies von Büllesheim*, 10.9.2015, ECLI: EU:C:2015:574, where the Court interpreted the same rule based on jurisdiction found in Regulation 44/2001. In Case C-47/14, *Holterman* para. 41, the CJEU clearly seems to indicate that the term 'employment' should be interpreted in light of the concept of worker as defined in Case 66/85, *Lawrie-Blum* and Case C-232/09, *Danosa*.
35. Case E-9/20, *EFTA Surveillance Authority v. the Kingdom of Norway*, 15.7.2021.
36. Private Limited Companies Act § 6-11(1) and Public Limited Companies Act § 6-11(1).
37. *See* E-9/20, *ESA v. Norway* para. 51.
38. *Ibid.*, para. 65.
39. *Ibid.*, paras 73-74.

it may not be sufficient as there may be other factors indicating that the managers are in fact not subordinated.

In Case C-232/09, *Danosa*, the CJEU also emphasised the importance of 'the nature of the duties entrusted to that person; the context in which those duties are performed; the scope of the person's powers'. It is clear that the duties and powers are important for evaluating the extent that the manager is subordinated, but it raises the question whether the Court may also think that a distinction should be drawn between the task of an executive and non-executive manager? However, in the cases mentioned, we cannot see that the CJEU makes a distinction between these two groups. Thus, in all cases except Case E-9/20, *ESA v. Norway*, the managers seeking protection under EU law were executive managers, and, therefore, it is not clear if the same inclination for granting worker status is applicable to non-executive managers. We know from Case E-9/20, *ESA v. Norway* that the Commission thinks that non-executive managers may also have worker status, but unfortunately neither the EFTA Court nor the CJEU has ruled on this matter.

In Case C-270/13, *Iraklis Haralambidis*, the president was appointed for a four-year period, but it was possible to reappoint him. We cannot read from this case that this fact had any impact on the result. If the person appointed (or elected) for a fixed period of time (which is often the case for non-executive but may also be the case for executive managers) can be dismissed or removed during the period, then it is likely that there is subordination. Only if a manager employed for a fixed time cannot be removed during this period or may only be removed in very serious cases would the temporary appointment impact the status of the manager.

So, if neither the status as non-executive or executive nor the fact that the employment or election is for a fixed period of time seems to be decisive, we are back to evaluate whether the sufficient degree of subordination is present, given that a body has the power to give instructions to the manager and/or given that a body may dismiss the manager. These features will often depend on the applicable company law. In the following, the focus is on the differences in company law that may have an impact on the evaluation of whether there is subordination or not.

For executive managers who are employed and supervised by either a supervisory board or a board of directors consisting of both executive and non-executive directors, it is likely that there is the necessary level of subordination to grant worker status.[40] In these cases, the executive manager will often also be obliged to seek the approval of the board for certain transactions. This, for instance, is the case for executive managers in the Nordic system, who will have to follow instructions from the board of directors and may also, at any time, be dismissed by the board.[41] This system seems similar to that found in Latvia where, according to Case C-232/09, *Danosa*, an executive director is likely to have worker status. But, in other Member States, it may not be that evident that the executive managers are workers. For instance, according to

40. The same is the case if a body outside the company has similar power, such as the minister in Case C-270/13, *Iraklis Haralambidis*.
41. *See* Per Lekvall, *Chapter III A Consolidated Nordic Governance Model*, 52-53 (Per Lekvall ed., SNS Förlag 2014) (https://papers.ssrn.com/sol3/papers.cfm?abstract_id=2534331).

German law, the executive management of an Aktiengesellschaft is not under the instruction of the supervisory board (who can only advise, not give orders).[42]

For non-executive and executive managers elected by the shareholders at the general meeting, a worker status seems less likely. It varies considerably to what extent the general meeting may be able to give instructions to such a person. In some jurisdictions for some corporate forms, the general meeting can only decide on topics that according to the law (and possibly the articles of association) have been allocated to them, whereas in other jurisdictions, the general meeting may, in principle, make decisions on any issue.[43] In many jurisdictions, public limited companies which are normally intended for larger companies, including listed companies, the general meeting will often have limited powers to give instructions. As public limited companies are often required to have a supervisory board (consisting exclusively of non-executive managers) or a board of directors (partly with non-executive managers), it may be less likely that non-executive managers are under the subordination required to have worker status. For private limited companies, the law will often give the shareholder a wider access to give instructions. In such companies, there are often only executive directors who are then likely to have the status as workers; *see* also the judgment in Case C-229/14, *Balkaya*, in relation to a German GmbH.[44]

To conclude, even though those elected by the general meeting may be less likely to be granted worker status, it cannot be excluded that in some jurisdictions the power of the general meeting may make it likely that the degree of subordination qualifies for worker status. This, in particular, may be the case when dealing with a jurisdiction that allows the general meeting room to give instructions, and when the general meeting has exercised this in a way where they are not only general instructions but also very detailed, and maybe even consecutive, instructions. Also, it is most likely that there is subordination if the general meeting is free to remove the manager at will. But even if a company is conductive for subordination, it may still be relevant to evaluate how the general meeting has exercised its power in the particular case.

To be a worker, there is also a requirement of remuneration. One may contemplate whether managers who are paid a share of the profit of the company, and who may therefore risk not being paid, can have worker status. The CJEU, however, has decided that fishermen who are paid a share of the proceeds of sale of their catches may have worker status, and, consequently, managers paid in this way may also qualify for

42. Additionally, the board may not be free to dismiss the executive manager, and this may also indicate that there is no necessary level of subordination. For instance, in Germany, managers can only be dismissed if there are sufficient grounds, *see* the German Public Companies Act § 84(3).
43. In the Nordic countries, the general meeting may normally engage on most issues apart from those expressly allocated to the board, *see* Lekvall, *supra* n. 41, at 53. In comparison, in German public companies, the general meeting can only engage in issues expressly allocated to them by law or by the articles of association, *see* Carsten Gerner-Beuerle & Michael Schillig, *Comparative Company Law*, 351 (Oxford University Press 2019).
44. For German law, it is also clear that the general meeting in companies formed as a GmbH has the option of interfering – and thus instructing – management, whereas in companies formed as Aktiengesellschaften the general meeting will only have limited power in this respect. This is also a trend in other jurisdictions.

worker status.[45] Non-executive managers will often be paid less than executive managers, but the CJEU has accepted that even a low salary will be enough to grant worker status.[46]

§6.04 THE PROTECTION OF SELF-EMPLOYED MANAGERS

As it seems possible that managers sometimes may have the status as self-employed persons, it needs to be decided whether managers with this status can invoke Article 49 TFEU or Article 56 TFEU or, if the matter is governed by the Service Directive, it must be decided whether Chapter III or IV of that Directive applies.

These questions would depend on whether the manager fulfils the requirement of having an establishment. This according to the CJEU, *inter alia*, requires premises or a fixed establishment in the Member State where the self-employed person takes up a position as manager.[47] The fact that he/she works in a company will hardly be enough to comply with the requirement of having some sort of office or location as the company's offices are not his/hers and are not there to represent the manager. So, it would require either that the manager have offices available in the state or that the manager decides to move his/her residence to the Member State. For managers, this is most likely to occur where the manager takes up an executive position as such a position will often require the manager to be present regularly at the premises of the company. Article 49 only applies if the managers are present in the Member State of establishment on a permanent basis. Often, managers are appointed for a specific period of time. However, given that they will often expect to be reappointed, such time-limited appointment need not mean that the requirement of permanency is not fulfilled.

Normally, a non-executive manager will only need to be at the company a few times a year, and this does not require him/her to take up residence. Therefore, self-employed non-executives will most likely benefit from Article 56 and Chapter IV of the Service Directive.

§6.05 HOW DOES THE STATUS OF MANAGERS MATTER?

To a large extent, the protection offered to managers under the free movement rules will be the same regardless of which protection is invoked: Article 45 TFEU or the alternative protections as self-employed persons under Articles 49, 59 TFEU or the Service Directive. A brief overview of this protection that applies disregarding the

45. *See* Case C-3/87, *The Queen v. Ministry of Agriculture, Fisheries and Food, ex parte Agegate Ltd*, 14.12.1989, ECLI:EU:C:1989:650, para. 36. For most managers, there will be a fixed remuneration which may be supplemented by bonuses and warrant/share option programmes. In this case, there is no doubt that they fulfil the requirement of a remuneration.
46. *See, e.g.*, Case 139/85, *R. H. Kempf v. Staatssecretaris van Justitie*, 3.6.1986, ECLI:EU:C:1986:223.
47. *See, inter alia*, Case 205/84, *Commission of the European Communities v. Federal Republic of Germany*, 4.12.1986, ECLI:EU:C:1986:463, para. 21 and Case C-221/89, *Factortame II*, para. 20.

status of the manager is given below, followed by a discussion of situations where the status given to managers may make a difference.

[A] Protection Against Discrimination and Restrictions

Managers will be protected against discrimination under any of the relevant free movement rights. There are several cases where it has been required that managers should either be a national of or have residence in the state where the company they manage is active, or even comply with both requirements. Such requirements are evidently likely to be either directly or covertly discriminating to nationals from other Member States and have been rejected in several cases by the CJEU.[48]

In Case C-206/19, SIA *'KOB'*, the CJEU set aside a requirement in Latvian law that managers of a company acquiring agricultural land needed to show some proficiency in Latvian language. Since this requirement was only imposed on non-Latvian citizens, it was easy to set aside as directly discriminatory.[49] But even if it had applied to all managers, disregarding nationality, it would have been indirect discrimination of managers from other Member States.

The CJEU has also applied the free movement rights and the Service Directive to protect managers and companies against unjustifiable restrictions. For there to be a restriction, there needs to be a restriction on market access. The Court has found that if a company is required to make changes to how it is organised, including changes in management, then market access will be restricted.[50] If there is a requirement as to where the real seat of the company should be placed, this may affect where the management should work from, and in turn this may also affect who may be engaged as managers. This type of requirement has been discussed in many cases, starting with the famous Case C-81/87, *Daily Mail*.[51] In this case, it was accepted that the state of incorporation may require that the company maintains its seat in that state. However, the Court has been very reluctant to accept a seat requirement in other states than the

48. Thus, nationality requirements were set aside in Case C-221/89, *Factortame II*, and in C-474/12, *Schiebel Aircraft GmbH v. Bundesminister für Wirtschaft, Familie und Jugend*, 4.9.2014, ECLI:EU:C:2014:2139. Residence requirement may be a bit more likely to be justified, even though the national requirement failed to meet the CJEU's requirements in Case C-350/96, *Clean Car* and Case C-114/97, *Commission v. Spain*.
49. *See* Case C-206/19, *SIA 'KOB' v. Madonas novada pašvaldības Administratīvo aktu strīdu komisija*, 11.6.2020, ECLI:EU:C:2020:463, para. 40.
50. *See* Case C-299/02, *Commission of the European Communities v. Kingdom of the Netherlands*, 14.10.2004, ECLI:EU:C:2004:620, para. 19; Case C-465/05, *Commission of the European Communities v. Italian Republic*, 13.12.2007, ECLI:EU:C:2007:781, para. 46 and Case C-89/09, *European Commission v. French Republic*, 16.12.2010, ECLI:EU:C:2010:772, para. 48. *See also* about the requirement for residence in EU or EEA for both executive and non-executive managers in the decision by the EFTA Court in E-9/20, *ESA v. Norway*, *see* Karsten Engsig Sørensen, *Nationality and residency requirements for corporate management – a comment to the EFTA Courts decision in E-9/20, ESA v. Norway*, 4 NTS – Nordic Journal of Company Law, 1-10 (2021).
51. Case 81/87, *The Queen v. H. M. Treasury and Commissioners of Inland Revenue, ex parte Daily Mail and General Trust plc*, 27.9.1988, ECLI:EU:C:1988:456.

state of incorporation,[52] but did accept that it may sometimes be required that a company has a place of business in the jurisdiction where it conducts certain types of activities.[53]

In another case, the CJEU set aside a requirement that the manager of a company holds a substantial shareholding in the company.[54] Finally, it is clear that the requirement as to the composition of the management may indirectly pose a barrier for the appointment of some members. These types of rules have proven to be an unacceptable restriction to the free movement of capital in several of the Golden-Share cases.[55]

[B] Differences in the Protection Given Different Status

There may be situations where a manager may not be able to invoke Article 45 TFEU but would have been able to apply either Article 49 or Article 56 TFEU. The best examples are the transitional rules that have been in place during the accession of new Member States, where old Member States have been allowed to restrict the free movement of workers from new Member States, but not the freedom of establishment or the freedom to provide services. During such transition periods, managers with the status of worker are cut off from benefitting, whereas a classification as self-employed may offer protection.

One may also contemplate whether managers who use little time on performing their duties may fall outside Article 45 TFEU, but not necessarily outside Article 49 or 56 TFEU. The question is whether the minimum work time requirement for being considered a 'worker' corresponds to a minimum time requirement for having 'a genuine economic activity'. The CJEU has required that to be a worker, the work must not be on such a small scale as to be purely marginal and ancillary.[56] The CJEU has never set a minimum, but it must be assumed that 10 hours or less may not be enough,

52. *See* Case C-208/00, *Überseering BV v. Nordic Construction Company Baumanagement GmbH (NCC)*, 5.11.2002, ECLI:EU:C:2002:632, which dealt with the application of the real seat theory in Germany which would have the effect that the Überseering would not be accepted as a plaintiff. However, a real seat requirement for the Portuguese airline company TAP was accepted in a case involving a condition set on privatisation of the company, *see* Case C-563/17, *Associação Peço a Palavra and Others v. Conselho de Ministros*, 27.2.2019, ECLI:EU:C:2019:144.
53. This was the case in Case C-221/89, *Factortame II*, but as we just saw, the Court also accepted such a requirement in Case C-299/02, *Commission v. Netherlands*, for reasons of control and jurisdiction, and a similar point was made by the Court in Case C-114/97, *Commission v. Spain*.
54. *See* Case C-209/18, *Commission v. Austria*. The Court found that the requirement infringed Art. 15(1)(c) of the Service Directive, *see* paras 83-84 of the judgment.
55. *See* Case C-112/05, *Commission v. Germany* (some members of the supervisory board should be appointed by the state and regional government) and Case C-212/09, *European Commission v. Portuguese Republic*, 10.11.2011, ECLI:EU:C:2011:717 (appointment of chair of board given to the state). In Case C-566/15, *Erzberger*, a shareholder tried unsuccessfully to challenge the German rules on election of worker participation.
56. *See* for instance Case 139/85, *Kempf*, para. 14 and Case C-357/89, *V. J. M. Raulin v. Minister van Onderwijs en Wetenschappen*, 26.2.1992, ECLI:EU:C:1992:87, para. 10.

unless there are special circumstances.[57] Since many non-executive managers work less than 10 hours a week, there is a risk that they may not have worker status. This raises the question whether they may be covered by either Article 49 or 56 TFEU if they have the status of being self-employed. As for Article 49 TFEU, there will only be an establishment if there is a genuine economic activity.[58] The CJEU has not had the chance to define more closely what it takes to have genuine economic activity, but a good guess is that this requirement is not that different from the required activities of workers. So, the application of Article 45 and Article 49 TFEU may be aligned in this regard. But if the self-employed managers rely on Article 56, there is no requirement as to the number of services that need to be supplied, and, consequently, Article 56 can be relied upon even by non-executive managers working less than 10 hours a week.

Finally, the protection provided by Article 45 TFEU may in one regard be more far-reaching than the protection offered by Articles 49 and 56 TFEU. Thus, according to Case C-281/98, *Angonese*,[59] Article 45 also protects workers against discrimination from the employer, even if that employer is a private company. In comparison, Articles 49 and 56 do not offer any protection to managers against acts committed by private companies.[60] This means that a manager who is discriminated against with regard to free movement, for instance, due to his or her nationality, residence or language abilities, may be protected under Article 45, given that he or she has worker status.

As the examples show, there are situations where it may have consequences whether a manager is granted the status as worker or self-employed under the free movement rights. It may also make a difference if a manager as self-employed is able to rely on the Service Directive. Even though the Service Directive is to a great extent aligned with the freedom of establishment and freedom to provide services, there are some areas where the Directive may offer a better protection. This is, for instance, the case with Article 14 of the Directive, entitled 'Prohibited requirements'. The requirement listed in this provision is prohibited without any reservation or exceptions.[61] Therefore, the CJEU could make short process of the residence requirement for management in companies acquiring agricultural land in Latvia in Case C-206/19, *SIA 'KOB'*.[62]

57. If, for instance, a person holds several jobs as non-executive manager, which is a very likely scenario, it is not likely to matter if each of these are for less than 10 hours as the overall amount of work is surely not marginal.
58. *See* Case C-196/04, *Cadbury Schweppes plc and Cadbury Schweppes Overseas Ltd v. Commissioners of Inland Revenue*, 12.9.2006, ECLI:EU:C:2006:544, para. 68.
59. Case C-281/98, *Roman Angonese v. Cassa di Risparmio di Bolzano SpA*, 6.6.2000, ECLI:EU:C:2000:296.
60. That is, unless the company is one of those who exercise 'autonomous power', *see* Catherine Barnard, *The substantive law of the EU* 231-233 (Oxford University Press 2022). It is also possible that the rules apply if the employer is a private company controlled by a Member State, and therefore not truly private.
61. *See* Case C-593/13, *Presidenza del Consiglio dei Ministri and Others v. Rina Services SpA and Others*, 16.6.2015, ECLI:EU:C:2015:399.
62. The issue was decided in two paragraphs, *see* paras 37-38.

§6.06 FREE MOVEMENT BETWEEN EU AND THIRD COUNTRIES

The free movement rights according to Articles 45, 49 and 56 TFEU as well as under the Service Directive do only to a limited extent protect free movement of managers between the EU and third countries.[63] However, free movement may be ensured – to some extent – by one of the many associations and trade agreements entered into between the EU and different third countries. It is not possible here to account for all these agreements, but the EU-UK trade and cooperation agreement that came into force on 1 January 2021 will be used as an illustration.[64]

Free movement of persons does not play a large part in the trade agreement entered into by the EU; not surprisingly, this is also the case with the EU-UK agreement. There are no rules that allow for free movement of workers (or persons in general), but there are a few provisions providing for a limited free movement of persons in connection with establishments and the provision of services. For our purpose, the rules allowing for establishments are the most interesting ones since they specifically aim to offer some protection to the managers of such establishments.

The rules are found in the chapter on investment liberalisation, e.g., Title II of Part Two. Investment covers establishment undertaken, *inter alia*, by companies. Such an establishment may take the form of setting up a subsidiary or a branch.[65] If it is an establishment undertaken by a person or company benefitting from the agreement, the following protection of managers applies:

> According to Article 131, a party to the EU-UK agreement must not introduce requirements that a company which constitutes an establishment should appoint individuals of any particular nationality as executives, managers, or members of the board of directors. The prohibition seems to cover all types of nationality requirements. For instance, a Member State cannot require that a company which constitutes an establishment should have some members of management who are from that Member State or who are either EU or EEA citizens. Such nationality requirements make an establishment more burdensome, and it may require that the investors use other persons in the management than those they prefer.

Additionally, there are rules in Chapter 4 of Title II that allow for a limited free movement of persons as part of an establishment. Temporary stays are possible for persons who are working in 'a senior position' and who are responsible for setting up an establishment. These are termed business visitors for establishment purposes.[66] Such persons working in senior positions would include managers. It is made clear that

63. As shown in Case 299/02, *Commission v. Netherlands* and E E-9/20, *ESA v. Norway*, in some situations the effort to ensure free movement of companies may protect the interest of non-EU/EEA nationals exercising free movement.
64. The Trade and Cooperation Agreement between the EU and the United Kingdom is published in OJ L 149/10 2021.
65. In fact, the chapter on investment has a broader coverage than the establishment covered by Art. 49 TFEU since it also includes investment of down to 10% of the capital of a company. For an analysis of the application of the chapter on investment and services, *see* Karsten Engsig Sørensen, *Free Movement of Companies under the New Trade and Cooperation Agreement Between the EU and the UK*, 4 ECL 117-124 (2021) DOI: 10.54648/eucl2021015.
66. *See* Art. 141(1)(a)(ii).

such persons are not allowed to engage in any other economic activity apart from setting up the establishment, nor are they allowed to receive remuneration from a source located within the party in whose territory the establishment is set up.[67] The chapter also facilitates intra-corporate transferees into the establishment of certain types of personnel after the establishment has been set up. This includes managers (as well as specialists) who are allowed to stay for three years. There is an extensive definition of the term 'manager', probably to avoid that the concept is extended to cover too many persons. A manager is a 'natural person working in a senior position, who primarily directs the management of the enterprise'. The rules allow him or her to do this under the general supervision or direction from the board of directors or from shareholders. However, the responsibility should include '(i) directing the enterprise or a subdivision thereof; (ii) supervision and controlling the work of other employees; and (iii) having the authority to recommend hiring, dismissing or other personnel-related actions'.[68] Additionally, the manager should be an intra-corporate transferee, which means that the manager must have been employed not less than one year in the company forming the establishment and must not already be residing in the territory of the party where the establishment is set up.[69]

During the temporary stay, the manager is protected against discrimination.[70] An Annex attached to these rules lists a number of measures that the Member States, the EU, and the UK can keep in place, even though these measures restrict the free movement of persons allowed in Chapter 4. Interestingly, the EU makes the reservation that the requirement of national treatment in Chapter 4 does not require the Member States or the EU to grant natural or legal persons the treatment granted under TFEU or secondary EU law to natural persons or companies from other Member States, *see* para. 4 of the Annex. This would indicate that the access to social benefits, the right to bring along your family, and other rights which Union citizens have when exercising free movement within the EU will not necessarily be extended to UK residents who exercise free movement under Chapter 4.

To sum up, the EU-UK agreement aims to offer the managers of establishment some protection in the state where the establishment is set up. The agreement does not rely on the distinction between workers and self-employed when delimitating these managers, but instead has a unique definition of the terms 'managers' and 'persons' working in senior positions. This definition aims to ensure that the persons benefiting from this protection are for the main part limited to executive managers.

§6.07 CONCLUSIONS

As illustrated, executive and non-executive managers may be protected as either workers or self-employed. It will require a case-by-case examination to establish their status, as the focus of this assessment is whether they are in a position of subordination

67. *See* Art. 140(5)(a).
68. *See* Art. 140(5)(e).
69. *See* Art. 140(5)(d).
70. *See* Art. 141.

or not. This case-by-case examination mainly focuses on the question whether the manager is subject to instruction from another corporate body (or even somebody outside the company, such as a minister) and whether the manager can be dismissed at any time by that body. Therefore, the company law rules applicable to the company employing or electing the manager will be essential for evaluating that. If the manager holds share in the company, this will also affect his or her status in the case where the shareholding may give the manager some degree of influence over the company. However, it does not seem decisive whether the manager is employed for a fixed period or not. The CJEU has often given executive managers the status as workers, but it has stressed that this need not always be the case. The CJEU has no rules on non-executive managers, but company law will often make it less likely that these have status as a worker, although this is by no means a given.

The protection granted to the managers and the companies that employ them will, for the most part, be the same, disregarding which free movement rights apply to the situation and disregarding whether or not the Service Directive applies. There are, however, some differences which make it important that they qualify their status correctly.

The rules protecting the free movement of managers between the EU and third countries are considerably different. As illustrated by the new EU-UK Trade and Cooperation Agreement, managers are allowed more free movement than most other groups of personnel; there is an extensive definition of managers, and this definition is unique for the trade agreements.

CHAPTER 7

The Qualification of Managers as Employees in Private International Law

Fieke van Overbeeke

§7.01 INTRODUCTION: THE IMPORTANCE OF A MANAGERIAL STATUS IN PRIVATE INTERNATIONAL LAW

An increasing number of managerial positions in the EU (today 9.4 million people) presumes an increasing number of managers as well engaging in cross-border working activities. These internationally active managers could provoke private international law (hereinafter 'PIL') questions when legal disputes arise between manager and company.[1] For example, which court would be internationally competent to hear the case, which law applies to the relation between manager and company, and under which criteria should a judgment of country X be recognized and executed in country Y. All these PIL questions are dealt with in EU legal instruments, such as the Brussels Ia Regulation (Brussels 1a),[2] the Rome I Regulation (Rome I)[3] and the Posting of Workers Directive.[4]

---

1. In this chapter, I will only focus on disputes between manager and company. Other, from a PIL point of view interesting, international legal disputes, such as liability claims of third parties against managers, fall outside the scope of this chapter. *See* for an overview of all sorts of international legal disputes relating to managers and the applicable PIL rules: T.M.C. Arons, *Verkenning van de internationale bevoegdheid en het toepasselijk recht bij geschillen over de aansprakelijkheid van bestuurders*, Ondernemingsrecht 2017/138 (2017).
2. Regulation (EU) No. 1215/2012 of the European Parliament and of the Council of 12 December 2012 on jurisdiction and the recognition and enforcement of judgments in civil and commercial matters, OJ L 351, 20.12.2012.
3. Regulation (EC) No. 593/2008 of the European Parliament and of the Council of 17 June 2008 on the law applicable to contractual obligations (Rome I), OJ L 177, 4.7.2008.
4. Directive 96/71/EC of the European Parliament and of the Council of 16 December 1996 concerning the posting of workers in the framework of the provision of services, OJ L 18, 21.1.1997.

As shown in this book, the importance of a managerial status differs considerably in the various legal systems of Member States, with some states providing a certain degree of protection for this group of workers, whereas in other states, protective provisions are lacking. This begs the question: How does PIL, as enshrined in EU instruments, deal with legal disputes between manager and company? Is the managerial status important in this context, and if so, how?

In principle, EU PIL does not recognize managers as a special category of persons for whom special PIL rules apply. EU PIL does however recognize employees as a special category with special protective PIL rules. In certain cases, managers could qualify as an employee that could invoke these special rules, whereas in other cases, the managerial status could block the application of the special rules. This chapter discusses under what circumstances a manager qualifies as an employee with access to the protective PIL rules and whether and to what extent the current PIL rules are adequate to deal with this special group of workers.

§7.02 THE IMPLICATIONS OF A MANAGER BEING AN EMPLOYEE IN PIL

[A] Introduction

Both the EEX Convention of 1989 (predecessor of Brussels Ia) and the Rome Convention of 1980 (predecessor of Rome I) form a reflection of the fact that employees should be recognized as weaker parties that should receive special protective PIL rules.[5]

As will be discussed thoroughly hereafter, the protective rules favour the employee as regards restricting the possibility to make choice-of-court and choice-of-law clauses, limiting jurisdiction venues for claims of the employer and prioritizing the 'locus laboris' (the place where the employee works) as a default connecting factor.

The terms 'individual contract of employment' and 'employee' are generally used in these special provisions and thus provide access to the protection of these rules. These terms have a broad scope, which could extend to various forms of labour relations, varying from blue- to white-collar work. Even though status- or sector-specific rules, e.g., for managers, agents, or transport workers, were common in PIL systems of national legislation of Member States in the EU, they were not embedded in EU PIL. This means that the title of manager in itself is not decisive for interpreting the

5. Treaty of 26 May 1989, OJ L 285/1 (Treaty of San Sebastian); Convention on the law applicable to contractual obligations opened for signature in Rome on 19 June 1980, OJ L 266, 9.10.1980. *See also* Case C-125/92, *Mulox IBC Ltd v. Hendrick Geels*, 13.7.1993, ECLI:EU:C:1993:306, in which the Court created such special jurisdiction rule for contracts of employment. *See*. Case C-133/81, *Roger Ivenel v. Helmut Schwab*, 26.5.1982, ECLI:EU:C:1982:199, no. 16: 'It emerges from an examination of the provisions of the Convention [EEX Convention] ..., that the rules on jurisdiction, too, are inspired by concern to afford proper protection to the party to the contract who is the weaker from the social point of view.' *See also* Case C-266/85, *Hassan Shenavai v. Klaus Kreischer*, 15.1.1987, ECLI:EU:C:1987:11; and Case C-32/88, *Six Constructions Ltd v. Paul Humbert*, 15.2.1989, ECLI:EU:C:1989:68.

scope of protective PIL rules; instead, the specific circumstances in which a manager operates within a company structure are assessed and the scope is defined.

[B] International Jurisdiction and Recognition and Enforcement Matters: Brussels Ia

The rules on jurisdiction and recognition and enforcement currently are enshrined in the Brussels Ia Regulation from 2012.

[1] International Jurisdiction

[a] General Rules

The default rule on jurisdiction is that regardless of nationality, persons shall be sued at the courts in the Member State where they are domiciled, Article 4 Brussels Ia.

Section 2 of Brussels Ia creates additional jurisdiction venues such as the provision of services under a contract. In this situation, a person domiciled in one Member State may be sued in another Member State if this is where, under the contract, the services were provided or should have been provided, Article 7(1)(b).

In addition, party autonomy is highly valued by the European legislators. Parties to a contract are given a wide margin to make their own preferred choice of forum, which may derogate from the default jurisdiction rules.[6]

The above-mentioned general rules apply to managers that do not qualify as employees falling under the special protective PIL provisions of section 5 of Brussels Ia.[7]

[b] Protective Rules for Individual Contracts of Employment

Section 5 of Brussels Ia contains special jurisdiction rules for individual contracts of employment.[8] The default rule for claims brought against the employer is that the employee can exercise three jurisdiction venues: the domicile of the employer, the habitual workplace, or the engaging place of business, Article 21. On the contrary, the employer is only granted one venue: the domicile of the employee, Article 22.

---

6. *See* for a discussion of the consequences of a choice of forum for a third state: L. van Bochove, *De herschikte EEX-Vo en derde landen: het formele toepassingsgebied van de Verordening nader bezien*, TCR 2017(1) (2017) DOI: 10.5553/tcr/092986492017025001001.
7. *See* Case C-47/14, *Holterman Ferho Exploitatie BV and Others v. F.L.F Spies von Büllesheim*, 10.9.2015, ECLI:EU:C:2015:574, paras 50-65, on the interpretation of the provision of services of a manager and where such services should be located. *See also* paras 66-79 of the case for claims based on tort against managers.
8. *See also* Michiel Poesen, *Concurrent Liabilities and Jurisdiction over Individual Contracts of Employment under the Brussels Ia Regulation*, 16 J. Priv. Int. L. 2, 320-333 (2020) DOI: 10.1080/17441048.2020.1762978.

Moreover, the choice-of-court clauses are limited such that they cannot derogate from the jurisdiction venues granted to the employee, Article 23. Additionally, regarding the so-called tacit choice of forum, the court is obliged to, before assuming jurisdiction, ensure that the defendant is informed of his right to contest the jurisdiction of the court and of the consequences of entering or not entering an appearance, Article 26(2).

[c] Implications for Managers of Being an Employee That Could Invoke the Protective Rules for Individual Contracts of Employment

When both the general rules and the protective rules for individual contracts of employment are compared, it is clear that the legislator provides more protection to employees. The implications for a manager to be qualified as an employee that could invoke the protective rules for individual contracts of employment may be summarized as:

- the employer can be sued on additional jurisdiction grounds;
- the employer can be sued in a Member State, even though he or she is not domiciled in that Member State (or in a Member State at all?);
- the employee can only be sued in the Member State of his or her domicile;
- choice-of-forum clauses are limited and only when they are beneficial for the employee;
- a tacit choice of forum gives extra obligations for a court to, before assuming jurisdiction, ensure the employee about his or her rights.

[2] International Recognition and Enforcement of Judgments

[a] General Rules on Recognition and Enforcement

The default rule on recognition and enforcement under Brussels Ia is that an EU judgment will be automatically recognized and enforced, as the requirement of an exequatur and declaration of enforceability are abolished, Articles 36 to 39 Brussels Ia.

Exceptions apply. Grounds for refusal of recognition and enforcement include the violation of public policy, problems relating to the serving of documents and irreconcilable judgments, Article 45 Brussels Ia. It is well established that these grounds should be seen as strict exceptions and that they should not be invoked easily.[9] These general rules apply to managers that do not qualify as employees.

9. *See* Case C-568/20, *J v. H Limited*, 7.4.2022, ECLI:EU:C:2022:264; Case C-559/14, *Rudolfs Meroni v. Recoletos Limited*, 25.5.2016, ECLI:EU:C:2016:349; Case C-394/07, *Marco Gambazzi v. DaimlerChrysler Canada Inc. and CIBC Mellon Trust Company*, 2.4.2009, ECLI:EU:C:2009:219.

[b] *Recognition and Enforcement of Rulings Concerning Contracts of Employment*

For the protection of employees, an extra refusal ground is added by Article 45 section 1 sub of Brussels Ia, namely, in case the judgment conflicts with the section for protection of contracts of employment when the employee was the defendant.

[c] *Implications for Managers of Qualifying as an Employee*

The additional refusal ground for contracts of employment indeed provides extra protection to employees. However, the practical implications seem rather low since the refusal grounds can only be applied restrictively.

[C] Conflict of Laws: Rome I and the Posting of Workers Directives

The Rome I Regulation and the Posting of Workers Directives regulate choice of law in international contracts of employment.[10]

[1] *Rome I Regulation*

[a] *General Rules*

Party autonomy is highly valued in Rome I, so the default rule is freedom of choice. A contract shall be governed by the law chosen by the parties, Article 3.[11]

In the absence of a choice of law, general conflict-of-law rules are provided in Article 4. Most relevant is Article 4(1)(b) Rome I that a contract for the provision of services shall be governed by the law of the country where the service provider has his/her habitual residence.[12] The applicable law can be overruled by mandatory rules, Article 9, or by the public policy exception, Article 16.

If a manager does not qualify as an employee under Rome I, these general rules apply.

---

10. *See* for the later enacted Directives: Directive 2014/67 of the European Parliament and of the Council of 15 May 2014 on the enforcement of Directive 96/71/EC concerning the posting of workers in the framework of the provision of services and amending Regulation 1024/2012 on administrative cooperation through the Internal Market Information System (Enforcement Directive), OJ L 159, 28.5.2014; Directive (EU) 2018/957 of the European Parliament and of the Council of 28 June 2018 amending Directive 96/71/EC concerning the posting of workers in the framework of the provision of services (Revision Directive), OJ L 173, 9.7.2018. These legal instruments enhance and correct the application of the Posting of Workers Directive considerably and mainly on the basis of social considerations. A detailed discussion of these Directives falls outside the scope of this chapter.
11. *See* for derogations: Rome I, Art. 3, sections 3 and 4.
12. *See* for derogations: Rome I, Art. 4, section 3.

[b] Protective Rules for Individual Contracts of Employment

Rome I provides protection for employees by limiting the choice of law clause, Article 8(1), and prioritizing the habitual working place of an employee, Article 8(2). Regarding the choice of law, the Court has confirmed that this provision is based on the 'favour principle'.[13] This means that if the chosen law is more favourable to the employee, then this law applies and vice versa; if the law of the habitual working place (or the law pursuant to the other connecting factors of Article 8) is more favourable, then this law applies.

[c] Implications for Managers of Being an Employee That Could Invoke the Protective Rules for Individual Contracts of Employment

An employee enjoys better protection by the provided restrictions to the choice-of-court clause.[14] If managers are qualified as employees, this provision prevents a company from choosing, in its relationship with the manager, a labour law system with little rights and duties for managers. As shown in this book, there are many legal systems of Member States with gaps regarding the protection of managers, which stresses the importance of this PIL provision.

Another implication of managers being considered employees is that the choice-of-court clause is based on the 'favour principle'. Given the difference in protection of managers in the various Member States, the applicability of the most favourable provisions to the manager would have a considerable impact on the rights of the individual manager.

[2] Posting of Workers Directives

[a] The Protective Rules of the Posting of Workers Directives

The Posting of Workers Directive applies to temporary work performed in another EU Member State.[15] The definition of a worker is determined by the law of the Member State to whose territory the worker is posted, Article 2 Posting of Workers Directive. This is in contrast with the autonomous definitions of 'workers' in Rome I and Brussels Ia.

The Posting of Workers Directive clarifies that a predetermined set of labour conditions, such as wages, in the country where a manager temporarily works will be respected, Article 3(1)-(7). More specifically, if a labour contract of a manager is

13. Joined Cases C-152/20 and C-218/20, *DG and EH v. SC Gruber Logistics SRL and Sindicatul Lucratorilor din Transporturi v. SC Samidani Trans SRL*, 15.7.2021, ECLI:EU:C:2021:600.
14. The objective applicable law provisions of Art. 8 of Rome I do not necessarily provide better protection if compared to the general Art. 4 of Rome I. Roughly said, in most cases, Art. 8 would lead to the application of the habitual workplace and Art. 4 to the habitual residence of the service provider.
15. However, companies established in a third state must not be given more favourable treatment than companies established in a Member State, *see* Posting of Workers Directive, Art. 1, section 4.

governed by the labour law of country X pursuant to Article 8 Rome I, any hard core of labour provisions in the 'host country' that are more favourable must also be observed.[16]

The Posting of Workers Directives was created to fill a gap that Rome I leaves in situations of labour mobility from high-wage Member States to low-wage Member States. Article 8(2) of Rome I considers the habitual workplace to be the applicable labour law, even when the employee temporarily works abroad. If this work abroad is performed in a high-wage Member State, within the EU, many concerns occur: social competition on labour conditions between employees in the high-wage Member State, protection of the posted worker and unrestricted freedom of services in the EU. The Posting of Workers Directives aims to balance these interests, and, in this way, they can be seen as a necessary component of Rome I. The joint application of both instruments contributes to a certain harmony in the applicable labour law.

[b] *Implications for Managers of Falling under the Posting of Workers Directives*

The Posting of Workers Directive is developed in the context of social competition issues in the EU and has a high practical importance to blue-collar working activities. This is due to the fact that these activities are highly labour intensive and often take place in the context of minima (minimum wages, etc.). In practice, the protection of a manager from this perspective does not seem to occur often.[17] However, the Posting of Workers Directive could be applicable to a manager and thus could bring about the above-mentioned implications.

§7.03 THE ASSESSMENT OF A MANAGER BEING AN EMPLOYEE IN PIL

[A] Introduction

For a manager to invoke the protective PIL rules for employees, it is important that the contract or relation between manager and company can be qualified as a contract of employment and that the manager qualifies as an employee. In general, this needs to be assessed in an autonomous manner, which means that the law of the Member States is not decisive, with the exception of the Posting of Workers Directive. Most scholars favour a broad autonomous interpretation of a contract of employment in PIL instruments.[18] Hereafter, it will be assessed how these terms are or could be interpreted in the various relevant PIL instruments.

16. *See* Posting of Workers Directive, Art. 3, sections 1 and 7. These latter provisions override the labour law of the contract.
17. Aukje van Hoek, *Detachering in het internationaal privaatrecht. Over de complexe verhouding tussen de Rome I-verordening en de Detacheringsrichtlijnen*, Detachering, 36 (Herwig Verschueren ed., Die Keure 2020).
18. *See* for an elaborative discussion of the advantages and disadvantages of various interpretation methods in this context (*lex fori, lex causae* or autonomous techniques): C.G.J Morse, *Contracts of employment and the EEC contractual obligations convention* 146-149 (1982). In German

[B] International Jurisdiction and Recognition and Enforcement Matters: Brussels Ia

[1] No Definition

The term 'individual contract of employment' is not defined in Brussels Ia, and the recitals do not include guidelines. The Court has provided more clarity in the context of an internationally active manager in Case C-47/14, *Holterman*.

[2] The CJEU Holterman Case

Case C-47/14, *Holterman*, concerned a legal dispute between manager Spies von Büllesheim and company Holterman.[19] Spies von Büllesheim, who lives in Germany, had joined Holterman, based in the Netherlands, as a manager in 2001. In addition, Spies von Büllesheim held 15% of the shares in Holterman. According to Dutch law, the legal position of a manager of a company in the case at hand is usually twofold: the manager has both a corporate and a contractual relationship with the company based on a contract of employment or a 'management agreement'.

In 2006, the relationship between the manager and Holterman came to an end. Because Holterman took the position that the manager had made serious errors in the performance of his duties, Holterman summoned the manager to appear before the Dutch court to claim damages. Holterman took up several positions by basing his claim primarily on a specific provision of liability of managers ex Article 2:9 Dutch Civil Code, alternatively on a provision of liability of employees and therefore breach of employment contract ex Article 7:661 Dutch Civil Code and more alternatively on tort ex Article 6:162 Dutch Civil Code. The Civil Code, Book 2, entitled 'Legal Persons', provides in Article 2:9:

1. Every manager has an obligation vis-à-vis the legal person to perform properly the duties assigned to him. All management tasks that have not been assigned

literature, the importance of labour protection in PIL is stressed and on the basis of this a broad 'funktionellen Qualifikationsmethode' is suggested. *See, e.g.*, Olaf Deinert, *Internationales Arbeitsrecht: Deutsches und europäisches Arbeitskollisionsrecht* 48 (Mohr Siebeck Tübingen 2013). In the same vein, in English literature, a broad qualification is favoured paralleled with references to the broad interpretation of the term 'employee' in EU law. *See* Uglješa Grušić, *The European Private International Law of Employment* 82-83 (Cambridge University Press 2015). In my Ph.D. on international employment contracts, I favoured this approach as well: Fieke van Overbeeke, *Sociale concurrentie en conflictenrecht in het Europees wegtransport* 195-196 (Universiteit Antwerpen 2018), https://repository.uantwerpen.be/docman/irua/f21992/155699.pdf.

19. In this case, the predecessor of Brussels Ia was applicable: Council Regulation (EC) No. 44/2001 of 22 December 2000 on jurisdiction and the recognition and enforcement of judgments in civil and commercial matters, OJ L 012, 16.1.2001. The provisions of both regulations are highly identical, and it is established case law of the Court that the interpretation of the provisions under Regulation No. 44/2001 is directly relevant to these identical provisions of Brussels Ia. To avoid unnecessary complexity when discussing Case C-47/14, *Holterman*, I will directly refer to the new provisions of Brussels Ia.

to one or more other directors, by or pursuant to the law or the articles of association, shall come within those duties.

2. Every manager is responsible for the general conduct of the business. He is liable for the full consequences of poor management, unless, having regard in particular to the duties assigned to others, he cannot reasonably be criticized for that poor management, and he did not act negligently in taking measures to avert the consequences of that poor management.

Book 7 of the Civil Code, entitled 'Particular contracts', Title 10 on 'Employment contracts' provides in Article 7:661:

1. An employee who, in the performance of his contract, causes loss or harm to his employer or to a third party to whom the employer is liable to pay damages is not liable in that respect vis-à-vis the employer unless the loss or harm results from his deceit or recklessness. Having regard, in particular, to the nature of the contract, a different conclusion from the one reached in the previous sentence may be drawn from the circumstances of the case.
2. Any derogation from paragraph 1 above or from Article 6:170(3) to the disadvantage of the employee is possible only by written agreement and only if the employee is insured in that respect.

Book 6 of the Civil Code, dealing with the 'General Rules of the Law of Obligations', Title 3, entitled 'Tort, delict and quasi-delict', provides in Article 6:162:

1. A person who commits a wrongful act against another, for which he may be held liable, must remedy the loss or harm suffered by the latter.
2. An infringement of a right or an act or omission contrary to a legal obligation or to an unwritten rule laying down what is generally accepted in social life shall be regarded as a wrongful act, save where there are grounds for justifying that infringement, act or omission.

The manager disputed the international jurisdiction of the Dutch court by stating that the claims fall within the context of an international contract of employment, and that in that case, the Brussels Ia only provides for a jurisdiction ground at the domicile of the employee: in this case, Germany.

Holterman, however, argued that the various claims could very well be initiated together. Additionally, according to Holterman, Article 7(1)(b) Brussels Ia could be invoked. This provision provides an additional jurisdiction ground, favouring the place where the manager is required to perform his duties properly, i.e., the court of the place where the company has its registered office: in this case, the Netherlands. This latter interpretation is in line with established case law in the Netherlands.

The Supreme Court of the Netherlands (Hoge Raad), however, questioned both interpretations. The Supreme Court, *inter alia*, states that under Netherlands law, a distinction must be made between, on the one hand, a person's liability in his capacity as a manager of a company on the basis of a breach of his duty to perform his tasks properly under company law pursuant to Article 2:9 of the Civil Code or on the basis of 'wrongful conduct' for the purposes of Article 6:162 of the Civil Code and, on the other, that person's liability as an 'employee' of that company, quite apart from his capacity as a manager, on the basis of deceit or recklessness in the performance of his contract of employment for the purposes of Article 7:661 Civil Code.

The question whether or not the Dutch courts have jurisdiction to hear and determine the case requires, in the opinion of the Supreme Court, an examination of the relationship between, on the one hand, the rules on jurisdiction in section 5 Brussels Ia and, on the other, the rules on jurisdiction laid down in Article 7(1)(a) and Article 7(2) Brussels Ia.[20] More particularly, the question arises as to whether section 5 precludes the application of these latter provisions in a case such as the present where the defendant is being sued by a company, not only in his capacity as manager on the basis that he performed his duties improperly or that he acted wrongfully, but also, quite apart from that capacity, on the basis of his deceit or recklessness in the performance of the contract of employment concluded with that company.

In those circumstances, the Supreme Court decided to stay the proceedings and refer preliminary questions to the Court of Justice of the EU. One of these questions is of particular relevance to discuss and reads as follows:

> Must the provisions of ... [section 5 Brussels Ia] be interpreted as precluding the application by the courts of ... [Article 7(1)(a) and Article 7(2) Brussels Ia] in a case such as the present where the defendant is being sued by the company of which he is the manager, not only in his capacity as manager on the basis that he improperly fulfilled his duties or that he acted wrongfully, but also, quite apart from that capacity, on the basis of his deceit or recklessness in the performance of the contract of employment concluded with that company?

The Court commences by considering that a manager only could invoke the special PIL rules of section 5 Brussels Ia if the manager can be considered to be bound, through an 'individual contract of employment' for the purposes of Article 20(1) Brussels Ia, to the company of which he was a director and manager, and could thus be classified as an 'employee' for the purposes of Article 20(2) Brussels Ia. The Court then continues by stating that a definition in Brussels Ia is lacking and that an autonomous interpretation should be employed to assess whether a situation falls under the protective section 5 Brussels Ia.[21]

Subsequently, the Court reiterates that it has been held in established case law that contracts of employment have certain particularities: they create a lasting bond that brings the worker to some extent within the organizational framework of the business of the undertaking or employer, and they are linked to the place where the activities are pursued, which determines the application of mandatory rules and collective agreements. The Court rules that in relation to the independent concept of a 'contract of employment', it may be considered that it presupposes a relationship of subordination of the employee to the employer.[22]

Regarding the term 'employee', the Court refers to established case law as well, yet case law regarding the interpretation of Article 45 TFEU and a number of EU legislative acts, and states that the essential feature of an employment relationship is that for a certain period of time, one person performs services for and under the direction of another in return for which he/she receives remuneration. These factors,

20. At that time: Art. 5(1)(A) and Art. 5(3) Regulation No. 44/2001.
21. Case C-47/14, *Holterman*, paras 35-38.
22. *Ibid.*, paras 39-40.

according to the Court, need to be taken into account as regards the notion of 'employee' for the purposes of Article 20(2) Brussels Ia.[23]

With reference to recital 13 Brussels Ia on the protection of weaker parties as employees, the Court considers that the provisions of section 5 Brussels Ia are not only specific but also exhaustive. This means that if the manager can be qualified as an employee that could invoke the protective rules for individual contracts of employment, the special jurisdiction rules of section 5 Brussels Ia are the only rules that can be applied. This means that no application could be made of Article 7(1) and (2) Brussels Ia regarding the other claims based on contract and tort.

The Court provides some additional guidelines regarding the assessment of the qualification of a manager as an employee. It rules that it is for the referring court to examine the extent to which Mr Spies von Büllesheim, in his capacity as a shareholder in Holterman, was able to influence the will of that company's administrative body, of which he was the manager. In that case, it will be necessary to establish who had the authority to issue him with instructions and to monitor their implementation. If it were to turn out that Mr Spies von Büllesheim's ability to influence that body was not negligible, it would be appropriate to conclude that there was no relationship of subordination for the purposes of the Court's case law on the definition of a worker. Additionally, according to the Court, if after examining all the factors mentioned above, the referring court were to find that Mr Spies von Büllesheim, in his capacity as director and manager, had a bond with Holterman through an individual contract of employment for the purposes of Article 20(1) Brussels Ia, it would be for that court to apply the rules on jurisdiction laid down in section 5 Brussels Ia.

[3] *The CJEU* **Bosworth and Hurley** *Case*

There is a parallel with the *Bosworth and Hurley* case that was ruled by the Court under the Lugano II Convention.[24] This PIL Convention basically reflects the mechanism of the predecessor of Brussels Ia: the EEX Regulation 44/2001. This means that most provisions of the Lugano Convention are identical with the EEX Regulation and also with Brussels Ia regarding the protective PIL rules for individual contracts of employment in section 5.

The Lugano II Convention applies in relation between the EU and Iceland, Norway and Switzerland.[25] The Court of Justice of the EU is competent to rule in matters relating to the Lugano Convention, and so it becomes clear in which legal context the Bosworth and Hurley case is embedded and that the considerations of the Court in this case could be relevant for the interpretation of Brussels Ia.

Mr Bosworth and Mr Hurley are British nationals who are domiciled in Switzerland and who, at the material time, were the chief executive officer (CEO) and chief financial

23. *Ibid.*, paras 41-42.
24. Case C-603/17, *Peter Bosworth and Colin Hurley v. Arcadia Petroleum Limited and Others*, 11.4.2019, ECLI:EU:C:2019:310.
25. On 8 April 2020, the United Kingdom applied to accede to the Lugano Convention, but it is not yet clear if and when the United Kingdom will accede to this Convention.

officer (CFO), respectively, of the internationally operating 'Arcadia Group'. The Arcadia Group extends to, *inter alia*, Arcadia London, Singapore and Switzerland. Mr Bosworth and Mr Hurley were also directors of those branches and were each party to a contract of employment with one of those companies drafted by themselves or at their direction.

On 12 February 2015, the Arcadia Group commenced proceedings in the High Court of Justice in the United Kingdom against a number of parties, including Mr Bosworth and Mr Hurley. Arcadia sought compensation for the damage that the Arcadia Group claimed to have sustained as a result of fraudulent transactions involving the companies in that group.

The proceedings brought by Arcadia were based on claims of unlawful means of conspiracy, breach of fiduciary duty and breach of express and/or implied contractual duties pursuant to Mr Bosworth's and Mr Hurley's contracts of employment.

Mr Bosworth and Mr Hurley challenged the jurisdiction of the United Kingdom courts to hear and determine Arcadia's damages claims against them on the ground that those claims fell within the provisions of section 5 of the Lugano II Convention concerning the rules on jurisdiction over individual contracts of employment, and that, under those rules, the claims should be brought before the courts of the State in which Mr Bosworth and Mr Hurley are domiciled, that is to say, the Swiss courts.

Eventually, the case was brought before the Supreme Court, which decided to ask a preliminary question regarding, *inter alia*, whether the provisions of section 5 of the Lugano II Convention must be interpreted as meaning that a contract between a company and a natural person can be treated as an 'individual contract of employment', within the meaning of those provisions, where that person is able to determine or does determine the terms of that contract and has control and autonomy over the day-to-day operation of that company's business and the performance of his own duties, but the shareholder(s) of that company has the power to procure the termination of that contract.

The Court first considers the parallel between the Lugano II Convention and the EEX Convention 44/2001 and points to their identical wording and thus the fact that the Court's interpretation of the latter provisions can be applied to the provisions of the Lugano II Convention. After that, the Court reiterates the *Holterman* case and other case laws.[26]

Subsequently, the Court states that the conclusion of a contract is not a condition for the application of the rules of special jurisdiction laid down in section 5, and therefore that the absence of any formal contract does not preclude the existence of an employment relationship that falls within the concept of 'individual contract of employment' within the meaning of those provisions. However, according to the Court, such a relationship can be treated as an 'individual contract of employment' within the meaning of the provisions of section 5 only if there is a relationship of subordination between the company and the director concerned.[27]

The Court first notes that, according to the information provided by the referring court, Mr Bosworth and Mr Hurley were, respectively, CEO and CFO of the Arcadia

26. Case C-603/17, *Bosworth*, paras 22-26.
27. *Ibid*., paras 27-28.

Group; that they were directors of Arcadia London, Arcadia Singapore and Arcadia Switzerland; that they were each party to a contract of employment with one of those companies drafted by themselves or at their direction; and that they acted at all material times on behalf of all Arcadia Group companies.

The Court highlights that it is also apparent from the order for reference that Mr Bosworth and Mr Hurley exercised control over by whom, where and on what terms they were employed. Furthermore, according to the Court, in the circumstances, it appears that Mr Bosworth and Mr Hurley had an ability to influence Arcadia that was not negligible and that, therefore, it must be concluded that there was no relationship of subordination, irrespective of whether or not they held part of the share capital of Arcadia. The fact that Mr Bosworth and Mr Hurley were answerable to the Arcadia Group's shareholders, who had the power to 'hire and fire' them, is irrelevant in that regard. The Court agrees with the Advocate General by ruling that neither the general directives which a director may be given by the shareholders of the company he directs for the orientation of that company's business nor the legal mechanisms for control by shareholders point, in themselves, to the existence of a relationship of subordination, and therefore the mere fact that the shareholders have the power to revoke a directorship is not sufficient for the conclusion to be drawn that such a relationship exists.

The Court concludes that it follows from this that a contract concluded between a company and the director of that company does not constitute, in circumstances such as those at issue in the main proceedings, an 'individual contract of employment' within the meaning of section 5 of the Lugano II Convention.

[4] Evaluation of the Assessment of Managers Qualifying as Employees under Brussels Ia

Case C-47/14, *Holterman* and Case C-603/17, *Bosworth and Hurley*, illustrate the implications for a manager to be qualified as an employee who could invoke the protective rules for individual contracts of employment. If the manager could be seen as an employee, he could only be sued in his place of domicile (Germany or Switzerland). If the manager was not qualified as an employee, he could be summoned at the place of establishment of the company (the Netherlands or the United Kingdom). In the rulings, the Court prioritizes the contract of employment over the company law-related issues of the relationship between manager and company, in contrast to the Dutch jurisprudence on that matter. In this way, a manager could receive a high level of protection in the PIL rules.

Not all managers, however, receive this protection. The assessment is broad and is carried out on a case-by-case basis, taking into account all the factors and circumstances characterizing the relationship between the parties. In line with the established case law of the Court relating to other EU PIL or labour law instruments, the Court navigates towards a qualification of the 'actual' or 'real' relationship, i.e., the actual manner in which parties execute their duties in practice, instead of the formal relationship, i.e., the existence and wording of contracts. Subordination seems to play a decisive role in this assessment.

The Court provides several factors relevant to assessing whether there is a relationship of subordination between the company and the manager. This includes whether a manager is able to influence the will of the company's administrative body of which he was the manager. In this context, it boils down to establishing who had the authority to issue the manager with instructions and monitor their implementation. If it turns out that the manager's ability to influence that body was not negligible, it would be appropriate to conclude that there was no relationship of subordination.

Elements that do point to a relationship of subordination would be that a person operates as a CEO or/and a CFO, that this person is a director as well and that he or she is party to a contract of employment that is drafted or directed by this director and that he or she acts at all material times on behalf of the company. The Court added that the fact that a manager is answerable to the shareholders of the company, who had the power to 'hire and fire' him or her, is irrelevant in this assessment. Neither is relevant the fact that general directives which a manager may be given by the shareholders of the company he or she directs for the orientation of that company's business nor the legal mechanisms for control by shareholders point, in themselves, to the existence of a relationship of subordination, and therefore the mere fact that the shareholders have the power to revoke a directorship is not sufficient for the conclusion to be drawn that such a relationship exists.

This broad interpretation leaves space to deal with all sorts of managerial positions that occur in current society and seems to ensure that managers with a relationship of subordination can invoke the protective rules of section 5 Brussels Ia. All in all, this seems like an adequate result that provides protection for managers who need it and exempts managers that enjoy all the freedom to arrange their own rights and duties and, thus, do not seem to be in need of protection on this level when it comes to choice of jurisdiction.

[C] Conflict of Laws: Rome I and the Posting of Workers Directives

[1] Rome I Regulation

[a] No Definition

Just like under Brussels Ia, Rome I does not define the term 'individual contract of employment' and there are no guidelines in the recitals. Unlike under Brussels Ia, the Court has not provided guidance on the definition of the term under Rome I. The preparatory works as well as other relevant institutional EU documents of Rome I also remain silent on the matter.[28] As mentioned, scholars favour a broad interpretation of the term, also according to Rome I.

28. Regarding the predecessor of Rome I, the Rome Convention, neither in the preparatory works nor in the explanatory report indications can be found. The explanatory report only states that the special conflict-of-laws rule for 'individual contracts of employment' also covers the case of void contracts and de facto employment relationships, which seems to indicate a broad interpretation, but it remains unclear when exactly a person can be qualified as an employee. *See*

[b] *Analogue Application of Case Law under Brussels Ia?*

Since there is little guidance on the interpretation of the term 'individual contract of employment' under Rome I, it can be examined to what extent the relevant case law of the Court under Brussels Ia – and by extension under other PIL and labour law instruments – could be used by analogy.

Recital 7 Rome I stipulates that the substantive scope as well as the provisions of Rome I should be interpreted consistent with, *inter alia*, Brussels Ia.[29] The idea behind such 'purposive' interpretation is procedural economy: in this way, the chances are higher that the competent court will apply its own law. Indeed, in that case, the court would apply the law with which it is most familiar, thereby reducing the possibility of erroneously applying (foreign) law and, at the same time, avoiding a confirmation of foreign law, which proves to be exacting from the viewpoint of time and also cost.[30]

In Case C-29/10, *Koelzsch*,[31] the Court recognized the importance of this 'purposive' interpretation between the predecessor of Rome I, the Rome Convention, and the predecessor of Brussels Ia, the Brussels Convention, when interpreting identical provisions for contracts of employment, relating to the connecting factor of the habitual workplace, Article 8(2) Rome I.[32]

The case law of the Court, in particular Case C-47/14, *Holterman* and Case C-603/17, *Bosworth and Hurley*, could provide guidance on the assessment of whether a manager would qualify as an 'employee' with an 'individual contract of employment' under Rome I.

However, the relevant provisions in Brussels Ia and Rome I are not completely identical. In particular, Article 1(2)(7) Rome I provides the exception. Disputes concerning the personal liability of managers for the obligations of the company are excluded from the scope of Rome I, but are included in Brussels Ia. This could mean that these claims are not regulated by Rome I and thus are regulated by national PIL rules. This could in turn lead to the application of different PIL rules within the EU, which then could lead to incoherencies with Brussels Ia.[33]

Yet, it could very well be possible that the Court eventually follows its case law under Brussels Ia also with regard to Rome I. This means prioritizing the existence of a contract of employment over other – more company law-related – factors and, thus,

Mario Giuliano and Paul Lagarde, *Report on the Convention on the Law Applicable to Contractual Obligations*, OJ C 282, 31.10.1980.

29. Reference is made to the predecessor of Brussel Ia, but Brussels Ia arranges that all references made to its predecessor should be read as a reference to Brussels Ia, *see* Brussels Ia, Art. 80.
30. *See* Opinion of AG Trstenjak in Case C-29/10, *Heiko Koelzsch v. Grand Duchy of Luxembourg*, 16.12.2010, ECLI:EU:C:2010:789, para. 80.
31. Case C-29/10, *Heiko Koelzsch v. Grand Duchy of Luxembourg*, 16.12.2010, ECLI:EU:C:2010:789.
32. *Ibid.*, paras 28, 33, 39 and 41.
33. The conflict-of-law rules regarding companies are not harmonized in the EU. National PIL rules therefore apply, which means that they could also employ different scope rules and different substantive conflict-of-law rules. And in fact, these rules in practice differ considerably in the Member States, varying from 'statutory seat' to 'real seat' connecting factors.

applying Article 8 Rome I after all. Arguments in favour of this could be the fact that the considerations behind section 5 Brussels Ia and Article 8 Rome I are, to a certain extent, similar: both rules by nature are a '*lex specialis*' for contracts of employment and, therefore, could apply to cases in which contracts of employment exist, notwithstanding other circumstances of the case. For Rome I, this means prioritizing the contract of employment and invoking Article 8 Rome I over the company-related issue that could trigger Article 1(2)(f) Rome I. The Court has not yet provided clarity on the matter. This issue remains uncertain for managers in the EU.

[c] Evaluation of the Assessment of Managers Qualifying as Employees under Rome I

If we assume that the Court prescribed assessment under Brussels Ia is directly relevant to assess whether managers qualify as an 'employee' with an 'individual contract of employment' under Rome I, the same considerations under Brussels Ia regarding the broad interpretation and possibilities to provide protection to managers that are in need of this apply here, as discussed *supra* §7.03[C][1][b]. The provisions of Rome I also provide extra protection that could make a difference for a manager compared with the general rules of Rome I. The fact that only managers with a relationship of subordination will be granted access to these provisions seems fair.

However, it could also be possible that the case law under Brussels Ia would not be applied to Rome I since, *inter alia*, the material scope of Rome I differs, cf. Article 1(2)(7) Rome I. Even though it is likely that the Court does draw a parallel with Brussels Ia because of the similarities in the system behind the *lex specialis* in both instruments, the uncertainty on this point for managers in the EU is undesirable and should be addressed.

[2] Posting of Workers Directives

[a] No Definition and Reference to the National Law of a Member State

As was shortly mentioned above, the national law of the Member State where the manager temporarily works determines whether a person is an employee that could invoke the protective PIL rules of the Directives, cf. Article 2(2) of the Posting of Workers Directive. The background of this provision is to prevent 'false self-employment', which seems logical from this point of view since only persons that are qualified as self-employed by the legislation of the temporary working state fall outside the scope of the protective Directives.[34] Article 4(5) of one of the Posting of Workers Directives, Directive 2014/67, provides additional guidelines.

34. *See also* M.S. Houwerzijl, *De Detacheringsrichtlijn: over de achtergrond, inhoud en implementatie van Richtlijn 96/71/EG* 130 (Deventer Kluwer 2005).

[b] *Evaluation of the Assessment of Managers Falling under the Posting of Workers Directives*

Given the variety of legislation in the Member States on the topic of managers and employee protection, the fact that this legislation primarily determines the scope of the Directives could lead to a different application of the Posting of Workers Directives within the EU. Besides concerns regarding the unity and uniform application of EU law, this could lead to a difficult assessment beforehand of the possible application of these Directives and thus which law will be applicable to an internationally active manager.

[3] *Evaluation of the Assessment of Managers in the Joint Application of Rome I and the Posting of Workers Directives*

Incoherencies can occur if Rome I is applied in conjunction with the Posting of Workers Directives. Under Rome I, the term 'employee' receives an autonomous interpretation, whereas the Posting of Workers Directive refers to the national law of the temporary working state to determine the status of a worker. In the case of a manager with a relation of subordination, and thus assuming that this manager needs a certain degree of protection, this could lead to undesirable results.

For example, a manager habitually works in Poland and at some point starts to temporarily work in Germany. Because of the relation of subordination with the company, the manager qualifies as an employee under Article 8 Rome I, and on the basis of the habitual workplace principle, the legislation of Poland applies to his contract of employment.

Certain provisions of the Posting of Workers Directives in Germany are more favourable to the manager, however, and yet, according to German law, he is not qualified as a worker falling under the Posting of Workers Directive. In this situation, the manager misses out on the protective mechanism of this Directive that the temporary working state shall ensure its hardcore provisions to the workers on its territory;[35] which is a necessary component to Rome I and together both instruments strike a certain balance in the applicable labour provisions. In this case, the harmony of a joint application of these instruments is breached, and thus the manager has to fall back on the unpredictable overriding mandatory rules of Article 9 Rome I. This practically means that, assuming that he can only initiate litigation in Poland cf. Article 21 Brussels Ia, it would be very hard to assert his alleged rights.[36]

35. Assuming that when the Posting of Workers Directive applies, it neutralizes the scope-rules of the hard core provisions of the host state and thus that it does not matter whether or not a manager is qualified as an 'employee' under that national law of the host state.
36. Rome I, Art. 9, section 3, deals with foreign mandatory rules and does not oblige the court to apply them. The Posting of Workers Directive on itself neither contains this obligation, but the Directive provides a jurisdiction ground at the temporary working state in which the application of their working conditions obviously would be ensured.

§7.04 CONCLUSIONS

By prioritizing the employment law aspects of the relation between manager and company, the jurisdiction rules of Brussels Ia enshrine a rather high degree of protection. At the same time, the interpretation given by the Court makes sure that only managers with a relation of subordination could successfully invoke these protective rules. This seems to strike an adequate balance between protection and the freedom of parties to arrange their rights and duties.

The conflict-of-law rules of Rome I have not been interpreted in the context of managers. If a certain purposive interpretation with Brussels Ia and, thus, with its case law can be assumed, also here an adequate balance seems to be struck. However, *inter alia*, given the different scope rules of the regulations, another interpretation could be possible as well. The legal uncertainty on this point for managers in the EU constitutes a statutory shortage and should be addressed either with legislation or in jurisprudence.

Furthermore, incoherencies can occur if Rome I is applied in conjunction with the Posting of Workers Directives, given the mismatch between definitions in their provisions. Another problem with the application of the Posting of Workers Directives to managers is the fact that the temporary working state (host state) determines the status of the worker. Combined with a variety of legislation in the Member States on the topic of managers and employee protection, this could have negative implications for the legal certainty and foreseeability of the application of these Directives.

Even though the practical implications of these Directives for managers are low, it would be recommendable to provide clarifications on the application of the Posting of Workers Directives to managers. With a growing group of managers with a relation of subordination within the EU, this recommendation would become more and more important.

CHAPTER 8

National Social Security Approaches to (Non)-executive Managers and Cross-Border Implications

Charlotte Bruynseraede, Gerard Everaet & Paul Schoukens

§8.01 INTRODUCTION

This chapter looks closer at the social security protection of managers in cross-border situations. Not only are the employment classification and applicable social security scheme often a topic of discussion within a given country but also the increasing international mobility of managers and misaligned employment classifications throughout states raise questions as to which extent manager's social security protection is affected when exercising mandates in different countries across Europe. We do not discuss sole proprietors[1] as they are uniformly considered being self-employed for social protection purposes. Instead, we focus on larger companies where multiple managers undertake different roles, and the applicable social security scheme is far less clear. Where relevant, a distinction is made between executive and non-executive managers.[2]

The first section of this chapter consists of a legal comparison of approaches to the status of managers in a number of national social security systems throughout the EU in order to uncover common trends. We ask ourselves whether managers are part of the employee, self-employed or a special social protection scheme, how and which part of their income is subject to social security contributions and whether exceptions apply. Albeit not an EU Member State, Switzerland is included in the comparison as it also falls under the European coordination rules on cross-border employment, laid down in Regulation (EC) No. 883/2004 and its implementing Regulation (EC) No.

1. Under sole proprietorship, we understand the situation in which a person is the sole owner of a business and considered an individual entrepreneur.
2. For a definition of both concepts, we refer to the definitions as used earlier in this book.

987/2009.[3] These rules are discussed in the second section, in which we examine closer the social security implications of taking up a managerial position abroad.

§8.02 APPROACHES IN NATIONAL SOCIAL SECURITY SYSTEMS

[A] The Difficult Assessment of the Applicable Social Security Scheme for Managers

Even though social security schemes across Europe differ in the way they are organized, we do see a strong adherence to the division between employees and self-employed persons. The division may be decisive for the level of social security protection since self-employed workers often enjoy a less extensive social protection than employees.[4]

Usually, it is not too difficult to draw a uniform line across states as to who qualifies as an employee and who qualifies as a self-employed person for social security purposes. Elements such as working in a subordinate manner and whether or not the economic risk is borne by the worker are indicators used in almost every country to assess the employment classification. The high diversity in company structures as well as the different tasks a manager may fulfil however make it difficult to unequivocally apply those indicators to them. The thin line between being bound by the company's statutes yet retaining a significant decision-making power is something that virtually every state struggles with. States apply their own logic to the classification of managers for social security purposes which consequently leads to the emergence of a variety of possibilities when exploring the situation in different jurisdictions.

[B] Applicable National Social Security Schemes and the Approach to the Remuneration for the Payment of Social Contributions

A manager can be subject to: (a) the employee social security scheme; (b) the self-employed social security scheme; (c) depending on the level of control or the nature of the company, the employee or self-employed scheme; or (d) a specific social security scheme, which is strictly speaking a modality of either the employee or self-employed scheme.

Connected to the classification question is the way in which the remuneration as a basis for social security contributions is approached. A manager's aggregate remuneration usually consists of both fixed parts and variable components, such as

3. Regulation (EC) No. 883/2004 of the European Parliament and of the Council of 29 April 2004 on the coordination of social security systems (Regulation 883/2004), 29.4.2004, and implementing Regulation (EC) No. 987/2009 of the European Parliament and of the Council of 16 September 2009 laying down the procedure for implementing Regulation (EC) No. 883/2004 on the coordination of social security systems (Regulation 987/2009), 16.9.2009.
4. Slavina Spasova et al., *Access to Social Protection for People Working on Non-standard Contracts and as Self-Employed in Europe: A Study of National Policies 2017*, European Social Policy Network (ESPN), European Commission, 1-97 (2017).

attendance fees for a board meeting. The type and level of compensation may in the first place give an indication of the employment relationship. Above that, the remuneration serves as a basis for the payment of social security contributions. A mandate, i.e., the position as a manager, is either remunerated or not. This duality allows for different approaches between countries: in case a remuneration is received for the performance of the mandate, social contributions are in principle due although some countries exempt workers from the payment of social contributions if the remuneration lies below a minimum threshold. In case no remuneration is given for the mandate, we distinguish two approaches (with possibly huge effects in cross-border situations): (1) the non-remunerated mandate leads to the exclusion from the obligation to pay social security contributions or (2) even if the mandate is not remunerated, the manager is obliged to contribute to the relevant social security scheme.

[C] A Closer Look at National Approaches

Having outlined the possible approaches as regards the manager's applicable social security scheme and remuneration, we now look at a number of states more in detail in order to document common practices. Switzerland, Belgium, Germany, the Netherlands and Italy are discussed in depth as examples of the above-mentioned distinctions in social security treatment.

[1] Managers Are Subject to the Employee Social Security Scheme: The Case of Switzerland

Although they do not qualify as employees for employment law, managers in Switzerland fall within the employee social security scheme.[5] The remuneration received for the execution of the mandate leads to the payment of contributions to the employee scheme and, hence, entitles the manager to corresponding social benefits.[6] This applies to both executive and non-executive managers, irrespective of the company structure. A few minor exceptions as to the level of protection apply: in contrast to other employees, managers are, for example, not entitled to temporary unemployment benefits.[7] Nevertheless, the protection they enjoy under the employee social security scheme is still more extensive than if they were covered under the self-employed scheme, which would not entitle them to accident insurance and unemployment insurance.[8]

Finally, it should be mentioned that a mandate in a company can never be considered a marginal activity (a concept applied in European coordination law and

5. Verordnung über die Alters- und Hinterlassenenversicherung (AHVV), 31.10.1947, Art. 7, lit. h, and Stefanie Meier-Gubser, *Selbständig oder nicht?*, VRPRAXIS UnternehmerZeitung, 48 (2017).
6. AHVV, 31.10.1947, Art. 7 lit. h.
7. Bundesgesetz über die obligatorische Arbeitslosenversicherung und die Insolvenzentschädigung (AVIG), 25.6.1982, Art. 31 Abs. 3 lit. c.
8. Mutual Information System on Social Protection (MISSOC), *Social Protection for the Self-Employed: Switzerland*, 3 (2021).

discussed further) according to Swiss law, so even when the remuneration is very low or the mandate contains very few obligations, it will be considered a substantial activity.[9] This will be relevant for the discussion of the implications for foreigners to take up a mandate in Switzerland (*see* §8.03 *infra*).

[2] Managers Are Subject to the Self-Employed Social Security Scheme: The Case of Belgium

In Belgium, the manager (*mandataris*) of a company is presumed to be self-employed, regardless of whether it concerns an executive or non-executive manager.[10] All managers are thus subject to the social security scheme for self-employed persons and are obliged to pay contributions on the remuneration they receive for their tasks. The presumption can be rebutted if they prove the unremunerated character of the mandate, in which case the manager is no longer subject to the self-employed scheme.[11] Rebutting the presumption, however, does not lead to the application of the employee scheme. It is not self-evident to prove the unpaid nature of the mandate. First and foremost, the remunerated character is approached very broadly; managers' fees, attendance fees and benefits in kind are all considered income from the mandate and thus exclude an unremunerated character.[12] Furthermore, the unremunerated character must be proven both legally (by referral to the statutes or official decision of the board competent for the payment of the remuneration) and factually.[13] This implies that even if a small remuneration is received for the execution of the mandate, the manager will have to contribute to the system. This may be disadvantageous since the contributions due are subject to a fixed minimum threshold, even if the actual income lies below this threshold.

It is possible to combine the position as a manager with a position as employee within the same company, but only when the tasks clearly differ. Clear, distinct tasks could be, by way of example, when a person is appointed as an accountant of the company through an employment contract and additionally has a seat on the board of directors as a non-executive director. Such a combination leads to the application of both the employee and self-employed social security scheme.[14]

---

9. Wegleitung über die Versicherungspflicht in der AHV/IUV (WVP), Gültig ab 01.01.2009, Stand: 01.01.2023, Rz. 3088.1.
10. Koninklijk besluit nr. 38 van 27. juli 1967 houdende inrichting van het sociaal statuut der zelfstandigen, 27.07.1967, Art. 3, § 1.
11. Koninklijk besluit van 19 december 1967 houdende algemeen reglement in uitvoering van het Koninklijk besluit nr. 38 van 27 juli 1967 houdende inrichting van het sociaal statuut der zelfstandigen (ARS), 19.12.1967, Art. 2.
12. Wetboek van de inkomstenbelasting 1992 (WIB92), 10.04.1992, Art. 31, tweede lid, 1°, 2°.
13. ARS, 19.12.1967, Art. 2.
14. *Sociale Zekerheid /Onderneming: Mandaathouders van vennootschappen*, Instructies 2022/3, https://www.socialsecurity.be/employer/instructions/dmfa/nl/latest/instructions/persons/specific/mandatariesorshareholders_commercialcompanies.html.

[3] *Depending on the Level of Control or the Nature of the Company, Managers Are Subject Either to the Employee Social Security Scheme or to the Self-Employed Social Security Scheme: The Case of Germany and the Netherlands*

Whereas labour law in Germany explicitly excludes managers from being employees,[15] social security law has a wider scope of application and, instead, looks at certain elements that might indicate subordinated employment, such as following instructions and integration into the employers' work organization.[16]

As regards the executive manager (*Geschäftsführer*) of a limited liability company (*GmbH*), the legal ability to avert other shareholders' decisions is decisive for the applicable social security scheme. When they have the ability to do so, the executive manager is considered a self-employed person for social security purposes.[17] In practice, this is usually assessed through the question of whether the person is a majority or minority shareholder. Majority shareholders, i.e., managers owning more than 50% of the shares in the limited liability company, are considered to have a significant influence on company decisions and are, therefore, considered to be self-employed.[18]*A contrario*, minority shareholders usually do not have this decisive power over the management of the company and should be considered employees for social security purposes. Only in case the minority shareholder has a blocking minority, they are also considered to be self-employed. A similar logic applies to the executive manager (*Vorstandsmitglied*) of a public limited company (*AG*), with the exception that even though they fall within the mandatory social protection scheme for employees, they do not enjoy social protection to the same extent as regular employees.[19] The executive manager (*Vorstandsmitglied)* is explicitly excluded from the mandatory pension and unemployment scheme.[20] Nevertheless, they do have the obligation to contribute to the sickness scheme[21] unless the income exceeds a yearly threshold.[22] In spite of the few exceptions, being subject to the employee scheme is still much more advantageous than being subject to the self-employed scheme. Self-employed workers enjoy far less coverage within statutory social insurance and are, for instance, exempted from unemployment benefits and accidents at work.[23]

15. Arbeitsgerichtsgesetz (ArbGG), 02.07.1979, § 5, (1) – as a result, executive board members or managers are not covered by a number of labour law guarantees, regardless of their social security status.
16. Sozialgesetzbuch Viertes Buch – Gemeinsame Vorschriften für die Sozialversicherung (SGB IV), 23.12.1976, § 7.
17. Franka Lau, *Sozialversicherungspflicht von GmbH-Geschäftsführern*, NZS 12, 452-480 (2019).
18. BSG, 14.3.2018, B 12 KR 13/17 R: Sozialversicherungsrechtlicher Status von Fremd- und Gesellschafter-Geschäftsführern, NZS 778 (2018).
19. Tobias Grambow, *Sozialversicherungspflicht von Vorständen der AG und geschäftsführenden Direktoren der SE*, AG 13/14, 479-481 (2010).
20. Sozialgesetzbuch Drittes Buch – Arbeitsförderung (SGB III), 24.03.1997, § 27 Abs. 1 Nr. 5, and Sozialgesetzbuch Sechstes Buch (SGB VI), 23.12.1976, § 1 Satz 4.
21. Sozialgesetzbuch Fünftes Buch – Gesetzliche Krankenversicherung (SGB V), 20.12.1988, § 5 Abs. 1 Nr. 1, and LSG Berlin-Brandenburg, Urteil v. 7.8.2013 – L 9 KR 269/11.
22. SGB V, 20.12.1988, § 6 Abs. 1 Nr. 1.
23. MISSOC, *Social Protection for the Self-Employed: Germany*, 1-35 (2021).

Non-executive managers (*Aufsichtsratsmitglieder*) in Germany have traditionally been considered self-employed workers.[24] Recent fiscal case law, however, made a turn in the assessment of the non-executive's remuneration. Following a judgment of the EU Court of Justice[25] and subsequent case law of the Federal Fiscal Court (*Bundesfinanzhof*),[26] the remuneration of a non-executive manager was, unlike before, explicitly considered not being self-employed income if it only consisted of a fixed fee and, thus, did not include variable remuneration for participation in meetings, among others. In 2021, the Federal Ministry of Finances (BMF, *Bundesministerium für Finanzen*) clarified that the remuneration of non-executive managers is not considered self-employed income if the non-executive manager receives a fixed remuneration for his tasks or, when combined with a variable remuneration, the variable remuneration is limited to a maximum of 10% of the entire income from the management tasks.[27] This new approach will however not immediately change the approach of the remuneration for social security purposes since the concepts of (self-employed) income are each time given an autonomous interpretation in social law, fiscal law and labour law.[28]

Combining the status as (self-employed) manager with the status as an employee within the same company is possible in both social security and labour law, but only in case the tasks performed as an employee can be clearly delineated as an employment relationship.[29]

In the Netherlands, the applicable social security scheme for managers also depends on other factors rather than the mere title. Instead of looking at the level of shares in the first place, as is done in Germany, the nature of the company is decisive. With respect to executive managers, the decisive fact is whether they work for a company listed on the stock market or not. Executive managers working for an unlisted company are in principle considered employees of the company, irrespective of whether they were appointed in the articles of the company or work under an employment agreement.[30] This is because of the formal interpretation of subordination: the fact that the executive manager remains subject to the board of directors presupposes a subordinated relationship according to Dutch case law.[31] Nevertheless, a minor exception applies to the directors – major shareholders – who are considered self-employed for social security purposes.[32]

24. LSG Nordrhein-Westfalen, Urteil v. 13.9.1966 – L 15 Kn U 156/64.
25. Case C-420/18, *IO v. Inspecteur van de rijksbelastingdienst*, 13.6.2019, ECLI:EU:C:2019:490.
26. BFH, Urteil v. 27.11.2019 – V R 23/19.
27. BMF, Urteil v. 08.07.2021 – III C 2 - S 7104/19/10001:003 BStBl 2021 I S. 919.
28. BFH, Urteil v. 2.12.1998 – X R 83/96, and BFH, Urteil v. 10.03.2005 – V R 29/03 BStBl 2005 II S. 730.
29. Wilhelm Moll, *Münchener Anwalts Handbuch: Arbeitsrecht*, n. 28 (Verlag C.H. Beck 5th ed. 2021).
30. Edward De Bock, *De bijzondere positie van de bestuurder van de NV of BV* (Gerdien Van Der Voet ed., Boom Juridisch 2021), and Loyens & Loeff, *Het vennootschaps- en arbeidsrechtelijk ontslag van statutair bestuurders*, 123 Genoteerd 3 (2019).
31. Guus J.J. Heerma Van Voss, *Mr. C. Assers Handleiding tot de beoefening van het Nederlands Burgerlijk Recht. 7. Bijzondere overeenkomsten. Deel V. Arbeidsovereenkomst*, 2020/40 (Wolters Kluwer 2020).
32. Wet van 6 november 1986, tot verzekering van werknemers tegen geldelijke gevolgen van werkloosheid (WW), 06.11.1986, Art. 6 Abs. 1 lit. d, and Wet van 5 juni 1913, tot regeling der arbeiders-ziekteverzekering (ZW), 05.06.1913, Art. 6 Abs. 1 lit. d.

Even though executive managers of an unlisted company are in principle subject to the social protection applicable to employees, their legal relationship with the company is relevant for the application of the unemployment scheme. In case the executive manager is appointed in the statutes, his protection in the event of dismissal is not as extensive as if he were employed on the basis of an employment agreement. When the executives' mandate is unremunerated, however, he is excluded from the social protection scheme for employees due to the fact that obtaining a wage is an essential requirement for an employment agreement.[33] Executive managers working in a listed company cannot be employed through an employment contract and are considered self-employed workers.[34]

A simultaneous employment relationship as an employee within the same company is possible, provided that the conditions of an employment relationship are met, i.e., the presence of a subordinate relationship in that capacity and the presence of a wage.[35]

[4] Managers Are Subject to a Special Scheme: The Case of Italy

In Italy, different social protection schemes apply depending on the type of manager. First of all, a subdivision into four categories of employees can be found in the Italian Civil Code, among which two types of so-called executives:[36] top managers (*dirigenti*) and middle managers (*quadri*), both regarded as employees but governed by different provisions.[37] In order to assess whether a person is considered a top or middle manager, corresponding national collective labour agreements must be consulted. Even though they take part in the employee social security scheme, their social protection is not as extensive as that of regular employees, especially with regard to unemployment benefits. The top or middle manager can only claim a limited amount of benefits, disproportionately low compared to the often high contributions paid.[38] It must be pointed out that these top and middle managers are still subject to the appointed executive manager of the entire company. The latter corresponds to what we have considered so far as the executive manager, according to the earlier defined concept.

Members of the board of directors – including non-executive managers and the appointed executive manager – are not considered employees for social security purposes. Instead, their social security rights are governed by the '*Gestione Separata*',[39] a specific approach within the social security scheme for self-employed, established to

33. Burgerlijk Wetboek (BW) Boek 7, 1.1.2020, Art. 7:610, 1.
34. Burgerlijk Wetboek (BW) Boek 2, 1.7.2017, Art. 2:132, 3.
35. BW Boek 7, Art. 7:610, 1, and Jan Dop, *Statutair bestuurder of titulair bestuurder?*, Russell Advocaten (25 juni 2020), https://www.russell.nl/publicatie/statutair-bestuurder-titulair-bestuurder/.
36. Codice Civile, 16.3.1942, Art. 2095.
37. Michele Tiraboschi, *Labour Law and Industrial Relations in Recessionary Times: The Italian Labour Relations in a Global Economy*, Adapt Labour Studies e-Book series no. 3, 313 (Adapt University Press 2012).
38. *Ibid.*, at 352.
39. Riforma del Sistema pensionistico obbligatoria e complementare, Legge 8 agosto 1995, n. 335, 08.08.1995, and MISSOC, *Social Protection for the Self-Employed: Italy*, 4 (2021).

accommodate the newly recognized employment status of para-subordinate workers, to be understood as a form of dependent-self-employed.[40] Para-subordinate workers are formally self-employed but enjoy some employment protection. The use of such an intermediate protection, however, raises multiple questions as to the application of the Regulation (*see* §8.03 *infra*).

A combination of board membership and an employment contract with the company is possible and allowed if the tasks differ in their nature and the tasks of the latter are clearly performed in a subordinated manner. Such a combination leads to the applicability of the social security system for employees to the total remuneration and is, in fact, common practice in order to enjoy a more extensive social protection.[41]

[D] Conclusion on National Approaches to Managers

Studying a number of countries teaches us that the applicable social security system for managers differs enormously from one state to another. We can conclude that a manager falls under the employee social security scheme, the self-employed social security scheme, or a special social security scheme. The classification can be established purely on the basis of the title, as observed in Switzerland and Belgium, or can depend on additional factors, such as the level of control or the nature of the company, as observed in Germany and the Netherlands. There is a slight tendency to place executive directors under the employee social security scheme – although this cannot be generalized. It is notable that when managers fall within the employee social security schemes, usually a number of exceptions eroding their protection apply to them, such as a less extensive unemployment protection. Nevertheless, their social protection remains more comprehensive than it would be if they were covered under the self-employed schemes. As far as non-executive managers are concerned, states tend to provide social protection under the self-employed regime, although this is again not always the case. Most states allow for the possibility of combining the mandate with an employment contract with the company under the condition that the duties clearly differ and the tasks under the employment contract are clearly performed in a subordinate manner. In some states (such as in Italy), this can lead to a complete absorption in favour of the employee's scheme. In other states (such as in Belgium), on the other hand, it leads to the application of two statuses.

The findings show that even though some general trends in approaches are discerned, every state still has its own way of treating managers for social security purposes, creating a patchwork of different possibilities across states. The variety of possibilities in itself is not necessarily problematic; only when managers move across borders it becomes complex to assess to which extent their social protection is affected.

40. Ministry of labour and social policy Italy: *National Plan for Access to Social Protection by Subordinate and Autonomous Workers*, 3 (2021), and Carlo Zoli et al., *National Report Italy – Executive Summary*, Working Yet Poor D3.2, 34 (2021).
41. Alessandro Varrenti & Fernando de las Cuevas, *Company Directors: Jurisdictional Comparisons*, 269 et seq. (Sweet & Maxwell 2012).

§8.03 IMPLICATIONS FOR CROSS-BORDER SITUATIONS

[A] Introduction to the Coordination Regulations

Social security is organized by each country in a different way. Also, within the EU, social security remains a core competence of the different Member States, cf. Article 153 TFEU. As a result, when EU citizens make use of their right to freedom of movement and work across Member States' borders, negative and positive conflicts of law may arise between the different social security systems of the Member States involved. Workers[42] – and in this context, managers – may be obliged, for example, to pay social security contributions in different Member States, or may opposingly lose benefits normally afforded to them if a social risk would arise. In order to deal with these discrepancies, the EU adopted Regulation 883/2004 on the coordination of social security and its implementing Regulation 987/2009. These Regulations lay down the rules of designation in an exclusive manner of the applicable social security legislation for EU citizens and their dependent family members who move across borders between EU Member States and who have been subjected to the social security legislation of one of the Member States.[43] This exclusive effect of the determination of the applicable social security legislation means that the Member State whose social security legislation is applicable is the only competent. As such, only the legislation of this Member State is applicable, not only for the professional activities performed within its jurisdiction but also for those performed in the other Member State(s), even if the professional activities are of a different nature.[44]

Since there is no universal accepted definition on what social security actually is within the different Member States, Article 3(1) of Regulation 883/2004 sets out the specific social security schemes that are covered by the Regulation.[45] In general, this includes the risks that are in most Member States considered to be part of social security, but Regulation 883/2004 explicitly excludes social and medical assistance.[46]

Regulation 883/2004 is also applicable – both concerning their territory and their citizens – to all the states which are part of the European Economic Area (EEA)[47] and

42. 'Workers' for the purposes of this contribution refer to both employed persons and self-employed persons.
43. *See* Regulation 883/2004 Art. 2: Next to EU citizens and their dependents or survivors, stateless persons and refugees are also included within the personal scope of the Regulation.
44. The Member State where a manager is professionally active as an employee is, for example, thus also responsible for the social security coverage of the activities said manager executes as a self-employed person in another Member State.
45. The included social security schemes are: (a) sickness benefits; (b) maternity and equivalent paternity benefits; (c) invalidity benefits; (d) old-age benefits; (e) survivors' benefits; (f) benefits in respect of accidents at work and occupational diseases; (g) death grants; (h) unemployment benefits; (i) pre-retirement benefits; (j) family benefits.
46. *See* Regulation 883/2004 Art. 3 section 5.
47. Next to the Member States of the EU, the European Economic Area also includes Iceland, Liechtenstein and Norway.

Switzerland. In 2010, the personal scope of Regulation 883/2004 was expanded by Regulation 1231/2010 to also include third-country nationals.[48]

The basic rule set forth by Regulation 883/2004 to determine the applicable social security legislation is the *lex loci laboris* principle. This means that the competent state is exclusively determined by the place where one actually works.[49] Managers who, for example, live in Germany but work in the Netherlands will thus be socially insured in the Netherlands. The main exemptions foreseen to this rule are 'posting', cf. Article 12, and 'simultaneous performance of activities in multiple Member States', cf. Article 13 *infra*.

[B] Simultaneous Performance of Activities

[1] Determining the Applicable Social Security Legislation: Four Possible Scenarios

Managers will in certain instances perform their professional activities in more than one Member State. For that reason, there might not be one single place where these managers are exclusively working. When dealing with social security coordination, depending on the facts of the case, managers who work in a cross-border context that involves more than one Member State could therefore make use of the exceptions foreseen by Articles 12 and 13 of Regulation 883/2004. Since in most cases the professional activities of managers who work in a cross-border context are not simply of a temporary nature, we will for the purposes of this book chapter not elaborate on the exception of posting and focus our attention on Article 13 of Regulation 883/2004.[50]

In its essence, Article 13 envisages four possible work scenarios where the worker involved performs simultaneously professional activities in more than one Member State.[51] Applied to managers, these four scenarios are:

(1) managers working as an employee for one or more employers.
(2) self-employed managers professionally active in a cross-border context;
(3) managers with mixed professional activities, working as both a self-employed and an employee;
(4) civil servants, who are working in addition as managers, as either self-employed or employees.

48. It is important to note however that Denmark opted out of Regulation 1231/2010, as a consequence of which Regulation 883/2004 does not apply to third-country nationals who move between Denmark and another Member State.
49. Regulation 883/2004 Art. 11 section 3 lit. a.
50. It has to be stressed however that managers could find themselves in situations where posting is the more suitable approach for the purposes of social security coordination. This is, for example, certainly the case when the professional activities that are carried out in cross-border context are of a temporary nature. The question of jurisdiction and choice of law for posted managers is addressed in Chapter 7 on International Private Law.
51. Eva Van Ooij, *Highly Mobile Workers Challenging Regulation 883/2004: Pushing or Opening Pandora's Box?*, 27 MJ 5, 578 (2020) DOI: 10.1177/1023263x20940137.

We now briefly elaborate on the legal consequences of each of these scenarios for the purposes of social security coordination.

[a] Managers Working as an Employee

When a manager works as an employee in two or more Member States, the applicable social security legislation is determined by either that of the Member State of residence or that of the Member State in which the registered office or place of business of his employer is situated. The former being the case when the manager pursues a substantial part of his activity in the Member State of his residence, or when there are no substantial activities in the Member State of residence and the manager is employed by several employers of whom at least two have their registered offices or places of business in different Member States other than the Member State of residence of the manager. The latter being the case, and specifically excluding the Member State of residence of the manager, when the manager does not pursue a substantial part of his activity in the Member State of his residence and either works for one employer or for several employers who have either their place of business or registered office in the same Member State, other than the one where the manager has his residence. It is also the case if he/she works for different employers who have their place of business or registered office in different Member States, one of which being the Member State of residence of the manager.[52]

In the overall assessment of the concept of a substantial activity, a share of 25% of the working time and/or remuneration (of the manager) is an important indicator for the qualification of an activity as substantial.[53]

[b] Self-Employed Managers Professionally Active in a Cross-Border Context

Managers who are self-employed in two or more Member States fall under the social security legislation of the Member State where they have their residence if they pursue a substantial part of their activities in that Member State.

If there is no substantial activity in their Member State of residence, the applicable legislation is that of the Member State where the centre of interest of the activities as a self-employed person is located.[54]

Also here, the 25% threshold is used as an important indicator: when the activity as a self-employed reaches a share of 25% of the turnover, working time, number of services rendered and/or the income, this indicates a substantial activity.[55]

52. Regulation 883/2004, Art. 13, section 1.
53. Regulation 987/2009, Art. 14, section 8.
54. Regulation 883/2004, Art. 13, section 2 – the concept 'centre of interest' for the purposes of social security coordination is defined by Art. 14 section 9 of Regulation 987/2009.
55. Regulation 987/2009, Art. 14, section 8.

[c] *Managers with Mixed Professional Activities*

If the manager works as both an employee and a self-employed person in more than one Member State, the social security legislation of the Member State where the manager works as an employed person is applicable.[56]

[d] *Civil Servants, Who Are in Addition Also Working as Managers*

In the fourth scenario, Article 13(4) of Regulation 883/2004 determines that the applicable social security legislation is that of the Member State where the person involved is a civil servant. This is the case even if the activities as a manager in another Member State are more substantial than the activities as a civil servant.

[2] ***Marginal Activities: The 5% Rule***

According to Article 14(5)(b) of Regulation 987/2009, marginal activities are not taken into account for the application of Article 13 of Regulation 883/2004. In other words, when a manager performs cross-border activities simultaneously in different Member States, activities of a marginal nature are not considered when assessing the competent Member State.[57] Marginal activities are disregarded for all situations covered by Article 13 of Regulation 883/2004, meaning thus also in case the person combined self-employed activities with (marginal) employee activities.[58]

The reason why the Regulation stipulates that marginal activities should not be taken into consideration to determine the competent Member State is to avoid that workers would manipulate the responsible jurisdiction with regard to their social protection.[59]

The concept of marginal activities as such is not defined in the Regulations, but the Practical Guide on the Applicable Legislation clarifies that:

> [m]arginal activities are activities that are permanent but insignificant in terms of time and economic return. It is suggested that, as an indicator, activities accounting for less than 5% of the worker's regular working time and/or less than 5% of his/her overall remuneration should be regarded as marginal activities.[60]

Also, the nature of the activities, such as activities that are of a supporting nature, that lack independence, that are performed from home or in the service of the main activity, can be an indicator that they concern marginal activities. In this respect, we can refer to the Swiss

---

56. Regulation 883/2004, Art. 13, section 3.
57. Grega Strban et al., *Analytical Report 2018 – Social Security Coordination and Non-standard Forms of Employment and Self-Employment: Interrelation, Challenges and Prospects*, 37 (European Commission 2020).
58. *See* Case C-89/16, *Radosław Szoja v. Sociálna poisťovňa and WEBUNG, s.r.o.*, 13.7.2017, ECLI: EU:C:2017:538.
59. Administrative Commission for the Coordination of Social Security Systems: *Practical guide on the applicable legislation in the European Union (EU), the European Economic Area (EEA) and in Switzerland*, 27 (2013).
60. *Ibid.*

interpretation of the nature of management activities: a mandate in a company is considered always to be a substantial activity due to its intrinsic character of giving leadership (managing responsibility).[61] Whether such an (*a contrario*) interpretation can be rooted on the definition of marginal activities as provided by the Practical Guide remains to be seen. The concept of marginal activities under Regulation 987/2009 is one of Union law, and its final interpretation is eventually to be determined by the European legislator or by the European Court of Justice in case a clear definition is not provided.[62]

[C] Challenges for Managers Active in Different Countries

Although the applicable rules may be clear in theory, the distinct social security classifications of the position of the manager across Member States sometimes make a practical application of Regulation 883/2004 challenging. Part of the challenges are related to the need to have the nature of the professional activities qualified for national social security law as it is still required to know whether the activities are considered wage-earner activities, self-employed activities or civil servant activities for the application of Article 14 of Regulation 883/2004. The outcome of these designation rules, indicating the eventual competent state, may differ depending on whether the manager performs activities of a similar nature or of a different nature. In the first situation, the country of residence normally prevails. In the latter situation, the state where the manager is considered to be an employee when simultaneously combined with self-employed activities in another state, or the state where the manager has a civil servant position, when simultaneously combined with employed or self-employed activities in another state. In other words, it is important to know under which status the manager works in the country, *see* §8.01 *supra*, as well as which country has the legal competence to qualify the management activity. Another challenge concerns the unclarity on a possible requalification of the management activities by other relevant Member States. The qualification problem becomes even more complicated when Member States apply an in-between category to managers that does not correspond fully to the traditional categories used in Title II of Regulation 883/2004 (employed activities – self-employed activities). Finally, the increasing possibilities to carry out management activities from a distance by means of online communication raise questions as to the applicable Member State. In what follows, the possible problems that may arise are discussed more in depth.

[1] Different National Classification of Professional Activities: Who Qualifies?

As the applicable legislation rules differ across working and non-working groups and across employees, self-employed workers and civil servants, it is important to know whether a manager is considered as an employee or self-employed worker for the

61. *See supra* §8.02[C][1]: the case of Switzerland.
62. *See also* Case C-137/11, *Partena ASBL v. Les Tartes de Chaumont-Gistoux SA*, 27.9.2012, ECLI: EU:C:2012:593.

application of Title II of Regulation 883/2004.[63] According to Case C-121/92, *Zinnecker*, each of the Member States involved is competent to determine the nature of the professional activities.[64] Those legal classifications are considered when assigning the competent Member State under the application of Title II of Regulation 883/2004. In the end, the assigned Member State is in charge of providing the social protection for the manager. An executive manager who conducts simultaneous activities in Belgium and in Germany may be classified differently: self-employed in Belgium and – depending on the number of shares – employee in Germany. In case the manager is deemed an employee under German social security law, Germany will be competent as a result of the application of Article 13(3) of Regulation 883/2004. This means that the manager will fall within the German social security scheme for employees, also for the activities performed in Belgium.

[2] Requalification

Even though each Member State is competent to determine whether the managerial tasks performed on its territory are subject to the employee or self-employed social security scheme, the question arises whether the competent Member State has the possibility to requalify the classification given by other Member States where cross-border managerial tasks are performed. Although some legal scholars are of the opinion that the competent Member State can requalify all the cross-border activities involved, it has to be pointed out that there is no legal basis in EU law to do so.[65] If Member States would be allowed to requalify, a manager performing activities in Belgium and Switzerland will be considered for all involved activities as a wage earner: Switzerland is the competent state and is allowed to requalify the self-employed activities performed in Belgium to wage-earner activities for the application of the Swiss system. If requalification is not followed, the eventual competent state must respect the classification given by the other Member State, in our example self-employment, on whose territory the manager is active. This can have serious consequences for the final substantive outcome of the allocation rules for the individual involved: still in our example, the said manager would not have access to the Swiss accident insurance for the part of his or her activities performed in Belgium.[66] When we follow the idea of requalification of the activities, the manager involved is also considered to be an employed person for the Belgian activities, and therefore these activities can be covered as well by the Swiss accident insurance.

In the Administrative Commission for the Coordination of Social Security Systems, the consensus drew on the more practical approach and to have the eventual competent Member State deciding on the qualification of all activities involved.[67] However, notwithstanding this common position, it was interesting to notice that, in

63. Strban et al., *supra* n. 57, at 29 et seq.
64. Case C-121/92, *Staatssecretaris van Financiën v. A. Zinnecker*, 13.10.1993, ECLI:EU:1993:840.
65. Strban et al., *supra* n. 57, at 30.
66. MISSOC, *Social protection for the self-employed: Switzerland*, 3 (2021).
67. Strban et al., *supra* n. 57, at 30.

some country reports, another interpretation was followed, which forces the competent Member State to respect the qualification given by the authorities on whose territory activities were performed. It appears that there is still no final consensus on how far the legal effect of national qualifications should reach.

[a] *Implications of the In-Between Categories of Workers for the Application of Title II*

Until this point, we have only discussed the classification of a manager as being either an employee or a self-employed worker. However, as seen *supra* §8.02, Italy does consider managers for the application of social security as working in an in-between category as belonging to the overall category of *parasubordinati* and as accommodated in the *Gestione separata* in the general system. Using an intermediate category, however, makes the application of Regulation 883/2004 difficult since the Regulation does not mention in-between categories; with the exception of civil servants, it distinguishes only two types of activities: activities as an employed person and self-employed activities. How then to qualify the activities of the manager belonging to an in-between category for the application of the Regulation? It has been argued that, in case the national legal classification of the professional activity is not clear in indicating whether the activity is to be considered as wage earner or self-employed activity, the formal insurance status could be considered, i.e., the formal belonging to a professional social security system for employees, respectively self-employed persons. The fact that *parasubordinati* are formally covered by the system of employees is then considered to be a decisive element, even though for some of these workers, specific rules are in place as *Gestione separata*.[68]

[b] *Performing Management Activities from a Distance: The Challenge of Telework*

A final challenge arising in the application of the Regulation to the managers' activities is the question of which Member State is competent in case work is performed from a distance. This is increasingly the case for both executive managers and for non-executive managers, but it is particularly relevant for the latter group, as they usually do not have to be physically present at the company on a regular basis. Attending a board meeting, for instance, can nowadays easily be done online. But what happens in

68. *Ibid.*, at 33-34. This interpretation is based upon older case law that extended Regulation No. 3 and Regulation 1408/71 to some self-employed groups, which at that time did not yet belong to the personal scope of the coordination regulations, when these groups were formally protected in the employee system. *See* Case C-75/63, *Mrs M.K.H. Hoekstra (née Unger) v. Bestuur der Bedrijfsvereniging voor Detailhandel en Ambachten (Administration of the Industrial Board for Retail Trades and Businesses)*, 19.3.1964, ECLI:EU:C:1964:19; Case C-19/68, *Giovanni de Cicco v. Landesversicherungsanstalt Schwaben*, 19.12.1968, ECLI:EU:C:1968:56; Case C-23/71, *Michel Janssen v. Landsbond der christelijke mutualiteiten*, 27.10.1971, ECLI:EU:C:1971:101; and Case C-143/79, *Margaret Walsh v. National Insurance Officer*, 22.5.1980, ECLI:EU:C:1980:134.

case management work is performed from another country than the country where the company is established?

The exact answer to this question is as such far from clear today. If we would follow the description of the place of work put forward by the *Partena* judgment[69] with its emphasis on the 'place where in practical terms, the person concerned carries out the actions connected with that activity', it seems to be logical that precedence has to be given to the actual place of work of the manager which than in any case supersedes the country where the company is established. However, the CJEU judgment on *X v. Staatssecretaris van Financiën*[70] provided some nuance. The court ruled in line with the opinion of AG Szpunar, in which attention to the situation of tele-homework was given:

> [i]t is one of the advantages – or, for some people, a curse – of the digital economy, that an employee may be asked or allowed to accomplish a part of his office tasks while away from the office, by working from home. The particularity of such working arrangement lies in the fact that it potentially undermines the concept of a particular place of employment, as a relevant factor for determining the Member State which has the closest link to the employment relationship.[71]

The Court eventually decided that when 'working from home is not explicitly reflected in contractual documents, does not constitute a structural pattern and amounts to a relatively small percentage of the overall working time, it is inappropriate to rely on that circumstance for the purposes of applying the designation rules'.[72] In these specific cases, telework, thus, does not have to be taken into consideration to determine the applicable social security legislation. But what if conversely the activities are not marginal (in kind), are followed in a structured manner and/or are agreed upon with the company? Should they then be considered for the application of Title II? Regulation 883/2004 will have to address in its designation rules the specific nature of virtual work underlying many telework and platform work activities.[73]

§8.04 CONCLUSIONS

When dealing with the social security legislation applicable to managers, it is clear that a wide variety exists as to how several jurisdictions approach the issue. There is no universal legal definition of managers across different jurisdictions, and as a consequence various approaches to determine their status as either an employed or self-employed person exist. There is a tendency to consider executive managers as

69. Case C-137/11, *Partena*.
70. Case C-570/15, *X v. Staatssecretaris van Financiën*, 13.9.2017, ECLI:EU:C:2017:182.
71. Opinion Advocate General Szpunar in Case C-570/15, *X*, paras 36-37.
72. Case C-570/15, *X*.
73. At the occasion of the Covid-19 pandemic, national administrations applied interpretations considering telework activities as if they were performed on the territory of the country where normally the work activities are conducted, this with an eye not to have the competent state changed to the country of residence of the worker – *see* for more information: European Commission, *Covid-19: Information for frontier workers and posted workers*, 6 (2020).

employees, while non-executive managers are more often considered to be self-employed persons. It has to be emphasized, however, that this tendency is rather a general trend with clear exceptions existing in some Member States.

With regard to managers who work in a cross-border context, there is a clear framework in place for those whose cross-border activities involve EU Member States, EEA Member States and Switzerland. Regulation 883/2004 and implementing Regulation 987/2009 provide for four scenarios to determine the applicable social security legislation in case managers perform simultaneous activities in several Member States. Although the rules to determine the applicable social security legislation seem straightforward at first glance, several challenges with regard to the implementation of these rules for managers still exist. This is partially due to the fact that Regulation 883/2004 gives precedence to wage-earner activities over self-employed activities to indicate the competent state for social security purposes. Consequently, the classification of the manager's activity has a major relevance: in case of simultaneous performance of mixed activities (employed and self-employed), the state where the manager works as an employee will eventually absorb the final social security competence for all activities; if in one of the states the manager is a civil servant, that state will eventually absorb the social security capacity. The national qualification of the managerial activity has a major impact on the coordination rules. One should not lose sight of the fact that the designation rules have an exclusive effect since the eventual competent state excludes in principle the application of systems of other non-competent states. Some of the legal issues even remain unresolved today, such as the question on the competence of the competent Member State to requalify the status of managers. Also, new forms of work pose challenges to the determination of the applicable social security legislation, be it because managers fall in between the status of employed and self-employed persons or be it because the place of their activities is difficult to determine. Both aspects are fundamental for the current coordination framework. Yet for the future, with the growing importance of telework, it however seems difficult to hold on to the actual location of the professional activities for the purpose of indicating the competent state.

Overall, we can conclude that the exact social protection of managers is not always straightforward and definitely does not fall within a 'one-size-fits-all' conceptualization, not on the comparative level between jurisdictions, nor on the level of social security coordination in a European context. With the growing digitalization of work, it will become even more challenging to indicate which system in the end is to be assigned as competent system for managers having simultaneous positions in different (companies in different) states.

CHAPTER 9

Information and Consultation from the Perspective of Managers: Rights Vis-à-Vis Duties

Andrea Iossa

§9.01 INTRODUCTION

The right of workers to take part in decision-making processes at company and workplace level is one of the many successes obtained by workers and trade unions during the course of the twentieth century.[1] The involvement of workers in decision-making processes has found legal expression in the rights of information and consultation for employees – and in some national contexts, even of a right of participation and co-determination.[2] It is generally acknowledged that the recognition of workers' information and consultation rights by national legal systems across Europe aims at promoting industrial democracy.[3] Unlike collective labour rights,[4] information and consultation are rights that imply and require certain mechanisms to be put in place and utilised at company level. The exercise of information and consultation rights

1. Ulrich Mückenberger, *Workers' Representation and Plant and Enterprise Level* (Bob Hepple and Bruno Veneziani eds, Hart Publishing 2009).
2. In industrial relation systems like the German and the Swedish ones, the right of co-determination entails a more substantial involvement of employees in running the business and participation in the making of a decision, *see* Reinhold Fahlbeck, *Lex Laboris – Quo Vadis? The Swedish Experience* (Roger Blanpain & Manfred Weiss eds, Kluwer Law International 2003).
3. Wanjiru Njoya, *The EU Framework of Information and Consultation: Implications for Trade Unions and Industrial Democracy* (Alan Bogg et al. eds, Edward Elgar 2016).
4. Collective labour rights can be deemed as 'unilateral' rights of workers to organise trade union activities and take up conflicts against their employers. In principle, they would not require any contribution or participation from the employer's side to be exercised except the obligation not to hinder or sanction their exercise. On collective labour rights in general, *see* Guy Mundlak, *Human Rights and Labor Rights: Why Don't the Two Tracks Meet?*, 34 CLLPJ 217 (2012).

entails, therefore, the presence of functioning procedures within the workplace, where management and employees discuss and, possibly, negotiate important aspects concerning the running of business. In light of the evolution of companies to complex organisations with many levels and establishments,[5] the position of managers is salient in this regard. Unlike business owners, who in the end profit from workers' labour, managers are the professionals who often exercise most of the functions and prerogatives usually associated with the employer.

In line with this view, this contribution reviews the legal status, entitlements, and responsibilities of managers under the EU legal framework for information and consultation rights of workers/employees. This framework has three dimensions: in the EU legal system, information and consultation rights have: (a) a fundamental rights dimension, (b) a national dimension, and (c) a transnational dimension. Each of these dimensions has specific – yet often intertwined – legal expressions defined by EU legal sources. The analysis carried out in this chapter examines the status of managers in relation to information and consultation rights, as well as the implications concerning their rights and duties, across these three dimensions. In a nutshell, the chapter explores whether and to what extent, according to EU law, managers are entitled to exercise information and consultation rights as employees in their companies and what duties and responsibilities they carry in relation to the good functioning of workplace machinery for information and consultation rights.

An examination of the rights and duties of managers in the context of mechanisms for the exercise of information and consultation rights is important in order to understand the relevance of these professional figures in workplace relations. Industrial relations research shows how the attitudes and actions of managers do actually matter for the effective functioning of mechanisms and procedures for the exercise of information and consultation rights.[6] Also, managers' views have the potential to influence workplace regulation by informing human resources practices, rules, and guidelines.[7] It follows that a scrutiny of managers' rights and duties in light of the EU legal framework for information and consultation rights contributes to a better understanding of workplace relations and regulations, with the aim of promoting the functioning of legal mechanisms for workers' voice in view of companies' needs to adapt to structural changes.[8]

The chapter is structured as follows: it starts with some preliminary considerations on the figure of managers within labour law (§9.02); it continues with an overview of the legal framework for information and consultation rights in EU law

---

5. *See* Giovanni Gaudio, *Adapting Labour Law to Complex Organisational Settings of the Enterprise: Why Rethinking the Concept of the Employer Is Not Enough*, 50 ILJ 2, 264 (2021) DOI: 10.1093/indlaw/dwaa007.
6. Valeria Pulignano & Jeremy Waddington, *Management, European Works Councils and Institutional Malleability*, 26 EJIR 1, 5 (2020); Nadia K. Kougiannou et al., *Inside the Meetings: The Role of Managerial Attitudes in Approaches to Information and Consultation for Employees*, 60 BJIR 3, 585-605 (2021) DOI 10.1111/bjir.12650.
7. Eleanor Kirk, *Law and Legalities at Work: HR Practitioners as Quasi-Legal Professionals*, 50 ILJ 4, 583 (2021) DOI: 10.1093/indlaw/dwab025.
8. Ruth Nielsen, *EU Labour Law* 181 (DJØF Publishing 2013).

(§9.03); then, it discusses questions of entitlements (§9.04) and obligations (§9.05) that managers might have on the basis of the EU legal framework for information and consultation rights. A final section concludes.

§9.02 PRELIMINARY CONSIDERATIONS: ROLE AND STATUS OF MANAGERS FROM A LABOUR LAW PERSPECTIVE

Managers represent a professional figure whose key significance was raised in connection with the emergence of large corporations in the first decades of the 1900s. This evolution in company structures was marked by a separation between 'ownership' and 'control' in which owners of growing companies started relying on professionals rather than on themselves or family members to run the business and to be present in the workplace to supervise production.[9] Managers became the 'link' between owners and employees – appointed by, and therefore accountable to, owners or shareholders of companies and corporations, while at the same time monitoring and controlling the employees, which are the traditional tasks that labour law recognises to the employer as expressions of managerial authority in the workplace.[10] Yet, a growing stream of research has shown how labour law has a 'flattened' and unidimensional conception of the employment relationship that fails to capture complexity in company structures and hierarchies. For instance, Davies and Freedland point to the failed attempt of labour (employment) law to comprehend the separation between 'capital' and 'management' that brought about the evolution in company structures and organisations mentioned above.[11] In the words of Davies and Freedland, 'the managers or bearers of employing functions may themselves be constituted as employees of or workers for the enterprise in question and this may even be true for those right at the top of a hierarchical structure'.[12] Consequently, they introduce the category of 'the dual-role manager/worker' to identify the employee who exercises employer's prerogatives on behalf of the enterprise while at the same time being employed by the enterprise itself. Building on Davies and Freedland's work, Prassl notices how '[t]he perception of companies as anthropomorphic individual units' brings about a unitary notion of the 'employer' that does not take into consideration complexity in company structures.[13]

9. Blanche Segrestin et al., *The Separation of Directors and Managers: A Historical Examination of the Status of Managers*, 25 JMH 2, 141 (2019) DOI: 10.1108/jmh-11-2018-0060. The authors also mention that it become common for family members of large corporations' owners to attend business schools as to become professional managers to be employed in family business.
10. *See* Luisa Corazza & Orsola Razzolini, *Who Is an Employer?* (Matthew W. Finkin & Guy Mundlak eds, Edward Elgar, 2015). For a discussion on labour law and employer's authority, *see also* Andrea Iossa, *Anti-authoritarian Employment Relations? Labour Law from an Anarchist Perspective* (Alysia Blackham et al. eds, Hart Publishing 2019).
11. Paul Davies & Mark Freedland, *The Complexities of the Employing Enterprise* 276 (Guy Davidov & Brian Langille eds, Hart Publishing 2006).
12. *Ibid.*, 278.
13. Jeremias Prassl, *Autonomous Concepts in Labour Law? The Complexities of the Employing Enterprise Revisited*, 153 (Alan Bogg et al. eds, Hart Publishing 2015).

This perception discards the 'multitude of actors, from employees and management to a board of directors and shareholders'.[14]

Davies and Freedland's as well as Prassl's analyses aim at disclosing the narrowness of a 'unitary' concept of employer in relation to core aspects of labour (employment) law.[15] For the purpose of this chapter, however, their analysis is functional to understand the role and status of managers in relation to the exercise of information and consultation rights. Through the prism of the 'dual-role manager/worker' category, managers might be entitled to employment rights in front of companies' owners and shareholders - including information and consultation rights - and at the same time they hold duties towards companies' employees concerning the effective and correct functioning of the mechanisms for informing and consulting company's employees according to the law - as if they were the employer. From a labour law perspective, a reflection on the dual role of managers brings about the need to reflect upon the boundaries - and therefore limitations - of the field and of the legal framework - how can labour law understand the complexity of companies' structure and make sense of the different roles a same employee would be possibly performing within it? In the context of information and consultation rights, the dual role of managers brings about questions concerning entitlement and exercise of those rights in relation to the legal status of managers and of their status and tasks within the company.

§9.03 THE EU LEGAL FRAMEWORK FOR INFORMATION AND CONSULTATION RIGHTS: AN OVERVIEW

Information and consultation rights constitute one of the social policy fields in which the Treaty on the Functioning of the EU (TFEU) calls the EU to 'support and complement the activities of the Member States' (Article 153(1)(e) TFEU). The achievement of machinery for the exercise of these rights is, therefore, included among the social policy objectives of the EU. In this context, however, management and labour are placed on opposite ends as representing different and opposite actors in industrial relations.

As mentioned in the Introduction, the EU legal framework for information and consultation rights can be understood as having a three-dimensional structure. In the context of the EU legal system, information and consultation rights have: (a) a fundamental rights dimension, (b) a national dimension, and (c) a transnational dimension. For each of these dimensions, there are specific EU legal sources that ensure, promote, and protect the exercise of workers' information and consultation rights.

As *fundamental rights*, information and consultation rights are expressed in Article 27 of the Charter of Fundamental Rights of the EU (CFREU) included in Title IV

14. *Ibid.*
15. *See also* Paul Davies & Mark Freedland, *Changing Perspectives upon the Employment Relationship in British Labour Law* (Catherine Barnard et al. eds, Hart Publishing 2004).

of the Charter dedicated to Solidarity. The provision states that '[w]orkers or their representatives must, at the appropriate levels, be guaranteed information and consultation in good time in the cases and under the conditions provided for by Union law and national laws and practices' (Article 27 CFREU). The article owes its formulation not only to the (Revised) European Social Charter[16] but also to various ILO Conventions and Recommendations dealing with and promoting workers' involvement.[17] The relevance of a social dimension of information and consultation rights in EU law is strengthened by their inclusion in the European Pillar of Social Rights, which at its Point 8(b) states '[w]orkers or their representatives have the right to be informed and consulted in good time on matters relevant to them, in particular on the transfer, restructuring and merger of undertakings and on collective redundancies'. In this sense, the Pillar 'operationalises' – perhaps by filling a gap left by Article 27 CFREU as for the subjects of information and consultation – the rights of employees to be informed and consulted by placing them in the context of company operations that have the potential to affect working and employment conditions.

While it cannot be disputed that information and consultation rights belong to the category of EU fundamental rights, Article 27 has been subject to a controversial interpretation by the Court of Justice of the EU (CJEU) in Case C-176/12, *Association de médiation sociale (AMS)*.[18] Here, the CJEU states that the wording of Article 27 lacks sufficient clearness to have a direct horizontal effect and, therefore, cannot be invoked in disputes between individuals, including in employment disputes.[19] According to the CJEU, 'to be fully effective', Article 27, 'must be given more specific expression in European Union or national law'.[20] In its reasoning, the CJEU implicitly accepts the argument suggested by the Advocate General who, in his opinion, draws a distinction between 'rights' and 'principles' in the CFREU.[21] In his interpretation, social rights mainly belong to the latter category. This would imply that social rights, in order to acquire effectiveness, require the adoption of legislation implementing specific social policies. According to the CJEU's decision, Article 27 would then fall into the latter category, entailing therefore the need for national legal orders to adopt implementing

16. Filip Dorssemont, *Article 27*, 752 (Steve Peers et al. eds, Nomos 2014). Dorssemont also notes how from the perspective of Art. 11 of the European Convention of Human Rights and its interpretation given by the Court a right to information and consultation appears quite mild as only a 'right to be heard' for the trade union, 754.
17. Bruno Veneziani, *Article 27 – Workers Right to Information and Consultation Within the Undertaking*, 432-435 (Filip Dorssemont et al. eds, Hart Publishing 2019).
18. Case C-176/12, *Association de médiation sociale v. Union locale des syndicats CGT and Others*, 15.1.2014, ECLI:EU:C:2014:2.
19. Employment disputes would also include disputes between public employees and the state in its quality as employer. This is confirmed by several cases of the CJEU concerning horizontal direct effect of directives, *see* Nicole Lazzerini, *The Horizontal Application of the General Principles of EU Law: Nothing Less than Direct Effect* 180-183 (Katja S. Ziegler et al. eds, Edward Elgar Publishing 2022).
20. Case C-176/12, *AMS*, para. 45.
21. Opinion of AG Cruz Villalón in Case C-176/12, *AMS*, para. 45. For a discussion on this distinction in relation with social rights, *see* Catherine Barnard, *Are Social 'Rights' Rights?*, 11 ELLJ 4, 4, 351 (2020) DOI: 10.1177/2031952520905382.

legislation and at the same time excluding the direct effect of the provision.[22] Such an interpretation seems to downgrade – arguably[23] – the relevance of the provision in the context of the EU legal framework. However, it cannot be denied that Article 27 CFREU enshrines information and consultation rights as fundamental rights for 'workers or their representatives'. The issue of holdership, i.e., the personal entitlement to exercise those rights, is relevant for the discussion on managers' rights, and it will be explored below.

The *national dimension* of information and consultation rights is primarily promoted and supported by Directive 2002/14/EC establishing a general framework for informing and consulting employees in the European Community[24] (hereinafter 'Information and Consultation Directive'). The Directive's purpose is 'to establish a general framework setting out minimum requirements for the right to information and consultation of employees in undertakings or establishments within the Community' (Article 1(1)). The Directive promotes a national dimension of information and consultation rights by referring to 'national law and industrial relations practices in individual Member States' as the sources to establish the general framework and procedures for the exercise of information and consultation rights at company level (Article 1(2)). The scope of the Directive includes 'undertakings' located in a Member State with at least fifty employees and 'establishments' located in a Member State with at least twenty employees (Article 3(1)(a) and (b)). The Directive then devolves to Member States the competence to define the method for operating these calculations (Article 3(1)). In line with several provisions included in Title X on Social Policy of the TFEU, the Directive places management and labour on two opposite sides and calls for their collaboration in enforcing information and consultation rights. Accordingly, managers would then be mostly deemed as holders of duties in relation to the procedures to ensure that employees at company level are properly informed and consulted.

The *transnational dimension* of information and consultation rights is mainly expressed and promoted by Directive 2009/38/EU on the establishment of a European Works Council or a procedure in Community-scale undertakings and Community-scale groups of undertakings for the purposes of informing and consulting employees[25] (hereinafter 'EWCs Directive').[26] This Directive has the ambition to promote the

22. For a critical comment on the ruling, *see* Filip Dorssemont, *Case Notes – The Right to Information and Consultation in Article 27 of the Charter of Fundamental Rights of the European Union: Less than a Right and Less than a Principle, Just an Ordinary Provision Lacking Direct Effect?*, 21 MJ 4, 704 (2014).
23. Dorssemont is very sceptic on this point, *see* Dorssemont, *supra* n. 16, at 717-718.
24. Directive 2002/14/EC of the European Parliament and of the Council of 11 March 2002 establishing a general framework for informing and consulting employees in the European Community – Joint declaration of the European Parliament, the Council and the Commission on employee representation, OJ L 080, 23.3.2002.
25. Directive 2009/38/EC of the European Parliament and of the Council of 6 May 2009 on the establishment of a European Works Council or a procedure in Community-scale undertakings and Community-scale groups of undertakings for the purposes of informing and consulting employees (Recast), OJ L 122, 16.5.2009.
26. A transnational dimension for information and consultation rights is also expressed in the Council Directive 2001/86/EC of 8 October 2001 supplementing the Statute for a European

establishment of specific bodies for the exercise of information and consultation rights in companies with a transnational outreach in the EU. The purpose of the EWCs Directive 'is to improve the right to information and to consultation of employees in Community-scale undertakings and Community-scale groups of undertakings' (Article 1(1)).[27] Unlike the Information and Consultation Directive, the material scope of the EWCs Directive limits the topics that can be subject to information and consultation to transnational issues (Article 1(3)). The EWCs Directive provides for a complex procedure to achieve the establishment of an EWC. The Directive requires the establishment of a Special Negotiating Body representing the employees with the mandate to negotiate with the central management of the transnational company the establishment of the EWC. In this regard, the role of managers is central, as it will be discussed below.

In addition, information and consultation rights are also promoted by a set of EU directives concerning company restructurings, transfers, and cross-border mergers, as well as those concerning insolvency of employers and collective redundancies. These directives are: Directive 98/59/EC on the approximation of the laws of the Member States relating to collective redundancies[28] (hereinafter 'Collective Redundancies Directive'); Directive 2001/23/EC on the approximation of the laws of the Member States relating to the safeguarding of employees' rights in the event of transfers of undertakings, businesses, or parts of undertakings or businesses[29] (hereinafter 'Transfer of Undertakings Directive'); and Directive 2008/94/EC on the protection of employees in the event of the insolvency of their employer[30] (hereinafter 'Insolvency Directive'). Those directives were originally adopted to deal at national level with the effects of the 1970s economic crisis. Since then, they have become the legal framework for protecting employees in cases of company crisis and restructuring. In parallel with the evolution of the internal market and of the transnational dimension for companies operating in it, a transnational dimension has also evolved for the scope of these directives.[31]

company with regard to the involvement of employees, OJ L 294, 8.10.2017, 22. This Directive is however not taken into account for the discussion elaborated in this chapter.

27. The Directive identifies the former as 'any undertaking with at least 1,000 employees within the Member States and at least 150 employees in each of at least two Member States' and the latter as 'a group of undertakings with [...] at least 1,000 employees within the Member States; at least two group undertakings in different Member States, and at least one group undertaking with at least 150 employees in one Member State and at least one other group undertaking with at least 150 employees in another Member State' (Art. 2.1).
28. Council Directive 98/59/EC of 20 July 1998 on the approximation of the laws of the Member States relating to collective redundancies, OJ L 225, 12.8.1998.
29. Council Directive 2001/23/EC of 12 March 2001 on the approximation of the laws of the Member States relating to the safeguarding of employees' rights in the event of transfers of undertakings, businesses or parts of undertakings or businesses, OJ L 082, 22.3.2001.
30. Directive 2008/94/EC of the European Parliament and of the Council of 22 October 2008 on the protection of employees in the event of the insolvency of their employer (codified version), OJ L 283, 28.10.2008.
31. Catherine Barnard, *EU Employment Law* 577 (4th ed. Oxford University Press 2012); Dorssemont, *supra* n. 16, at 755.

Finally, in 2019, two further directives with links to information and consultations rights have been adopted: Directive (EU) 2019/1023 on restructuring and insolvency[32] and Directive (EU) 2019/2121 on cross-border conversions, mergers and divisions.[33] Both directives introduce amendments to Directive (EU) 2017/1132 relating to certain aspects of company law.[34] Among the various novelties, both directives contain provisions that aim at strengthening and protecting information and consultation rights for workers in situations of company restructuring, mergers, and divisions in accordance with the Information and Consultation Directive and the EWCs Directive (Article 13 Directive 2019/2013 and Article 86k Directive 2019/2121).

§9.04 MANAGERS AS HOLDERS OF INFORMATION AND CONSULTATION RIGHTS

In light of the discussion above, a question emerges: are managers entitled to exercise information and consultation rights as employees in their companies? The question requires exploring the issue of holdership and entitlement of information and consultation rights in EU law, also in order to understand whether EU law excludes managers from the entitlement of information and consultation rights. To discuss this question from the perspective of the managers is not an easy task. The social policy provisions of the TFEU place 'management' in opposition to 'labour' – for instance, in relation to the possibility for the two sides to establish a dialogue on adopting and implementing EU legislation in social policy fields (Articles 151, 153(3), 154 TFEU). This is not unexpected. As an industrial relations actor, 'management' represents the employer, especially at company level. The juxtaposition with 'labour' – as the organised social power representing workers – is consequential and is reflected in labour law and EU law too. As explained above, however, managers can also have the status of employees from a labour law perspective as well as if considered within the company structure. In this sense, managers might also be entitled to exercise and enjoy certain employment and labour rights.

A preliminary observation in this regard concerns whether certain categories of workers may be excluded from the entitlement to and enjoyment of EU information and consultation rights. In this regard, the Information and Consultation Directive and the EWCs Directive give Member States the possibility to introduce limitations to the application of information and consultation rights to merchant navy crews (Article 3(3)

32. Directive (EU) 2019/1023 of the European Parliament and of the Council of 20 June 2019 on preventive restructuring frameworks, on discharge of debt and disqualifications, and on measures to increase the efficiency of procedures concerning restructuring, insolvency and discharge of debt, and amending Directive (EU) 2017/1132, OJ L 172, 26.6.2019.
33. Directive (EU) 2019/2121 of the European Parliament and of the Council of 27 November 2019 amending Directive (EU) 2017/1132 as regards cross-border conversions, mergers and divisions, OJ L 321, 12.12.2019.
34. Directive (EU) 2017/1132 of the European Parliament and of the Council of 14 June 2017 relating to certain aspects of company law, OJ L 169, 30.6.2017, 46.

and Article 1(7), respectively).[35] In addition, the Information and Consultation Directive provides for the Member States to introduce measures that limit the application of the Directive to 'undertakings or establishments which pursue directly and essentially political, professional organisational, religious, charitable, educational, scientific or artistic aims, as well as aims involving information and the expression of opinions' (Article 3(2)). A further *ratione personae* exclusion is to be found in the Collective Redundancies Directive, which excludes from its scope of application 'workers employed by public administrative bodies or by establishments governed by public law' (Article 1(2)(b)). None of these provisions specifically address managers. Therefore, excluding possibly civil servants in case of collective redundancies and high-rank officers in certain (non-profit) organisations, it seems that managers cannot be automatically excluded from the entitlement of information and consultation rights.

A further consideration that goes in this direction concerns the definition of the notion of 'employee' in relation to the application of those directives. A common feature of the several directives concerning information and consultation rights is that they refer to Member States' national legal definitions for identifying the concept of 'employee' for the application of the directives. For instance, both the Information and Consultation Directive and the Transfer of Undertaking Directive state that, as regards their scope of application, '"employee" means any person who, in the Member State concerned, is protected as an employee under national employment law and in accordance with national practice' (Article 2(d) and Article 2(d), respectively). Similarly, the EWCs Directive prescribes that 'part-time employees, employed during the previous two years calculated according to national legislation and/or practice' are included in the calculation for the threshold above which the Directive applies (Article 2(2)). The CJEU has also provided a wide interpretation of Article 2(d) of the Information and Consultation Directive, in which the Court specifies that all workers that are protected by employment legislation under national law are to be considered as employees for the application of the Directive, and no exemptions are allowed for Member States.[36] No distinction seems to be derived from EU law about the qualification of the employees as for their entitlement to be covered by those directives ensuring the exercise of information and consultation rights in different contexts and situations. If managers have to be excluded from the exercise of information and consultation rights, this has to derive from national law and practice, for instance, depending on the type of contract a manager might have with the company they manage (it might be a contract as a consultant instead of as an employee) or if stated in collective agreements.

Looking then towards Article 27 CFREU, the entitlement of information and consultation rights is reserved to 'workers or their representatives'. Accordingly, employers are excluded from the exercise of information and consultation rights. Once again, this is not surprising since workers' information and consultation rights

35. Directive 2001/23/EC on transfers of undertakings excludes from its scope transfers of vessels that would not involve a transfer of business (Art. 1.3). In this sense, the Directive applies in case the crew would be transferred to a new employer.
36. C-385/05, *Confédération générale du travail (CGT) and Others v. Premier ministre and Ministre de l'Emploi, de la Cohésion sociale et du Logement*, 18.1.2007, ECLI:EU:C:2007:37, para. 34.

correspond to employers' duties to inform and consult the employees and their representatives on company matters. For instance, in Swedish labour law, where information, consultation, and co-determination rights have a prominent role, workers' information and consultation rights are framed as 'employer's obligation to negotiate' (*arbetsgivares förhandlingsskyldighet*).[37] Therefore, information and consultation rights constitute restrictions to the managerial prerogatives and cannot be considered in the same way as, for instance, the rights to collective bargaining and to collective action, which instead can be equally exercised by both industrial relations parties as expressions of collective autonomy.[38] This observation is also relevant in the context of EU fundamental rights. Unlike Article 27 CFREU, the right to collective bargaining and the right to collective action are, according to Article 28 CFREU, attributed to '[w]orkers and employers, or their respective organisations'. In this regard, Veneziani stresses how Articles 27 and 28 CFREU share 'the same ideological roots' but have different functions.[39] Similarly, Dorssemont highlights how the exercise of information and consultation rights 'precedes the adoption of a unilateral decision by management, the right to negotiate amounts to a legal act, i.e., an agreement, which will be concluded by management and labour'.[40] To be informed and consulted on company developments are, therefore, rights that primarily benefit the employees of the company. Regarding this aspect, Dorssemont explains that information and consultation rights 'are best described as *collective freedoms*', which are held by individual workers but exercised collectively.[41] While it is in the interest of the individual employee to be aware of managerial decisions, such a right, as well as the right to provide opinions to the employer on those decisions, can only be exercised by a collective – a works council or a local union club – that represents the company's employees.

Even though this interpretation would not exclude managers as employees among the holders of information and consultation rights under EU law, the question remains open if we reflect upon collective organising of managers and managerial unionism. Often, for the group of managers employed by a company, it might be enough to receive information and provide opinions through the board of the company, in which they usually sit. To exercise information and consultation rights at company level in the 'classical' way – that is, through an established collective of employees' representatives (managers in this case) – might be redundant and difficult to achieve due to the possibly limited number of professional figures in the company structure. Managerial trade unionism is, however, an established phenomenon. For instance, and just to consider the EU context, the Council of European Professional and Managerial Staff (Eurocadres) has existed since 1993. Eurocadres represents national trade unions for the higher rank of 'white-collar workers', it is affiliated with the European Trade

37. *See* Jenny Julén Votinius, *Employee Representation at the Enterprises: Sweden* 131-155 (Roger Blanpain ed., Kluwer Law International 2012).
38. *See* Filip Dorssemont & Marco Rocca, *Article 28 – Right of Collective Bargaining and Action* 465-504 (Filip Dorssemont et al. eds, Hart Publishing 2019).
39. Veneziani, *supra* n. 17, at 441.
40. Dorssemont, *supra* n. 16, at 751.
41. *Ibid.*, at 756, emphasis is in the original.

Union Confederation (ETUC), and it participates in cross-sectoral EU social dialogue. Though, as mentioned on its website, Eurocadres 'voice[s] the cross-sectoral interests of Professionals and Managers through advocacy, social dialogue, collective bargaining and joint work with member organisations and cooperation partners'.[42] Information and consultation rights might then be outside the strategic means used by Eurocadres to promote the collective interest of managers, which might be better promoted through cooperation with civil society organisations, cross-sectoral collective bargaining with employers' associations, and lobbying activities towards Member States in implementing EU law.[43]

§9.05 MANAGERS' DUTIES TO INFORM AND CONSULT EMPLOYEES

The issue of managers' duties in relation to the exercise of information and consultation rights by employees appears, to a certain degree, easier to explore. Information and consultation rights constitute, as said earlier in the chapter, restrictions to managerial prerogatives. EU law places a series of obligations upon management in this regard. Not all obligations will be discussed here, though. The aim of this section is to provide an overview of the major duties that managers have to perform as representatives of the employer in relation to the exercise of employees' information and consultation rights.

Certain specific obligations can already be derived from the definitions of 'information' and 'consultation' provided by the Information and Consultation Directive. Here, 'information' is defined as 'transmission by the employer to the employees' representatives of data in order to enable them to acquaint themselves with the subject matter and to examine it' (Article 2(f)), while 'consultation' is defined as 'the exchange of views and establishment of dialogue between the employees' representatives and the employer' (Article 2(g)). Given that, in medium- and large-size companies, managers perform the tasks that labour law assigns to the 'employer', they have then the duty to establish and supervise those machinery and conducts to fulfil the tasks of informing and consulting the employees' representatives.

The exercise of information and consultation rights requires procedures to be put in place – or, as defined by Article 4 of the Information and Consultation Directive, 'Practical arrangements'. The provision specifies in which cases is the employer called to inform and consult employees' representatives. According to the provision, information and consultation cover: 'recent and probable development of the undertaking's or the establishment's activities and economic situation'; 'the situation, structure and probable development of employment within the undertaking or establishment and on

42. Eurocadres: *about us*, https://www.eurocadres.eu/about-us/.
43. A recent case in this regard concerns the implementation of Directive (EU) 2019/1937 of the European Parliament and of the Council of 23 October 2019 on the protection of persons who report breaches of Union law, *see* Vigjilenca Abazi, *The European Union Whistleblower Directive: A 'Game Changer' for Whistleblowing Protection?*, 49 ILJ 4, 640-656, 646 (2020) DOI: 10.1093/indlaw/dwaa023.

any anticipatory measures envisaged, in particular where there is a threat to employment'; 'decisions likely to lead to substantial changes in work organisation or in contractual relations' (Article 4(a), (b), (c)). The inclusion of information and consultation procedures in directives regulating situations such as transfers of undertaking, merges, collective redundancies and the like goes therefore in the direction indicated by the Information and Consultation Directive, that is to keep employees (through their representatives) informed about company developments and give them the possibility to express opinions in that regard.

The information and consultation rights refer then to the obligation for employers (or managers) to inform and consult employees' representatives for certain decisions to be made concerning the company's economic and financial situation and/or development. A central question in this regard concerns the timing: shall employees' representatives be informed and consulted before or after the decision is taken? The distinction is of utmost relevance. To be informed and consulted before a decision is made would imply the possibility for employees' representatives to study the situation, inform the employees, and, possibly, suggest alternative ways to proceed than those proposed by the management. Drawing again a parallel with Swedish labour law, it is an established interpretation of the Labour Court that the employers' duty to inform and consult employees' representatives (provided by sections 11, 12, and 13 of the Co-Determination Act[44]) has to be performed in good time and at an early stage of the process that would lead to the decision in order to give employees' representatives room to negotiate the decision with the employer.[45]

In the context of EU law, a similar interpretation can be found in relation to collective redundancies. Article 2(1) of the Collective Redundancies Directive places the obligation to 'begin consultations with the workers' representatives' not only 'in good time' but also already when the employer is 'contemplating' the implementation of collective redundancies. In practice, this aspect has been interpreted by the CJEU as entailing that consultations shall begin when no decision about the actual implementation of collective redundancies has been taken yet.[46] Accordingly, the CJEU specifies that no dismissal can be completed or finalised until the process of consultation provided by the Directive has taken place since the provision requires the employer to begin consultation 'with a view of reaching an agreement' (Article 2(1) Collective Redundancies Directive). In this sense, '[t]he effectiveness of such an obligation would be compromised if an employer was entitled to terminate contracts of employment during the course of the procedure or even at the beginning thereof'.[47] In a later ruling, the Court indicates that the obligation to start consultations 'would arise in connection with the existence of an intention on the part of the employer to make collective

44. Lag (1976:580) om medbestämmande i arbetslivet.
45. Swedish Labour Court judgments AD 2008 No. 3 and AD 2012 No. 26. In Swedish labour law, the employer's obligation to inform and consult employees' representatives at company level implies the obligation to negotiate the decision to be taken, although no obligation to reach an agreement is included.
46. Case C-188/03, *Irmtraud Junk v. Wolfgang Kühnel*, 27.1.2005, ECLI:EU:C:2005:59, para. 36.
47. *Ibid.*, para. 44.

redundancies'.[48] The interpretation given by the CJEU seems to aim at ensuring the involvement of workers' representatives in the decision-making process – by attributing to consultations the prerogatives of steering the decision by the employer to make collective redundancies and how.[49] In this regard, it is worth noting that the Collective Redundancies Directive also contains obligations on the contents of the information that the employer has to communicate to workers' representatives, which include reasons for the redundancies, number and categories of workers affected, time frame, criteria for the selection, and others (Article 2(3) Collective Redundancies Directive). The employer has also the obligation to inform the competent public authority about 'any projected collective redundancies' by providing the same information (Article 3 Collective Redundancies Directive).

In case of transfer of undertaking, both the transferor and the transferee have obligations towards the employees affected by the transfer. Managers of two companies or groups have thus the same obligations towards the same group of employees who are formally about to change employer.[50] Article 7 of the Transfer of Undertaking Directive lists matters about which employees' representatives need to be informed by both the current and future employers. In this regard, Article 6 is interesting too. It aims at safeguarding the 'status and function' of employees' representatives who might be affected by the transfer. The objective is then to prevent a situation in which the transfer would reset employees' representation in the new company structure.[51] When one of the two managements intends to adopt measures that affect the employee, the Directive states the obligation to consult the employees' representatives 'with the view of reaching an agreement' (Article 7(2)). It goes without saying that information and consultation have to happen 'in good time'. The Directive contemplates a specific situation, though: the transferee has the obligation to inform employees' representatives 'in any event before his employees are directly affected by the transfer as regards their conditions of work and employment' (Article 7(1)). From the perspective of managers, an interesting provision concerns the level at which decisions of transfer might be taken and the ensuing obligation of informing and consulting employees (Article 7(4)). Following the ratio of the Directive, which enshrines information and consultation rights in situations of transfer, the management of a company that is subject to a (partial or total) transfer would be exempted from the obligation to inform and consult employees' representatives if the decision has been taken by the management of a controlling company or group.[52]

In relation to the establishment of EWCs in transnational companies, managers have more specific duties and obligations. The EWCs Directive indicates that the 'central management' is responsible 'for creating the conditions and means necessary for the setting-up of' an EWC (Article 4(1)). In this regard, the duty of informing

48. Case C-44/08, *Akavan Erityisalojen Keskusliitto AEK ry and Others v. Fujitsu Siemens Computers Oy*, 10.9.2009, ECLI:EU:C:2009:533, para. 39.
49. Filip Dorssemont, *Case C-55/02, Commission of the European Commission v. Portuguese Republic; Case C-188/03, Imtraud Junk v. Wolfgang Kühnel*, 43 CML Rev. 1, 225-241 (2006).
50. Barnard, *supra* n. 31, at 579.
51. *Ibid.*, 618.
52. Nielsen, *supra* n. 8, at 452.

employees' representatives by providing all the relevant information has a wide reach. It includes the obligation for the central management of a company located in a Member State to provide such information when the central management of the company group is located outside the EU, as well as it covers the obligation of central management of the other companies belonging to the same group that are located within the EU to provide the relevant information to each other.[53] As part of this responsibility, the central management 'shall initiate negotiations' that would lead to the establishment of a Special Negotiating Body (Article 5(1)) that would negotiate with them 'the scope, composition, functions, and term of office of the European Works Council(s)' (Article 5(3)). Once the Special Negotiating Body has been established, the central management has the duty to convene a meeting to start the negotiations for the formation of the EWC. At the same time, the management shall refrain from taking part in the preliminary and follow-up meetings held by the employees' representatives who sit in the Special Negotiating Body (Article 5(4)). Finally, it is interesting to mention how the central management is also the holder of a right to be informed in relation to the establishment of the Special Negotiating Body: along with 'competent European workers' and employers' organisations', it has the right to 'be informed of the composition of the special negotiating body and of the start of the negotiations' (Article 5(2)(b)).

§9.06 CONCLUDING REMARKS

In light of the discussion above, EU law does not exclude managers from the entitlements of information and consultation rights. However, it is clear that the scope of their duties in relation to employees' representatives is more far reaching and wider. On the one hand, managers are, legally speaking, entitled to exercise those rights within the company, while, on the other hand, acting on behalf of the employer, they have a set of obligations to fulfil in order for the employees of their company to exercise information and consultation rights. This applies especially in situations of company crisis and/or restructuring. This twofold position derives from the twofold position managers have in company structures: they manage the company without being its owners, but they 'represent' the employer in front of the employees. This latter function is codified by labour law (and EU law), which instead fails to recognise the complexity of company structures and to adjust rights and duties accordingly. This does not mean that managers are excluded from rights that might derive from labour law (and EU law). Rather, it means that managers are in the position of having certain entitlements as employees but mostly of having to perform employers' duties.

Company structures make it difficult for managers to look after their interests vis-à-vis the interests of the company by exercising information and consultation rights. Managers seem to possess an individual power to make their voice heard by the

---

53. *See* Case C-62/99, *Betriebsrat der bofrost* Josef H. Boquoi Deutschland West GmbH & Co. KG v. Bofrost* Josef H. Boquoi Deutschland West GmbH & Co. KG, 29.3.2001*, ECLI:EU:C:2001:188; Nielsen, *supra* n. 8, at 203.

company, for instance, by taking an active part in the decision-making process on the management side or by negotiating on an individual level terms and conditions of work due to their bargaining power. No specific procedure for involving managers in decision-making or mechanisms to ensure their collective representation at company level are provided by EU law, which only recognises 'management' and 'workers' as wide legal categories. Protection of managers' rights happens mostly via business organisations and industrial relations channels.

If, in principle, EU law does not exclude managers from the entitlement to information and consultation rights, the question of the opportunity for managers to exercise those rights needs to be resolved in the realm of industrial relations. Managerial trade unionism is an established phenomenon, and managers have their own trade union organisations to promote their interest - at national and European levels. However, information and consultation rights seem to be outside the range of strategies adopted by managerial trade unions, which instead privilege other strategies such as social dialogue, collective bargaining, lobbying, and cooperation with other organisations. In relation to the rights of information and consultation for employees as defined by the EU legal framework, the duties that managers have to fulfil as representing the employer are instead well defined and strict.

CHAPTER 10

Oscillating Between Labour Law and Corporate Law: The Status of Employee Representatives in the Boards

Achim Seifert

§10.01 EMPLOYEE REPRESENTATION IN COMPANY BOARDS

In various EU Member States, employees or their unions have the right to elect or to appoint a certain number of employee representatives to the board of directors (in one-tier systems), or to its supervisory board in companies that have a two-tier structure of corporate governance.[1] Well-known examples of European countries that have established such board-level employee representation schemes are Germany, France, Luxembourg, The Netherlands, Denmark, and Sweden. Beyond these national models, the EU has established a legal framework for a negotiated participation of employees in the board of directors or the supervisory board of a European Company (*Societas Europaea* (*SE*))[2] that has successively been extended to other forms of cross-border corporate restructuring such as cross-border mergers,[3] conversions and

1. For an instructive overview on the national board-level representation schemes in the EU Member States, *see* e.g., the country reports in: *Unternehmens-Mitbestimmung der Arbeitnehmer im Recht der EU-Mitgliedstaaten – Employees' Co-Determination in the Member States of the European Union* (Theodor Baums & Peter Ulmer eds, de Gruyter 2004). *See also* Jeremy Waddington & Aline Conchon, *Board-Level Employee Representation in Europe – Priorities, Power and Articulation* (Routledge 2016).
2. *See* Directive 2001/86/EC of 8 October 2001 supplementing the Statute for a European company with regard to the involvement of employees, OJ L 294, 15.11.2022.
3. *See* Art. 133 Directive 2017/1132 of the European Parliament and of the Council of 14 June 2017 relating to certain aspects of company law. The provision has replaced Art. 16 Directive 2005/56/EC of the European Parliament and of the Council of 26 October 2005 on cross-border mergers of limited liability companies.

divisions:[4] In the event that the parties do not have reached an agreement on employee involvement, so-called subsidiary rules apply which guarantee to employees their acquired rights of board-level representation as applied before the establishing of the European Company.[5]

Such board-level representation schemes give employees a voice in the corporate structure of companies and are embedded in corporate law. In two-tier systems, as in Germany, board-level employee representation takes place in the supervisory boards (*Aufsichtsräte*), whereas it is integrated into the boards of directors in one-tier systems of corporate governance. In contrast to employee representation through works councils, workers' delegates or joint committees that are primarily dealing with workplace-related issues such as discipline, working time schemes or health and safety at work, the representation in the boardroom gives employees the power to participate in the decision-making process of the company and goes well beyond work-related issues.

Through these participatory schemes, employees normally become non-executive directors on the board of directors; it is unusual that one or even more of them become executive directors.[6] In two-tier systems, employee representation takes place on a supervisory board. These employee representatives do not have the status of directors, but their role is similar to a non-executive director, as the supervisory board not only controls the managing board but also has a considerable influence in the determination of the company's strategy. The same applies to board-level representation schemes under EU law, namely in the European Company and in companies resulting from a cross-border merger.

The legal status of these employee representatives in boards of directors or supervisory boards is twofold. On the one hand, it is in many Member States determined by national labour law that employee representatives shall be employees of the company: only in Member States, where employee representatives shall be appointed or proposed by a trade union, it is often not a requirement for the representatives to be employees of the company.[7] Even though their status as employees of the company is being modified – they are, for instance, released from their contractual duty to work insofar as they are exercising their board mandate – they remain bound by the duties resulting from their employment contract. On the other hand, the legal status of the employee representative is also fixed by company law: as

4. *See* Art. 86l and Art. 160m Directive 2017/1132 relating to certain aspects of company law which were introduced by the 'Company-Law-Package' cf. Directive 2019/2121 of 27 November 2019 amending Directive (EU) 2017/1132 as regards cross-border conversions, mergers and divisions, OJ L 321 12.12.2019, 12.
5. *See* Part 3 'Standard rules of participation' of the Annex to Directive 2001/86/EC of 8. October 2001.
6. One example of an executive director coming from the employees' side is the German 'Works Director' (*Arbeitsdirektor*) under section 33 German Act on Co-determination (*Mitbestimmungsgesetz* (MitbestG)) of 1976 who is the HR chief executive of the company: even though the law allows that the 'Works Director' has been elected against the votes of the employees' bench in the supervisory board, it is widespread practice that he or she comes from the employees' side.
7. In Germany, the MitbestG reserves some of the seats on the employees' bench within the supervisory board to trade unions which are represented in the company: they have the right to propose candidates for a number of seats on the employees' bench in the supervisory board; *see* section 7(2) MitbestG.

board members, they are embedded in a net of rights and duties resulting from company law, such as the loyalty duty by which board members are bound. In most Member States, having established a board-level representation scheme, employee representatives on boards of directors or supervisory boards are generally deemed to have the same rights and duties as board members representing shareholders.[8] As a result, they have, for instance, the right to vote and shall receive the same remuneration for the exercise of their board mandate as the shareholders' representatives do; as to their duties, they are bound - as representatives of shareholders are - to the loyalty duty, to duties of care and may be held liable for breaches of their duties of care. Their legal position under company law is not only determined by statutory law but is also influenced by corporate governance principles that have been set out in Corporate Governance Codes adopted in EU Member States, and also at international level, although not all of these principles have been enshrined in compulsory rules but only in recommendations, normally for listed companies.[9] The legal position of employee representatives in board-level representation schemes, determined by labour law as well as by company law, is therefore Janus-faced.

Labour law and company law as the two areas of law that determine the legal status of employee representatives on boards do not always live together in harmony and may come into conflict with each other. A full subordination of employee representatives to company law may create tensions with their key function to give the workforce a voice within the company's corporate structure. The following lines aim to analyse some of these conflicts between labour and company law arising from the double legal status of employee representatives on boards. The question behind this is how labour and company can be reconciled in order to resolve these conflicts between them. When analysing this question, it is not possible to take into account the national laws of all Member States. Instead, emphasis shall be laid on selected national laws in Europe such as German, Dutch, Luxembourgish, and French law.

A fundamental question in the present context, to be dealt with in §10.02, is whether employee representatives in boards have to be considered as board members, only representing the interests of the workforce in the board and accordingly the interests of one stakeholder group within the company, or as independent board members, as the Commission Recommendation of 15 February 2005 on the role of non-executive or supervisory directors of listed companies and on the committees of the (supervisory) board[10] supposes. The answer to this question necessarily has implications for the understanding of the company's interest to be promoted by board members. Section 10.03 raises the question of the duties of care employee representatives in boards are submitted to and will exemplify the problem by analysing whether employee

8. Pars pro toto, I only refer to the German context, *see* Bundesgerichtshof (BGH), *judgment of 25 February 1982 – II ZR 123/81*, in Arbeitsrechtliche Praxis (AP) MitbestG § 25 No. 2, and section 3(3) Act on the Co-determination in the Coal- and Mining Sector (*Montan-Mitbestimmungsgesetz*).
9. The existing Corporate Governance Codes are accessible at the website of the European Corporate Governance Institute (ECGI), at: https://ecgi.global/content/codes.
10. Commission Recommendation of 15 February 2005 on the role of non-executive or supervisory directors of listed companies and on the committees of the (supervisory) board (Text with EEA relevance), OJ L 52, 25.02.2005, 51.

representatives bring with them the necessary skills to exercise their board mandate and analyses mechanisms to purchase them on the job. Section 10.04 examines whether the confidentiality duty which also board members from the employees' side are submitted to allow the employee representatives in the boards to disclose information about the deliberations of the board to employee representatives at other levels (e.g., works councils). The fifth and final section of the chapter shifts from conflicts between employee representatives on boards and their company to a loyalty conflict between employee representatives on the boards and the workforce which they are supposed to represent and which may arise from the payment of a (considerable) remuneration for serving on a board of directors or a supervisory board.

§10.02 INDEPENDENCE OF EMPLOYEE REPRESENTATIVES IN BOARDS?

Employee representatives have been elected by the company's workforce or, as it is the case in some national schemes, have been appointed by a trade union represented within the company. They may therefore be considered as persons who authentically represent the interests of the employees by whom they have been elected; the only exception is the Dutch model of the *Struktuurregeling*, where the company committee (*ondernemingsraad*), representing the employees of the company, has the right to propose only candidates who are not employed by the company to the general meeting of shareholders.[11] Leaving aside the Dutch case, board members of the employees' side seem to represent the interests of one specific stakeholder group within the company and do not seem to belong to the independent board members of which a sufficient number should be elected to the board of directors or the supervisory board according to corporate governance principles. Nonetheless, it has been controversially discussed whether employee representatives are independent board members.[12] The response to this question is of particular interest in the present context since it may inform us on whether board members elected or appointed by the employees' side (only) represent the particular interest of the workforce or the interest of the company as a whole.

[A] Independence of Employee Representatives Despite Their Employment Relationship?

Since the 1990s, it has been recognised as an element of a good corporate governance that a minimum of directors or members of a supervisory board should be

11. Article 2:153(2) and 2:263(2) Dutch Civil Code (*Burgerlijk Wetboek*).
12. For those who consider employee representatives as independent, *see, e.g.*, Jan Lieder, *Das unabhängige Aufsichtsratsmitglied: Zu den Änderungen des Deutschen Corporate Governance Kodex*, 8 NZG 569, 571 (2005). The majority of doctrine does not see them as independent board members: *see, e.g.*, Marco Staake, *Arbeitnehmervertreter als unabhängige Aufsichtsratsmitglieder?* 19 NZG 853 et seq. (2016); Markus Roth, *Unabhängige Aufsichtsratsmitglieder*, 175 ZHR 605, 630 et seq. (2011).

independent.[13] These independent directors shall increase the quality of decision-making in boards by avoiding *a priori* potential conflicts of interest in which board members may be involved. Paragraph 13.1. of Recommendation 2005/162/EC of the European Commission of 15 February 2005 on the role of non-executive or supervisory directors of listed companies and on the committees of the (supervisory) board[14] requires for the independence of directors that they are 'free of any business, family or other relationship, with the company, its controlling shareholder or the management of either, that creates a conflict of interest such as to impair [their] judgment'. In order to ensure an 'impair' decisions of boards, the Commission recommends that 'a sufficient number of independent non-executive or supervisory directors should be elected to the (supervisory) board of companies to ensure that any material conflict of interest involving directors will be properly dealt with' but does not propose a fixed number or percentage of independent directors. Pursuant to the Commission Recommendation, it is up to the autonomy of the corporation to determine which number of independent directors is appropriate. This Commission Recommendation has been implemented by many Corporate Governance Codes in the Member States.[15]

Paragraph 1 of Annex 2 to the Commission Recommendation provides various criteria, concretising the independence of directors. Of particular interest in the present context is subparagraph (b) of the Recommendation, pursuant to which directors shall 'not be an employee of the company or an associated company, and not having been in such a position for the previous three years, except when the non-executive or supervisory director does not belong to senior management and has been elected to the (supervisory) board in the context of a system of workers' representation recognised by law and providing for adequate protection against abusive dismissal and other forms of unfair treatment'.

There is no doubt that directors on the board need to be independent of management.[16] As far as external employee representatives such as trade union representatives not employed by the company are concerned, their independence vis-à-vis the company's management is not in question since they are not in an employment relationship with the company. If one takes seriously the Commission Recommendation, employee representatives who are employed by the company would have to be considered as not independent of management, as their status of employees is one of dependence on the company as their employer: as a matter of fact, it must be doubted that employees who are subjected to the company's power to direct their work are able to independently control as board members the management of their company. However, the Commission Recommendation recognises as an exception from this dependence of employees that the board member 'has been elected to the (supervisory) board in the context of a system of workers' representation recognised by

13. For a recent example, *see* OECD, *G20/OECD Principles of Corporate Governance* 57-58 (VI.E. 2015), available at: https://ecgi.global/content/codes.
14. *Supra* n. 10.
15. *See, e.g.*, Recommendation C.6. German Corporate Governance Code, Principle 10 French Corporate Governance Code of Listed Corporations and Principle 2.1. Dutch Corporate Governance Code.
16. *See, e.g.*, Theodor Baums, *Unabhängige Aufsichtsratsmitglieder*, 180 ZHR 697 (2016).

law and providing for adequate protection against abusive dismissal and other forms of unfair treatment'; normally, employee representatives will meet these requirements of the Recommendation since most of the existing national systems provide a protection against unfair dismissal or 'other forms of unfair treatment'.[17]

The explanation for this exception is the Commission's intention to avoid that statutory employee representation schemes come under pressure by this recommendation that an appropriate number of board members shall be independent: The Commission Recommendation has therefore the intention to safeguard existing employee board-level representation schemes in the Member States.[18]

[B] Inevitable Conflicts of Interest

Despite this qualification as independent board members by Commission Recommendation 2005/162/EC, it cannot be denied that employee representatives on boards of directors or supervisory boards nonetheless pursue the interests of the workforce of the company they are representing. They have been directly or indirectly elected by the workforce or – in some of the national participation schemes – have been appointed by trade unions which are represented within the company. Their appointment may be revoked under certain conditions when the workforce considers that one of its representatives does not pursue its interests.[19] This function to give the workforce a voice in boardroom deliberations inevitably expose employee representatives to conflicts.

One good example is employment protection in the case of a corporate restructuring process. Employee representatives will normally try to protect existing employment within the company even though a corporate restructuring might be necessary and require a reduction of the workforce. In this event, employee representatives will typically prioritise employment protection. Closely related to their attitude towards corporate restructuring processes in the company is their typical behaviour within the board in the case of a hostile takeover bid referring to their company. In this situation, the employees' interest in safeguarding employment in the company will often be opposed to takeovers that may be reasonable from an economic perspective. In some countries with a high level of board-level representation of employees such as Germany, where half of the seats in the supervisory boards of corporations with two

17. For example, section 26 MitbestG 1976 or Article L.426-9 Labour Code of Luxembourg.
18. The Commission Recommendation is certainly a reaction to the US-American Sarbanes-Oxley-Act of 2002. Since this Act, the 'Listed Company Manual' of the New York Stock Exchange (NYSE) requires in its section 303A.01 that the majority of members of a board of directors in a listed company are independent directors. Through their qualification as independent board members, European companies, applying a board-level employee representation, shall preserve the capacity to be listed at the NYSE.
19. Under German law, for instance, a revocation of an employee representative in the supervisory board requires a majority of 75% of the workforce for a revocation: *see, e.g.*, section 23 MitbestG. In Luxembourg, a simple majority of the votes within the company's délégations du personnel seems to be enough for a revocation; cf. Art. L. 426-7(2) Code du travail lux. And for France Art. L. 225-32 Code de Commerce provides that employee representatives in boards may only be revoked in case of a serious breach of duties by judicial decision.

thousand or more employees are reserved to employee representatives,[20] these employee participation schemes may become a structural obstacle to the growth of a takeover market.[21]

Another example of inevitable conflicts of interest that employee representatives may be exposed to is their involvement in collective bargaining procedures or their participation in a strike. In these cases, the right to bargain collectively and the right to strike need to be reconciled with the corporate duty of board members to act in the interest of the company. This conflict is not only of a theoretical nature as one famous case in Germany, the so-called Case *Bsirske*,[22] may show. In 2002, *Frank Bsirske*, then president of the German services' trade union *Vereinte Dienstleistungsgewerkschaft* (ver.di) and at the same time vice-president of the supervisory board of the German Airline *Lufthansa*, was one of the promoters of a strike movement against *Fraport*, the owner of Frankfurt International Airport. Due to the strikes, led by ver.di, *Lufthansa* lost more than EUR 20 million of turnover. Various shareholders challenged *Bsirske*'s role in the organisation of the strike against *Fraport*, which indirectly affected *Lufthansa*, and argued that his behaviour was in breach of the company's interest and that he would therefore be liable for the damages caused to the company. The case did not come before the courts, but in the following annual shareholders' meeting, the majority of the shareholders refused to discharge him.[23]

The balancing of the right to collective bargaining and to collective action on the one side and the duty of directors to act in the company's interest under corporate law on the other remains therefore an open question. Even though the case is peculiar, and one must doubt whether it might happen in other European countries, it is not without interest to briefly sketch how the German legal doctrine has been dealing with the *Bsirske* case. It is not surprising that there has been a wide range of assessments and that particularly company lawyers have opined that *Bsirske*'s duty to respect the company's interest would outweigh the right to strike. The majority of labour lawyers seem, however, to take a different stance and consider that employee representatives on boards have the right to participate in a lawful strike even though the strike is directed against the company. The details of the exercise of their right to strike are still controversial. In the 1970s and 1980s, a number of authors only considered a 'passive' strike participation of employee representatives in boards as lawful and not their 'active' participation, i.e., the involvement in the organisation of the strike within the trade union. By now, the prevailing opinion in the labour law doctrine seems to be that also those employee representatives in boards are entitled to go on strike who have been involved, due to their function within the trade union calling for the strike, in the

20. *See* section 1(1) MitbestG.
21. *See, e.g.*, Klaus Hopt, *Vergleichende Corporate Governance*, 175 ZHR 444, 505 et seq. (2011) with further references.
22. For a fuller account of the facts of this case, *see* Otto Ernst Kempen, *Fernwirkungen von Arbeitskämpfen auf die Unternehmensmitbestimmung? (Der Fall Bsirske)* 537, 442 (Alfred Söllner et al eds, Verlag C.H. Beck 2005).
23. This refusal of discharge had no direct impact on the position of Bsirske. Lufthansa did not sue him for the damages caused by the strike.

organisation of the strike.[24] Thus, company law and labour law doctrines seem to be divided upon this question.

It is clear from this doctrinal debate in Germany, however, that the participation of employee representatives in a strike does impede a normal exercise of their mandate in the supervisory board.[25] Although their mandate does not end or is going to be suspended due to their participation in a strike, they are excluded from all decisions to be taken within the board regarding the strike. Otherwise, employee representatives on boards would be able to influence the decisions of the board which refer to the strike, including the company's negotiation strategy; this would obviously affect the independence of the company during a strike. It seems that this conflict between board-level representation and the right to strike has not been dealt with in other European legal orders so far. Nor does Directive 2001/86/EC provide a solution to this conflict for the European Company. Hence, it depends on the interpretation of national law whether employee representatives may invoke their right to strike and to which extent the participation in a strike affects their legal status within a board of directors or a supervisory board. Since the right to strike is a fundamental right, guaranteed by Article 11 ECHR,[26] Article 28 EU Charter of Fundamental Rights[27] and by Article 3 ILO Convention No. 87 on Freedom of Association and the Right to Organise,[28] due consideration shall be given to it though.

In the light of these inevitable conflicts, employee representatives on boards cannot be considered as independent board members. Although they are bound by the duty to respect the interest of the company, as all other board members, their presence in the boardrooms – be it in companies according to the applicable national board-level representation scheme or in European Companies – aims at giving the interests of the company's workforce a voice in the control of management and in strategic decisions of the board. However, this restraint must not be a contradiction to the duty of board

24. In this sense Martin Henssler *§ 26 Mitbestimmungsgesetz* (Matthias Habersack & Martin Henssler eds, Verlag C.H. Beck 4th ed. 2018) para. 30 with further references; for a more detailed analysis, *see* Peter Hanau & Ulrich Wackerbarth, *Unternehmensmitbestimmung und Koalitionsfreiheit: Interessenkonflikte von Gewerkschaftsvertretern im Aufsichtsrat* 70 et seq. (Nomos Verlagsgesellschaft 2004). *See also* Achim Seifert, *Unternehmensinteresse und Aufsichtsratsmitbestimmung im Spannungsverhältnis* 258, 270 et seq. (Ulrich Jürgens et al, eds, Nomos Verlagsgesellschaft 2007).
25. Seifert *supra* n. 24, at 275.
26. Since its judgment of 21 April 2009 in the Case *Enerji Yapi-Yol Sen v. Turkey*, application No. 68959/01, [2009] ECHR 2251, the ECtHR considers that the right to strike is part of the right to freedom of association within the meaning of Art. 11 ECHR. For a fuller analysis of the ECtHR's case law on the right to strike, *see* Filip Dorssemont, *The Right to Take Collective Action under Article 11 ECHR* (Filip Dorssemont et al. eds, Hart Publishing 2013) with further references.
27. Due to Art. 51(1) ECFR, the fundamental rights of the Charter are only limited in scope as they are only addressed to the institutions, bodies, offices and agencies of the Union with due regard for the principle of subsidiarity and to the Member States only when they are implementing Union law.
28. For an overview on the right to strike under Art. 3 ILO Convention No. 87, *see* Jean-Michel Servais, *International Labour Law* 107 (Wolters Kluwer 6th ed. 2020) with further references. For the case law of the Freedom of Association Committee, concretising the right to strike within the meaning of Convention No. 87, *see* ILO, *Freedom of Association – Compilation of the Decisions of the Freedom of Association Committee* paras 751 et seq. (International Labour Office 6th ed. 2018).

members to act in the company's interest. As a matter of fact, more and more national company law systems have been recognising that the employees' interest is one element of the company's interest and that board members shall also take into consideration the interests of the company's employees in their decision-making process. Examples for this legal evolution are section 172, paragraph 1, point (b) of the UK's Companies Act[29] and Article 1833, paragraph 2 of the French Civil Code, introduced by the '*Loi PACTE*' of 2019,[30] according to which a company shall be managed in its best interest, taking into account, *inter alia*, the social relevance of the decisions; equally, under German company law is recognised that the employees' interest shall be one element to be taken into account by the board of directors (*Vorstand*).[31] But leaving aside this recent evolution of company law, it results from the statutory recognition of employee voice in boardrooms that the duty of board members to promote the company's interest when exercising their mandate undergoes a profound change from an essentially substantive to a rather procedural content, obligating shareholders' and employees' representatives within boards to cooperate in good faith:[32] thus, the company's interest marks the duty of all board members to reconcile the different group interests, represented within the boardroom, in a constructive way and a spirit of cooperation.

§10.03 DUTIES OF CARE AND DIRECTORS' DUTIES OF SKILL

Board members are submitted to a number of duties of care when exercising their mandate. Breaches of these duties of care may have far-reaching consequences. Board members may be held liable by the company for their wrongdoing; in many cases, however, the effects of liability have been softened by Directors' & Officers' Insurances.[33] In some cases, the breach of a duty of care fulfils the conditions of a criminal offence and may be subject to a criminal prosecution of the board member.[34] Another consequence may be the removal of the board member by the general meeting of shareholders in the one-tier system and by the general meeting of shareholders[35] or by the court in two-tier systems.[36] This chapter does not aim at exhaustively treating the various duties of care which employee representatives on the boards are submitted to. Instead, emphasis shall be laid on one specific duty of care that has a particular

29. For an analysis of this new provision, *see* Paul L. Davies et al., *Gower Principles of Modern Company Law* 286-287 (Thomson Reuters 11th ed. 2021).
30. *LOI n° 2019-486 du 22 mai 2019 relative à la croissance et la transformation des entreprises (1)*, Journal Officiel de la République Française of 22 May 2019.
31. *See, e.g.*, Gerald Spindler, *Münchener Kommentar zum Aktiengesetz: AktG*, § 76, para. 66 (Verlag C.H. Beck 5th ed. 2019).
32. For the German context, *see* Seifert, *supra* n. 24, at 264-265.
33. For a detailed analysis of D & O insurances, *see* Simon Deakin, Helmut Koziol & Olaf Riss, *Directors' & Officers' (D & O) Liability* (Verlag De Gruyter 2018).
34. For example, a breach of the confidentiality duty of board members under German law: cf. section 404 AktG.
35. For example, Art. L. 225-75(2) French Commercial Code.
36. *See, e.g.*, section 103(3) AktG. The removal by the Court requires an important reason (*wichtiger Grund*).

relevance for employee representatives: the board members' duty of skills and to dispose of the necessary knowledge to exercise their mandate.

That board members shall have the necessary skills and knowledge to complete their tasks properly is widely recognised.[37] To put it in the words of the Commission Recommendation, the board 'should ensure that it is composed of members who, as a whole have the required diversity of knowledge, judgment and experience [...]'.[38] Thus, the skills and knowledge of board members may vary depending on various factors such as the size of the company, the sector the company is operating in and the task a specific board member shall complete within the board: a board member who forms part of the board's audit committee needs to have another expertise than a board member who is going to become a member of the board's remuneration committee or who shall control management in the field of production or marketing.

Only a few examples will suffice in the present context: there have to be board members experienced in the technology of products or services the company is offering, in the situation and evolution of the markets in which the company is operating, and some of the board members need to have a specific expertise in accountability or risk management. In companies without an employee board-level representation, the shareholders may fulfil these skill expectations of corporate governance by proposing to the general meeting of shareholders a list of candidates for the board of directors or the supervisory board, disposing collectively of the necessary knowledge, skills, and experience.

Needless to say, this duty of skill also applies to employee representatives on boards. However, it has been repeatedly questioned that employee representatives normally meet these requirements and are sufficiently prepared for their membership in boards. As a matter of fact, they have been elected by the workforce of the company: these elections are more of a political decision of the workforce on who is considered the most apt among the candidates to pursue the employees' interests in the boardroom, their skills to exercise a board mandate being of minor relevance. The skills employee representatives bring to boardroom discussions are normally different from those of shareholders' representatives. As employees of the company, they may bring their professional experiences and expertise, often acquired to a considerable extent within the company, and a sound knowledge of the workflow. Only in a few cases, employee representatives will have the necessary skill to exercise their board mandate when acceding to the board, such as employee representatives who belong to the executive staff, having a sufficient expertise to effectively control management; employees who have been working in the accountability or the controlling of the company will even have the expertise to become a member of the audit committee.

---

37. This duty of care is supposed by para. 11.1. Commission Recommendation 2005/162/EC on the role of non-executive or supervisory directors of listed companies and on the committees of the (supervisory) board. Equally, national company laws have recognised this duty: cf. section 174 UK Company Act 2006; for Germany, cf. BGH, *Urt. v. 15.11.1982 – II ZR 27/82*, 36 NJW 991 (1983).
38. *See* Commission Recommendation of 15 February 2005 on the role of non-executive or supervisory directors of listed companies and on the committees of the (supervisory) board (Text with EEA relevance), 2005/162/EC, para. 11.1.

Leaving aside these cases, the normal employee representatives will not have the necessary skills to control management decisions on strategy, compliance or accountability, when becoming a board member unless he or she brings in specific experiences in these fields such as employees of the company's finance department, experienced in accountability. Their duties of care in their capacity as board members, resulting from corporate governance principles, and the purpose to give employees a say in boardroom decision may therefore come into conflict.

The typical board member on the employees' side normally needs therefore training to comply with the duty of skill under corporate law and to be able to exercise their mandate in an appropriate manner. Having said that, it is surprising that only a few national board-level-representation schemes entitle employee representatives to training measures aiming at preparing them for the exercise of their board mandate.[39] It is therefore in most Member States up to trade unions to organise workshops, seminars and other training measures for employee representatives. One example are the seminars organised by the German Hans-Böckler-Foundation, an organism of the German Trade Union Federation (*Deutscher Gewerkschaftsbund* (DGB)) and subsidised by unionised employee representatives who shall transfer most of their remuneration as board members to the foundation:[40] these seminars, for which no fees have to be paid, may also be attended by non-unionised employee representatives.[41] Another example is the 'European Worker Participation Competence Centre' (EWPCC) within the European Trade Union Institute (ETUI) and financed by the 'European Workers Participation Fund' (EWPF).[42] The advantage of these seminars, offered by trade union institutions, is that they are tailored to the specific needs of employee representatives on boards and that the content is taught from an employee perspective. Nonetheless, it must be doubted whether these seminars are sufficient for them since they are limited to one or two days and may only give a general overview on relevant subjects like accountability, risk management, etc. Their length will normally not be enough to enable employee representatives to effectively exercise their mandate as board members or as members of one of the board's committees (e.g., the audit committee).

What is actually needed are additional training measures for (all) board members, taking account of the requirements of board membership in a specific company from which also employee representatives on boards would benefit. Such training should be funded by the company itself. For the time being, there is no general duty of the company to devote the necessary resources for the training even though such duty has been recognised by corporate governance. The OECD, in its 2015 'Principles of

39. One example is Art. L. 225-30-2 of the French Code de Commerce.
40. *See infra* §10.05.
41. *See, e.g.*, the seminar programme for 2022, available at: https://www.mitbestimmung.de/html/bockler-seminare-fur-aufsichtsrate-11989.html. According to section 2(1) Statutes of the Hans-Böckler-Foundation, the purpose of the foundation – 'the promotion of research and training and the idea of worker participation' – shall be realised, *inter alia*, by financing and promoting seminars and workshops for employees of companies submitted to a statutory board-level representation scheme.
42. For further information on the EWPCC, *see*: https://www.worker-participation.eu/About-WP/European-WP-Competence-Centre.

Corporate Governance', recommends, for example, providing 'training for employee representatives, so that this representation is exercised effectively and best contributes to the enhancement of board skills, information and independence'; various national corporate governance codes have followed this example.[43] Only for the financial sector, there is a duty to fund training measures: Article 91(9) of Directive 2013/36/EG of 26 June 2013 on access to the activity of credit institutions and the prudential supervision of credit institutions and investment firms provides, for instance, that 'institutions shall devote adequate human and financial resources to the induction and training of members of the management body'. Not only this statutory rule of EU law, limited in its scope, but also the French rule of Article L. 225-30-2 Code de Commerce[44] might be points of departure for the adoption of a general rule in the national laws of Member States, entitling (all) board members to sufficient training measures.

§10.04 THE CONFIDENTIALITY DUTY OF EMPLOYEE REPRESENTATIVES

Another controversial field of conflict between the status of employee representatives and company law refers to the confidentiality duty to which all board members are submitted. According to the national company laws of Member States, members of a board of directors or of a supervisory board shall respect the confidentiality of the deliberations within the board.[45] This duty to preserve the confidentiality of the deliberations within the boards implies that board members, including employee representatives, do not disclose information on the deliberations of the board, namely information on the board's decision-making, to thirds.

[A] Information Disclosure to Other Employee Representatives

However, one of the controversial questions still is whether this duty also forbids a disclosure of information on board deliberations to other employee representatives within the company, such as works councils,[46] personnel delegates,[47] joint committees[48] or officials of a trade union, represented within the company. As a matter of fact, the exchange of information between employee board members and other employee representatives is necessary for both sides: it enables employee representatives at the different levels of representation (workplace, plant or company) to give coherence to

43. *See, e.g.*, Recommendation D.11 German Corporate Governance Code: 'The company shall support Supervisory Board members sufficiently upon their appointment and during training and professional development measures, and shall disclose such measures in the report of the Supervisory Board.' *See also* 14.1. French Corporate Governance Code of Listed Corporations.
44. Article L. 225-30-2 Code de commerce entitles employee representatives in boards to participate in training measures adapted to the exercise of their board mandate and to be taken in charge by the company.
45. *See, e.g.*, section 116 German Act on Public Limited Companies (*Aktiengesetz*).
46. For example, the German or Austrian works councils (*Betriebsräte*).
47. As, for example, the personnel delegates (*délégations du personnel*) under Luxembourgish law.
48. For example, the French Social and Economic Committee (*Comité social et économique*).

their activities and to avoid thereby conflicts which may arise between different bodies of employee representation within the company. In a number of European countries (e.g., Austria, Germany and Luxembourg), employee representatives are or may be at the same time board members and members of a works council.[49] Such communication and exchange between employee representatives on the boards and other levels of employee representation has been facilitated in some national systems, which require or at least allow that employee representatives on boards of directors or supervisory boards are at the same time members of the works council or the worker delegation.[50] The extreme opposite is the French case where the board membership is incompatible with other representation mandates like the *délégué du personnel*, the *délégué syndical* or the membership in the social and economic committee.[51]

Such information channels on the employees' side may come into conflict with the company's interest for confidentiality. As far as can be seen, the question has played an important role in German law; the following observations will therefore focus on the German example, in particular on the relationship between employee representatives in the supervisory boards and the works councils. Section 79(1)(iv) of the German Works Constitution Act (*Betriebsverfassungsgesetz*) explicitly authorises works council members to disclose confidential information to the employee representatives in the supervisory board. In this direction, a communication between employee representatives on plant and company level is explicitly authorised. However, employee representatives in the supervisory boards shall respect their confidentiality duty also towards works councils or other employee representatives: The Federal Labour Court (*Bundesarbeitsgericht*)[52] does not recognise an exception in this case, even though also works council members are submitted to a specific confidentiality duty.[53] As a result, employee representatives in the boards are practically not authorised to communicate with other employee representatives or employees on their work in the supervisory board. This case law may lead to a disconnection between the different levels of employee representation and may hinder a coherent and effective defence of employee interests in the company.[54]

---

49. For the German case, *see*, *e.g.*, Kurt Biedenkopf, Wolfgang Streeck & Hellmut Wißmann, *Bericht der wissenschaftlichen Mitglieder der Kommission zur Modernisierung der deutschen Unternehmensmitbestimmung* 27 et seq. (Hans Böckler Stiftung 2006). Regarding Austria, *see* section 110 of the Austrian Act on the Works Constitution (*Arbeitsverfassungsgesetz*) which provides that the Works Council is entitled to send several of his members in the supervisory board of the company.
50. For the German case, *see* Biedenkopf *supra* n. 49. Regarding Austria, *see* section 110 of the Austrian Act on the Works Constitution (*Arbeitsverfassungsgesetz*).
51. Article L. 225-30 Code de commerce.
52. *See* BAG 23.10.2008 - 2 ABR 59/07, NZA 855 et seq. (2009).
53. *See* section 79(3) of the Works Constitution Act (*Betriebsverfassungsgesetz* (BetrVG)). It must be admitted, however, that the confidentiality duty of works council members under section 79(3) BetrVG is not identical with that of members of the supervisory board as section 79(3) BetrVG is limited to the disclosure of trade secrets (*Betriebsgeheimnisse*) that have been declared as such by the employer.
54. For a more in-depth analysis of this important aspect, *see* Otto Kahn-Freund, *Industrial Democracy*, 6 ILJ 65, 77 et seq. (1977), referring to the Report of the Committee of Inquiry on Industrial Democracy, London 1977 ('Bullock-Report').

[B] Specific Requirements of Insider Law

The question of confidentiality may also have a capital market law dimension when companies with a board-level employee representation scheme are listed on the stock market. In this case, the disclosure of information on board meetings to other elected employee representatives such as works councils or trade union representatives may infringe the prohibition of insider dealing under Article 10 of Regulation (EU) 596/2014 of 16 April 2014 on market abuse (market abuse regulation).[55] Pursuant to this provision, the disclosing of inside information to any third party is forbidden 'unless such disclosure is made in the normal course of the exercise of the employment, profession or duties' by the person in question.

In Case C-384/02, *Grøngaard*, the Grand Chamber of the CJEU[56] had to decide whether Article 3(a) of Directive 2003/6/EC on insider dealing and market manipulation, which entirely corresponds to Article 10 of Regulation (EU) 596/2014 of 16 April 2014 on market abuse, allows the disclosure of inside information by an employee representative in the board of directors to other employee representatives outside the board. The dispute in the main proceedings came from a Danish context. Following an extraordinary meeting of *RealDanmark*'s board of directors, whereof Mr *Grøngaard* was a member as employee representative, he disclosed to the General Secretary of his trade union, Mr *Bang*, the *RealDanmark*'s plans to merge with *Danske Bank*. Mr *Bang* then consulted his two deputy General Secretaries as well as one of his colleagues in the trade union secretariat, Mr *Christensen*, on the planned merger. Mr *Christensen* bought shares in *RealDanmark* after having received this information and purchased additional shares when he got the planned date of the merger through Mr *Grøngaard*. When the merger was made public, the market price of *RealDanmark* shares rose by about 65%, and Mr *Christensen* sold his shares with considerable profit; he was subsequently sentenced for this insider dealing. But Mr *Grøngaard* and Mr *Bang* were also being prosecuted before the criminal court for having disclosed inside information.

The Grand Chamber of the CJEU ruled that the prohibition of insider dealing precludes in principle an employee representative on a board of directors from disclosing inside information which he has received in his capacity as board member to officials of his trade union 'unless there is a close link between the disclosure and the exercise of the employment, profession or duties, and that disclosure is strictly necessary for the exercise of that employment, profession, or duties' (paragraph 48). The Court of Justice emphasised that national courts 'must, in the light of the applicable national rules, take particular account of' the fact that this exception to the prohibition of disclosure of inside information must be interpreted strictly by national courts, that each additional disclosure is liable to increase the risk of that information being exploited for a purpose contrary to the prohibition and the sensitivity of the inside information.

55. Regulation (EU) 596/2014 of 16 April 2014 on market abuse OJ L 173, 12 June 2014, p. 1.
56. Case C-384/02, *Criminal proceedings against Knud Grøngaard and Allan Bang*, 22.11.2005, ECLI:EU:C:2005:708. CJEU (Grand Chamber).

Following this decision of the CJEU, the Member States dispose of a limited discretionary power when it comes to determining whether or not employee representatives on the boards of listed companies shall be allowed to disclose information, resulting from their board membership, to other employee representatives such as works councils or a trade union which is represented within the company. Hence, the answer to the question whether an employee representative on the board is in breach of his or her duty of confidentiality when disclosing insider information to other employee representatives outside the board depends on national law. The national laws of the Member States resolve this conflict in different ways. On the one hand, the Danish Supreme Court (*Højesteret*), for instance, which had to decide the case underlying the CJEU Case C-384/02, *Grøngaard*, considered that such a right to disclose information to a trade union representative is in line with Danish law and found the accused not guilty of insider dealing.[57] On the other hand, German law is much more severe in this respect, given that employee representatives on boards are not entitled to disclose information on board deliberations to other employee representatives within the company or to trade union representatives, without any exception (*see* §10.04[A] *supra*). In the latter case, the employee representative may be held liable for this breach of his or her duty of confidentiality and may be prosecuted before a criminal court for having disclosed inside information as the disclosure of insider information is a criminal offence.[58] Furthermore, he or she may be revoked from his office.

§10.05 REMUNERATION OF EMPLOYEE REPRESENTATIVES IN BOARDS

A third potential conflict that may arise from the presence of employee representatives on boards relates to the remuneration they receive when acting as members of the company's board of directors or the supervisory board.

In most national systems that have established board-level representation schemes, employee representatives are entitled to the same remuneration as board members representing shareholders.[59] This is a consequence of the principle underlying most employee board-level representation schemes that all board members have the same rights and duties. There are only a few schemes in which employee representatives exercise an honorary office and are therefore not entitled to a specific remuneration beyond their wage which they receive as employees of the company: one example is employee representation on the boards of so-called mixed corporations (*sociétés mixtes*), i.e., State-owned corporations, in France.[60] Although EU law does not explicitly provide such equal treatment, it is furthermore widespread that in agreements on employee participation in European Companies and in companies, resulting from a cross-border merger, the principle of equal treatment between shareholder and employee representatives in the boards has not been challenged. As far as the German

57. *See* Højesteret, judgment of 14 May 2009 - U 2009.2142 H.
58. *See* section 404 AktG.
59. For the German context *see, e.g., supra* n. 8, pp. 106, at 112 et seq.
60. Article 11(2) French Act of 26 July 1983 on the democratisation of the public sector (*Loi relative à la democratisation du secteur public*).

context is concerned, for instance, there seems to be no single case where a European Company agreement on employee participation in the board differentiates between shareholder and employee representatives concerning the payment.

As a result, employee representatives on boards of directors or supervisory boards may earn considerable remunerations, often exceeding their wages. This additional payment may cause distrust and envy within the workforce towards their representatives in the boards, suspected to exercise the representation mandate in order to increase their income and not for the sake of the best interest of the workforce, represented by them; moreover, the payment of a high remuneration as board member may further the sentiment within the workforce that its representatives rather belong to the managers' side and have lost contact with those who shall be represented by them. Such sentiments may lead to an erosion of solidarity on the employees' side, affecting the effectiveness of employee participation in the boards. In some cases, such 'alienation' between the workforce and its representatives in the board may also have negative impacts on strike movements against the company[61] if employee representatives in the board are at the same time trade union representatives, involved in the organisation of the strike. The equal treatment between shareholder and employee representatives may therefore turn into the opposite of what employee participation on the boards has created for.

On a national level, trade unions have tried to correct these potentially delegitimising effects of this strict application of the principle of equal treatment by imposing on their members who have been elected representatives in a board of directors or in a supervisory board to transfer a part of their remuneration to a fund, created by the unions. In Germany, for instance, unionised employee representatives in supervisory boards are required to transfer a significant part of their remuneration as board members to the Hans-Böckler-Foundation which funds research projects in the field of labour and industrial relations, gives scholarships to doctoral or postdoctoral researchers in social sciences and offers seminars to employee representatives in order to improve their skills.[62] German courts have recognised this model as lawful.[63] A similar model exists in various other countries that have established board-level representation schemes, such as France or Luxembourg.[64]

This model has also been adopted by the European Trade Union Confederation (ETUC). According to a resolution of October 2008, adopted by the Executive Committee of the ETUC, employee representatives in the board of directors or the supervisory board of a European Company and unionised in one of the trade unions, affiliated to the

61. Cf. §10.02[B].
62. For more details on the activities of the Hans-Böckler-Foundation, *see* https://www.boeckler.de/en/index.htm.
63. For an overview, *see* Achim Seifert, *Abführungspflichten von Arbeitnehmervertretern im Aufsichtsrat* BB, 1784 et seq. (2019) with further references.
64. On the French context, *see, e.g.*, Marie-Noelle Auberger, *Perceptions et représentations des représentants du personnel au conseil d'administration ou de surveillance: le cas des administrateurs salariés C.F.D.T.*, 113, 119 (Aline Conchon & Marie-Noelle Auberger eds, Documentation Française 2009); for Luxembourg, cf. Henri Goedert, *La représentation des salariés dans les organes des sociétés en droit luxembourgeois et en droit allemand*, 551 (Université de Nancy II 1983).

ETUC, shall transfer a part of their board member remuneration to their trade union: more precisely, they are obliged to 'transfer 10 percent of their remuneration if the remuneration is less than or equal to 3,500 Euros' and shall, 'in addition to this deduction [...], transfer 90 percent of any remaining remuneration over and above 3,500 Euros'.[65] These funds support, on the one hand, trade unions in the Member States, belonging to the ETUC, and their institutions (e.g., training facilities for employee representatives). On the other hand, more than 50% of the fund subsidises the EWPF, created by the ETUC, and administering the EWPCC of the ETUI.[66] The activities of the EWPCC are centred around the organisation of seminars and legal aid for employee representatives on boards.[67]

The effectiveness of this model, set up by the ETUC and by various national trade unions, heavily relies on the unionisation of employee representatives in boards. Only if they are submitted to these trade union rules by virtue of their union membership, trade unions are entitled to the transfer of a part of the remuneration which employee representatives receive in their capacity as directors or members of a supervisory council. The overall decreasing union density may limit the scope of this model. But even if most employee representatives are unionised, the model may be confronted with problems since it also depends on the loyalty of unionised employee representatives in the boards: as a matter of fact, there have always been unionised board members who have not been respecting the union rules and have not transferred part of their remuneration to their union. Hence, the model can only be an imperfect solution to the problem described above.

§10.06 CONCLUDING REMARKS

Systems with established employee board-level representation schemes tie together labour and company law. These schemes fulfil first and foremost functions closely related to labour law when ensuring that the interests of employees are represented within the board of directors or the supervisory board of the company. But the task to represent employees' interests in boardrooms is exercised in the legal forms of company law, as employee representatives become part of a body which is governed by company law. The chapter has tried to develop how these two areas of law, bound together in employee board-level representation schemes, and the logic behind each of them may come into conflict: on the one hand, the idea of labour law to give employees a voice in boardrooms and to enable them to pursue their interests collectively in boards of directors or supervisory boards of companies, and the purpose of company law to ensure a good corporate governance of companies on the other. In all conflicts that have been discussed above, these conflicting purposes of labour law and company

65. Cf. para. 7 Resolution of the Executive Committee of the ETUC on the European Worker Participation Fund of 15-16 October 2008, available at: https://www.worker-participation.eu/About-WP/European-WP-Competence-Centre/Documents.
66. *Supra* §10.03.
67. Further information on the EWPCC is available at: https://www.worker-participation.eu/About-WP/European-WP-Competence-Centre.

law need to be reconciled. There is certainly no general rule deciding whether one or the other of these two areas of law shall prevail in case of a conflict. It depends on the national legislature, establishing a board-level representation scheme, to dissolve tensions between the two fields of law.

CHAPTER 11

Occupational Safety and Health: A Fundamental Principle and Right at Work on Its Way to Include Managers

Ana Cristina Ribeiro Costa

§11.01 INTRODUCTION

Managers are seen as representing or embodying the employer, and thus are very important for the promotion of occupational safety and health (OSH) within the workplace. Their duties are usually statutorily defined, their responsibilities are high, and they are often jointly liable with the employer for any breach of OSH legislation.[1]

However, as individuals that perform their work and share the same working environment of the employees, they too may be subject to professional risks and may suffer occupational contingencies. In fact, not only experienced executives from large companies face occupational hazards[2] but also first-time managers and executives of

1. About the criminal, civil, administrative, and labour liability of the *alto directivo* in what concerns prevention of risks, cf. Juan García Blasco & Manuel González Labrada, *Alta dirección y prevención de riesgos laborales* 300-305 (José L. M. Pérez & Ángel L. De Val Tena eds, Granada Publishing Ltd 2010).
2. Among other interesting stories is the one of António Horta Osório, a Portuguese banking executive, CEO of Lloyds Banking Group from 2011 to 2021, who acknowledged he suffered from burnout, and admitted himself to a medical facility after days of sleep deprivation and symptoms like extreme exhaustion. Cf. Louise Carpenter, *The CEO of Lloyds Bank Turned Its Fortunes Around – But the Anxiety Almost Broke Him*, The Times (7 October 2017, 12.01 AM BST), https://www.thetimes.co.uk/article/the-ceo-of-lloyds-bank-turned-its-fortunes-around-but-the-anxiety-almost-broke-him-fg970cpjr.

small and medium enterprises cope with significant professional risks, particularly psychosocial risks, such as stress and burnout.[3]

Nevertheless, the nature of their relationship is relevant to analyse the protection they have regarding OSH. In fact, managers may be employees and, as such, protected by employment law standards, including OSH. If, on the contrary, they have a status of self-employed, contractor or independent workers, they may be protected regarding OSH but are subject to different rules. Within some jurisdictions, there is also a third concept of 'economically dependent workers', who are generally protected under OSH law.[4] Finally, in case they have contractual relationships exclusively governed by corporate law and if they are purely members of the board or executive and non-executive managers, they will likely not be protected.[5]

This chapter will thus analyse the risks to which managers are particularly exposed within their job performance. The international legal framework, particularly the European, regarding the protection of OSH will be analysed in order to assess whether they are protected within it. Afterwards, some national legal regimes will be compared, in order to realise to what extent managers benefit or not from different levels of regulation, depending on their status.

§11.02 MANAGERS AND OSH

As stated above, managers are subject to occupational risks. Such risks include not only ergonomic hazards - due to awkward postures, stationary positions, repetitive movements, among other risk factors - but also psychosocial risks.[6] The latter are eased by circumstances such as: (i) factors related to working conditions, (ii) social factors and (iii) personal factors.

---

3. Ben Laker et al., *What First-Time Managers Can Do to Address Burnout*, Harvard Business Review (19 June 2022), available at https://hbr.org/2022/03/what-first-time-managers-can-do-to-address-burnout. A Spanish court classified the death of the company's People Manager as a result of a heart attack as a work-related accident, on the understanding that it was due to the aggravation of the nervous stress from which he had been suffering, cf. *Sala de lo Social del Tribunal Superior de Justicia de Madrid*, STSJ de Madrid, 19-06-1990.
4. Francisco Liberal Fernandes refers there is a current openness from the EU Member States and social partners to acknowledge economically dependent work as a reality that should be subject to a certain degree of regulatory harmonisation, *see* Francisco L. Fernandes, *O conceito de trabalhador no direito social comunitário, Gestlegal* 104 (Gestlegal 2019). Emanuele Menegatti also emphasises that the Member States will 'be forced to move beyond the rigid dichotomy "employee"/"self-employed" and the attached outmoded approach to employment rights of "all or nothing"', *see* Emanuele Menegatti, *The Evolving Concept of 'Worker' in EU Law*, 12 ILLEJ 1, 82 (2019).
5. Discussing the interesting intersections between Corporate Law and Employment Law, Cristóbal Molina Navarrete, *La actualidad de la cuestión de las 'zonas concurrentes' entre el Derecho Mercantil y el Derecho del Trabajo. Apuntes a propósito del libro 'La representación orgánica y voluntaria en las sociedades de capital', del profesor Dr. Angel Martínez Gutiérrez*, 4 RGLJ 573-588 (2005).
6. Among other professional risks, such as the ones related to the physical environment, ergonomic and *in itinere* risks. The latter are enhanced, for example, by the business travels that the manager may have to do to perform the job, to which fatigue may be added, as well as risk factors associated with driving. José Antonio Fernández Avilés et al., *El trabajo en la economía colaborativa y la prevención de riesgos laborales* 93 (Borpi S. L. 2018).

Among factors related to working conditions and organisation that may facilitate the emergence of occupational risks are prolonged exposure to electromagnetic fields and display screens,[7] the participation of the manager in decision-making and the autonomy the managers have in their position. Besides, intra-group phenomena such as reciprocal conflicts (between colleagues, superiors and subordinates), as well as perversion of personal conduct and relationships, caused by rivalry, for example, and depending on the extent to which managers can rely on the other stakeholders, may also contribute to occupational risks, and particularly psychosocial risks.[8] Inter-group phenomena (with customers, between departments) which affect the whole organisation, such as organisational culture, methods of organisational change, leadership style, level of development of formal working groups, degree of participation, decision-making processes and negotiation,[9] may lead to professional risks. Finally, events such as the dismissal or resignation of an employee, serious disease or death of an employee, or judicial proceedings, may be specific risk factors for managers.[10]

Besides, external organisational factors may also contribute to occupational risks. Examples are static circumstances that affect the size and organisational structure of the company, such as the hierarchical organisation chart or conflicts with the administration, as well as dynamic events, such as changes in that organisation chart, company transformations, the financial situation of the company, loss of a client, conflict with a client, poor performance of the company, conflicts among partners or shareholders, or exposure to uncertainty due to phenomena such as Covid-19. Corporate restructurings include phenomena such as downsizing, merger, incorporation, acquisition, spin-off, outsourcing, temporary work, relocation, filing for bankruptcy or shutdown.[11]

Another important issue to address is the fact that the legislation, such as the Working Time Directive,[12] usually exempts managers from the limits provided for the maximum weekly working hours, mandatory daily or weekly rest periods or breaks. However, these exemptions may pose a harm to the safety and health of managers, who usually have an intensive rhythm and long working hours; are subject to high

7. Cf. the Council Directive 90/270/EEC of 29 May 1990, on the minimum safety and health requirements for work with display screen equipment.
8. Ángel Sánchez-Anguita Muñoz, *Psicopatologías laborales* 45 (Publicaciones Universidad Pontificia 2008).
9. *Ibid.*, 31.
10. Thomas Lechat & Olivier Torrès, *Les risques psychosociaux du dirigeant de PME: typologie et échelle de mesure des stresseurs professionnels*, 29 PME 3-4, 145 (2016), available at DOI: 10.7202/1038335ar.
11. Pilar Rivas Vallejo, *La prevención de los riesgos laborales de carácter psicosocial* 25 (Editorial Comares, 2009).
12. Cf. Art. 17 a), on the admissible derogations to certain provisions of Directive 2003/88/EC of the European Parliament and of the Council of 4 November 2003 concerning certain aspects of the organisation of working time, regarding 'managing executives or other persons with autonomous decision-taking powers'. However, we have to enhance that the concept of worker within this Directive has been broadly considered by the Court of Justice of the EU (CJEU) in cases such as Case C-428/09, *Union Syndicale Solidaires Isère v. Premier ministre and Others*, 14.10.2010, ECLI:EU:C:2010:612, and C-316/13, *Gérard Fenoll v. Centre d'aide par le travail 'La Jouvene' and Association de parents et d'amis de personnes handicapées mentales (APEI) d'Avignon*, 26.3.2015, ECLI:EU:C:2015:200.

levels of time pressure, short deadlines and short work cycles; and are constantly controlled on their progress and results.[13] In Case C-84/94, *United Kingdom of Great Britain and Northern Ireland v. Council of the EU*,[14] the CJEU recognised that damage is caused to workers' health by the amount of work requested, either by excessive working hours without a break or by the absolute absence of a rest break, particularly in intensive work that has to be completed in short periods of time.

Managers are also exposed to the continuous use of certain tools and new technologies of information and communication. These foster an uninterrupted connectivity that enables their users the freedom to self-exploit, not allowing themselves enough rest time and contributing to a poorer work-life balance.[15]

Social factors include the relations with third parties inside or outside the business organisation, whether they are clients, suppliers, patients, users, or any of those with whom the manager is required to establish contact. These relationships are a source of emotional destabilisation depending on their intensity, typology and the individual affected, and may trigger emotional imbalances. Besides, dynamic and non-structural factors can result from personal, emotional, or family-related circumstances, as well as from extraordinary, sporadic, and extreme situations of a professional nature. Some examples include conflicts arising from strikes, social, commercial or tax issues, or within companies affected by significant crises.[16]

Personal factors that relate to the manager's work, such as their personal engagement, competitiveness and work addiction, are also relevant. The latter is indeed more frequent among executives involved in economic or international activities, people aged 30-50 years old and upper-middle class, and managers, as the time they dedicate to work depends exclusively on them.[17]

Within these factors, we may also distinguish biological issues such as age. Indeed, health problems that prevent individuals from working long periods of time tend to increase significantly, like musculoskeletal disorders of the neck and back.[18] Besides, there are also non-static, transitory factors of the individual, motivated by

13. Stavroula Leka, et al., *Work-Related Psychosocial Risks: Key Definitions and an Overview of the Policy Context in Europe* 3 (Loic Lerouge ed., Springer Editions 2017).
14. Case C-84/94, *United Kingdom of Great Britain and Northern Ireland v. Council of the EU*, 12.11.1996, ECLI:EU:C:1996:431.
15. Avilés *supra* n. 6, at 88-93. Recently, the Spanish legislator defined that the employees that have managing functions shall be encompassed by the policies designed by the employer to define the exercise of the right to disconnect. About the need to enforce this right to employees with responsibilities, *see* Francisco Trujillo Pons, *Las personas trabajadoras que ocupan 'puestos directivos' y su derecho a la desconexión digital en el trabajo*, 1 Iuslabor 148-167 (2022) DOI: 10.31009/iuslabor.2022.i01.06. *See also* Directive (EU) 2019/1158 of the European Parliament and of the Council of 20 June 2019 on work-life balance for parents and carers and repealing Council Directive 2010/18/EU.
16. *Supra* n. 11, 28, 44.
17. *Ibid.*, 6, 27, 86.
18. Lourdes Tortosa Latonda et al., *Trabajo y envejecimiento. Mejora de las condiciones ergonómicas de la actividad laboral para la promoción de un envejecimiento saludable* 1 (Instituto de Biomecánica de Valencia 2002) http://envejecimiento.csic.es/documentos/documentos/imserso-estudiosidi-01.pdf.

health,[19] emotional changes or a biological state, which may influence and determine the emergence of psychosocial risks.

Moreover, the personal circumstances that the manager goes through, such as the death of a relative or close friend, a divorce, or other events of lesser intensity such as continuous family disputes, conflicting professional and family demands or little support at home, may influence the way the individual faces the job and psychological disposition towards its demands or requirements.[20] Alcohol and drug abuse and dependence also influence occupational health problems, as they usually lead to behavioural problems.[21] Finally, treatment for infectious diseases, nutritional aspects, physical activity, healthy sleep, stress related to personal financial circumstances, family distribution of household chores and mobility to work are all aspects that relate to personal well-being and may contribute to occupational risks.[22]

As such, it is obvious that managers – particularly executive managers, due to the specifics of their position and tasks – may be exposed to circumstances that may result in occupational risks that, in turn, may lead to consequences for their health, for their personal and family relationships, as well as for the company and the society. What we will assess is whether the OSH law provides for the prevention of those risks and reparation of the said consequences when their subjects are managers.

§11.03 INTERNATIONAL LEGAL FRAMEWORK OF OSH

Labour Law had its grounds in the mid-nineteenth century, with the development of industrialisation. OSH law emerged simultaneously with the recognition of the need to effectively regulate working conditions and improve the working environment.[23]

Hence, this theme has been the subject of attention from the International Labour Organization (ILO) almost since its establishment in 1919.[24] Convention No. 155 from 1981 is one of the most important instruments within OSH field, requiring States to implement a national policy of OSH.[25] It defines workers as 'all employed persons, including public employees' (Article 3(b)). However, States may exclude, in part or in

19. *Supra* n. 8, 39.
20. *Supra* n. 13, 3.
21. *Supra* n. 8, 107.
22. Manuel Velázquez, *Comparative Study of the Psychosocial Risks Prevention Enforcement by the European Labour Inspectorates* 40 (Loic Lerouge ed., Springer Editions 2017).
23. Manuel M. Roxo, *Direito da segurança e saúde no trabalho. Da prescrição do seguro à definição do desempenho, uma transição na regulação* 15 (Almedina 2011).
24. Although the first conventions excluded persons holding positions of supervision or management from their subjective scope – cf. e.g., Art. 2, a), Convention No. 1 (1919) on Hours of Work (Industry) – or allowed States to exempt them from the application of certain instruments, such as Art. 1, no. 3, c) of Convention No. 30 (1930) Hours of Work (commerce and offices). Some other Conventions allow exceptions with a broader wording, such as the Convention No. 189 (2011) Domestic Workers, Art. 13 where there is the possibility of 'excluding wholly or partly from its scope: (a) categories of workers for whom other protection is provided which is at least equivalent; and (b) limited categories of workers in respect of whom special problems of a substantive nature arise'.
25. On the importance of ILO's Conventions to the theme of OSH, cf. Antonio Ojeda Avilés, *Derecho Transnacional del Trabajo* 128 (Tirant lo Blanch 2013).

whole, limited categories of workers which may present particular difficulties (Article 2(2)), such as managers. A sole reference to managers is made in Article 20, where it is recognised that 'Co-operation between management and workers and/or their representatives within the undertaking shall be an essential element of organisational and other measures taken in pursuance of Articles 16 to 19 of this Convention.' In this context, managers are seen as embodying the employer.

Later in 2006, Convention No. 187 on the Promotional Framework for OSH demands that the national systems for OSH shall include, among others, '(d) arrangements to promote, at the level of the undertaking, cooperation between management, workers and their representatives as an essential element of workplace-related prevention measures' (Article 4). Again, managers are regarded as parties acting on behalf of the employer, but not particularly as subjects of the Convention's protection.

Convention No. 190 on violence and harassment, approved in 2019, seems to have a broader subjective approach.[26] Article 2 refers to the protection of 'workers and other persons in the world of work, including employees as defined by national law and practice, as well as persons working irrespective of their contractual status (...) and individuals exercising the authority, duties or responsibilities of an employer'. This latter category of the definition clearly opens the window for managers to be considered within the Convention's scope of protection.[27] It thus adopts an ambitiously broader concept compared to previous Conventions within OSH.

In 2022, the International Labour Conference approved a resolution to add the principle of a safe and healthy working environment to the ILO's four Fundamental Principles and Rights at Work, adopted in 1998.[28] As such, ILO's MS, regardless of their level of economic development, commit to respect and promote OSH within the working environment, even if they have not ratified the new Fundamental Convention no. 155 or 187.[29]

26. About this Convention, *see* Ana Cristina Ribeiro Costa, *El contenido del Convenio n.º 190 de la Organización Internacional del Trabajo: definiciones y ámbito de aplicación – 'vino nuevo en odres viejos'* 29-59 (Maria G. Q. Lima & Manuel C. Carrasco eds, Dykinson 2021), available at https://e-archivo.uc3m.es/bitstream/handle/10016/32437/violencia_correa_quintero_2021.pdf?sequence = 3&isAllowed = y.

27. This was however not entirely new. Among others, Convention No. 31 (1931) on Hours of Work (coal mines), revised by Convention No. 46 (1935) already clarified the concept of worker excluded 'persons engaged in supervision or management who do not ordinarily perform manual work', which allows us to conclude that the ones who did perform manual work would be encompassed by the concept (Art. 2 a) and b)). Similarly, Art. 8 of Convention No. 41 (1934) on Night Work (women) referred it did 'not apply to women holding responsible positions of management who are not ordinarily engaged in manual work' and Art. 3, a) of Convention No. 45 (1935) on Underground Work (women) allowed national laws or regulations to exempt females holding positions of management who did not perform manual work from the prohibition of employment on underground work in mines.

28. As can be read in *International Labour Conference adds safety and health to Fundamental Principles and Rights at Work*, International Labour Organization (10 June 2022) https://www.ilo.org/global/about-the-ilo/newsroom/news/WCMS_848132/lang--en/index.htm.

29. Cf. the table on ratifications of fundamental instruments per country at *Ratifications of fundamental instruments by country*, International Labour Organization, https://www.ilo.org/dyn/normlex/en/f?p = NORMLEXPUB:10011:0::NO::P10011_DISPLAY_BY,P10011_CONVENTION_TYPE_CODE:1,F.

There therefore seems to be an evolution, in terms of issues related to health and safety at work, to include any person working, irrespective of their contractual status. This development may in the future lead to a clearer inclusion of managers within subjects protected by the scope of the new Fundamental Conventions.

§11.04 EUROPEAN LEGAL FRAMEWORK OF OSH

At the regional level, EU Law as well as the Council of Europe (CoE) address OSH.

[A] EU Legal Framework

Within EU law, the historical evolution of OSH took place in several stages.[30] The first Action Program of the European Communities on safety and health at work was created for the period of 1978-1982.[31] Later on, the Single European Act of 1986 introduced Article 118-A, now Article 153 on the Treaty on the Functioning of EU (TFEU), which states that the Union shall support and complement the Member States' activities in fields such as the improvement of the working environment to protect workers' health and safety. Directives would be the preferred mean to achieve that goal, defining minimum requirements for gradual implementation and considering each Member States' conditions and technical rules.[32] A reference to managers was made in the third programme of social action. It addressed areas such as safety and ergonomics in the workplace and managers' and workers' training.[33]

At this point, the Framework Directive 89/391 on safety and health of workers at work[34] (hereinafter 'the OSH Framework Directive') was approved, followed by a number of specific individual Directives enacted under Article 16(1) of the OSH Framework Directive.[35] The OSH Framework Directive sets minimum standards to be implemented by the Member States, as well as general principles and rules that must be incorporated in each national legislation and practice. The main ideas of the OSH

30. Four phases, according to some legal doctrine - Magdalena Nogueira Guastavino et al., *Lecciones de Derecho Social de la Unión Europea* 366 (Tirant lo Blanch 2012); three phases are mentioned by Bruno Caruso & Silvana Sciarra, *Il lavoro subordinato* 78-82 (G. Giappichelli Editorem 2009); other authors stand for two phases, first being the one until the Framework Directive, and the other from that moment on, even though some legal doctrine considers that the first phase ends in 1987, with the entry into force of the Single European Act. Cf. Antonio Costa Reyes, *Manual de Derecho Social de la Unión Europea* 365 (Tecnos 2011).
31. Guastavino, *ibid.*, 367-375.
32. *Supra* n. 25, 202.
33. Guastavino, *supra* n. 30, at 367. Vicente Lafuente Pastor & Ruth Vallejo Dacosta, *Marco jurídico de la seguridad y salud en el trabajo* 65 (Prensas Universitarias de Zaragoza 2010).
34. Council Directive 89/391/EEC of 12 June 1989 on the introduction of measures to encourage improvements in the safety and health of workers at work, OJ L 183, 29.6.1989, p. 1-8.
35. The specific Directives would regulate the workplace, the working equipment, and individual protection equipment, specific risks, specific activities, and specific groups of workers (young people, pregnant women, workers in temporary working companies, among others).

Framework Directive are the universality of its application and the harmonisation of national legislation.[36]

Its scope defines worker as 'any person employed by an employer, including trainees and apprentices but excluding domestic servants' (Article 3, a). Despite the reference to *employment by an employer,* which could lead to exclusion of self-employed or autonomous workers, the CJEU has been following a broad interpretation of the concepts provided by the OSH Framework Directive,[37] with the intention of covering all workers in all sectors.

This was the situation in Case C-232/09, *Dita Danosa,*[38] that discussed the personal scope of Directive 92/85 on health and safety of pregnant workers,[39] a special Directive under the OSH Framework Directive. The CJEU stated that a member of a capital company's board of directors may be a 'worker' for the purposes of Directive 92/85 considering the specifics of the relationship, particularly 'if that activity is carried out, for some time, under the direction or supervision of another body of that company and if, in return for those activities, the board member receives remuneration', cf. paragraph 56. The sui generis nature of the employment relationship under national law does not have consequences for the meaning of worker for the purposes of Union law.[40] Emanuele Menegatti argues that, along with Case C-47/14, *Holterman,*[41] Case C-232/09, *Dita Danosa* clarifies that the adoption of a shared concept of worker that may differ from the national ones, even if within different legal contexts, is justified by common social protection goals.[42]

CJEU's case law helps to draft other criteria that would lead to the application of secondary law to members of the board of directors, where subordination seems to be unveiled.[43] These criteria have not been outlined regarding the application of OSH law

36. As states Brian Bercusson, 'the provision of the Framework Directive ... demonstrate how health and safety law has been "Europeanised" by EU Law' – *see* Brian Bercusson, *European Labour Law* 346 (Cambridge University Press 2009). In fact, this 'comunitarization' of the national systems in the field of OSH is based on the convergence that is intended by the EU legislation. Cf. Reyes, *supra* n. 31, 369.
37. Joaquín Huelin Martínez De Velasco, *El acervo comunitario sobre prevención de riesgos laborales* 100 Estudios de Derecho Judicial 49-82, 54 (2006).
38. Case C-232/09, *Dita Danosa v. LKB Lizings SIA*, 11.11.2010, ECLI:EU:C:2010:674.
39. Council Directive 92/85/EEC of 19 October 1992 on the introduction of measures to encourage improvements in the safety and health at work of pregnant workers and workers who have recently given birth or are breastfeeding (tenth individual Directive within the meaning of Art. 16(1) of Directive 89/391/EEC), OJ L 348, 28.11.1992, p. 1-7.
40. A critical analysis of this case can be read in Siniša Petrović & Petar Ceronja, *Corporate Effects of the Danosa Case: Is the Termination of Membership of the Board of Directors Allowed in the Case of a Pregnant Board Member?,* 8 CYELP 1, 437-456 (2012) DOI: 10.3935/cyelp.08.2012.139. The authors suggest the protection of the Court within the EU legislation should have been restricted to the contractual relationship between the pregnant member of the board and the company, leaving the corporate relationship to be regulated by the rules of company law.
41. Case C-47/14, *Holterman Ferho Exploitatie BV and Others v. F.L.F. Spies von Büllesheim,* 10.9.2015, ECLI:EU:C:2015:574.
42. Menegatti *supra* n. 3, at 76. Another case that reflects the broad concept of workers adopted by the CJEU within the context of the Framework Directive is Case C-428/04, *Commission of the European Communities v. Republic of Austria,* 6.4.2006, ECLI:EU:C:2006:238.
43. An ETUI report on the concept of worker has outlined the criteria based on the CJEU's case law. On the contrary, the CJEU has decided that when a person is the director of a company of which

in particular, but may guide us on what the Court finds as leading to a situation where the member of the board of directors is worth of a treatment similar to that of an employee.

There are however other instruments within EU OSH law that either compare self-employed workers to employers or suggest they should be regarded as employees. An example of the first is Directive 92/57 on minimum safety and health requirements at temporary or mobile construction sites,[44] where self-employed persons are compared to employers in what concerns some obligations. Among instruments that compare them to employees are Council Recommendation of 18 February 2003[45] on protection of the health and safety of self-employed workers, where the extension of the OSH Framework Directive to self-employed workers is discussed, and Directive 2002/15[46] on the organisation of working time in mobile road transport activities, which protects self-employed drivers in similar terms of the protection granted to mobile workers. Finally, Regulation 561/2006[47] on the harmonisation of certain social legislations, which defines 'driver' as 'any person who drives the vehicle even for a short period, or who is carried in a vehicle as part of his duties to be available for driving if necessary' (Article 4(c)), thus protecting working conditions and road safety regardless of the nature of the relationship.[48]

---

they are the sole shareholders, they do not carry out their activity in the context of a relationship of subordination and will be considered as self-employed people. Even so, 'the personal and property relations between spouses that result from marriage do not rule out the existence, in the context of the organisation of an undertaking, of a relationship of subordination characteristic of an employment relationship between the company and the spouse of the director of a company of which he is the sole shareholder', cf. Martin Risak & Thomas Dullinger, *The Concept of 'Worker' in EU Law: Status Quo and Potential for Change* 36-37 (2018). Besides Case C-232/09, *Dita Danosa*, the report bases its conclusions on Case C-47/14, *Holterman*, para. 47; Case C-229/14, *Ender Balkaya v. Kiesel Abbruch*, 9.7.2015, ECLI:EU:C:2015:455, para. 40; C-107/94, *P.H. Asscher v. Staatssecretaris van Financiën*, 27.6.1996, ECLI:EU:C:1996:251, para. 26; and Case C-337/97, *C.P.M. Meeusen v. Hoofddirectie van de Informatie Beheer Groep*, 8.6.1999, para. 15. Another interesting case is Case C-334/92, *Teodoro Wagner Miret v. Fondo de Garantía Salarial*, 16.12.1993, ECLI:EU:C:1993:945 where the CJEU decided that higher management staff could not be excluded from the scope of Council Directive 80/987/EEC of 20 October 1980, on the approximation of the Member States' laws relating to the protection of employees in the event of the insolvency of their employer.

44. Council Directive 92/57/EEC, of 24 June 1992, on the implementation of minimum safety and health requirements at temporary or mobile construction sites (eighth individual Directive within the meaning of Art. 16(1) of the Framework Directive).
45. Council Recommendation of 18 February 2003, concerning the improvement of the protection of the health and safety at work of self-employed workers.
46. Directive 2002/15/EC of the European Parliament and of the Council, of 11 March 2002, on the organisation of the working time of persons performing mobile road transport activities.
47. Regulation (EC) No. 561/2006 of the European Parliament and of the Council of 15 March 2006 on the harmonisation of certain social legislation relating to road transport and amending Council Regulations (EEC) No. 3821/85 and (EC) No. 2135/98 and repealing Council Regulation (EEC) No. 3820/85 (Text with EEA relevance) - Declaration, OJ L 102, 11.4.2006, p. 1-14.
48. There is a tendency to the approximation of the regimes of self-employed and employment also within the themes of equal treatment and non-discrimination: Council Directive 2000/43/EC of 29 June 2000 implementing the principle of equal treatment between persons irrespective of racial or ethnic origin and Council Directive 2000/78/EC of 27 November 2000 establishing a general framework for equal treatment in employment and occupation, cf. Sofía Olarte Encabo, *Trabajadores autónomos* 217 (Tecnos 2009).

Thus, though not directly addressed by the Court's case law, the protection of a relevant subject, such as OSH, seems to justify the adoption of a broad concept of worker within the OSH Framework Directive, inclusive of managers, particularly when certain circumstances are verified, such as their economic dependency and subordination to the direction or supervision of another company's body.

Besides, the Charter of Fundamental Rights of the EU (CFREU), signed in 2000,[49] includes a provision on the right to personal dignity, emphasising the inviolability of the person (Article 1) and a precept on the integrity of the person, proclaiming the right of all to physical and mental integrity (Article 3(1)). Article 31(1) reveals the concern that all workers should have healthy, safe and dignified working conditions. Finally, in Article 35, it is provided that all citizens – 'everyone' – shall have 'the right of access to preventive health care and the right to benefit from medical treatment under the conditions established by national laws and practices'.

No specific references to managers are done within the CFREU. However, the link of the CFREU to the European Social Charter (ESC) adopted by the CoE, affirmed in its preamble, shall lead us to the conclusion that all workers, including non-employees, must be covered by health and safety at work regulations, as the European Committee of Social Rights (ECSR) points out.[50]

Finally, we cannot forget to address this issue from the social security perspective. In fact, the dimension of reparation of OSH law is usually implemented by social security mechanisms. As mentioned above, the CJEU case law recognises that 'there is no single definition of worker in Community law: it varies according to the area in which the definition is to be applied',[51] and as such, the concept of 'person covered' by Regulation (EC) No 883/2004 on the coordination of social security systems may not coincide with the one of employee or even be conditional on the pursuit of a professional activity.[52]

Indeed, Article 36 of Regulation 883/2004 on the right to benefits in kind and in cash related to accidents at work and occupational diseases refers to 'A person who has sustained an accident at work or has contracted an occupational disease.'[53] Thus, the regime shall apply to any person covered by the regulation (Article 2), which does not exclude any type of work and includes all the insured persons mentioned in Articles 17, 18(1), 19(1) and 20(1), pursuant to 36(1). Thus, we conclude managers are not

49. It became legally binding with the Treaty of Lisbon, which requires that it has the same legal value as the Treaties, cf. Art. 6(1) Treaty on European Union.
50. Nicola Kountouris, *The Concept of 'Worker' in European Labour Law: Fragmentation, Autonomy and Scope*, 47 Industrial Law Journal 2, 218, n. 120 (2018) DOI: 10.1093/indlaw/dwx014.
51. Case C-85/96, *María Martinez Sala v. Freistaat Bayern*, 12.5.1998, ECLI:EU:C:1998:217 para. 31.
52. Case C-623/13, *Ministre de l'Économie et des Finances v. Gérard de Ruyter*, 26.2.2015, ECLI: EU:C:2015:123, para. 30. About these concepts, along with the concept of EU citizen, *see* Belén Alonso-Olea García, *Los conceptos de trabajador por cuenta ajena, asegurado social y ciudadano de la Unión Europea según la jurisprudencia del Tribunal de Justicia de la Unión Europea. Sus consecuencias y controversia*, 62 REDE 93-125 (2017).
53. It does not refer to employees, self-employed or any other subjects, but to 'a person'. They are not defined by each Member States' legislation as they are not limited to the definition of 'insured person' enshrined in Art. 1, c).

excluded from the protection of the Regulation regarding accidents at work and occupational diseases.

As such, there is apparently a movement of EU law and its interpretation by the case law to be progressively inclusive of managers within the scope of protection of the core worker's rights, similar to the trend that has been recognised within ILO.[54]

[B] Council of Europe Legal Framework

The CoE's European Convention on Human Rights (ECHR) does not directly provide for a catalogue of labour rights.[55] In particular, it does not expressly protect citizens from hazardous working conditions or concrete occupational risks. However, case law from the European Court of Human Rights (ECtHR), such as *Brincat and others v. Malta* (2014),[56] has shown that OSH can be safeguarded as part of other rights, including the right to life (Article 2) and the right to respect for private and family life (Article 8).[57]

Instead, OSH assumes special prominence in the CoE's ESC, which is reflected in several provisions. Even though in some legal scholars' view, the ESC made only very general efforts of merely formal character,[58] it was nonetheless the first European legislative instrument to provide for a human right to healthy and safe working conditions, allowing such a right to be claimed before an international body.[59]

Article 3 of the ESC is devoted exclusively to OSH. It is written in 'rather general terms',[60] which allows it to be 'readily adaptable' to changes within this field.[61] The ECSR has imposed a wide objective and subjective protection,[62] as well as geographically, throughout the national territories.[63] The Committee has taken a broad personal

54. Including soft law. In fact, Community Charter of Fundamental Social Rights (1989), which would boost European social policy, was an important element in the development of a European soft law regarding OSH – Sara Brimo, *L'État et la protection de la santé des travailleurs* 160-163 (Lextenso Éditions 2012).
55. Except for ECHR Art. 4 on the prohibition of slavery and forced labour.
56. European Court of Human Rights, Case of *Brincat and others v. Malta*, Applications nos. 60908/11, 62110/11, 62129/11, 62312/11 and 62338/11, judgment of 24 July 2014.
57. About this case, *see* Ana C.R. Costa, *Brincat and Others vs Malta: Occupational Health and Safety under the Guise of the Rights to Life and to Respect for Private and Family Life (European Court of Human Rights, 60908/11, 62110/11, 62129/11, 62312/11 and 62338/11)* 133-143 (M. Łaga et al. eds, Gdansk University Press 2017).
58. Ana Belén Muñoz Ruiz, *El sistema normativo de la prevención de riesgos laborales* 70 (Lex Nova 2009).
59. Katarzyna Lasak, *Health and Safety in the European Social Charter*, 25 IJCL 2, 110 (2009) DOI: 10.54648/ijcl2009010.
60. *Ibid.*, 111.
61. John Darcy & David Harris, *The European Social Charter* 67 (Transnational Publishers Inc. 2001).
62. Even though the legislation and control procedures may be distinct – *supra* n. 53, 74. About the broad approach of the workers, activities and risks covered by the ESC, *see* Ana C. R. Costa, *A tutela da segurança e saúde no trabalho no âmbito da Convenção Europeia dos Direitos do Homem e da Carta Social Europeia* 275-300 (Manuel M. Roxo ed., 2017).
63. European Committee of Social Rights (ECSR), Conclusions 2013, Portugal. All the conclusions of the ECSR may be found at https://hudoc.esc.coe.int/eng#{%22sort%22:[%22ESCPublicationDate%20Descending%22],%22ESCDcType%22:[%22FOND%22,%22Conclusion%22,%22Ob%22]}.

approach that employees should be protected under national laws and practices regardless of the nature of their contractual relationship.

For example, the ECSR has clarified that farmers and homeworkers should be covered by OSH standards,[64] as well as workers from the fishing industry. The ECSR is also interested in the practical application of the legal provisions to workers within the Government service, judges, domestic,[65] temporary, agency, interim and fixed-term workers and details on how this category of workers is represented.[66]

The Committee has moreover concluded the legislation on the protection of self-employed workers in France and Estonia, for example, was insufficient, in violation of Article 3(2), particularly considering they are usually employed in high-risk sectors.[67] In the 2009 report on the conformity of Spanish legislation and practices, the ECSR concluded, likewise, that the scope of the legislation and provisions on OSH for autonomous workers was not sufficient.[68] Finally, in 2017, the Committee's report led to the conclusion on non-conformity of Germany's regulations on the grounds that certain categories of self-employed workers are not sufficiently covered.[69]

As such, this provision demands legislation to encompass risks in a broad sense, protecting all forms of work, irrespective of the nature of their relationship. Although there are no known cases addressed to the ECSR under the collective complaints mechanism that address the manager's position, it is clear that in case a specific proceeding would debate the duty of the Member States to protect managers under OSH law, the Committee would likely be favourable to that idea, considering its previous conclusions under the reporting procedure.

Besides, by assuming both employees and self-employed shall be protected by the Member States' legislation, the ECSR clearly undertakes a position that is aligned with the more recent ILO's instruments. As the Committee's position is based on the grounds that both statuses are normally exposed to the same risks, it can be anticipated that the criteria for the managers to be considered as subjects of protection would be assessing whether they are indeed exposed to the same risk factors or not. In this case, executive managers, involved in the day-to-day activity of the company, are most likely to be considered to perform a comparable situation to the subjects of protection, and will be covered in any case if they are either employees or self-employed workers.

64. ECSR, Conclusions XIII-4, Belgium and XIV-2, Belgium.
65. ECSR, Conclusions 2017, Hungary. These were reaffirmed by the ECSR regarding domestic workers and self-employed – ECSR, Conclusions 2021, Hungary. Albania had the same outcome, which was found by the ECSR not in conformity with the Charter due to inadequate protection of temporary agency workers and lack of information on domestic and home workers – ECSR, Conclusions 2021.
66. ECSR, Conclusions XIV-2, Portugal; 2013, Portugal; 2017, Portugal; and 2021, Serbia. Temporary agency workers had been addressed by the ECSR previously, in 2003, when the ECSR concluded that France would have to take into account the protection of these precarious workers, particularly concerning their medical surveillance and the articulation between temporary-work agency and user undertaking – ECSR, Conclusions 2003, France.
67. ECSR, Conclusions 2003, France and 2005, Estonia.
68. ECSR, Conclusions 2009, Spain.
69. ECSR, Conclusions 2017, Germany. The ECSR also found Andorra not in conformity with the Charter due to an inadequate protection of self-employed workers – Conclusions 2021.

§11.05 SOME NATIONAL LEGAL FRAMEWORKS OF MANAGERS' PROTECTION WITHIN OSH

In France, Law no. 2021-1018, of 2 August 2021, to strengthen occupational health prevention was amended, and now it states on Article L. 4621-4 that the manager of an undertaking which is a member of an inter-company occupational health and prevention service may benefit from the services offered to employees. Traditionally, in France, the *cadre dirigeant* were already very protected in terms of working time, for the purposes of allowing exceptions to these provisions.[70]

In Italy, the category of the *dirigenti* is not included in the protection conferred statutorily, but it is common for collective bargaining to contain provisions on such a protection, as long as those managers are no longer within the probationary period. Usually, the right to maintain the job post in case of workplace accident is provided, as well as a duty to have an insurance that covers reparation occupational contingencies, payment of salary and any indemnities. If the manager provides for their own insurance, they may have a right to redress against the employer.[71] Regarding working time, the Italian case law also appeals to limits of reasonability, in order to guarantee their physical and psychological integrity.[72]

In what concerns Portugal, the law extends the scope of protection of work-related accidents, occupational diseases and OSH to other individuals without an employment contract, among whom the administrator, director, manager or equivalent, provided they are remunerated, and to the providers of work without legal subordination but with economic dependence.[73] For social security purposes, regardless of being a manager with or without exercise of activity, their contributions will always include protection within social security for occupational disease events.[74] Thus, in Portugal, in the wake of Case C-232/09, *Dita Danosa* of the CJEU, the criterion of receiving remuneration is solely considered for the *administrators, directors, managers or equivalent* to be protected within OSH law. However, we cannot disregard the

70. Hervé Gosselin, *Le temps de travail. Jurisprudence récente de la chambre sociale de la Cour de cassation*, 4 Droit Social 375 (2010).
71. Mariangela Cistaro & Stefano Cui, *La malattia del lavoratore: Diritti e doveri delle parti* 179-180 (Giuffré Editore 2012).
72. In fact, the law also states that though they are exempted from the protection, the general principles of protection of safety and health of workers shall apply to managers (Art. 17, no. 5, a) of Decreto Legislativo 8 April 2003, no. 66.
73. Article 4, no. 1 of Law no. 7/2009 refers to Arts 283 and 284 of the Labor Code (CT), which in turn refer to the specific legislation that regulates the chapter on prevention and remedying of accidents at work and occupational diseases legislation. Though it is not clear, we believe it includes Law no. 98/2009 of 04-09, on work-related accidents and occupational diseases and Law no. 102/2009 of 10-09, on the legal regime for the promotion of safety and health at work (LSST). The extension to economically dependent workers is also enshrined in Art. 4, a) LSST. In any case, Art. 4, no. 2 of Law 7/2009 provides that the self-employed must have insurance that guarantees the payment of the benefits set out in Arts 283 and 284 of the CT and respective regulatory legislation, which, in turn, is regulated by Decree-Law 159/99, of 11 May.
74. Apelles J. B. Conceição, *Segurança Social* 219 (Almedina 2014).

fact that within the working time regime, they are still exempted from some limitations.[75]

In Spain, there are no references to OSH within the special legal framework of the *alto directivo*. Being arguable that the *Ley de Prevención de Riesgos Laborales* applies directly regardless of an agreement within the employment contract, the legal doctrine sustains that the grounds for their protection are the EU legislation and the Spanish Constitution.[76] However, within the Spanish jurisdiction, it is recognised that in what concerns the prevention activities, the manager is liable for his own security, being both debtor and creditor of security, and thus there is a confusion of both plans. Moreover, the manager is entitled to a protection against harassment, arising not only from superiors but also from other employees, thus both vertically and horizontally. The manager is also entitled to a reparatory protection. Besides this, it is hard to envisage how to apply reasonable accommodation and conciliation mechanisms, including the possibility of change of work position. Thus, suspension of the employment contract may be the only option, in certain cases.[77] In what concerns social security protection, in Spain, directors who perform ordinary duties and do not control the company shall be covered by the general system of social security as employees, provided that they do not perform management functions and their duties are limited to those of an ordinary nature.[78]

We may thus conclude that some specific national legislations already provide for some protection for managers regarding OSH, particularly of individuals we would consider as executive managers, regardless of the nature of their relationship, although that protection is usually not exactly the same as the one granted to employees.

§11.06 CONCLUSIONS

As Jeffrey Pfeffer states, 'professional and C-suite executives are scarcely immune to the effects of poor working conditions on their health and wellbeing'.[79] It is indeed clear that managers are exposed to risk factors to the same (or even greater) extent as

75. For example, managers, who work under working hour exemption regime, are not entitled to benefit from the limitation of maximum working hours provided for workers (Art. 211, no. 4 CT), they may work for more than six consecutive hours without a rest break (Art. 213, no. 5 CT), they are not entitled to have a rest period of at least 11 hours between two different daily working periods (Art. 214, no. 2, a) CT), and they may work within that working hour exemption regime without being additionally paid for it, in case they waive that compensation (Arts 218, no. 1, a) and 265 no. 2 CT). About these exceptions, cf., Maria Irene Gomes & Catarina de Oliveira Carvalho, *La relación laboral del trabajador dirigente en el ordenamiento jurídico portugués*, IV Revista de Derecho del Trabajo 11, 236-237 (2016) DOI: 10.17658/issn.2058-5462/issue-21//p22.
76. *Supra* n. 1, 292.
77. *Ibid.*, 297-299.
78. *Manual del Personal de Alta Dirección* (Raquel Serrano & Alex Valls eds, Thomson Reuters 2012).
79. The author mentions a Swisscom CEO and a Zurich Insurance Group CFO that have committed suicide in 2013, allegedly related to having trouble with being on-call 24/7 and to a conflict with the CEO, respectively. *See* Jeffrey Pfeffer, *Dying for a Paycheck. How Modern Management Harms Employee Health and Company Performance – And What We Can Do about It* 10 (Harper Collins Publishers 2018).

employees. However, they are usually not considered by national legislations as such and are thus given an autonomous regime in what concerns OSH law.

In any case, European legal instruments, as well as CJEU case law, seem to be recently willing to allow them to access the same benefits as employees in what concerns some minimum employment standards that shall include OSH. This appears to be aligned with the intention disclosed by the ILO around its centenary[80] to establish a universal labour guarantee for all workers, regardless of their contractual regime, which includes the right to, *inter alia*, the protection of health and safety at work.[81]

80. International Labour Organization, *Work for a Brighter Future: Global Commission on the Future of Work* 12 (2019), https://www.ilo.org/wcmsp5/groups/public/---dgreports/---cabinet/documents/publication/wcms_662410.pdf.
81. Among legal doctrine, the study led by Alain Supiot had already concluded that a certain set of social rights of economically dependent workers needed to be protected, regardless of their statute - Alain Supiot, *Au-delà de l'emploi: Les voies d'une vraie réforme du droit du travail* 293 (Flammarion 2016).

CHAPTER 12

Non-discrimination Against Persons in Management

Peter Ahlberg

§12.01 INTRODUCTION

The applicability of EU labour law rights to persons in higher management is usually dependent on the manager's status as a 'worker'. In some contexts, this is determined by the autonomous and uniform EU law notion of 'worker' originating from Article 45 of the Treaty on the Functioning of the European Union (TFEU). In other contexts, EU legislation leaves the precise demarcation of the notion of worker, and thus the extent to which managers fit in, to national law. When the notion of 'worker' is crucial for the applicability of EU law to management, the key issue is usually whether the manager in question can be considered to perform her or his activities under the supervision of others.

However, recent case law has made it clear that managers and others can benefit from other parts of EU anti-discrimination law regardless of whether they are workers. Specifically, when it comes to the protection against discrimination under Directive 78/2000 establishing a general framework for equal treatment in employment and occupation (the Framework Directive 78/2000),[1] the Court ruled in Case C-587/20 *HK/Danmark*[2] that a person is protected under the Framework Directive 78/2000 regardless of whether said person qualifies as a worker under Article 45 TFEU.

In this chapter, we discuss this ruling, its rationale, context and implications for the protection of managers' labour law rights with regard to being protected against discrimination on grounds of religion or belief, disability, age or sexual orientation.

1. Council Directive 2000/78/EC of 27 November 2000 establishing a general framework for equal treatment in employment and occupation, OJ L 303, 2.12.2000.
2. Case C-587/20, *Ligebehandlingsnævnet som mandatar for A mod HK/Danmark og HK/Privat*, 2.6.2022, ECLI:EU:C:2022:419.

§12.02 PROTECTION UNDER THE FRAMEWORK DIRECTIVE 78/2000

The Framework Directive 78/2000 lays down a general prohibition against discrimination on the grounds of religion or belief, disability, age or sexual orientation as regards employment and occupation. Together with Directive 54/2006 on gender equality in the labour market[3] (Directive 54/2006) and Directive 43/2000 on equal treatment irrespective of racial or ethnic origin,[4] it forms the backbone of EU anti-discrimination law on the job market.

The prohibition in the Framework Directive 78/2000 Article 2 covers direct and indirect discrimination. The latter occurs when an apparently neutral criterion - such as a ban on all religious and political symbols at the workplace[5] or a rule permitting the termination of employees who are absent too often[6] - has the effect of putting certain protected groups at a disadvantage. In general, the Directive leaves narrow room for the Member States to provide possible exemptions from the prohibition against direct discrimination, while indirect discrimination can be justified by a legitimate aim when the means to achieve the aim are appropriate and necessary.

Harassment is also prohibited according to the Framework Directive 78/2000. Article 2(3) defines harassment as unwanted conduct related to any of the protected grounds that takes place with the purpose or effect of violating the dignity of a person and of creating an intimidating, hostile, degrading, humiliating or offensive environment. The concept of harassment may be defined in accordance with the national laws and practices of the Member States.

The areas in which the prohibition applies are very broad and extend far beyond traditional cases of discriminatory dismissals or rejections, which many would intuitively associate with anti-discrimination law. According to Article 3, all persons are protected in relation to, *inter alia*, conditions for access to employment, self-employment and occupation, access to vocational training, employment conditions and involvement in labour organizations and professional organizations. For managers in particular, being covered by the protection under the Framework Directive 78/2000 would mean among other things that any discriminatory conditions for access to a managerial position - whether direct or indirect - would have to be justified under the exemptions in the Directive and could potentially be held unlawful. This includes not

3. Directive 2006/54/EC of the European Parliament and of the Council of 5 July 2006 on the implementation of the principle of equal opportunities and equal treatment of men and women in matters of employment and occupation (recast), OJ L 204, 26.7.2006.
4. Council Directive 2000/43/EC of 29 June 2000 implementing the principle of equal treatment between persons irrespective of racial or ethnic origin, OJ L 180, 19.7.2000.
5. Cf., for example, Case C-188/15, *Asma Bougnaoui and Association de défense des droits de l'homme (ADDH) v. Micropole SA*, 14.3.2017, ECLI:EU:C:2017:204, and Case C-157/15, *Samira Achbita and Centrum voor gelijkheid van kansen en voor racismebestrijding v. G4S Secure Solutions NV*, 14.3.2017, ECLI:EU:C:2017:203. The Court found that the rules applied equally to all religions and therefore did not entail direct discrimination. However, the Court noted that the rule would entail indirect discrimination if it had the effect of putting persons adhering to a particular religion or belief at a particular disadvantage. This was left for the national court to decide.
6. Cf., for example, Case C-270/16, *Carlos Enrique Ruiz Conejero v. Ferroser Servicios Auxiliares SA and Ministerio Fiscal*, 18.1.2018, ECLI:EU:C:2018:17.

only discrimination in the selection process itself but also provisions in the bylaws of a company. Even national legislation that sets certain requirements for specific managers or board members, etc., would have to comply with the rules in the Directive if these categories fall within its personal scope.

§12.03 WORKER STATUS AND SUBORDINATION IN EU LABOUR LAW

The question of applicability of EU labour law rights to persons in higher management is usually a question of whether the manager qualifies as a worker under the relevant EU legislation. In particular, it has been of importance whether or not the manager can be considered to perform her or his activities under the supervision of others.[7]

Secondary EU legislation in the field of labour law can be roughly divided into two categories, namely those that leave it to the national legislation - with certain limitations - to define a 'worker', and those that employ a harmonized concept of worker based on Article 45 TFEU.[8]

In the first category falls, notably, Directive 2001/23 on employees' rights in the event of transfer of undertakings,[9] which defines an 'employee' as any person who is protected as an employee under national employment law in the Member State concerned, as well as Directive 96/71 on the posting of workers,[10] according to which the definition of a worker is that which applies in the law of the Member State to whose territory the worker is posted.[11] In the second category falls Directive 2003/88 on organization of working time[12] and Directive 92/85 on safety and health of pregnant workers[13] as examples. In its interpretations of the scope of directives without reference to the national concept, the Court of Justice of the EU (hereinafter 'CJEU') has

7. Case C-232/09, *Dita Danosa v. LKB Lizings SIA*, 11.11.10, ECLI:EU:C:2010:674, paras 38-56, and Case C-229/14, *Ender Balkaya v. Kiesel Abbruch und Recycling Technik GmbH*, 9.7.2015, ECLI:EU:C:2015:455, paras 31-48.
8. Nicola Countouris, *The Concept of 'Worker' in European Labour Law: Fragmentation, Autonomy and Scope*, 47 ILJ 2, 201-202 (2018) DOI: 10.1093/indlaw/dwx014.
9. Council Directive 2001/23/EC of 12 March 2001 on the approximation of the laws of the Member States relating to the safeguarding of employees' rights in the event of transfers of undertakings, businesses or parts of undertakings or businesses, OJ L 82, 22.3.2001.
10. Directive 96/71/EC of the European Parliament and of the Council of 16 December 1996 concerning the posting of workers in the framework of the provision of services, OJ L 18, 21.1.1997.
11. In Case C-393/10, *Dermod Patrick O'Brien v. Ministry of Justice*, 1.3.2012, EU:C:2012:110, and Case C-216/15, *Betriebsrat der Ruhrlandklinik gGmbH v. Ruhrlandklinik gGmbH*, 17.11.2016, EU:C:2016:883, paras. 25-43, the CJEU noted with regard to Directive 97/81 on part-time work and Directive 2008/104 on temporary agency work - where similar definitions apply - that the Member States' discretion with regard to defining workers covered by the directives is not unlimited. The discretion cannot be used in a way which would jeopardize the achievement of the objectives pursued by those directives.
12. Directive 2003/88/EC of the European Parliament and of the Council of 4 November 2003 concerning certain aspects of the organization of working time, OJ L 299, 18.11.2003.
13. Council Directive 92/85/EEC of 19 October 1992 on the introduction of measures to encourage improvements in the safety and health at work of pregnant workers and workers who have recently given birth or are breastfeeding (tenth individual Directive within the meaning of Article 16(1) of Directive 89/391/EEC), OJ L 348, 28.11.1992.

continuously held that the concept of 'worker' must be given an autonomous and independent meaning in the EU legal order.[14]

The Framework Directive 78/2000 does not contain a definition of the concept of 'worker' that leaves discretion to the national legislatures like those in Directive 2001/23 on employees' rights in the event of transfer of undertakings or Directive 96/71 on the posting of workers. On this basis, it could be assumed that the scope of Directive 54/2006 on gender equality in the labour market would be defined in a manner similar to that established by the CJEU with regard to Directive 2003/88 on organization of working time and Directive 92/85 on safety and health of pregnant workers among others – i.e., on the basis of a uniform concept of 'worker' based on TFEU Article 45. The CJEU alluded to this approach in Case C-143/16, *Abercrombie*,[15] where the worker status of the plaintiff in a case concerning age discrimination was examined with reference to classical case law on TFEU Article 45. However, it is not clear from the ruling precisely why this question was deemed relevant to examine.

If worker status was in fact a prerequisite for protection under the Directive, the fate of the manager would likely be determined by the subordination criteria developed in Case C-232/09, *Danosa*, and Case C-229/14, *Balkaya*. In Case C-232/09, *Danosa*, the Court – while leaving the final assessment to the national court – was very sceptical towards an argument that a member of a capital company's board of directors was not in a relationship of subordination and thus did not qualify as a 'pregnant worker' within the meaning of Directive 92/85 on protection of pregnant workers. The deciding factor for the CJEU seemed to be the fact that while no single person could give Ms Danosa binding instructions on how to do her work, she had to report to and cooperate with a supervisory board within the company and, ultimately, the shareholders could remove her from her position.[16] If similar criteria applied for the Framework Directive 78/2000, many managers and executives would likely benefit from protection against discrimination under that directive. For others, some ambiguity would remain, in particular for top management – both executive and non-executive. For this group of managers, it would be up to each manager to prove that he or she was in fact subordinated to another body within the company.

However, this approach to demarcating the Framework Directive 78/2000 assumes that the Directive pursues essentially the same objectives as the traditional EU employment legislation. On closer inspection, the Framework Directive 78/2000 reveals broader objectives which go beyond the economic and social integration and development of the Union as set out in Article 151 TFEU and, instead, focuses on the

14. Case C-256/01, *Debra Allonby v. Accrington & Rossendale College, Education Lecturing Services, trading as Protocol Professional and Secretary of State for Education and Employment*, 13.1.2004, ECLI:EU:C:2004:18, Case C-428/09, *Union syndicale Solidaires Isère v. Premier ministre and Others*, 14.10.2010, ECLI:EU:C:2010:612, and Case C-229/14, *Balkaya*, para. 33.
15. Case C-143/16, *Abercrombie & Fitch Italia Srl v. Antonino Bordonaro*, 19.7.2017, ECLI:EU:C:2017:566, paras 19-23.
16. In Case C-229/14, *Balkaya*, paras 49-51, the CJEU similarly ruled that a member of the board of directors of a capital company should be regarded as a 'worker' within the meaning of the Transfer of Undertakings Directive. In this case, the CJEU also emphasized the fact that the board member in the case was appointed and could have his mandate taken away by the general meeting of shareholders of the company.

rights of the Union's citizens as individuals. This shows not only in the wording of the provisions in the Directive but also in its legal basis in the Treaty. Much of the typical EU labour law secondary acts have their basis in TFEU provisions in Part Three (Union Policies and Internal Actions), Title X (Social Policy) which specifically concern worker's rights. The Framework Directive 78/2000, however, is based on TFEU Article 19, which is found in Part Two (Non-Discrimination and Citizenship of the Union). This suggests that something more fundamental is at stake when it comes to the principle of non-discrimination. Essentially, this principle encompasses a *human* right - not a *worker's* right.

This different heritage is also reflected in the wording of the Directive, which does not limit the personal scope to 'workers'. In fact, the term 'worker' only appears *en passant* in Article 3(1)(c) regarding organizations of 'workers' and in Article 6(1)(a) regarding the possibility of justifying a difference in treatment on grounds of age in the form of special conditions on access to employment for older 'workers'. On the contrary, Article 3 on the scope of the Framework Directive 78/2000 specifically states that the Directive shall apply to 'all persons' in relation to access to 'conditions for access to employment, to self-employment or to occupation' and - notably - 'at all levels of the professional hierarchy'. Especially, the last phrase indicates that the EU legislator did not intend to limit the protection against discrimination to relationships of subordination. After all, by definition, no relationship of subordination can exist at the very top of the 'professional hierarchy' - yet the Framework Directive 78/2000 explicitly also applies there.

These differences between the Framework Directive 78/2000 and traditional EU labour law directives were the focal point in the recent Case C-587/20, *HK Danmark*.

[A] The *HK Danmark* Case

Case C-587/20, *HK Danmark*, concerned a woman, A, who was precluded from running for re-election for the post of chair of the sector board of HK Privat (a sector of the trade union HK Denmark) because of an age limit in the bylaws of the trade union. According to the age limit in force at the time, anyone above the age of 60 could not run for election. At the time where she was precluded from running for re-election because of this age limit, she had held the position of chair of the board for seventeen years as her only full-time occupation, having been re-elected every four years. She contested this age limit as direct discrimination before the Equal Treatment Board and subsequently before the Danish courts.

The trade union argued that A did not fall within the scope of section 2(1) of the Danish Anti-Discrimination Act,[17] which provides that an 'employer' may not discriminate against 'employees' with regard to employment, termination, transfers or with regard to salary and employment conditions in general. The trade union held that the chair of the sector board was not in a relationship of subordination to anyone else, as she could not be instructed in how to do her work by anyone and only had a political

17. Act No. 1001 of 24/08/2017, act on prohibition of discrimination in the labour market, etc.

obligation towards the voters who elected her for the post. They also argued that the post could not be characterized as 'self-employment' within the meaning of section 3(3) of the same Act, which provides that the prohibition against discrimination also applies to anyone who 'lays down rules or makes decisions on access to self-employment'.

The Anti-Discrimination Act does not contain a verbatim transposition of the provision in Article 3 of the Framework Directive 78/2000 which, in addition to 'employment' and 'self-employment', also lists a third category of 'occupation' and explicitly provides that the protection extends to 'all levels of the professional hierarchy'. Instead, in the implementation of the Framework Directive 78/2000, the Danish Anti-Discrimination Act could appear at the surface to rely on a narrower and more traditional Danish labour law approach, which essentially imposes obligations on an 'employer' vis-à-vis an 'employee'.[18]

The main question in the case was how the Framework Directive 78/2000 should affect the interpretation of these provisions. The Danish Eastern High Court opted to refer the case to the CJEU. The main reasons for the referral were first the questions of the relevance of subordination, and second, the fact that the position of chair of the sector board was obtained – in the words of the High Court – through 'political elections'. The emphasis on this latter term seems to suggest that the Danish High Court harboured some concern that the prohibition on age discrimination would apply to (politically) elected officials – perhaps, one might speculate, due to the implications that such an interpretation could have on, e.g., other elected occupations, such as for members of parliaments.

However, neither the Advocate General's opinion[19] nor the CJEU's subsequent ruling in the case show any signs of this concern.

In its ruling of 2 June 2022, the CJEU first stated that the Framework Directive 78/2000 does not refer to the law of the Member States for the purpose of defining the scope of the Directive concerning 'conditions for access to employment, to self-employment or to occupation' in Article 3(1)(a). As such, and in accordance with its recent ruling in Case C–507/18, *Associazione Avvocatura per i diritti LGBTI*,[20] the CJEU concluded that this notion should be given an autonomous and uniform interpretation throughout the EU.[21]

The CJEU then examined the wording of Article 3(1)(a) of the Framework Directive 78/2000 and surmises that the use together of the terms 'employment',

18. In European Commission, Directorate-General for Justice, Nicola Countouris and Mark Freedland, *The Personal Scope of the EU Sex Equality Directives* (Publications Office 2013), the authors have gathered country reports that address the differences in personal and material scope between Directives 2006/54/EC, 2000/43/EC and the Framework Directive 78/2000. It seems that the Danish approach to the Framework Directive 78/2000 is also found in many Member States, while others have opted for a verbatim transposition of Art. 3.
19. Opinion of Advocate General Richard de la Tour in Case C-587/20, *HK Danmark*, 13.9.2022, ECLI:EU:C:2022:29.
20. Case C-507/18, *NH v. Associazione Avvocatura per i diritti LGBTI - Rete Lenford*, 23.4.2020, ECLI:EU:C:2020:289.
21. Case C-587/20, *HK Danmark*, para. 25.

'self-employment' and 'occupation' means that Article 3(1)(a) covers conditions for access to any occupational activity, whatever the nature and characteristics of such activity.[22]

This textual interpretation was, according to the CJEU, confirmed by the purpose and context of the Directive. Notably, the CJEU remarked – as did the Advocate General – that Directive 54/2006 on equal treatment is adopted on the basis of Article 19 TFEU, which confers on the Union the power to take appropriate action to combat discrimination based, *inter alia*, on age. As noted above, Article 19 is placed in Part Two of the Treaty, which concerns Non-Discrimination and Citizenship of the Union. In this respect, the Directive differs from much of the traditional secondary EU labour law legislation, which is based, in particular, on Article 153(2) TFEU found in Part Three, Title X on Social Policy. Accordingly, the CJEU indeed confirmed that, as opposed to much of the 'traditional' EU labour law secondary legislation, the purpose of the Framework Directive 78/2000 is not 'to protect only workers as the weaker party in an employment relationship', but rather 'to eliminate, on grounds relating to social and public interest, all discriminatory obstacles to access to livelihoods and to the capacity to contribute to society through work, irrespective of the legal form in which it is provided'.[23]

Interestingly, the Court could likely have arrived at the same result using the traditional and mutually exclusive concepts of 'worker' and 'self-employed'. The Court has held on several occasions that workers and self-employed persons form a continuum that covers all economic services, so that 'any activity which a person performs outside a relationship of subordination must be classified as an activity pursued in a self-employed capacity'.[24] For the purposes of answering the referred question, it might have been sufficient to copy the reasoning made in Case C-232/09, *Danosa*, where the Court concluded that, even if Ms Danosa did not qualify as a worker, she would – by way of exclusion – have to be considered a self-employed person and, thus, still be protected due to her pregnancy (albeit under a different directive, in that case).[25] Thus, in Case C-587/20, *HK/Danmark*, the Court could have ruled that the hotly contested topic of subordination would only be relevant for establishing under which exact part of Article 3(1)(a) she fell, but that it was not of practical importance for her right not to be discriminated on grounds of age. Instead, the Court chose to emphasize the broader social objectives of the Framework Directive 78/2000. On this background, the Court stated that as in so far as the post of sector convenor of *HK/Privat* constituted 'real and genuine professional activity', the conditions for access to that post would be covered under the Framework Directive 78/2000 regardless of whether or not the person occupying the post was characterized as a worker.

22. *Ibid.*, para. 27.
23. *Ibid.*, para. 34.
24. Case C-268/99, *Aldona Malgorzata Jany m.fl. v. Staatssecretaris van Justitie*, 20.11.2001, ECLI:EU:C:2001:616, para. 34.
25. Case C-232/09, *Danosa*, para. 70.

§12.04 'UPWARDS' AND 'DOWNWARDS' LIMITS IN SCOPE?

In the English translation of the CJEU ruling, the plaintiff, A, is described as a 'convenor' of the organization, which the dictionary defines as a trade union official of high rank who works in a particular factory. This terminology is somewhat unclear and might leave the impression that the judgment only applies to trade unions or that it must be read in the light of some very specific facts of the case. However, it is important to note that the position of 'convenor' in the case was, in terms of responsibilities, similar to a typical position of chairman of the board or other upper/top management positions in a company. The plaintiff in the case did not work at a particular office or factory. She was the manager of (a sector of) the trade union itself and was therefore ultimately in charge of a large business and responsible for hundreds of employees. As such, the conclusions in the ruling are not limited to labour organizations but are applicable to any type of manager or executive.

The judgment in Case C-587/20, *HK Danmark*, no doubt signals a broad and inclusive approach to the scope of the Framework Directive 78/2000. However, the CJEU did seem to establish some limits by stating that the Directive applied in the case 'in so far as the post of sector convenor of HK/Privat constitutes real and genuine professional activity'.[26] This notion is new and has not been used in previous case law. It clearly draws inspiration from a consistent case law on the concept of worker, where one of the key criteria is that a person pursues 'activities which are real and genuine, to the exclusion of activities on such a small scale as to be regarded as purely marginal and ancillary'.[27] In the worker definition, that criteria serves, broadly speaking, to distinguish the real economic activities whose free movement the Treaty gives special protections from activities that are more private in nature and therefore are not as important to the economic integration of the Union as a whole.

With the CJEU's adaptation of this criteria in the scope of the Framework Directive 78/2000 in Case C-587/20, *HK Danmark*, it is clear that despite being founded on human rights principles rather than the traditional objectives of economic and social integration pursued by EU employment law, the Framework Directive 78/2000 does not apply to everyone and everything. In order to enjoy protection under the Directive, the activity needs to be both 'professional' (as opposed to leisure, amateur, private, unpaid occupations?) and 'real and genuine' (i.e., have some degree of substance to it?). These criteria seem to establish a 'downwards' limit of applicability when the activity is too insignificant to a person's professional life to warrant protection.

In its ruling, the CJEU noted that the position in question qualified as a real and genuine professional activity 'in particular in so far as it concerns a full-time occupational activity which is remunerated by monthly salary'.[28] However, one should be careful not to overstate the importance of this interposed sentence. It cannot be taken to mean that only full-time jobs with a monthly salary are covered – only that such

26. Case C-587/20, *HK Danmark*, para. 35.
27. Cf., *inter alia*, Case C-658/18, *UX v. Governo della Repubblica italiana (Status of Italian Magistrates)*, 16.7.2020, ECLI:EU:C:2020:572, para. 93.
28. Case C-587/20, *HK Danmark*, para. 35.

positions quite obviously qualify. The seeming connection to the known criteria of 'real and genuine activity' in the worker concept suggests that some type of remuneration is a prerequisite for falling within the scope of Article 3(1)(a). But in that case, some unpaid positions would likely just fall under Article 3(1)(b) instead, which includes, *inter alia*, 'practical work experience'. When these two provisions are read together and in light of the broad objectives of the Directive as outlined in Case C-587/20, *HK Danmark*, it may well be that the CJEU would opt for a more holistic assessment of whether a given activity - paid or unpaid - is undertaken in a professional capacity or not.

Nevertheless, excluded from the scope of the Framework Directive 78/2000 appears to be, e.g., unpaid occupations that are undertaken in the private sphere and not as a means to achieve a livelihood or otherwise in a professional capacity, including, presumably, even unpaid top management positions in certain associations, etc. Even if such unpaid occupations may contribute just as much to society, the wording, context and purpose of the Directive limit its scope to activities that are economic in nature.[29]

The ruling raises a question on the position of non-executive managers who are far from being occupied full time in any one such position - such as professional board members who are involved in multiple companies and have a full-time job besides this activity. It seems hard to find valid reasons in the ruling that such board members should be excluded from the scope of the Directive as long as the activity is in fact undertaken in some sort of professional capacity - even if the direct remuneration for each position might be insignificant. Such activities are no doubt a way of 'contributing to society through work',[30] and it seems difficult to accept that companies and organizations should be given carte blanche to exclude persons of a certain sexuality or religion from their board just because the position is not very time-demanding.[31]

Even though the ruling leaves some room to speculate on this 'downwards' limit in scope of the Directive, it has undoubtedly clarified that this particular Directive is not limited 'upwards' in scope in the sense that it ceases to apply once the person in question has so much autonomy that he or she can no longer be considered a worker. The CJEU unambiguously rejected the relevance of the criteria of subordination. This means that any restriction of access to top management positions can be examined under the Directive, regardless of whether these restrictions follow from company bylaws or from national legislation, and regardless of whether the discrimination in question is direct or indirect.

29. The preparatory works of the Directive show that the Parliament suggested an addition to Art. 3, which would have meant that the Directive would also apply to 'unpaid and voluntary work' (European Parliament, *Report on the proposal for a Council directive establishing a general framework for equal treatment in employment and occupation*, A5-0264/2000, 21.9.2000). This suggestion was not included in the final version of the Framework Directive 78/2000.
30. Case C-587/20, *HK Danmark*, para. 34.
31. This consequence was also highlighted in Opinion of AG Richard de la Tour, *supra* n. 19, para. 70.

§12.05 DISCRIMINATION IN THE ELECTION PROCESS?

The prohibition against discrimination is not affected by the fact that a management position is achieved through an election. In this regard, the CJEU noted in its ruling – in line with previous case law – that the method of recruitment to a post has no bearing on the application of that directive.[32] The fact that the chairwoman in question achieved her post through an election on the general assembly could not disqualify the position as an 'occupation' within the meaning of the Framework Directive 78/2000.[33]

On the one hand, it seems to follow logically that, in principle, the prohibition against discrimination would also apply to the selection process itself, which in this case is the election. On the other hand, this seems to give rise to some complicated issues since each individual voter – whether it be the members of a general assembly electing a board member or the board electing an executive manager – might have different and private motivations for their vote. The rules on burden of proof in Article 10 of the Framework Directive 78/2000 make the matter even more delicate. In theory, if the prohibition on discrimination does apply in this situation, and a manager could establish facts from which it might be presumed that there had been direct or indirect discrimination, then it would fall on the company or the organization to prove that the collective decision of the general assembly did not carry discriminatory motivations (or that such motivations at least were not decisive to the outcome?), which would likely be difficult. It remains to be seen whether such a situation would indeed be covered by the Directive, and in that case how the rules on burden of proof would be applied.

32. Case C-587/20, *HK Danmark*, para. 38.
33. Neither could the argument that the position was 'political' in nature.

CHAPTER 13

The Protection of Managers in the Event of Employer Insolvency: The Scope of European Union Law

Mette Søsted Hemme & Line Herman Langkjær

§13.01 INTRODUCTION

In the event of employer insolvency, employees and managers (executive or non-executive) may have claims for unpaid remuneration. Remuneration provides the means to uphold the general livelihood of the recipients, and, thus, claims for unpaid remuneration have a different character than ordinary creditor claims. Employees are not, unlike other contracting parties, in a position to protect themselves from the consequences of the contracting party's insolvency by demanding the provision of security.[1] Insolvency proceedings often take a very long time, and distributable assets are in many cases not sufficient to cover employees' outstanding claims.[2] Thus, with the aim of improving the working and living conditions of employees, the Council of the European Communities adopted the Insolvency Directive in 1980.[3] The main feature of the Directive was the obligation for Member States to establish a body, which guarantees payment of outstanding claims of employees in the event of employer insolvency. The Insolvency Directive requires that the guarantee institution covers employees' claims arising from contracts of employment or employment relationships, but the Directive does not define who should be considered an employee. The

1. Proposal for a Council Directive on the approximation of the laws of the Member States concerning the protection of employees in the event of the insolvency of their employer, COM(78) 141 final, preamble (Proposal for Directive 80/987/EEC).
2. *Ibid.*
3. Council Directive 80/987/EEC of 20 October 1980 on the approximation of the laws of the Member States relating to the protection of employees in the event of the insolvency of their employer, OJ L 283, 28.10.1980.

definition of the term 'employee' is left for national law, cf. Article 2(2). In this contribution, the personal scope of the Insolvency Directive is examined closer in order to assess the status of *managers* in the event of employer insolvency under EU law.

In §13.02, we first analyse the personal scope of the Insolvency Directive in general, including a discussion on whether EU law sets any limitations on the discretion of national law. In §13.03, it is examined whether Member States – in accordance with EU law – can exclude a manager of a company from the protection laid down in the Insolvency Directive. In §13.04, we briefly address the implications for the manager, who may not be covered by the protection offered by the Insolvency Directive. Finally, in §13.05, we conclude this chapter by addressing the possible consequences of the different national solutions in this area of law.

§13.02 THE INSOLVENCY DIRECTIVE

[A] Introduction to the Insolvency Directive

With the adoption of the Insolvency Directive, Member States were required to establish a body to guarantee payment of outstanding claims of employees in the event of employer insolvency.[4] Since the adoption, the Directive has been amended several times and is now codified in Directive 2008/94/EC.[5] The Insolvency Directive is a partial harmonization directive, laying down a minimum degree of protection for the outstanding claims of employees.[6]

The main reason for adopting the Directive was to improve the inadequate protection of employees' claims in the event of employer insolvency across the different Member States.[7] Moreover, the aim was to approximate the laws of Member States in this particular field, in order for employees to receive equal protection in all Member States.[8] At the time of adoption, some Member States had already established national guarantee institutions, whereas other Member States had not. The terms for being granted a guarantee for unpaid claims varied widely.[9] Even between those Member States who already had guarantee institutions the terms for being granted a guarantee for unpaid claims varied widely. The existing differences in legislation across Member States were regarded as reinforcing social imbalances within the Union, and approximation of laws in this field was seen as a tool to combat these social imbalances.[10]

The Insolvency Directive pursues a social objective as it aims to ensure a minimum degree of protection of employees in the event of the insolvency of their

4. *Ibid.*
5. Directive 2008/94/EC of the European Parliament and of the Council of 22 October 2008 on the protection of employees in the event of the insolvency of their employer, amended by Directive 2015/1794/EU.
6. *Ibid.*, recital 3 of the preamble.
7. Proposal for Directive 80/987/EEC, preamble.
8. *Ibid.*
9. *Ibid.*
10. *Ibid.*

employer, cf. recital 3 of the preamble. Claims relating to salary are, by their very nature, of great importance to the individual concerned.[11] In order to avoid excessive demands on the financial resources of the guarantee institutions, Member States are, nonetheless, allowed to set limitations on the responsibility of the institutions, cf., *inter alia*, Article 4(3). This provision stipulates that Member States may set ceilings on the payments made by the guarantee institution.[12] Thus, it is clear that the Directive is not limited to welfarist objectives.[13] The Directive aims to secure a balanced economic and social development in the European Union.

[B] The Scope of the Insolvency Directive

Insolvency law is an area of law in which harmonization has been met by political scepticism, making it difficult politically to find agreement.[14] This is also clear from the Insolvency Directive, where several core concepts have been left for national law to define, including the personal scope of the Directive.

The Insolvency Directive applies to employees' claims arising from contracts of employment or employment relationships and existing against employers who are in a state of insolvency, cf. Article 1(1). The Directive does not define who should be considered an employee and, therefore, who is protected. The term 'employee' is defined by reference to national law, cf. Article 2(2).[15] By letting national law be decisive for defining who is an employee, the European legislator refrained from using the autonomous EU concept of an employee, which has been applied in areas such as free movement of workers and non-discrimination, etc.[16] This also means that who will be protected by the Directive could potentially vary greatly among the Member States and is almost entirely dependent on where the person concerned is working. One person working in Member State A could be protected in Member State A, whereas a person performing the exact same tasks and holding the same position in Member State B would not be protected. Although this lack of harmonization of the personal scope results in divergences across Member States, it is not surprising in light of the mentioned political setting.

After the adoption of the Directive, the Commission became increasingly concerned that the reference to national definitions of 'employee' could limit the scope of

11. As recognized by the CJEU in Case C-125/01, *Peter Pflücke v. Bundesanstalt für Arbeit*, 18.9.2003, EU:C:2003:477, para. 37.
12. Limitations must, however, be compatible with the social objective of the Directive, cf. recital 7 of the preamble.
13. *See* similar, Catherine Barnard, *EU Employment Law*, 647 (4th ed., Oxford University Press 2012).
14. Emilie Ghio et al., *Harmonising Insolvency Law in the EU: New Thoughts on Old Ideas in the Wake of the COVID-19 Pandemic*, 30 INSOL 3, 427-459 (2021).
15. Other core concepts, such as 'employer', 'pay', 'right conferring immediate entitlement' and 'right conferring prospective entitlement' are also left for national law to define, whereas the Directive defines, when an employer is in a state of insolvency.
16. T. Davulis, *Chapter 6: 2008/95/EC – Employer Insolvency 459* (Monika Schlachter ed., Kluwer Law International 2014).

the protection provided by the Directive in an unsatisfactory way.[17] Although the scope is (still) generally left for the Member States, the national room of manoeuvre was limited with the adoption of some minimum requirements in amendment Directive 2002/74/EC. The Directive now requires that certain characteristics about the employment cannot be used to reduce the scope. According to Article 2(2), Member States cannot exclude part-time employees, fixed-term employees and employees with a temporary employment relationship.[18] This is also in line with the principle of non-discrimination in these atypical work directives. Furthermore, Member States cannot set a minimum duration for the contract of employment or the employment relationship in order for an employee to qualify for claims, cf. Article 2(3).

In general, all employees must be protected under the Directive, but the Directive does contain several options to *exclude* particular employees. Since these are exceptions to the general rule, they must be construed and applied narrowly.[19] First, Member States may exclude claims by certain categories of employees from the scope of the Directive, by virtue of the existence of *other forms of guarantee*, if it is established that these offer the persons concerned a degree of protection equivalent to that resulting from the Directive, cf. Article 1(2). As evident from the (now repealed) Annex to the Directive, only four Member States excluded a few particular types of employees under this exception, when the Insolvency Directive was adopted.[20] This exclusion is, thus, assumedly of limited relevance in the Member States overall.

Second, Member States may continue to exclude *domestic servants* employed by a natural person from the scope of the Directive, where such provision already applies in national legislation, cf. Article 1(3).[21]

Third, according to Article 12(a), Member States are allowed to take necessary measures to avoid *abuse*. This allows for the exclusion of employees from the scope of the Insolvency Directive due to risk of abusive or unjustifiable circumstances. The abuse referred to in Article 12(a) is 'abusive practices that adversely affect the guarantee institutions by artificially giving rise to a claim for salary, thereby illegally triggering a payment obligation on the part of those institutions'.[22]

---

17. COM(2000) 832 final, section 4.1.2.
18. Within the meaning of, respectively, Directive 1997/81/EC, Directive 1999/70/EC, Directive 1991/383/ EEC. With Directive 2008/94, the term 'worker' was replaced with 'employee'.
19. Case C-201/01, *Maria Walcher v. Bundesamt für Soziales und Behindertenwesen Steiermark*, 11.9.2003, EU:C:2003:450, para. 38. Similar in Case C-435/10, *J.C van Ardennen v. Raad van bestuur van het Uitvoeringsinstituut werknemersverzekeringen*, 17.11.2011, EU:C:2011:751, para. 34, where the CJEU ruled that Article 4 of the Insolvency Directive 'must be interpreted strictly and in conformity with its social objective, which is to guarantee a minimum of protection to all employees'. Similar in Case C-309/12, *Maria Albertina Gomes Viana Novo and Others v. Fundo de Garantia Salarial IP*, 28.11.2013, EU:C:2013:774, para. 31.
20. As an example, Greece, United Kingdom and Italy excluded the crews of sea-going vessels. The Insolvency Directive was amended in 2015 with regard to the exclusion of seafarers, *see* immediately *infra*.
21. The possibility to exclude share-fishermen was repealed with Directive 2015/1794/EU of the European Parliament and of the Council of 6 October 2015.
22. Case C-201/01, *Walcher*, para. 39.

Fourth, Member States can refuse or reduce the liability or the guarantee obligation if it appears that fulfilment of the obligation is *unjustifiable* because of the existence of *special links* between the employee and the employer and of common interests resulting in *collusion* between them, cf. Article 12(b). This provision is intended to prevent fraud or fictitious employment contracts, as indicated by the Commission.[23] The rejection or reduction of liability based on this provision requires at least two elements to be present: (1) special links between employee and employer and (2) common interests resulting in collusion. An example of the existence of special links is the employment of close relatives or spouses. As argued in Danish Law, creditors could find it offensive and unfair if a person who, due to the special link between the debtor and the employee, i.e., a spouse, has benefitted (in)directly from the company in good times should also be treated preferentially during bad times.[24] The exclusion of close relatives or spouses was an opt-in possibility for Member States in the former Annex to the Directive. In connection with the amendment of the 2002 directive, the Commission considered that the possible exclusion of close relatives or spouses should be derived from the Directive itself and not the Annex (which was repealed with the 2002 directive).[25] The Directive does not contain a specific exclusion of claims raised by close relatives or spouses, and so it seems that in order to reduce or reject guarantee protection for this special group of employees, the conditions in Article 12(b) must be met. In other words, the special nature of the relationship is not enough; there must also be common interests resulting in collusion, i.e., fraud or fictitious employment contracts. The provision does seem somewhat ambiguous, as it is not clear what is meant by 'special links' in the provision or whether all types of fraud or fictitious employment relationships fall under the scope of Article 12(b), irrespective of the nature of the 'link' between employee and employer.

Finally, Member States may refuse or reduce the liability or the guarantee obligation in cases where the employee, on his or her own or together with his or her close relatives, was the *owner of an essential part* of the employer's undertaking or business *and* had a *considerable influence* on its activities, cf. Article 12(c). This provision is, *inter alia*, based on the implicit assumption that an employee who, simultaneously, owned an essential shareholding in the undertaking concerned and had a considerable influence on its activities could, thereby, be partly responsible for its insolvency.[26] It is worth noting that the latter provision does not require any abusive practice by the employee. By default - it appears - the Directive recognizes that it may be unjustifiable to give (full) protection to this specific category of employees.

Whether managers can be excluded from the protection offered by the Insolvency Directive with reference to Article 12 is dealt with in §13.03 *infra*.

23. COM(2000) 832 final, Explanatory Memorandum, section 4.1.2.
24. Cf. Report 1 of 1958-Committee of the Ministry of Justice, *Betænkning nr 423/1966 Betænkning I Konkursordenen*, 31.
25. COM(2000) 832 final, Explanatory Memorandum, section 4.1.2.
26. Case C-30/10, *Lotta Andersson v. Staten genom Kronofogdemyndigheten i Jönköping, Tillsynsmyndigheten, 10.2.2011*, EU:C:2011:66, para. 24.

[1] EU Law Limitations to the Scope

As mentioned above, the employee definition in the Insolvency Directive has been left for the Member States. The Member States are, however, not entirely free to set a national scope of application. EU law may set certain limits to the national definition of who is protected by a directive, when the Directive refers to the national concept of employee.[27] In this section, we examine which EU law limitations can be derived from CJEU case law to the national scope of protection in the Insolvency Directive.[28] First, we focus on the concept of employee and, second, on the possible exclusions from the scope in Article 12.

[a] EU Limitations to the Concept of Employee

CJEU has consistently held that the Insolvency Directive is intended to apply to 'all categories of employees' defined as such by the national law of a Member State, e.g., in Case C-334/92, *Wagner Miret*.[29] Here, the referring court had asked if higher management staff could be excluded from the scope of protection.[30] Mr Wagner Miret was a member of the higher management staff of an undertaking that became insolvent, and he claimed unpaid salary and severance payments from the Spanish guarantee institution. His application was dismissed on the ground that he had been a member of the higher management staff. According to the CJEU, this was not allowed since higher management staff were regarded as employees according to Spanish law.[31] In other words, CJEU relies heavily on the term 'employee' in the text of the Directive and the national definition of the term.

In Case C-311/13, *Tümer*,[32] CJEU clarified that national law cannot define at will the term 'employee' for the purpose of the Insolvency Directive. The *social objective* of the Directive must not be undermined by national definitions. In *Tümer*, the Dutch legislator explicitly exempted third-country nationals who were not legally resident in the Netherlands from the scope of protection of the payment guarantee. Whereas Mr

27. CJEU's judgment in Case C-216/15, *Betriebsrat der Ruhrlandklinik gGmbH v. Ruhrlandklinik gGmbH*, 17.11.2016, EU:C:2016:883, which concerns the scope of the Temporary Agency Work Directive 2008/104/EC, is one of the most prominent examples of EU law setting such limitations to Member State discretion.
28. For a broad exploration of the concept of employee in EU law, *see*, *inter alia*, Martin Risak & Thomas Dullinger, *The Concept of 'Worker' in EU Law: Status Quo and Potential for Change* (ETUI 2018), and Nicola Kountouris, *The Concept of 'Worker' in European Labour Law: Fragmentation, Autonomy and Scope*, 47 Industrial Law Journal 2, 192 (2017) DOI: 10.1093/indlaw/dwx014.
29. Case C-334/92, *Teodoro Wagner Miret v. Fondo de Garantía Salarial*, 16.12.1993, EU:C:1993:945, para. 12; and Case C-201/01, *Walcher*, para. 30.
30. Spain had not requested to include the category of higher management staff in the Annex to the Directive, which – until amendment of Directive 2002/74/EC – was a possibility to exclude certain categories of employees from the scope of the Directive.
31. *See* the Opinion of Advocate General Lenz delivered on 15 July 1993, Case C-334/92, *Wagner Miret*, EU:C:1993:322, note 8.
32. Case C-311/13, *O. Tümer v. Raad van bestuur van het Uitvoeringsinstituut werknemersverzekeringen*, 5.11.2014, EU:C:2014:2337.

Tümer was not regarded an employee within the meaning of the Dutch guarantee scheme, Mr Tümer was regarded as an employee under Dutch civil law and could, in that capacity, bring judicial proceedings for payment of wages against the employer. The CJEU stated that the discretion enjoyed by Member States for the purposes of defining the term 'employee' is not 'wholly unfettered'.[33] The CJEU concluded that the Directive must be interpreted as precluding such national legislation. First, the CJEU relied on the wording and the context of the Directive by stating, 'neither Article 1(1) nor the other provisions of Directive 80/987 exclude third-country nationals from the scope of the Directive; nor do they expressly permit Member States to do so'.[34] Second, the CJEU relied on the objective of the Directive by stating, 'the first subparagraph of Article 2(2) must be interpreted in light of the social objective of that directive, and, therefore, *Member States cannot define at will the term employee in such a way as to undermine that social objective*'.[35]

Even though the Court does not expressly refer to the principle of effectiveness in the ruling, the Court essentially deploys an effective protection of the social objective of the Directive. This is in line with the overall tendency of those EU directives that refer to employment relationships as defined in national law. Here, CJEU has tended to apply the concept of *effet utile* (principle of effectiveness).[36] The aim is to limit Member States from applying rules that are liable to impede the objectives pursued by a directive, and, therefore, deprive it of its effectiveness.[37] The principle of effectiveness is a general principle of EU law that is strongly linked to the authority and primacy of EU law over national law.[38] It may be added that CJEU has referred to the principle of effectiveness in relation to national definitions of employee in the context of other labour law directives (such as in Case C-393/10, *O'Brien*,[39] and Case C-216/15, *Ruhrlandklinik*).[40]

An interesting aspect of the case in Case C-311/13, *Tümer*, is that Advocate General Bot argued for a *wider application of EU law limitations*, including the duty to exercise that right consistently with EU law as such:

> it is important to emphasise that that discretion cannot have the effect of compromising either the general scheme or the effectiveness of Directive 80/987 and *must be exercised consistently with EU law and, in particular, with the*

33. *Ibid.*, para. 35.
34. *Ibid.*, para. 36.
35. *Ibid.*, para. 42. Emphasis added.
36. European Commission, Directorate-General Employment, *Report Expert Group, Transposition of Directive (EU) 2019/1152 on transparent and predictable working conditions in the European Union* (2021), 10.
37. *Ibid.*
38. M. Elvira Mendez-Pinedo, *The Principle of Effectiveness of EU Law: A Difficult Concept in Legal Scholarship*, 11 Juridical Tribune 1, 6 (2021).
39. Case C-393/10, *Dermod Patrick O'Brien v. Ministry of Justice*, 1.3.2012, EU:C:2012:110, which concerned Directive 1997/81/EC on part-time work.
40. Case C-216/15, *Ruhrlandklinik*, which concerned Directive 2008/104/EC on temporary agency work.

fundamental principles enshrined therein, which include the principle of equal treatment and non-discrimination.[41]

Even though CJEU did not refer to any of these EU law limitations in Case C-311/13, *Tümer*, it is worth noting that the CJEU has 'gone further' in the interpretation of other provisions in the Insolvency Directive. In Case C-442/00, *Caballero*,[42] the CJEU stated in general terms that 'where national rules fall within the scope of Community law, and reference is made to the Court for a preliminary ruling, the Court must provide all the criteria of interpretation needed by the national court to determine whether those rules are compatible with the fundamental rights the observance of which the Court ensures'. The case specifically concerned the general principle of equality and non-discrimination. Later, in Case C–498/06, *Robledillo Núñez*, the CJEU stated that the power of national law, recognized by the Insolvency Directive, to specify the benefits payable by the guarantee institution is conditional upon the requirements flowing from the general principle of equality and non-discrimination.[43] That principle precludes comparable situations from being treated in a different manner unless the difference in treatment is objectively justified. The CJEU has (so far) only extended its interpretation to limit Member State discretion with reference to the general principle of equality and non-discrimination with regard to material rights in the Directive, not the personal scope. The overall objective of the CJEU in deploying the principle of effectiveness is to prohibit Member States from arbitrarily excluding persons who are comparable to (or not substantially different from) workers under the national concept.[44] Thus, it seems natural that the general principle of equality and non-discrimination may also (in the future) be relied on in the context of the personal scope of the Directive. Perhaps, the CJEU did not extend its interpretation in Case C-311/13, *Tümer* further, as it was not deemed necessary in the specific case.

In Case C-311/13, *Tümer*, the CJEU also refrained from stating that the national definition of employee must be exercised consistently with 'EU law as such'. This was, however, proposed by Advocate General Bot as stated above. Such broad reference could lead to the notion that the national definition of employee should be interpreted in conformity with the autonomous EU law concept of employee deployed under Article 45 TFEU. Such a development would likely be seen as a challenge to the principles of subsidiarity and legitimacy of the CJEU. The restraint exercised by the

41. Opinion of Advocate General Bot in Case C-311/13, *Tümer*, 12.6.2014, EU:C:2014:1997. Emphasis added.
42. Case C 442-00, *Ángel Rodríguez Caballero v. Fondo de Garantía Salarial (Fogasa), 12.12.2002*, EU:C:2002:752, para. 31.
43. Case C-498/06, *Maira María Robledillo Núñez v. Fondo de Garantía Salarial (Fogasa)*, 21.2.2008, EU:C:2008:109, para. 30. Similar in Case C-198/13, *Víctor Manuel Julian Hernández and Other v. Reino de España and Others*, 10.7.2014, EU:C:2014:2055, para. 32, as well as older case law such as Case C-520/03, *José Vicente Olaso Valero v. Fondo de Garantía Salarial (Fogasa)*, 16.12.2004, EU:C:2004:826, para. 34, and Case C-81/05, *Anacleto Cordero Alonso v. Fondo de Garantía Salarial (Fogasa)*, 7.9.2006, EU:C:2006:529, paras 35-37.
44. The wording used *supra* n. 36, 12, is also closely associated with the principle of anti-discrimination: '... it is still open which differences between groups of working persons could have a justifying effect for excluding a particular group from the scope of protection...'.

CJEU in this regard could be considered wise in order for the CJEU to avoid allegations of judicial activism.[45]

Finally, the CJEU in Case C-311/13, *Tümer,* clarified another separate 'limitation' or criteria relating to the concept of employee in the Insolvency Directive. The Court highlighted that the definition of the term 'employee' in the Insolvency Directive refers to an employment relationship that gives rise to a right, held vis-à-vis the employer, to *receive payment for work done.*[46] The CJEU uses the criterion - the entitlement to pay - to classify a relationship as an employment relationship specifically under the Insolvency Directive. Thus, it was contrary to the social objective of the Insolvency Directive to deny claims for guarantees of remuneration to individuals, who under national legislation are attributed the status of employees with a right to claim wages against their employer.[47] The criterion of a right to claim wages is natural, as it would not be logical to demand the inclusion of persons who are not able to direct a wage claim against the employer under the national payment guarantee scheme. This rationale has now been reiterated in CJEU's recent judgment in Case C-101/21, *HJ.*[48]

[b] Exclusions to the Scope Stemming from Article 12

As stated *supra* §13.02[A], Article 12 allows for Member States to refuse or reduce protection offered by the Directive due to either: (a) abuse, (b) special links and collusion, or (c) ownership and considerable influence. As demonstrated below, the CJEU has on multiple occasions interpreted to which extent Article 12 allows Member States to reduce the protection.

In Case C-201/01, *Walcher,* the CJEU referred to the *principle of effectiveness* as setting limits for national rules that aim to prevent abuse of the national guarantee schemes. The case concerned Miss Walcher, who was an employee as well as a significant shareholder (with no dominant influence) in the company that became insolvent. Miss Walcher's right to guarantee for her unpaid salary was lost under Austrian law, as she had not made a genuine demand for payment of salary or resigned within sixty days from the time she was in a position to know that the company was no longer creditworthy.[49] It was undisputed in the case that Miss Walcher was an employee. Taking into account the considerations behind the Austrian case law, the CJEU considered that that case law did not relate to practices liable to constitute abuses within the meaning of Article 10(a) of the Insolvency Directive (now Article 12(a)). The CJEU pointed out that 'a national rule intended to prevent abuse must not prejudice the *full effect and uniform application of Community law in the Member States.* In particular, it is not open to national courts to compromise the objectives pursued by the

45. Similar, Kountouris, *supra* n. 28, at 204-205.
46. Case C-311/13, *Tümer,* para. 44.
47. *Ibid.,* para. 45.
48. Case C-101/21, *HJ v. Ministerstvo práce a sociálních věcí,* 5.5.2022, EU:C:2022:356, para. 35.
49. Miss Walcher's outstanding claims arising out of her employment relationship were, according to Austrian case law, regarded as equivalent to a capital contribution to the company.

directive in question'.[50] Thus, the principle of effectiveness sets limits as to whom Member States can exclude with reference to Article 12 (*see also* §13.03 *infra*).

The same guiding principles were stated again by the CJEU in Case C-30/10, *Andersson,*[51] where, however, the Court came to the conclusion that the Swedish provision in question *was* in conformity with Article 12(c) of the Insolvency Directive.[52] The provision excluded an employee from entitlement on the ground that the employee, alone or together with close relatives, within the *six months preceding the application for a declaration of insolvency,* was the owner of an essential part of the undertaking or business concerned and had a considerable influence on its activities.

Moreover, as seen most recently in Case C-101/21, *HJ,* the CJEU may deploy a proportionality test in relation to Member State action under Article 12. The principle of proportionality normally entails three stages of enquiry: whether the measure is suitable to achieve the desired result, whether it is necessary to achieve the desired result, and whether the measure imposes a burden that is excessive in relation to the objective sought after.[53] In Case C-101/21, *HJ,* the specific question was whether it was lawful for national case law to lay down a non-rebuttable presumption of abuse, thereby excluding certain types of managers. The ruling is commented on in more detail in §13.03 *infra*. But for the sake of this section, we may conclude that the CJEU in that ruling applied the general principle of proportionality in the context of Article 12(a) in the Insolvency Directive.

To summarize on the EU law limitations to the scope of the Directive, it must be noted that there are several limitations to the national freedom to determine the scope of the Insolvency Directive. The limitations include the principle of effectiveness, the social objective of the Directive, the general principle of equality and non-discrimination, the principle of proportionality, and a restrictive interpretation of the exceptions in Article 12. Not all limitations have (yet) been expressly used for the personal scope of the Directive, but the CJEU has relied on them in other contexts of the Insolvency Directive and corresponds to the overall framework of effectiveness.

§13.03 MAY MANAGERS BE EXEMPT FROM THE SCOPE OF THE DIRECTIVE?

Managers are not mentioned as a category of their own that must be covered by the scope of the Directive, such as fixed-term employees, and they are not mentioned as a category that can be excluded either. According to the system of the Insolvency Directive, whether a manager (executive or non-executive) falls under the personal scope of the Insolvency Directive is therefore dependent on: (1) is the manager

50. Case C-201/01, *Walcher,* para. 37. Emphasis added.
51. Case C-30/10, *Andersson,* paras 25-26.
52. The principle of effectiveness has also been deployed by the CJEU in Case C-125/01, *Pflücke,* in an assessment of national time limits for lodging applications. Such provisions must respect the general principles of EU law, notably the principles of equivalence and effectiveness, cf. paras 33-36.
53. Paul Craig & Gráinne de Búrca, *EU Law – Text, Cases, and Materials,* 583 (7th ed. Oxford University Press 2020).

considered an employee under national law and (2) if so can the manager be excluded with reference to one of the exceptions mentioned in §13.02 *supra.*

The Insolvency Directive rests on the assumption that such a national (universal) definition of employee exists and that it is possible to establish whether a manager falls inside or outside the scope of such a definition. It may, however, be challenging in some Member States to establish one universal employee concept under national law. In section A, the implications and practical issues related to this assumption of a universal employee concept are discussed. In section B, it is examined whether a manager that is considered an employee under national law may nonetheless be excluded on the basis of Article 12 in the Insolvency Directive.

[A] The Manager as an Employee?

If managers fall within the overall (or universal) concept of employee in a Member State, they fall as a general rule within the scope of the Insolvency Directive, cf. CJEU in Case C-334/92, *Wagner Miret*. This is the case, even if managers under national law are treated as a separate category of employees. This is clear from the wording and social objective of the Directive and is further supported by the principle of effectiveness – and perhaps even the general principle of equal treatment.

There are various national solutions for defining who is an employee in a Member State and, in particular, who is an employee covered by the national guarantee scheme. From the Commission's report in 1995 on the national transposition of the Insolvency Directive, it is evident that national solutions vary greatly with regard to defining who is an employee in this regard.[54]

For the sake of this chapter, we can distinguish between two main 'models'. In some Member States, the term 'employee' is defined by legislation ('legal statutory definition').[55] This is the case, e.g., in Germany and Poland.[56] However, in many Member States, there is no singular legal definition in legislation. It may instead have been left to the courts to assess the definition of employee on a case-by-case basis ('case-by-case assessment'). It will often be assessed for each individual legislation or area of law who is defined as an employee, i.e., a heterogeneous definition depending on the source of law. This is the case in Denmark, where many sources, however, refer to a more or less generic employee concept that is defined by general criteria. At least in borderline cases, the term 'employee' is still dependent on the specific statutory act or collective agreement in question.[57] It may be added that, at least in Denmark, the

54. COM(95) 164 final, sections 4-9.
55. Bernd Waas, *Comparative Overview*, xxxv (Bernd Waas & Guus Heerma von Voss eds, Hart Publishing 2017).
56. In Germany, a legal singular definition of an employee was introduced in 2017, cf. section 611a para. 1 BGB (*Bürgerliches Gesetzbuch*). In Poland, there is also a legal definition of an employee, which has universal scope in the area of labour law, *see* Leszek Mitrus, *The Concept of 'Employee': The Position in Poland*, 532 (Bernd Waas & Guus Heerma von Voss eds, Hart Publishing 2017).
57. Jens Kristiansen, *The Concept of 'Employee': The Position in Denmark*, 136 (Bernd Waas & Guus Heerma von Voss eds, Hart Publishing 2017).

scope of some statutory acts is intentionally wide. This latter 'model' may be described as a selective approach to the employee definition, as the specific source of law is – at least in borderline cases – decisive for the scope.

When turning more specifically to the legal definition of managers (as employees or not employees), this is also dealt with in different ways in the Member States. In German law, different legal definitions of executive managers apply in different legal contexts.[58] As stated by Weiss et al., '[t]hese differences are partly due to the functional necessity of treating executive staff in a way which may vary in different fields of labour law'.[59] Although some Member States may define a position as a 'manager' position (executive or non-executive) in national legislation, the decisive question is whether such a manager qualifies as an employee. This test will depend on the character of the work/position rather than the title of the position. The CJEU has taken a functional approach and looks at the underlying relationship between the employee and employer (person/organization receiving his or her work) irrespective of the legal characterization of the employment relationship under national law.[60] In some jurisdictions such as Denmark, it is widely accepted that executive managers are not covered by the ordinary employee concept across various legislation. Essentially, however, it depends on the actual circumstances and the personal scope of the legislation in question of whether a manager is an employee. Managers' status as employees may – in other words – intentionally vary across national legislation.

[1] The Implications for Member States?

The assessment of who is to be considered an employee under national law, with a view to establishing the scope of the Directive, may be challenging for Member States using either of the two models.

As for those Member States that apply a legal statutory definition, this model may ensure some foreseeability and uniform application (in principle), but it does not necessarily limit the court's discretionary interpretation or reduce legal uncertainty. It may be added that the definition of an employee is not static, and new types of work may challenge the (traditional) scope of national employee legislation. As visible on EU level, there is currently a proposal to introduce a new mechanism with regard to the assessment of employee status in platform work.[61]

In those Member States, where no universal employee concept exists, other issues arise. As one general national concept of employee may not be possible to establish, the Directive rests on an assumption that may be hard to reconcile with

58. Bernd Waas, *Restatement of Labour Law in Europe, Volume 1: The Concept of Employee*, 258 (Bernd Waas & Guus Heerma von Voss eds, Hart Publishing 2017).
59. Manfred Weiss et al., *Labour Law and Industrial Relations in Germany*, 52 (5th ed. Kluwer Law International 2020).
60. *See* the characteristics brought forward by the CJEU in Case C-216/15, *Ruhrlandklinik*, para. 43.
61. Proposal for a Directive of the European Parliament and of the Council on improving working conditions in platform work (2021/0414 (COD)), Art. 4(1). Without changing the definition of employee, a legal presumption rule in favour of employee status is proposed due to the specific challenges present in the context of atypical work.

national law in these situations. This may pose a challenge not only to national authorities (legislators) but also to the courts when assessing whether the national interpretation is inside or outside the margin of appreciation for Member States. The question then arises whether EU law lays down requirements as to which national definition of employee is the applicable one in the context of the Insolvency Directive.

Although Member States enjoy a broad discretion when defining the concept of employee, that discretion is not unlimited. As stated by the CJEU numerous times, and latest in Case C-101/21, *HJ*, the concept of employee must be interpreted so as to ensure the effectiveness of the social objective of the Directive.[62] But does the social objective and the principle of *effet utile* then prescribe that managers should be included in the concept of employees? The answer to the question is not particularly clear.

On the one hand, the social objective of the Insolvency Directive would be an argument in favour of a more encompassing definition of employees to include managers. On the other hand, especially Article 12 of the Insolvency Directive demonstrates that a close connection between a person and the running of the (insolvent) company may make protection unreasonable or involve risk of abuse. Thus, relying on the scheme of the Directive itself, arguments could be made in favour of the exclusion of managers from the concept of employee in this context. The argument can also be put forward that the purpose of the legislation in question should be given due regard, especially at the outer boundaries of the traditional concept of employee status.[63]

Neither the Directive, nor case law from the CJEU,[64] nor the EU law principles seem to require a specific employee concept when the Member State applies a case-by-case assessment (multiple definitions). Neither does existing EU law suggest that a fictitious universal employee concept is construed, when there intentionally is none. From our point of view, one should rather rely on the employee concept in the relevant parts of national law that reflect the same or similar underlying principles and aims as in the Insolvency Directive.

As has also been put forward by Guy Davidov, the question is 'whether we need one single test – a unified meaning of the term "employee" for all labour law purposes – or rather allow room for variations and nuances'.[65] What is 'lost' in legal certainty is perhaps gained in nuanced results, taking into consideration the underlying (different) aims of different regulations of labour law issues.

In conclusion, the interpretation of the scope of the Insolvency Directive is far from straightforward in Member States, where there is no universal definition of who is to be considered an employee under national law, e.g., as one legal statutory definition. Rather than resorting to construe fictitious employee concepts in national law, we

62. Case C-101/21, *HJ*, para. 34, and Case C-311/13, *Tümer*.
63. Other authors arguing for a purposive approach when defining worker status under EU law, *see, e.g.*, Risak and Dullinger, *supra* n. 28, at 46. For an elaborate work on a purposive approach in labour law per se (not only EU-related), *see* Guy Davidov, *A Purposive Approach to Labour Law* (Oxford University Press 2016).
64. The issue that no universal employee concept could be meaningfully construed in a given Member State has not surfaced in CJEU case law.
65. Davidov, *supra* n. 63, at 122.

propose that (in those situations) the employee concept in other relevant parts of national law could be taken into account in the interpretation of whether a manager falls within the employee concept in terms of the guarantee protection. Finally, it must be underlined that even though a legal singular definition on the surface seems easier to apply, for those Member States, it could prove harder to achieve nuanced results, e.g., in the case of managers, who hold a special position when a company becomes insolvent.

[B] Exclusion of Managers, Who Are Employees, Cf. Article 12 of the Insolvency Directive?

Next, we turn to the question of whether *an employee* under national law may be excluded from the protection offered by the Directive because that person is a manager.

It is first recalled that, as a general rule, the exclusion of certain categories of employees is not in accordance with the social objective of the Insolvency Directive, as stated by CJEU in Case C-311/13, *Tümer*. As the Court held in Case C-334/92, *Wagner Miret*, higher management cannot be excluded from the scope of the Directive if they are regarded as employees under national law, albeit a special group of employees.[66]

However, when it comes to a top-level manager, they may hold a different position in the company than most ordinary employees. The manager will most likely have great insight into the company's affairs and will potentially also be partly responsible for the insolvency of the company. Based on Article 12, could this special position of the manager then justify an exclusion from protection despite being considered an employee under national law?

Those arguments were put forward in Case C-101/21, *HJ*.[67] The referring Czech court asked if national case law, according to which a person who, on the basis of a contract of employment, performs concurrently the duties of CEO and member of a statutory body of a company, is *not* protected by the Directive, is compatible with Article 12(a) on abusive practices and Article 12(c) on ownership. The person concerned held two positions as manager – one as executive and one as non-executive.

The CJEU found that the national Czech case law was not compatible with Article 12.[68] First, the CJEU briefly declined the referring court's argument relating to Article 12(c) simply because its two cumulative conditions were not fulfilled. The person in question did not own an essential part of the company.[69] Second, and more interesting for the question raised above, the CJEU assessed the national case law in light of Article 12(a). Article 12(a) enables Member States to take the measures necessary to avoid abusive practices. The CJEU confirmed that a national case law, which seeks to prevent a situation in which persons, who may be partly responsible for the insolvency of the company, obtain payment of outstanding claims on account of the insolvency of that company, follows 'the logic behind Article 12(a)'.[70] The aim pursued by excluding

66. *See* §13.02[B], *supra*.
67. Case C-101/21, *HJ*.
68. *Ibid.*, paras 44 and 47.
69. *Ibid.*
70. *Ibid.*, para. 42.

persons who concurrently perform the duties of CEO and management board members was, in other words, legitimate according to the Directive. The reason for exclusion could perhaps, in principle, qualify as abuse in the context of the Directive.

The problem was, however, that the Czech case law established a *non-rebuttable presumption* according to which such person (performing the mentioned concurrent functions) in fact leads the company concerned, and that, consequently, granting that person the guarantees offered by the Directive would constitute abuse. According to the CJEU, this general presumption of abuse was disproportionate.[71] On this ground, the Czech case law was not compatible with Article 12(a).

Thus, the main point is that, while setting aside the national case law with reference to the principle of proportionality, the CJEU has not explicitly ruled out the possibility that a person may be excluded from the scope of protection offered by the Directive, due to the fact that that person may be partly responsible for the company's insolvency. This means that when an employee may be partly responsible for the insolvency and he/she subsequently tries to obtain payment from the guarantee institution due to the same company's insolvency, it could amount to an abusive practice as referred to in Article 12. The recent ruling in Case C-101/21, *HJ*, may be understood as the CJEU in fact possibly allows Member States to operate with a presumption rule, as long as the presumption is in fact rebuttable, according to which managers, who may be partly responsible for the insolvency, are excluded from the protection offered by the Directive.

It must also be recalled that Article 12(b) allows for Member States to reduce or refuse guarantee protection if it appears that fulfilment of the obligation is *unjustifiable* because of the existence of *special links* between the employee and the employer and of common interests resulting in *collusion* between them. Notwithstanding the ambiguity of the provision, one can imagine that claims brought forward by a (genuine) manager, who is given (fictitious) employee status leading up to the insolvency, may be reduced or refused under this provision. Such arrangement will be aimed at establishing a false claim for guarantee of unpaid remuneration, etc., in forthcoming insolvency proceedings. This situation is very different than the one imagined under Article 12(a) that the manager is not excluded from protection due to the managerial position itself, but rather because the manager falsely claims to be an employee.

To conclude on the application of Article 12 on managers, the CJEU has not exactly departed from the general rule laid down in Case C-334/92, *Wagner Miret*, that a manager who is considered an employee according to national law must be protected by the Directive. The new ruling in Case C-101/21, *HJ*, clarifies to what extent managers – even though covered by the personal scope – may nonetheless be excluded from the protection offered by the Insolvency Directive due to their special position and responsibilities in the company. On the basis of Article 12(a), a manager who is partly responsible for the company's insolvency may be excluded from protection, but on the condition that national law does not apply a non-rebuttable presumption rule for

71. This reasoning is in alignment with existing case law regarding disproportionality relating to abuse, cf. in Case C-17/17, *Hampshire*, and Case C-106/17, *Polbud*.

managers in that regard. The ruling in Case C-101/21, *HJ*, shows that a manager may hold a special position compared to other employees in the event of employer insolvency and that under those special circumstances, some nuances and variations in protection must be accepted due to the specific purpose and goals of the Directive. This recent development in CJEU case law provides an important clarification of the Insolvency Directive in that it strikes a proper balance of the particular interests at stake when the employee is a manager.

§13.04 THE PROTECTION OFFERED FOR MANAGERS BY THE INSOLVENCY DIRECTIVE (IMPLICATIONS)

As seen above in §13.03, managers may be excluded from protection in some Member States but included in others. The legal position for managers, therefore, depends on the Member State in which they work.[72]

For the manager, *the benefit of being covered by the scope of the Insolvency Directive* is that unpaid remuneration related to the insolvency of the employer is protected through the national guarantee scheme, independently of whether his claim is privileged or not in the insolvency proceeding. The manager's claim for unpaid remuneration does not depend on sufficient funds in the insolvent employer's estate.

The fact that a manager's claim is included in the scope of protection does not necessarily result in full payment of the claim, however. The outpayment from the guarantee institution may represent a lower percentage of the salary for a manager than for the average employee. This is related to the fact that Member States may set a ceiling on the payments made by the guarantee institution, cf. Article 4(3) of the Insolvency Directive. For a high-earning manager position, the guarantee outpayment may not resemble an ordinary income level. Furthermore, it should be recalled that the Insolvency Directive allows for national law to reduce a manager's claim in accordance with Article 12(c) when the manager, on his own or together with his or her close relatives, was also the owner of an essential part of the employer's undertaking or business and had a considerable influence on its activities. A reduction based on Article 12(c) requires active participation of the employee in the managerial decision-making of the company.[73] Managerial decision-making is not enough to exclude claims from protection in itself but is assumedly a precondition to exclude claims with reference to ownership.[74]

---

72. It is the guarantee institution in the Member State in which the employee works that is responsible for the meeting of the claim, and the extent of the right is determined by the law governing that institution, cf. Art. 9 of the Insolvency Directive. *See also* Robert Van Galen, *An Introduction to European Insolvency Law*, 131 (Wolter Kluwer 2021).
73. Schlachter, *supra* n. 16, at 486. The denial of protection to those persons may also be done indirectly through the definition of 'employee'; i.e., persons owning part of the undertaking and having considerable influence on its activities are not considered to be 'employees', cf. COM(2011) 84 final, sections 6-7.
74. COM(2011) 84 final, sections 6-7. *See* in particular, the Commission's assessment of the Bulgarian transposition of the Insolvency Directive and its assumed lack of compatibility with the Directive. *See also* Case C-101/21, *HJ*, para. 47.

For the manager, *the consequence of not being covered by the scope of the Insolvency Directive* is that a claim for unpaid remuneration may only be directed at the insolvent employer, who might already have entered into insolvency proceedings. Many Member States have given privilege to employee claims in the rank of creditors, but this is not the case in all Member States.[75] Furthermore, the manager's claim may not be covered by any privilege if the manager is not considered an employee under national law or in another way given privilege over ordinary creditors, which often will be the case. The manager's claim for remuneration is, therefore, in competition with all unsecured creditors. Thus, only rarely does the manager receive payment in full when directing a claim for remuneration against an insolvent employer. Even if the manager is able to obtain preferential treatment or receive dividend as an unsecured creditor, the time scale will provide implications for the manager. In many countries, dividend is not paid to the creditors until the time of closing of the insolvency proceeding.

§13.05 CONCLUSION

The adoption of the Insolvency Directive ensured that all Member States established a body, which guarantees payment of outstanding claims of employees in the event of employer insolvency.

While the Directive mandates that Member States ensure the protection of these claims, it also leaves it to national law to define its scope of application. As demonstrated above, the reference to national law in the Insolvency Directive results in national differences when defining who is an employee, hence covered by the scope of protection. The legal position for managers, therefore, depends on the Member State in which they work.

The CJEU has in its case law reiterated that while respecting the national definition of an employee, the Member State's discretion laid down in the Insolvency Directive is not unlimited. Member States must take into account the principle of effectiveness and social objective of the Insolvency Directive, when defining who is an employee under national guarantee schemes. Moreover, Member States must observe the general principles of proportionality and equality and non-discrimination, although it must be underlined that the CJEU is yet to apply the latter two principles directly in the interpretation of the personal scope.

For managers, their protection under the Insolvency Directive is linked to their status as employee (or non-employee) in national law. Two different national scenarios for managers have been examined above and may in short be summarized as follows.

First, managers may be excluded in general from the national (universal) concept of employee, and, thus, Member States would be allowed to exclude them from protection under the Insolvency Directive. Even in those situations where it is not possible to establish *one* employee concept in national law, relying on the scheme of the Insolvency Directive itself, arguments could be made in favour of excluding managers in this specific context, i.e., as non-employees. At the current state of

75. *Ranking and Priority of Creditors* (Dennis Faber et al. eds, Oxford University Press 2016).

development of EU law (and keeping in mind the 'combined definitions' in the four recent directives),[76] the CJEU limits to Member States' discretion have not taken over the national definition of employee in this situation.

Second, a manager may be covered by the national (universal) concept of employee but specifically excluded from the protection of the national guarantee scheme. In this situation, the CJEU case law mandates that managers cannot be excluded as a specific category of employees (no general exclusion). However, based on Article 12, a specific manager may probably be excluded from the scope of protection if the manager may be partly responsible for the insolvency of that company while observing that any presumption rule in that regard must in fact be rebuttable (specific exclusion).

In conclusion, the classification and protection of managers in relation to unpaid remuneration, when the employer becomes insolvent, give rise to various scenarios and therefore various legal qualifications and results. The answer to the question of whether managers are protected by the Insolvency Directive is not clear-cut.

The potential different treatment across Member States can be especially challenging for cross-border group companies. One can imagine that a manager in Member State A performs work with the same tasks and responsibilities (and under the same working conditions) as a manager in Member State B *before* the company becomes insolvent. The legal protection of the two managers' unpaid remuneration *after* the insolvency may, however, be very different if their status as employees varies between the two Member States. These national differences may also lead to certain forms of speculation. A manager accepting a position in a company in financial distress would be, at least in principle, more inclined to agree to such position in a Member State, where a manager is considered an employee with financial protection in case of insolvency.

In conclusion, the reference to the national employee concept in the Insolvency Directive results in national differences as to whether a manager is protected by that directive. Recalling that one of the aims of the Directive was to approximate the laws of Member States in order for employees to receive equal protection in all Member States, this seems unfortunate. To some extent, the EU law limitations deployed by CJEU in its case law may eventually reduce differences at national level. This may potentially even pave the road to political consensus on a more unified employee definition in the context of the Insolvency Directive in the future.

76. *See* Directive 2019/1158 on work-life balance for parents and carers, Directive 2019/1152 on transparent and predictable working conditions in the EU, Directive (EU) 2023/970 to strengthen the application of the principle of equal pay for equal work or work of equal value between men and women through pay transparency and enforcement mechanisms, and Proposal for a Directive on improving working conditions in platform work (2021/0414 (COD)).

PART III Overall Conclusions

CHAPTER 14

Overall Conclusions

Natalie Videbæk Munkholm, Vincenzo Pietrogiovanni & Karsten Engsig Sørensen

This chapter attempts to tease out a few overall conclusions across the book chapters, addressing the questions raised in the introduction.

As has become evident in the foregoing chapters, the situation of managers - executive and non-executive managers - is special. Many legitimate interests create a tension, which can be traced to the details of EU law. There is the interest of the manager as an employee in enjoying certain rights and protections, such as freedom of movement, a right to non-discrimination, and the right to a safe and healthy work environment. There is the interest of an open internal market, which is not open to abuse or unreasonable results, where managers as a result of their influence in decisions of the company sometimes are sanctioned and sometimes are exempt from certain employee rights under EU law. And there is the interest of leaving corporate governance structures to be decided by the Member States, just to name a few.

We have seen that the regulation at EU level as well as across Member States converge towards two central principles: that an exclusion or a liability should pursue a legitimate interest of the market, such as to counteract abuse, and that such exclusions or liability should be placed on the persons, who de facto carry out influences or decisions.

In other aspects, there has been less convergence across the areas investigated. The fluctuating status of managers may not follow an underlying rationale, in particular when status is left to be determined by the Member States, and do not take Article 45 TFEU as the starting point. This creates not only fluctuating status across Member States but also the complications are exacerbated whenever companies or persons use their right to free movement within the open internal market of the EU, and thus create cross-border work situations. This in turn is further complicated by new opportunities to perform work digitally, including telework where - as a result - a person can perform work in several other Member States simultaneously.

As stated in the introductory chapter, if the status of a person varies substantially across different aspects of European law, and these variations do not follow an underlying rationale or purpose of the different fields of European law, this would lead to uncertainty about rights and duties not only for the person performing work as a manager but also for companies employing managers. Indeed, uncertainties or legal conflicts in the rights and duties of managers could create room for speculations as to how and where to organize and structure companies in the European markets. These issues will be further discussed in this chapter.

In the following, we will first look closer at the status of managers in the situations where the concept of employee is harmonized, where the concept of employee is referred to the Member States and the limits for this national margin, and finally where an issue is not addressed by EU law at all and thus by default left entirely to be solved nationally.

Then, we will take a look at specific problems surfacing in the area of extending rights to managers, including exceptions to such rights, as well as specific problems surfacing in the area of enforcing duties and liabilities to managers for any breach of duties.

Finally, we will sum up potential problems and gaps and give a few constructive comments on avenues to move forward.

§14.01 HARMONIZED CONCEPTS, ARTICLES 45 AND 19 TFEU

[A] The Concept of 'Worker' in Article 45 TFEU

The concept of 'worker' in Article 45 TFEU is an autonomous uniform concept at EU level defined by the CJEU.

The level of subordination of a manager to a superior is oftentimes decisive for status as 'worker' under Article 45 TFEU. In the CJEU's functional approach, the organization in national company law that regulates the mechanisms for instructions and dismissals of managers from another corporate body thus becomes decisive. As seen in Chapters 2 and 3, the national organization of corporate governance structures as well as the tasks allocated to the various forms of 'managers' differ considerably under national law. These differences thus strongly influence the status of 'worker'. Therefore, the choice of corporate form may affect the rights and duties of managers, and potentially this could affect the choice of corporate form and the choice of jurisdiction to incorporate.

The Court has given the concept of 'workers' a broad scope, with a view to enable free movement within the market. For executive managers who are employed and supervised by either a supervisory board or a board of directors consisting of both executive and non-executive directors, it is likely that there is the necessary level of subordination to grant worker status and national rules can be challenged as hindrances of the free movement as workers. For non-executive and executive managers elected by the shareholders at the general meeting, a worker status under Article 45 TFEU is less likely.

When secondary EU instruments do not refer to the definition of 'worker' under national law, the scope of application is defined by the CJEU which uses the concept of worker in Article 45 TFEU as the starting point. For the selected secondary EU instruments analysed in this book, this is the case for private international law rules in Brussels Ia and Rome I, the rules governing Occupational Health and Safety and the Pregnancy Directive. In this, the broad scope that led the interpretation of Article 45 TFEU, with a view to support the internal market, becomes influential in the broad scope of EU rules, which have a clear social purpose of protecting employees.

For the uniform concept in Article 45 TFEU and the directives, the CJEU takes a functional approach and equates de facto and de jure participation in management organs, which prevents circumvention and promotes effective sanctioning of hindrances for the free movement or the fundamental social purposes of the Union.

A uniform and autonomous concept at EU level will override national concepts of 'employee' in the application of specific employee rights vis-à-vis an employer, which differ somewhat from the market freedoms enjoyed under TFEU Article 45. It could be argued that the adoption of an autonomous concept of worker that may differ from the national concepts could be justified by common social protection goals. And the same would be true for the free movement within the market. This aligns well with the fact that the Union pursues several overall goals, as stated in Treaty on European Union (TEU) Article 3, with social as well as economic purposes.

[B] The Scope of Acts Adopted under Article 19 TFEU

The Framework Directive 78/2000, prohibiting discrimination on grounds of religion or belief, disability, age, or sexual orientation, is enacted under Article 19 TFEU in Part Two of the Treaty, which concerns Non-Discrimination and Citizenship of the Union. The CJEU established that the term 'occupation' used to define the scope of the Directive includes all positions constituting a 'real and genuine' 'professional' activity. The CJEU has clarified that the Directive applies to persons who are in employment, as well as to persons who are not in a subordinate position. As stated by the CJEU, the essential element is that the person 'contributes to society through work' and thus deserves protection against discrimination in this capacity.

The right to non-discrimination on grounds of religion or belief, disability, age, sexual orientation in the Framework Directive 78/2000, and on grounds of race and ethnicity in the Non-Discrimination Directive 43/2000, both with legal basis in Article 19 TFEU, thus applies to managers as a human right, not as a 'worker's' right. The supra-national - overall Union's - interest in extending fundamental rights to its citizens in all aspects of life is not limited to protection against abuse from an employer in a work situation. The right to not be discriminated against protects against abuse and limitations from any source, including from bylaws and internal rules, and does not only restrain an abuse of power of employers.

For executive and non-executive managers, the protection against discrimination on grounds covered by secondary law enacted under Article 19 TFEU is the most clear and strong protection. It is a right granted to all 'humans', in this case all those performing work – in any capacity and at any hierarchical level.

This becomes the third underlying interest that justifies the uniform application of an autonomous scope of application of a directive, even when it overrides national scopes of protection against discrimination in relation to employment and occupation.

The strongest protections, where the scope of protections and rights include most managers, are the harmonized concept of 'worker' in Article 45 TFEU, as well as the harmonized concept of employment and occupation in Article 19 TFEU, which pursue free movement within the internal market, the private international law rules addressing jurisdiction in cross-border work situations, and the fundamental rights for workers to health and safety as well as to non-discrimination.

§14.02 NOT HARMONIZED CONCEPTS IN EU LAW AND LIMITS TO NATIONAL EXEMPTIONS OF MANAGERS

As outlined by many of the authors, EU secondary law often defers the scope of an act to be determined by Member States' concept of 'employee' or 'worker'. When directives or regulations delegate the definition of the scope to national law, Article 45 TFEU or other EU definitions may not influence the definitions.

The directives where this solution is applied instead align their scope of protection with the existing employment rules in the Member States. As a result, managers can be excluded from the scope of application of these directives.

Among the areas of EU law discussed in this book, a national scope of 'employee' is used in the EU acts on posting of workers, coordination of social security in cross-border work situations, information and consultation of employees, European Works Councils, employee rights in case of collective redundancies, employee rights in case of transfer of undertakings, and protection of employees in the event of employer insolvency.

However, although not harmonized, the CJEU has insisted that national concepts defining the scope of these acts should nonetheless observe certain minimum principles in their application.

First, the requirement of equivalence dictates that the Member States must interpret the scope of application of the EU directives in the same manner and with the same vigour as they would interpret the scope of application of national rules applicable to employees. If a manager would be protected by employment legislation under national law, he or she should also have the status of employee under EU directives. This principle of equivalence in application under national law entails that EU protections should receive the same status and treatment under national law as protections originating from national legislators. For managers, this means that EU law requires that national legislation is not allowed to *en bloc* or by a non-rebuttable presumption exclude managers from the scope of application of EU law if a manager according to the test under national law would be considered a worker. It also means that the status of a manager must be assessed on the facts of the relationship with the company, rather than being excluded by a formal delimitation of the application of the rights in the EU directives to (certain) management positions.

Second, the principle of effectiveness of EU law requires that the scope of a directive cannot be limited in a manner that undermines the (social) objective of a directive. This requirement is not one of equivalence but one of ensuring the results of a directive, as stated in Article 288 TFEU. For managers, this could mean that directives promoting fundamental social rights could require inclusion of managers in their scope. However, as put forward by the authors of Chapter 12, even strong social rights would still have to be weighed against certain legitimate considerations to exempt managers, such as considerations of abuse or reasonableness. This would present a more difficult balancing exercise, particularly in the directives that address the market as well as social rights, such as the Insolvency Directive, the Transfer of Undertaking Directive, and the Collective Redundancies Directive.

The directives that leave it to the Member State to define their scope create a fluctuating application of the rights of managers across Member States, bearing in mind not only national legislation but also national variations in governance structures as well as functions of 'managers'.

Many of the mentioned directives pursue dual purposes where the act strikes a balance between competing legitimate interests, such as in the case of transfer of undertaking, where the directive not only provides social protection to employees but also ensures flexibility for undertakings in the market; likewise in the situation of posting of workers, where the directive aims to give workers who temporarily perform work in another Member State basic employment rights, as well as aims to stimulate the free movement of services.

However, there seem to be no clear line or underlying functional or balancing rationale explaining why this diverse group of acts all defers the scope to be defined by the national concepts.

§14.03 UNREGULATED AT EU LEVEL, THUS, BY DEFAULT, LEFT TO THE MEMBER STATES

For quite a few labour-related issues, the EU legislator has not yet been able to reach an agreement to regulate at EU level. Such issues are still regulated entirely by national law. This includes corporate governance structures as well as the roles and functions of managers in corporate structures in Member States. This also includes sanctioning of national persons for breach of competition law, rules on disqualification of managers, as well as the rights and duties of employee representatives on company boards. The legal position of non-executive and executive managers will depend on which national jurisdiction(s) that undertake(s) the enforcement of a particular cross-border competition law infringement, a disqualification procedure, or where the employee becomes a board member.

However, on the issues of disqualification and sanctioning, a convergence can be seen in the national solutions. Sanctioning of natural persons is often directed at individuals in managerial positions that may influence the conduct of the undertaking even if they do not have a formal position that allows this. Thus, it is enough to order or exercise de facto leadership in relation to the company's infringement of competition law. The rules on disqualification also apply to de facto managers.

This is not the case for the national systems on board-level employee representation. The rights, duties and liabilities of employee representatives apply to de jure representatives only and are regulated by both labour law and company law. There is no convergence in the approach of Member States to deciding whether one or the other area of law shall prevail in situations of tension caused by the conflicting purposes of the two fields of law. This matter is left to be solved entirely by national law which results in multiple solutions across the Member States.

Overall, issues not regulated at EU level may lead to varying national solutions. This does not mean, however, that Member States' freedom to regulate is unlimited. National solutions must respect general principles of EU law, such as equal pay, non-discrimination on grounds of age and religion, and must not hinder the free movement of workers or establishments.

Nonetheless, the varying national solutions for the issues left unregulated by the EU complicate matters in particular for managers in cross-border work situations.

Overall, the chapters have demonstrated that the status of managers is most clear in areas of EU law that use an autonomous concept defined at EU level. This includes the EU rules protecting the right to free movement and those providing jurisdiction (and perhaps choice of law) in cross-border situations. This also includes EU rules providing a fundamental social right to protection of health and safety, and a human right to non-discrimination of persons performing work in any capacity. However, these rationales do not seem to be followed consistently in other areas of secondary legislation at EU level, where the same strong internal market mechanisms, social protections, or fundamental human rights are present. For many directives in the same areas, the scope is deferred to the national concepts of 'employee' or 'worker', or even special rules for managers are provided, as in the coordination of social security rules. This may give rise to very complicated legal situations in cross-border work for managers, which questions the legal certainty of both managers and companies.

§14.04 RIGHTS, SANCTIONS, AND DUTIES: CHALLENGES

[A] Rights

Turning now to take a closer look at general problems surfacing in the chapters on the rights of managers as employees. The problems not only relate to exempting managers from certain rights because of market considerations but also stem from the variations of corporate governance structures as well as variations of employee concepts (when applicable) in national law.

Directives with a clear social purpose should in many situations enjoy a wide definition of employees, extending to include executive managers. However, specifically for persons in management roles, exceptions may be justified by a number of opposing legitimate interests, such as the need to prevent abuse and speculation as outlined in Chapters 4, 5, 6, and 13.

First, the CJEU has taken a functional instead of a formalistic approach to address general exemptions. Exemptions for managers in top positions are allowed for rights deriving from changes to the company, such as insolvency, transfer of undertaking, collective redundancies, out of considerations for potential abuse and close connectedness to the decisions taken. But these exemptions must be rebuttable; i.e., it must be possible to test before national courts whether a particular manager has in fact abused his or her position or otherwise been unreasonably connected to any of the strategic decisions resulting in the situation triggering the rights.

Second, some of the EU acts use a uniform concept, but with a national margin for exemptions for managers. Where the Framework Directive on Occupational Health and Safety (OSH Framework Directive) and the OSH Pregnancy Directive use a wide uniform concept at EU level, the Working Time Directive expressly allows exceptions for persons in executive managerial positions. Hence, the national scope of application may vary for managers concerning breaks and daily and weekly rest periods depending on whether the Member State has chosen to use some or all of the exceptions for managers. Also, the rationale for excluding managers may be questioned when exceptions are justified by a presumption of the manager as a specific type and function in a hierarchy. As mentioned in the introduction, the image of managers as autonomous in most matters, and thus able to significantly influence not only company decisions but also their own working conditions, may no longer represent all managers in Europe. Exceptions still in existence at EU level based on assumptions about an archetype manager profile should at least be revisited in light of new developments and perhaps adjusted more clearly to aim for the underlying issue, namely that of significant levels of influence and autonomy.

Third, some rights surface as a protection for the employees in the event of changes/problems at the undertaking, such as guarantee of remuneration in case of insolvency, guaranteed information and consultation in the event of collective redundancies, guaranteed continued rights and protection against dismissal in the event of transfers of undertaking. In these situations, the CJEU has allowed the legitimate expectations at EU level of hindering risks of abuse and the unreasonableness of close links between a manager and the undertaking to influence the scope of application at national level. The requirement from the CJEU is, however, that exemptions also in these situations are based on genuine concerns of risks – either of abuse or of a close connection with the decisions. These balances resemble considerations that are legitimate also in other areas of EU law, as demonstrated in the book, *see* the below section.

A separate issue is that of enforcement of rights, which is brought to the surface in Chapters 7, 8, 9 and 11.

Many rights in EU Employment Directives are enforced vis-à-vis an employer, such as occupational health and safety protection, physical as well as psychological, and information and consultation rights. Even if managers are considered employees under the wide scope of application of the OSH Framework Directive, or under national law granting information and consultation rights, the enforcement of these rights may be problematic due to the role of the manager as both the holder of the right and the guarantor of the right on behalf of the employer. In reality, the health and safety concerns for managers would often be a matter to be settled by themselves, which is then at the personal level weighed against many other considerations in the job as top manager. Such a dual role of the manager is a blind angle in securing genuine health and safety for managers, in particular for their psychosocial risks. In addition, the right to information and consultation, as a collective right for managers, would in practice be better secured by engaging trade unions to negotiate their rights at sector level rather than the managers engaging in this right at company level. Trade unions for managers could be invited to play a stronger role in the future to promote and operationalize this right for managers.

Some rights are determined and interpreted by public authorities. This is the case for the coordination of social security measures and for the determination of status under private international law. One problem here is that in the event of simultaneous work in several Member States, a classification by one authority cannot be challenged by another authority. Thus, the status of a manager as classified by the competent Member State may be an anomaly in another Member State's social security system – but cannot be challenged under the current set of rules. A similar issue may arise when the competent jurisdiction determines the status of a manager under Private International Law rules. As long as the EU regulations do not address the issue of reclassification, this question remains unsolved.

[B] Sanctions and Duties

Looking at the enforcement of duties for managers at national level, some convergence can be detected in the jurisdictions compared.

Sanctions are often extended from de jure managers to de facto managers or shadow managers, placing the focus on who actually performs functions as a manager. This is done to prevent circumvention of the law, to ensure more effective sanctioning of duties, and to ensure that the correct person is held liable for wrongdoings.

This is seen in national rules on disqualification, where the public interest is a cross-cutting theme. The public interest in ensuring that qualified management is prevented from acting as managers applies to both de jure and de facto management, and for a disqualification order to be effective, it is necessary to counteract circumvention by the use of formally appointed 'straw men' taking orders from *shadow* managers.

This is also seen in the sanctioning of natural persons for a cross-border competition law infringement of an undertaking. Sanctioning is most often directed at the individuals that in reality may influence the conduct of the undertaking, e.g., by ordering or by exercising de facto leadership in relation to the company's infringement of competition law.

This aligns very clearly with the same legitimate interests that can justify exceptions to rights granted to managers, *see* section above.

[C] Potential Conflicts, Which Are Not Resolved

As has been highlighted in the sections above, the legal framework for companies as well as persons taking on work in managerial positions is not always clear. The EU legislators take an arm's-length approach to corporate governance and corporate governance structures as well as to the roles and functions designated to managers. However, this arm's-length approach has – as is clear from the chapters in this book – a spill-over effect on managers and their rights and duties. This spill-over effect creates legal uncertainty for managers as well as for companies.

The level of complication in cross-border situations is already high for rights that are provided at EU level, and where national law, including national governance structures, decides the level of protection granted to managers. These national variations become even more significant in areas where EU law does not provide a solution to situations where authorities in two or more Member States reach different conclusions. For instance, the question of the competence of a competent Member State to requalify the status of managers in cases of social security in cross-border work situations remains unresolved. The same is the case in areas where the EU has not yet regulated scope or content of rights, such as for disqualification, or for sanctioning natural persons for infringement of competition law. On the one hand, this may create complicated situations for the individual manager in question. On the other hand, these complications result in the manager being entitled only to part of the social security benefits in some of the Member States, where he or she has connections, and result in the manager's behaviour being sanctioned with quarantine not in all Member States. Although complicated, such types of variations for a manager in cross-border situations may be acceptable.

As highlighted in Chapter 9, the whole setup of the dual role of managers, on the one hand acting on behalf of the company and on the other hand also being employees of the same company, has not yet been clearly nuanced or narrowed down, not in legislation at EU level nor by the CJEU. The dual role in essence strongly reduces the use of certain fundamental rights at work for persons because they perform work as a manager, as – even if the scope includes managers – the right is very difficult to execute and enforce in practice at company level. As the manager influences the decisions at company level because of his or her position as manager, exercising a right to information and consultation collectively as managers may seem superfluous. This could instead call for a more active role and function of trade unions that specialize in promoting the interests of managers.

An unresolved issue in Private International Law rules concerns choice of jurisdiction. The term 'employee' in Brussels Ia on *jurisdiction* has been given a uniform autonomous interpretation by the CJEU in light of the concept of 'worker' in Article 45 TFEU, where subordination between the manager and the company is key. The choice-of-law rules of Rome I have not yet been interpreted in the context of managers. Rome I could be interpreted to align with the Posting of Workers Directive, a *lex specialis* for choice-of-law rules, which uses the national concept of employee. If so, this could create inconsistencies, as the Member State, where the work is temporarily carried out (host state), then would determine the status of the posted manager in relation to national employment rights. Combined with the national varieties in Member States on the role and functions of managers and their entitlement to employee rights, this could have negative implications on the legal certainty and foreseeability of posted managers, stemming from the varying application of both Rome 1 and the Posting of Workers Directives.

As is clear, these complications are exacerbated by cross-border elements, where concepts or exceptions are not harmonized. Freedom to work and establish undertakings across Member States is the core element of the internal market. When this element creates a situation of sincere complexity and legal uncertainty, it begs for improvement. Lack of legal certainty and variations in scope of application for rights as well as duties and sanctions give ground for speculation in establishing cross-border situations, in order to benefit from national variations in governance structures by organizing the company. The management may have an interest in registering the company in the Member States, where their rights are best protected. The owners/general assembly may have interest in registering the company in a Member State where freedom of contract between the individual manager and the undertaking is predominant.

§14.05 OVERALL CONCLUSIONS AND WAYS FORWARD

[A] Overall Conclusions

For some areas of EU law, we have seen that the scope of application is determined by an underlying rationale of the EU legislation. This is the case for the wide scope of workers applied in Article 45 TFEU, in the Directive on Occupational Health and Safety, and – the widest, most clear scope not depending on status as employee – in the Framework Directive 78/2000 on non-discrimination in employment and occupation. When a right to perform work is played out within the framework of the internal market, this right is extended to a wide group of persons performing work. When a right to perform work is allocated to a person as a human being, the protection applies even regardless of subordination.

Another point worth noting is that for the autonomous concept, the protection is functional, not focusing on the formal designation but on the activities of a person. This is the case concerning liabilities and sanctions. The assessment can cut across different governance structures and focus on the activities and functions of a person, rather than on titles or terminology.

For other areas of EU employment law, the rights unfold only in the sphere of a workplace and by way of the dynamics of employment. The scope of application is fundamentally different for secondary acts based on Article 19 TFEU as these acts apply to all work and occupation at any level in an organization, as well as self-employment. For secondary acts based on Article 153 TFEU, the scope of application is either harmonized taking its starting point in the definition of worker in Article 45 TFEU which requires a level of subordination or is not harmonized leaving it in the hands of national jurisdictions, including to strike a balance between corporate law and labour law for managers in executive and non-executive positions. Employee rights are promoted with the underlying rationale of the employee being the weaker party, and subordinate to an employer's prerogative to instruct or dismiss the employee. The individual person in a management position may have a fluctuating status depending on the level of subordination determined by national law, and as such, for these rights, the legal situation of the manager is less clear.

The interesting question is where to strike the balance - not all complications are problems that must be solved. Sometimes, the situation obtained is acceptable, and, thus, is the best balance between competing interests. Managers are the personification of a tension in the EU, where on the one hand the Member States in the area of corporate governance structures have a high level of autonomy and where on the other hand a number of both primary and secondary EU law sources obligate the Member States to extend social rights to employees.

The arm's-length principle for interfering with national corporate governance structures is a strong consideration. Even in cases of tension between the underlying interests of labour law (interfering with certain rights to employees as the weaker party), and the underlying interests of company law (ensuring national autonomy), this tension must still be resolved by national law. This results in a variety of results, with a lack of guiding principles across the Member States. This is most clear in the situation of board-level employee representation schemes, where a variety in national solutions is so far deemed acceptable.

In other areas, a balance has been struck by the CJEU between the interests of the individual manager and the interests of free movement within the internal market. This is the case in private international law concerning choice of jurisdiction, as highlighted in Chapter 7, where the CJEU case law clarifies that the decisive element for activating the protection for managers is the manager's level of influence on the company. The CJEU extends the protection to managers whose influence on the company is negligible and thus are in need of protection, whereas the CJEU exempts managers who enjoy all the freedom to arrange their own rights and duties and, thus, do not seem to be in need of protection when it comes to choice of jurisdiction. This balancing is acceptable, bearing in mind that the alternative for the more autonomous manager is not lack of protection, but that jurisdiction is determined by the general rules in Brussels Ia, not by the rules aiming to protect the 'weaker' party. As such, this result seems both balanced and reasonable.

A balance between arm's-length principle for corporate structures and the social rationale behind EU employment law can furthermore develop over time. This could be happening these years for the occupational health and safety of managers as highlighted in Chapter 11. The CJEU has set the threshold for 'subordination' - also for non-executive managers - at a very low level. The alternative here is also less acceptable, namely, that managers would become responsible for their own health and safety at work, physical as well as psychosocial.

The scope seemingly can depend not only on the strength of the social right promoted but also on whether the alternative to being included is acceptable or not. When the alternative is, e.g., that a person does not have access to certain managerial positions due to their race, ethnicity, age, disability, sexual orientation, religion or faith, that result is highly unacceptable under EU law. Whereas, when the alternative is that a person must live with a less protective legal framework, perhaps more complicated or more varied across Member States, this moves the balance in the direction of more discretion for the Member States.

[B] Potential Avenues Forward

Many of the existing variations are caused by the misalignment of the roles of managers across the EU Member states. This calls for an increased focus on possible tensions between on the one hand the interest in promoting an internal market or the autonomy for national corporate structures and on the other hand the social purpose often underlying EU employment law. The latter has since the adoption of the Amsterdam Treaty slowly seeped into all aspects of EU law and trickled into the national law governing also positions perhaps traditionally governed by national company law. The tension and misalignment so far are ongoing, creating complicated situations as well as a certain level of uncertainty for both managers and companies. This in turn allows room for speculation when choosing where to establish undertakings, taking into consideration the national corporate structures which directly affect the rights and duties under EU law of the company's managers in executive and non-executive positions. In areas where the scope of EU law is left to the Member States, or where issues are even yet unregulated at EU level, this avenue for speculating on where to incorporate companies is much wider.

The freedom of establishment and the open internal market are cornerstones of the EU, and the costs to the individual manager in relation to differing levels of rights in cross-border situations may seem minor in comparison. However, as rights at work are becoming increasingly fundamental, including general principles of the EU against age discrimination, principles of legal certainty and of proportionality, it may seem timely for legal actors to take a second look at the regulatory framework at EU level, as well as the case law under the CJEU.

Problems with conflicts or overlapping national legislation are that it affects the legal certainty for an increasing group of persons in the EU who perform work in managerial positions. Questions which could be further examined are whether the role and autonomy of managers has changed, in step with increasing numbers? Is the impression of who is a manager a remnant from times passed, and managers are now more varied, less autonomous and with less force? Are the balances acceptable, taking into consideration the actual level of influence on their own working terms or the company decisions – and also taking into consideration whether the alternative is reasonable? Based on the answers to these questions, EU law allowing exemptions to managers could be revisited with a view to modernize. This could be the case for *en bloc* exceptions to the Working Time Directive for managers in executive positions, as well as for secondary law that gives no guidance to lawful exemptions for persons influencing the decisions of the company.

Instead, the legislation should reflect more closely which functions and roles should be covered and which level of influence and autonomy should be exempted. The genuine level of autonomy determines the degree of need for rights and depends on several factors.

The level of autonomy and influence on the company's decisions are influenced by several factors. In this contribution, we have focused on legal structures at international, EU, national and company levels. Many other factors influence the company hierarchy and the level of influence and/or subordination of managers. Workplace culture, organizational structures chosen, management and organizational theories, as well as political preferences highly influence the setup of corporate governance structures – and thus the level of subordination or autonomy of the individual manager. Consequently, developments may be initiated from several angles, including improved or clarified regulation.

Additionally, new forms of work pose challenges to some of the existing frameworks. This is the case for the determination of the applicable social security legislation, be it because managers fall in between the status of employed and self-employed persons or be it because the place of their activities is difficult to determine. Both aspects are fundamental for the current coordination framework for social security. Yet, with the growing importance of telework, it seems difficult to hold on to the location of the actual performance of the professional activities for the purpose of indicating the competent state.

There is room for improvement in this situation challenging the general principle of legal certainty, the *effet utile* of directives extending rights to persons performing work, as well as the legitimate interest of protecting against abuse of companies.

In recent years, the EU legislators have had a focus on distinguishing 'genuine' self-employed from 'false' self-employed to counteract circumvention of EU employment law by simple formalities in the contract, with a view to codify and further strengthen the case law of the CJEU on the concept of 'worker'. This has resulted in extensive political negotiations and have so far resulted in a new 'hybrid' definition of scope in Directive 2019/1158 on work-life balance for parents and carers, Directive 2019/1152 on transparent and predictable working conditions in the EU, and Directive (EU) 2023/970 to strengthen the application of the principle of equal pay for equal work or work of equal value between men and women through pay transparency and enforcement mechanisms. Furthermore, proposal for a Directive on improving working conditions in platform work (COM (2021) 762) includes a rule of presumption for status as employee – which is still being negotiated. Although the focus of employed vis-à-vis self-employed does not entirely translate to the situation for managers, perhaps a similar attention could be provided to include managers performing work in top positions in the EU and – with inspiration from the Insolvency Directive Article 12 – more clearly describe lawful exemptions by Member States based on functions rather than roles or titles, which are moving targets.

In light of the increasing numbers of persons in managerial positions, in light of the developing markets, and in light of new forms of work where the issues are expected to become even more complicated, with the overall view of ensuring acceptable balances, perhaps certain clarifications would be welcomed not only by managers but also by undertakings.

Bibliography

Books

Antonio Ojeda Avilés, *Derecho Transnacional del Trabajo* (Tirant lo Blanch 2013).
José Antonio Fernández Avilés, Silvia Fernández Martínez, Lourdes Mella Mendez, Victoria Rodríguez-Rico Roldán & Adrián Todolí Signes, *El Trabajo en la Economía Colaborativa y la Prevención de Riesgos Laborales* (Borpi S. L. 2018).
Ulrik Rammeskow Bang-Pedersen et al., *Konkurs* (Jurist- og Økonomforbundets Forlag 2d ed. 2020).
Catherine Barnard, *EU Employment Law* (4th ed. Oxford University Press 2012).
Catherine Barnard, *The Substantive Law of the EU* 228-230 (Oxford University Press 2019).
Brian Bercusson, *European Labour Law* (Cambridge University Press 2009).
Kurt Biedenkopf, Wolfgang Streeck & Hellmut Wißmann, *Bericht der Wissenschaftlichen Mitglieder der Kommission zur Modernisierung der Deutschen Unternehmensmitbestimmung* (Hans Böckler Stiftung 2006).
Hanne S. Birkmose, *Shareholders' Duties* (Kluwer Law International 2017).
Sara Brimo, *L'État et la Protection de la Santé des Travailleurs* (Lextenso Éditions 2012).
Bruno Caruso & Silvana Sciarra, *Il Lavoro Subordinato* (G. Giappichelli Editorem 2009).
Mariangela Cistaro & Stefano Cui, *La Malattia del Lavoratore. Diritti e Doveri delle Parti* (Giuffré Editore 2012).
Apelles J. B. Conceição, *Segurança Social* (Almedina 2014).
Maurice Cozian, Alain Viandier & Florence Deboissy, *Droit des Sociétés* 345 (no. 861) (LexisNexis, 33rd ed. 2020).
Paul Craig & Gráinne de Búrca, *EU Law – Text, Cases, and Materials* (7th ed. Oxford University Press 2020).
Guy Davidov, *A Purposive Approach to Labour Law* (Oxford University Press 2016).
Paul L. Davies & Sarah Worthington, *Gower's Principles of Modern Company Law* (Sweet & Maxwell 10th ed. 2016).
Paul L. Davies, Sarah Worthington & Christopher Hare, *Gower's Principles of Modern Company Law* (Thomson Reuters 11th ed. 2021).

John Darcy & David Harris, *The European Social Charter* (Transnational Publishers Inc. 2001).

Simon Deakin, Helmut Koziol & Olaf Riss, *Directors' & Officers' (D & O) Liability* (Verlag De Gruyter 2018).

Olaf Deinert, *Internationales Arbeitsrecht: Deutsches und europäisches Arbeitskollisionsrecht* (Mohr Siebeck Tübingen 2013).

Alan Dignam & John Lowry, *Company Law* (Oxford University Press 11th ed. 2021).

Adriaan F. M. Dorresteijn et al., *European Corporate Law* (Kluwer Law International 3d ed. 2017).

Vanessa Edwards, *EC Company Law* (Oxford University Press 1999).

Sofía Olarte Encabo, *Trabajadores autónomos* (Tecnos 2009).

Francisco Liberal Fernandes, *O Conceito de Trabalhador no Direito Social Comunitário, Gestlegal* (Gestlegal 2019).

Robert Van Galen, *An Introduction to European Insolvency Law* (Wolters Kluwer Deventer 2021).

Carsten Gerner-Beuerle & Michael Schillig, *Comparative Company Law* (Oxford University Press 2019).

Carsten Gerner-Beuerle, Philipp Paech & Edmund Schuster, *Study on Directors' Duties and Liability* (London School of Economics 2013).

Henri Goedert, *La Représentation des Salariés dans les Organes des Sociétés en Droit Luxembourgeois et en Droit Allemand* (Université de Nancy II 1983).

Stefan Grundmann, *European Company Law* (Intersentia 2007).

Uglješa Grušić, *The European Private International Law of Employment* (Cambridge University Press 2015).

Magdalena Nogueira Guastavino, Olga Fotinopoulou Basurko & José María Miranda Boto, *Lecciones de Derecho Social de la Unión Europea* (Tirant lo Blanch 2012).

Matthias Habersack & Martin Henssler, *Mitbestimmungsrecht* (Verlag C.H. Beck 4th ed. 2018).

Peter Hanau & Ulrich Wackerbarth, *Unternehmensmitbestimmung und Koalitionsfreiheit: Interessenkonflikte von Gewerkschaftsvertretern im Aufsichtsrat* (Nomos Verlagsgesellschaft 2004).

Brenda Hannigan, *Company Law* (Oxford University Press 4th ed. 2016).

M.S. Houwerzijl, *De Detacheringsrichtlijn: over de achtergrond, inhoud en implementatie van Richtlijn 96/71/EG* (Deventer Kluwer 2005).

Kristian Huser, *Gjeldsforhandling og konkurs, vol. 2* (Juristinformasjon 1987).

ILO, *Freedom of Association – Compilation of the Decisions of the Freedom of Association Committee* (International Labour Office 6th ed. 2018).

Reinier Kraakmann, John Armour, Paul Davis, Luca Enriques, Henry B. Hansmann, Gérard Klaus J. Hopt Hertig, Hideki Kanda & Edward B. Rock, *The Anatomy of Corporate Law* (Oxford University Press 2d ed. 2009).

Reinier Kraakman et al., *The Anatomy of Corporate Law* (Oxford University Press 3d ed. 2017).

Lourdes Tortosa Latonda; Purificación Castelló Mercé; Alicia Piedrabuena Cuesta; Carmen Cortés Villalba; Álvaro Page del Pozo; Alberto Ferreras Remesal; Carlos

Vicente García Molina; *Trabajo y envejecimiento. Mejora de las condiciones ergonómicas de la actividad laboral para la promoción de un envejecimiento saludable* 1 (Instituto de Biomecánica de Valencia 2002) http://envejecimiento.csic.es/documentos/documentos/imserso-estudiosidi-01.pdf

Loyens & Loeff, *Het vennootschaps- en arbeidsrechtelijk ontslag van statutair bestuurders*, 123 Genoteerd 3 (2019).

Manual del Personal de Alta Dirección (Raquel Serrano & Alex Valls eds., Thomson Reuters 2012).

Wilhelm Moll, *Münchener Anwalts Handbuch: Arbeitsrecht* (Verlag C. H. Beck 5th ed. 2021).

C.G.J Morse, *Contracts of Employment and the EEC Contractual Obligations Convention* (1982).

Ángel Sánchez-Anguita Muñoz, *Psicopatologías Laborales* (Publicaciones Universidad Pontificia 2008).

Ruth Nielsen, *EU Labour Law* (DJØF Publishing 2013).

Fieke van Overbeeke, *Sociale Concurrentie en Conflictenrecht in het Europees Wegtransport* (Universiteit Antwerpen 2018).

Vicente Lafuente Pastor & Ruth Vallejo Dacosta, *Marco jurídico de la seguridad y salud en el trabajo* (Prensas Universitarias de Zaragoza 2010).

Ranking and Priority of Creditors (Oxford International and Comparative Insolvency Law) (Dennis Faber et al. eds, Oxford University Press 2016).

Antonio Costa Reyes, *Manual de Derecho Social de la Unión Europea* (Tecnos 2011).

Knut Ro & Håvard Wiker, *Konkursloven: Kommentarutgave* (Universitetsforlaget 2003).

Manuel M. Roxo, *Direito da segurança e saúde no trabalho. Da prescrição do seguro à definição do desempenho, uma transição na regulação* (Almedina 2011).

Ana Belén Muñoz Ruiz, *El sistema normativo de la prevención de riesgos laborales* (Lex Nova 2009).

Jeffrey Pfeffer, *Dying for a Paycheck: How Modern Management Harms Employee Health and Company Performance: And What We Can Do about It* (Harper Collins Publishers 2018).

Kjetil Schonhowd, *Konkurskarantene* (Juristforbundets Forlag 2001).

Jean-Michel Servais, *International Labour Law* (Wolters Kluwer 6th ed. 2020).

Jan Skåre, *Lov om aksjeselskaper med kommentarer* (Tanum-Norli 1980).

Gerald Spindler, *Münchener Kommentar zum Aktiengesetz: AktG* (Verlag C.H. Beck 5th ed. 2019).

Alain Supiot, *Au-delà de l'Emploi: Les Voies d'une Vraie Réforme du Droit du Travail* (Flammarion 2016).

Gitte Søgaard et al., *Business Law, Europe* (2d ed. Ex Tuto 2021).

Gitte Søgaard, *Aspects of Structural Risk Management in Groups* (Ex Tuto Publishing 2d ed. 2021).

Christoph Teichmann, *Binnenmarktkonformes Gesellschaftsrecht* (De Gruyter 2006).

The Nordic Governance Model (Per Lekvall ed., SNS Förlag 2014).

Unternehmens-Mitbestimmung der Arbeitnehmer im Recht der EU-Mitgliedstaaten – Employees' Co-Determination in the Member States of the European Union (Theodor Baums & Peter Ulmer eds., de Gruyter 2004).

Michele Tiraboschi, *Labour Law and Industrial Relations in Recessionary Times: The Italian Labour Relations in a Global Economy*, Adapt Labour Studies e-Book series n. 3 (Adapt University Press 2012).

Pilar Rivas Vallejo, *La prevención de los riesgos laborales de carácter psicosocial* (Editorial Comares, 009).

Guus J. J. Heerma Van Voss, *Mr. C. Assers Handleiding tot de beoefening van het Nederlands Burgerlijk Recht. 7. Bijzondere overeenkomsten. Deel V. Arbeidsovereenkomst* (Wolters Kluwer 2020).

Alessandro Varrenti & Fernando de las Cuevas, *Company Directors: Jurisdictional Comparisons* (Sweet & Maxwell 2012).

Jeremy Waddington & Aline Conchon, *Board-Level Employee Representation in Europe: Priorities, Power and Articulation* (Routledge 2016).

Adrian Walters & Malcolm Davis-White QC, *Directors' Disqualification & Insolvency Restrictions* (Sweet & Maxwell 3d ed. 2010).

Manfred Weiss et al., *Labour Law and Industrial Relations in Germany* (5th ed. Kluwer Law International 2020).

Kristin van Zwieten, *Goode on Principles of Corporate Insolvency Law* (Sweet & Maxwell 5th ed. 2018).

Book Chapters

Marie-Noelle Auberger, *Perceptions et représentations des représentants du personnel au conseil d'administration ou de surveillance: le cas des administrateurs salariés C.F.D.T.* (Aline Conchon & Marie-Noelle Auberger eds., Documentation Française 2009).

Fabrizio Barca & Marco Becht, *Introduction* (Fabrizio Barca & Marco Bech eds, 2010).

Juan García Blasco & Manuel González Labrada, *Alta dirección y prevención de riesgos laborales* 300-305 (José Luis Monereo Pérez & Ángel Luis De Val Tena eds., Granada Publishing Ltd 2010).

Edward De Bock, *De bijzondere positie van de bestuurder van de NV of BV* (Gerdien Van Der Voet ed., Boom Juridisch 2021).

Pierre-Henri Conac, *La société par actions simplifiée: une revolution démocratique*, 9 (Pierre-Henri Conac & Isabelle Urbain-Parleani eds. Dallos 2016).

Luisa Corazza & Orsola Razzolini, *Who Is an Employer?* (Matthew W. Finkin & Guy Mundlak eds, Edward Elgar 2015).

Ana Cristina Ribeiro Costa, *Brincat and Others vs Malta: Occupational Health and Safety under the Guise of the Rights to Life and to Respect for Private and Family Life (European Court of Human Rights, 60908/11, 62110/11, 62129/11, 62312/11 and 62338/11)* 133-143 (M. Łaga, S. Bellomo, N. Gundt & J.M.M. Boto eds, Gdansk University Press 2017).

Ana Cristina Ribeiro Costa, *A tutela da segurança e saúde no trabalho no âmbito da Convenção Europeia dos Direitos do Homem e da Carta Social Europeia* 275-300 (Manuel M. Roxo ed., 2017).

Ana Cristina Ribeiro Costa, *El contenido del Convenio n.º 190 de la Organización Internacional del Trabajo: definiciones y ámbito de aplicación – 'vino nuevo en odres viejos'* 29-59 (Maria Gema Quintero Lima & Manuel Correa Carrasco eds., Dykinson 2021). https://e-archivo.uc3m.es/bitstream/handle/10016/32437/violencia_correa_quintero_2021.pdf?sequence=3&isAllowed=y.

Paul Davies & Mark Freedland, *Changing Perspectives upon the Employment Relationship in British Labour Law* (Catherine Barnard et al. eds, Hart Publishing 2004).

Paul Davies & Mark Freedland, *The Complexities of the Employing Enterprise* (Guy Davidov & Brian Langille eds, Hart Publishing 2006).

T. Davulis, *Chapter 6: 2008/95/EC: Employer Insolvency* (Monika Schlachter ed., Kluwer Law International 2014).

Filip Dorssemont, *The Right to Take Collective Action under Article 11 ECHR* (Filip Dorssemont, Klaus Lörcher & Isabelle Schömann eds, Hart Publishing 2013).

Filip Dorssemont, *Article 27* (Steve Peers et al. eds, Nomos 2014).

Filip Dorssemont & Marco Rocca, *Article 28 – Right of Collective Bargaining and Action* (Filip Dorssemont et al. eds, Hart Publishing 2019).

Adriaan Dorresteijn & Cornelis de Groot, *Corporate Governance Codes: Origins and Perspectives* (Steef M. Bartman ed. 2006).

Reinhold Fahlbeck, *Lex Laboris – Quo Vadis? The Swedish Experience* (Roger Blanpain & Manfred Weiss eds, Kluwer Law International 2003).

Martin Henssler *§ 26 Mitbestimmungsgesetz* (Matthias Habersack & Martin Henssler eds, Verlag C.H. Beck 4th ed. 2018).

Aukje van Hoek, *Detachering in het internationaal privaatrecht. Over de complexe verhouding tussen de Rome I-verordening en de Detacheringsrichtlijnen* (Herwig Verschueren ed., Die Keure 2020).

Klaus J. Hopt & Patrick C. Leyens, *The Structure of the Board of Directors: Boards and Governance Strategies in the US, the UK and Germany* 116 et seq. (Afra Afsharipour & Martin Gelter eds, European Corporate Governance Institute 2021).

Klaus Hopt, *Vergleichende Corporate Governance*, 175 ZHR 444, 505 et seq. (2011).

Andrea Iossa, *Anti-Authoritarian Employment Relations? Labour Law from an Anarchist Perspective* (Alysia Blackham et al. eds, Hart Publishing 2019).

Otto Kahn-Freund, *Industrial Democracy*, 6 ILJ 65, 77 et seq. (1977).

Otto Ernst Kempen, *Fernwirkungen von Arbeitskämpfen auf die Unternehmensmitbestimmung? (Der Fall Bsirske)* (Alfred Söllner, Wolfgang Gitter, Raimund Waltermann, Richard Giesen & Oliver Ricken eds, Verlag C.H. Beck 2005).

Jens Kristiansen, *The Concept of 'Employee': The Position in Denmark*, 136 (Bernd Waas & Guus Heerma von Voss eds, Hart Publishing 2017).

Stavroula Leka, Aditya Jain & Loïc Lerouge, *Work-Related Psychosocial Risks: Key Definitions and an Overview of the Policy Context in Europe* 3 (Loic Lerouge ed., Springer Editions 2017).

Per Lekvall, *Chapter III A Consolidated Nordic Governance Model*, Nordic & European Company Law Working Paper No. 14-12 (Per Lekvall ed., SNS Förlag 2014), https://papers.ssrn.com/sol3/papers.cfm?abstract_id=2534331.

Leszek Mitrus, *The Concept of 'Employee': The Position in Poland*, 532 (Bernd Waas & Guus Heerma von Voss eds, Hart Publishing 2017).

Ulrich Mückenberger, *Workers' Representation and Plant and Enterprise Level* (Bob Hepple & Bruno Veneziani eds, Hart Publishing 2009).

Wanjiru Njoya, *The EU Framework of Information and Consultation: Implications for Trade Unions and Industrial Democracy* (Alan Bogg et al. eds, Edward Elgar 2016).

Jeremias Prassl, *Autonomous Concepts in Labour Law? The Complexities of the Employing Enterprise Revisited* (Alan Bogg et al. eds, Hart Publishing 2015).

Alexander Schall, *Power to Directors to Bind the Company* 97 et seq. (Alexander Schall, David Günther, Veronika E. Korom, Michael Lamsa, Wolf-Georg Ringe, Mathias Siems, Michael Stöber, Christoph Thole & Christoph Wiegand eds, 2014).

Alexander Schall & David Günther, *Article 9 Acts of the Organs of a Company and Its Representation* (Peter Kindler & Jan Lieder eds, Nomos Verlagsgesellschaft, Hart Publishing, and Verlag C.H.Beck 2021).

Achim Seifert, *Unternehmensinteresse und Aufsichtsratsmitbestimmung im Spannungsverhältnis* (Ulrich Jürgens, Dieter Sadowski, Folke Gunnar Schuppert & Manfred Weiss eds, Nomos Verlagsgesellschaft 2007).

Achim Seifert, *Abführungspflichten von Arbeitnehmervertretern im Aufsichtsrat*, BB (2019).

Karsten Engsig Sørensen, *Konkurskarantæne* (Mette Neville & Karsten Engsig Sørensen eds, Jurist- og Økonomforbundets Forlag 2013).

Manuel Velázquez, *Comparative Study of the Psychosocial Risks Prevention Enforcement by the European Labour Inspectorates* (Loic Lerouge ed., Springer Editions 2017).

Bruno Veneziani, *Article 27: Workers Right to Information and Consultation Within the Undertaking* (Filip Dorssemont et al. eds, Hart Publishing 2019).

Jenny Julén Votinius, *Employee Representation at the Enterprises: Sweden* (Roger Blanplain ed., Kluwer Law International 2012).

Bernd Waas, *Comparative Overview*, xxxv (Bernd Waas & Guus Heerma von Voss eds, Hart Publishing 2017).

Eddy Wymeersch, *A Status Report on Corporate Governance Rules and Practices in Some Continental European States* 1045 et seq. (Klaus Hopt, Hideki Kanda, Mark Roe, Eddy Wymeersch & Stefan Prigge eds, European Corporate Governance Institute 1998).

Periodicals

Vigjilenca Abazi, *The European Union Whistleblower Directive: A 'Game Changer' for Whistleblowing Protection?*, 49 ILJ 4 (2020).

T.M.C. Arons, *Verkenning van de internationale bevoegdheid en het toepasselijk recht bij geschillen over de aansprakelijkheid van bestuurders*, 138 Ondernemingsrecht 768 (2017).

Gregor Bachmann, Horst Eidenmüller, Andreas Engert, Holger Fleischer & Wolfgang Schön, *Regulating the Closed Corporation* 4 ECFR (2014).

Catherine Barnard, *Are Social 'Rights' Rights?*, 11 ELLJ 4 (2020).

Theodor Baums, *Unabhängige Aufsichtsratsmitglieder*, 180 ZHR 697 (2016).

L. van Bochove, *De herschikte EEX-Vo en derde landen: het formele toepassingsgebied van de Verordening nader bezien*, TCR 2017(1) (2017).

P. Castelló et al., *Trabajo y envejecimiento. Mejora de las condiciones ergonómicas de la actividad laboral para la promoción de un envejecimiento saludable*, 30 Seguridad y Salud en el Trabajo, 29-36, 31 (2004), available at http://www.insht.es/InshtWeb/Contenidos/Documentacion/TextosOnline/Rev_INSHT/2004/30/artFondoTextCompl.pdf.

Nicola Countouris, *The Concept of 'Worker' in European Labour Law: Fragmentation, Autonomy and Scope*, 47 ILJ 2 (2018).

Paul L. Davies & Klaus J. Hopt, *Boards in Europe: Accountability and Convergence*, ECGI - Law Working Paper No. 205/2013 (2013).

Filip Dorssemont, *Case C-55/02, Commission of the European Commission v. Portuguese Republic; Case C-188/03, Imtraud Junk v. Wolfgang Kühnel*, 43 CML Rev 1 (2006).

Filip Dorssemont, *Case Notes: The Right to Information and Consultation in Article 27 of the Charter of Fundamental Rights of the European Union: Less than a Right and Less than a Principle, just an Ordinary Provision Lacking Direct Effect?*, 21 MJ 4 (2014).

Forum Europaeum Corporate Group Law, *Corporate Group Law for Europe* 1 EBOR 165-264 (2000).

Thomas Garber, *Zur Arbeitnehmereigenschaft von Organpersonen einer Gesellschaft*, GPR 229-232 (2019).

Belén Alonso-Olea García, *Los conceptos de trabajador por cuenta ajena, asegurado social y ciudadano de la Unión Europea según la jurisprudencia del Tribunal de Justicia de la Unión Europea. Sus consecuencias y controversia*, 62 REDE 93-125 (2017).

Giovanni Gaudio, *Adapting Labour Law to Complex Organisational Settings of the Enterprise: Why Rethinking the Concept of the Employer Is Not Enough*, 50 ILJ 2 (2021).

Carsten Gerner-Beuerle et al., *Study on Directors' Duties and Liability*, Department of Law, London School of Economics (2013).

Emilie Ghio, Gert-Jan Boon, David Ehmke, Jennifer Grant, Line Langkjaer & Eugenio Vaccari, *Harmonising Insolvency Law in the EU: New Thoughts on Old Ideas in the Wake of the COVID-19 Pandemic*, 30 INSOL 3 (2021).

Maria Irene Gomes & Catarina de Oliveira Carvalho, *La relación laboral del trabajador dirigente en el ordenamiento jurídico portugués*, IV Revista de Derecho del Trabajo 11, 236 (2016).

Hervé Gosselin, *Le temps de travail. Jurisprudence récente de la chambre sociale de la Cour de cassation*, 4 Droit Social 375 (2010).

Tobias Grambow, *Sozialversicherungspflicht von Vorständen der AG und geschäftsführenden Direktoren der SE*, AG 13-14/2010 (2010).

Jesper Lau Hansen, *Udfordringerne fra EU-retten til den nordiske ledelsesmodel*, 4 NTS 13 (2019).

Peter Hommelhoff, *Aktuelle Impulse aus dem europäischen Unternehmensrecht: Eine Herausforderung für Deutschland*, NZG 1329 (1333) (2015).

Klaus J. Hopt & Patrick C. Leyens, *Board Models in Europe: Recent Developments of Internal Corporate Governance Structures in Germany, the United Kingdom, France, and Italy*, ECGI - Law Working Paper No. 17/2004 (2004).

Klaus J. Hopt, *Der Aufsichtsrat – Bedeutungswandel, Konvergenz, unternehmerische Mitverantwortung, Pflichten- und Haftungszuwachs*, ZGR 507 et seq. (2019).

Eleanor Kirk, *Law and Legalities at Work: HR Practitioners as Quasi-Legal Professionals*, 50 ILJ 4 (2021).

Nadia K. Kougiannou, BAdrian Wilkinson & Tony Dundon, *Inside the Meetings: The Role of Managerial Attitudes in Approaches to Information and Consultation for Employees*, 60 BJIR 3 (2021), https://doi.org/10.1111/bjir.12650.

Nicola Kountouris, *The Concept of 'Worker' in European Labour Law: Fragmentation, Autonomy and Scope*, 47 ILJ 2 (2018).

Katarzyna Lasak, *Health and Safety in the European Social Charter*, 25 IJCL 2, 110 (2009).

Franka Lau, *Sozialversicherungspflicht von GmbH-Geschäftsführern*, NZS 12 (2019).

Thomas Lechat & Olivier Torrès, *Les risques psychosociaux du dirigeant de PME: typologie et échelle de mesure des stresseurs professionnels*, 29 PME 3-4, 145 (2016), https://doi.org/10.7202/1038335ar.

Jan Lieder, *Das unabhängige Aufsichtsratsmitglied: Zu den Änderungen des Deutschen Corporate Governance Kodex*, 8 NZG 569, 571 (2005).

Troels Michael Lilja, *Konkurskarantæne og kapitalselskaber: Om ejerbeføjelser og ledelsesbeføjelser*, 16 NTS 1 (2014).

Stefanie Meier-Gubser, *Selbständig oder nicht?*, VRPRAXIS UnternehmerZeitung (2017).

M. Elvira Mendez-Pinedo, *The Principle of Effectiveness of EU Law: A Difficult Concept in Legal Scholarship*, 11 Tribuna Juridica 1 (2021).

Emanuel Menegatti, *The Evolving Concept of 'Worker' in EU Law*, 12 ILLE-J 1, 82 (2019).

C.G.J. Morse, *The EEC Convention on the Law Applicable to Contractual Obligations*, 2 YEL 1, 107-171 (1982).

Guy Mundlak, *Human Rights and Labor Rights: Why Don't the Two Tracks Meet?*, 34 CLLPJ (2012).

Mihir Naniwadekar, *The Law of Agency as Applied in Company Transactions*, 5 ECFR 280, 286 (2008).

Cristóbal Molina Navarrete, *La actualidad de la cuestión de las 'zonas concurrentes' entre el Derecho Mercantil y el Derecho del Trabajo. Apuntes a propósito del libro*

"La representación orgánica y voluntaria en las sociedades de capital", del profesor Dr. Angel Martínez Gutiérrez, 4 RGLJ 573-588 (2005).

Eva Van Ooij, *Highly Mobile Workers Challenging Regulation 883/2004: Pushing or Opening Pandora's Box?*, 27 MJ 5 (2020).

Joaquim Vieira Peres & Catarina Vieira Peres de Fraipont, *Non-compete Clauses and Fines on Natural Persons: The Blueotter and EGEO Case (Portugal)*, 13 JECLAP 4 (2022), https://doi.org/10.1093/jeclap/lpab087.

Siniša Petrović & Petar Ceronja, *Corporate Effects of the Danosa Case: Is the Termination of Membership of the Board of Directors Allowed in the Case of a Pregnant Board Member?*, 8 CYELP 1, 437-456 (2012).

Michiel Poesen, *Concurrent Liabilities and Jurisdiction over Individual Contracts of Employment under the Brussels Ia Regulation*, 16 J. Priv. Int. L. 2 (2020).

Francisco Trujillo Pons, *Las personas trabajadoras que ocupan 'puestos directivos' y su derecho a la desconexión digital en el trabajo*, 1 Iuslabor 148-167 (2022).

Valeria Pulignano & Jeremy Waddington, *Management, European Works Councils and Institutional Malleability*, 26 EJIR 1 (2020).

Stephan Rammeloo, *Companies & Firms in a Cross-Border EU Context: The Hybrid Legal Status of Managers in Cross-Border Civil Procedural Law ... and Further*, 16 ECL 4 (2019).

Stephan Rammeloo, *CJEU C-603/18 (Bosworth & Hurley V. Arcadia & Others): The Status of Company Officers (or Employees?) in Cross-Border Civil Proceedings & Jurisdictions of Courts under the 2007 'Lugano II' Convention*, 17 ECL 2 (2020).

Jonathan Rickford, *Fundamentals, Developments and Trends in British Company Law: Some Wider Reflections* ECFR 391, 405 (2004).

Georg Ringe, *German Versus Nordic Board Models: Form, Function, and Convergence*, 65 NJB 1, 27 et seq. (2016).

Markus Roth, *Unabhängige Aufsichtsratsmitglieder*, 175 ZHR 605, 630 et seq. (2011).

Blanche Segrestin et al., *The Separation of Directors and Managers: A Historical Examination of the Status of Managers*, 25 JMH 2 (2019).

Marco Staake, *Arbeitnehmervertreter als unabhängige Aufsichtsratsmitglieder?*, 19 NZG 853 et seq. (2016).

Eva Staal & Jens Røn, *Konkurskarantæne – en status*, UfR B 25 (2020).

Karsten Engsig Sørensen *Front' or 'Straw Men' Directors: A Missing Element in the Effort to Prevent Abuse of Companies?* ECFR 749 (2021).

Karsten Engsig Sørensen, *Nationality and Residency Requirements for Corporate Management: A Comment to the EFTA Courts Decision in E-9/20, ESA v. Norway*, 4 NTS 1-10 (2021).

Karsten Engsig Sørensen, *Free Movement of Companies under the New Trade and Cooperation Agreement Between the EU and the UK*, 4 ECL 117-124 (2021).

Karsten Engsig Sørensen, *The Legal Position of Parent Companies: A Top-Down Focus on Group Governance*, Nordic and European Company Law Working Paper No. 19-05 (2021).

Christoph Teichmann, *Towards a European Framework for Cross-Border Group Management* 150-157 13 ECL 5 (2016).

Christoph Teichmann, *Die digitale GmbH-Gründung: Ein Entwicklungssprung für die vorsorgende Rechtspflege*, GmbHR 1237 (2021).

Joaquín Huelin Martínez De Velasco, *El acervo comunitario sobre prevención de riesgos laborales* 100 Estudios de Derecho Judicial 49-82 (2006).

Reports

Administrative Commission for the Coordination of Social Security Systems: *Practical Guide on the Applicable Legislation in the European Union (EU), the European Economic Area (EEA) and in Switzerland* (2013).

BAG 23.10.2008 - 2 ABR 59/07, NZA 855 (2009).

BGH, Urt. v. 15.11.1982 - II ZR 27/82, 36 NJW 991 (1983).

Deutscher Gewerkschaftsbund, *Stellungnahme zum Entwurf eines Gesetzes zur Umsetzung der zweiten Aktionärsrechterichtlinie (ARUG II)*, 13 May 2019.

European Commission 'green paper' on Employee Participation and Company Structure, COM (75) 570 final, Bulletin of the EC, Supplement 8/75, in particular of 'Sociétés Anonymes'.

European Commission, *Green Paper – Corporate Governance in Financial Institutions and Remuneration Policies*, COM (2010) 285 final.

European Commission, *GREEN PAPER The EU Corporate Governance Framework*, COM(2011) 164 final.

European Commission, Directorate-General Internal Market: Holly J. Gregory, Robert T. Simmelkjaer, II, *Comparative Study of Corporate Governance Codes Relevant to the European Union and Its Member States* (2002).

European Commission, *Covid-19: Information for Frontier Workers and Posted Workers* (2020).

European Commission, Directorate-General for Justice, Nicola Countouris and Mark Freedland, *The Personal Scope of the EU Sex Equality Directives* (Publications Office 2013).

European Parliament, *Report on the proposal for a Council directive establishing a general framework for equal treatment in employment and occupation*, COM (1999) 565 final, A5-0264/2000, 21.9.2000.

European Commission, Directorate-General Employment, *Report Expert Group, Transposition of Directive (EU) 2019/1152 on transparent and predictable working conditions in the European Union* (2021).

Betænkning nr 423 (1966) Konkursordenen, Betænkning I, Afgivet af det Justitsministeriet den 29. januar 1958 nedsatte udvalg.

Mario Giuliano & Paul Lagarde, *Report on the Convention on the Law Applicable to Contractual Obligations*, OJ C 282, 31.10.1980.

Ministry of labour and social policy Italy, *National plan for access to social protection by subordinate and autonomous workers* (2021).

Mutual Information System on Social Protection (MISSOC), *Social protection for the self-employed: Germany* Mutual Information System on Social Protection (MISSOC), *Social protection for the self-employed: Italy* (2021).

Mutual Information System on Social Protection (MISSOC), Social protection for the self-employed: Switzerland (2021).

Oberlandesgericht Düsseldorf, NZG 1385 (2019).

OECD, *OECD Corporate Governance Factbook* (2021), https://www.oecd.org/corporate/corporategovernance-factbook.htm.

OECD, *G20/OECD Principles of Corporate Governance* 57-58 (VI.E. 2015), available at: https://ecgi.global/content/codes.

Martin Risak & Thomas Dullinger, *The concept of 'worker' in EU law: status quo and potential for change*, The European Trade Union Institute, Report 140 (ETUI 2018).

Slavina Spasova, Denis Bouget, Dalila Ghailani & Bart Vanhercke, *Access to Social Protection for People Working on Non-standard Contracts and as Self-Employed in Europe: A Study of National Policies 2017*, European Social Policy Network (ESPN), European Commission (2017).

Grega Strban, Dolores Carrascosa Bermejo, Paul Schoukens & Ivana Vukorpa, *Analytical Report 2018 – Social Security Coordination and Non-standard Forms of Employment and Self-Employment: Interrelation, Challenges and Prospects* (European Commission 2020).

Carlo Zoli, Andrea Lassandari, Ester Villa, Cinzia Carta, Giulia Marchi, Nicola De Luigi, Giovanni Guidetti & Luca Cattani, *National Report Italy: Executive Summary*, Working Yet Poor D3.2 (2021).

Electronic Sources

Dariusz Aziewics, *Antitrust Penalties for Individuals in Poland*, Kluwer Competition Law Blog (14 Jan. 2022), http://competitionlawblog.kluwercompetitionlaw.com/2022/01/14/antitrust-penalties-for-individuals-in-poland/.

Australian Competition Authority, The Australian Competition Authority secures a guilty plea from the former CEO of a waste management company for price fixing (Daniel Tartak), e-Competitions October 2022, Art. no. 109173 (20 Oct. 2022), https://www.concurrences.com/en/bulletin/news-issues/october-2022/the-australian-competition-authority-secures-a-guilty-plea-from-the-former-ceo.

Berlingske: *To firmaer er tiltalt for kartelaftale på vejstribe-opgaver*, Ritzau (25 November 2021), https://www.berlingske.dk/samfund/to-firmaer-er-tiltalt-for-kartelaftale-paa-vejstribe-opgaver.

Canadian Competition Bureau, The Canadian Competition Authority secures a fifth guilty plea and $25,000 from an engineering executive implicated in the Gatineau bid rigging scandal (Francois Paulhus / Genivar), e-Competitions October 2022, Art. no. 109129 (14 Oct. 2022), https://www.concurrences.com/en/bulletin/news-issues/october-2022/the-canadian-competition-authority-secures-a-fifth-guilty-plea-and-25-000-from.

Louise Carpenter, *The CEO of Lloyds Bank Turned Its Fortunes Around: But the Anxiety Almost Broke Him*, The Times (7 October 2017, 12.01 AM BST), https://www.thetimes.co.uk/article/the-ceo-of-lloyds-bank-turned-its-fortunes-around-but-the-anxiety-almost-broke-him-fg970cpjr.

Corporate Governance Codes, European Corporate Governance Institute (ECGI) https://ecgi.global/content/codes.

Danish Competition and Consumer Authority: *National Judgements*, https://www.en.kfst.dk/competition/national-judgements/.

Danish Competition and Consumer Authority, *Virksomheders oplysningspligt og beskyttelse mod selvinkriminering* (October 2021). https://www.kfst.dk/media/ysdir2vq/ekstern-vejledning-om-selvinkriminering-a.pdf.

Jan Dop, *Statutair bestuurder of titulair bestuurder?*, Russell Advocaten (25 juni 2020), https://www.russell.nl/publicatie/statutair-bestuurder-titulair-bestuurder/.

Eurocadres: *about us*, https://www.eurocadres.eu/about-us/.

Ben Laker, Vijay Pereira, Ashish Malik & Marcello Mariani, *What First-Time Managers Can Do to Address Burnout*, Harvard Business Review (19 June 2022), https://hbr.org/2022/03/what-first-time-managers-can-do-to-address-burnout.

Pinsent Masons: *Individual Liability for UK Competition Law Infringements*, OUT-LAW GUIDE (1 December 2020), https://www.pinsentmasons.com/out-law/guides/individuals-liability-uk-competition-law-infringements.

The Insolvency Service, *Insolvency Service Enforcement Outcomes: 2020/21* (30 October 2022), https://www.gov.uk/government/statistics/insolvency-service-enforcement-outcomes-202021.

International Labour Organization, *International Labour Conference Adds Safety and Health to Fundamental Principles and Rights at Work* (10 June 2022) https://www.ilo.org/global/about-the-ilo/newsroom/news/WCMS_848132/lang--en/index.htm.

International Labour Organization, *Ratifications of Fundamental Instruments by Country*, https://www.ilo.org/dyn/normlex/en/f?p=NORMLEXPUB:10011:0::NO::P10011_DISPLAY_BY,P10011_CONVENTION_TYPE_CODE:1,F.

International Labour Organization, *Work for a Brighter Future – Global Commission on the Future of Work* (2019), https://www.ilo.org/wcmsp5/groups/public/---dgreports/---cabinet/documents/publication/wcms_662410.pdf.

Mariska van de Sanden & Tialda Beetstra, *Dutch Court Holds Former Director Personally Liable for North Sea Shrimps Cartel Fine*, Kluwer Competition Law Blog (13 October 2020), http://competitionlawblog.kluwercompetitionlaw.com/2020/10/13/dutch-court-holds-former-director-personally-liable-for-north-sea-shrimps-cartel-fine/.

Marco Slotboom, *Individual Liability for Cartel Infringement in the EU: An Increasingly Dangerous Minefield*, Kluwer Competition Law Blog (25 April 2013), http://competitionlawblog.kluwercompetitionlaw.com/2013/04/25/individual-liability-for-cartel-infringements-in-the-eu-an-increasingly-dangerous-minefield/.

Sociale Zekerheid/Onderneming: Mandaathouders van vennootschappen, Instructies 2022/3, https://www.socialsecurity.be/employer/instructions/dmfa/nl/latest/instructions/persons/specific/mandatariesorshareholders_commercialcompanies.html.

US Department of Justice Antitrust Division: The US District Court for the Eastern District of North Carolina sentences a former engineering executive for rigging bids and defrauding the North Carolina Department of Transportation (Brent Brewbaker), e-Competitions September 2022, Art. no. 108585 (8 September 2022), https://www.concurrences.com/en/bulletin/news-issues/september-2022/the-us-district-court-for-the-eastern-district-of-north-carolina-sentences.

Table of Cases

European Case Law

[A] Court of Justice of the European Union (CJEU)

[B] Advocate-General opinions

[C] EFTA Court

[D] European Court of Human Rights (ECHR)

[E] European Committee of Social Rights (ECSR)

National Case Law

[A] Denmark

[B] Germany

[C] Norway

[D] Spain

[E] Sweden

[F] United Kingdom

BCLR - BULLETIN OF COMPARATIVE LABOUR RELATIONS

Vol. Author/Title/Year/ISBN

1. Roger Blanpain, *Individual Employment Contracts: Collective Agreements*, 1970.
2. Roger Blanpain, *Social Planning*, 1971 (ISBN 90-312-0018-2).
3. Roger Blanpain, *Guaranteed Income Funds*, 1972 (ISBN 90-312-0019-0).
4. Roger Blanpain, *Employee Participation at the Level of the Enterprise*, 1973 (ISBN 90-312-0020-4).
5. Roger Blanpain, *Vastheid van Betrekking: Staking en Bezetting*, 1974.
6. Roger Blanpain, *Labour Law and Industrial Relations (International Bibliography)*, 1975 (ISBN 90-312-0023-9).
7. Roger Blanpain, *Multinational Enterprises*, 1976 (ISBN 90-312-0024-7).
8. Roger Blanpain, *Worker's Participation in the European Company*, 1977 (ISBN 90-312-0044-1).
9. Roger Blanpain, *Women and Labour*, 1978 (ISBN 90-312-0077-8).
10. Roger Blanpain, *European Conference on Labour Law and Industrial Relations: Multinational Enterprises*, 1979 (ISBN 90-312-0091-3).
11. Roger Blanpain, *Job Security and Industrial Relations*, 1980 (ISBN 90-312-0147-2).
12. Roger Blanpain, Greg Bamber & Russell Lansbury, *Technological Change and Industrial Relations: An International Symposium*, 1983 (ISBN 90-312-0205-3).
13. Roger Blanpain, James Janssen van Raay & A. Moulty, *Worker's Participation in the European Community: The Fifth Directive*, 1984 (ISBN 90-654-4187-5).
14. Roger Blanpain, *Equality and Prohibition of Discrimination in Employment*, 1985 (ISBN 90-654-4215-4).
15. Roger Blanpain, *Restructuring Labour in the Enterprise: Law and Practice in France, F.R. of Germany, Italy, Sweden and the United Kingdom*, 1986 (ISBN 90-654-4283-9).
16. Roger Blanpain & E. Kassalow, *Unions and Industrial Relations: Recent Trends and Prospect: A Comparative Treatment*, 1987 (ISBN 90-654-4294-4).
17. Roger Blanpain & Marco Biagi, *Trade Union Democracy and Industrial Relations*, 1988 (ISBN 90-654-4394-0).
18. Roger Blanpain & Jelle Visser, *In Search of Inclusive Unionism*, 1990 (ISBN 90-654-4439-4).
19. Roger Blanpain, *Flexibility and Wages: A Comparative Treatment*, 1990 (ISBN 90-654-4461-0).

20. Roger Blanpain, Stephen Frenkel & Oliver Clarke, *Economic Restructuring and Industrial Relations in Industrialised Countries,* 1990 (ISBN 90-654-4488-2).
21. Roger Blanpain & Friedrich Fürstenberg, *Structure and Strategy in Industrial Relations,* 1991 (ISBN 90-654-4559-5).
22. Roger Blanpain, Amira Galin & Ozer Carmi, *Flexible Work Patterns and Their Impact on Industrial Relations,* 1991 (ISBN 90-654-4572-2).
23. Roger Blanpain, *Workers' Participation: Influence on Management Decision-Making by Labour in the Private Sector,* 1992 (ISBN 90-654-4600-1).
24. Roger Blanpain, Brian Brooks & Chris Engels, *Employed or Self-Employed,* 1992 (ISBN 90-654-4613-3).
25. Roger Blanpain & Tiziano Treu, *Industrial Relations Developments in the Telecommunications Industry,* 1993 (ISBN 90-654-4642-7).
26. Roger Blanpain & Marco Biagi, *Industrial Relations in Small and Medium Sized Enterprises,* 1993 (ISBN 90-654-4696-6).
27. Roger Blanpain & Marco Biagi, *Participative Management and Industrial Relations in a Worldwide Perspective,* 1993 (ISBN 90-654-4769-5).
28. Roger Blanpain, Jacques Rojot & Hoyt N. Wheeler, *Employee Rights and Industrial Justice,* 1994 (ISBN 90-654-4804-7).
29. Roger Blanpain & Ruth Ben-Israel, *Strikes and Lock-Outs in Industrialized Market Economies,* 1994 (ISBN 90-654-4841-1).
30. Roger Blanpain, Kazuo Sugeno & Yasuo Suwa, *The Harmonization of Working Life and Family Life,* 1995 (ISBN 90-411-0064-4).
31. Roger Blanpain & Laszio Nagy, *Labour Law and Industrial Relations in Central and Eastern Europe,* 1996 (ISBN 90-411-0298-1).
32. Roger Blanpain, *Labour Law and Industrial Relations in the European Union,* 1997 (ISBN 90-411-0527-1).
33. Taco Van Peijpe, *Employment Protection under Strain,* 1998 (ISBN 90-411-0528-8).
34. Roger Blanpain, Takashi Araki & Ryuichi Yamakawa, *The Process of Industrialization and the Role of Labour Law in Asia,* 1999 (ISBN 9-041-1104-7-X).
35. Roger Blanpain & Marco Biagi, *Non-standard Work and Industrial Relations,* 1999 (ISBN 90-411-1117-4).
36. Roger Blanpain, *Private Employment Agencies: The Impact of ILO Convention 181 (1997) and the Judgment of the European Court of Justice of 11 December 1997,* 1999 (ISBN 90-411-1118-2).
37. Roger Blanpain, *Multinational Enterprises and the Social Challenges of the XXIst Century: The ILO Declaration on Fundamental* Principles *at Work, Public and Private Corporate Codes of Conduct,* 2000 (ISBN 90-411-1280-4).
38. Roger Blanpain, Ryuichi Yamakawa & Takashi Araki, *Deregulation and Labour Law: In Search of a Labour Concept for the 21st Century,* 2000 (ISBN 90-411-1370-3).
39. Roger Blanpain, *The Council of Europe and the Social Challenges of the XXIst Century,* 2001 (ISBN 90-411-1543-9).

40. Roger Blanpain, *On-Line Rights for Employees in the Information Society, Use & Monitoring of E-Mail & Internet at Work*, 2002 (ISBN 90-411-1626-5).
41. Roger Blanpain, *The Evolving Employment Relationship and the New Economy: The Role of Labour Law & Industrial Relations*, 2001 (ISBN 90-411-1691-5).
42. Roger Blanpain, *Involvement of Employees in the European Union, Works Councils, Company Statute, Information and Consultation Rights*, 2002 (ISBN 90-411-1760-1).
43. Michele Colucci, *The Impact of the Internet and New Technologies on the Workplace: A Legal Analysis from a Comparative Point of View*, 2002 (ISBN 90-411-1824-1).
44. Roger Blanpain, *White Paper on the Labour Market in Italy: The Quality of European Industrial Relations and Changing Industrial Relations*, 2002 (ISBN 90-411-1841-1).
45. Roger Blanpain, Russell D. Lansbury & Young-Bum Park, *Impact of Globalisation on Employment Relations: A Comparison of the Automobile and Banking Industries in Australia and Korea*, 2002 (ISBN 90-411-1850-0).
46. Roger Blanpain & Antoine Jacobs, *Employee Rights in Bankruptcy: A Comparative-Law Assessment*, 2002 (ISBN 90-411-1942-6).
47. Roger Blanpain, Takashi Araki & Shinya Ouchi, *Corporate Restructuring and the Role of Labour Law*, 2003 (ISBN 90-411-1949-3).
48. Roger Blanpain, *Collective Bargaining, Discrimination, Social Security and European Integration*, 2003 (ISBN 90-411-2010-6).
49. Roger Blanpain & Luis Aparicio-Valdez, *Labour Relations in the Asia- Pacific Countries*, 2004 (ISBN 90-411-2239-7).
50. Roger Blanpain & Ronnie Graham, *Temporary Agency Work and the Information Society*, 2004 (ISBN 90-411-2252-4).
51. Roger Blanpain, *The Actors of Collective Bargaining: A World Report*, 2004 (ISBN 90-411-2253-2).
52. Roger Blanpain & Michele Colucci, *The Globalisation of Labour Standards: The Soft Law Track*, 2004 (ISBN 90-411-2303-2).
53. Roger Blanpain, Takashi Araki & Shinya Ouchi, *Labour Law in Motion: Diversification of the Labour Force & Terms and Conditions of Employment*, 2005 (ISBN 90-411-2315-6).
54. Roger Blanpain, *Smoking and the Workplace*, 2005 (ISBN 90-411-2325-3).
55. Roger Blanpain, *Confronting Globalization: The Quest for a Social Agenda*, 2005 (ISBN 90-411-2381-4).
56. Roger Blanpain, Thomas Blanke & Edgar Rose, *Collective Bargaining Wages in Comparative Perspective: Germany, France, the Netherlands, Sweden and the United Kingdom*, 2005 (ISBN 90-411-2388-1).
57. Roger Blanpain & Anne Numhauser-Henning, *Women in Academia & Equality Law: Aiming High - Falling Short?*, 2006 (ISBN 978-90-411-2427-6).
58. Roger Blanpain, *Freedom of Services in the European Union: Labour and Social Security Law: The Bolkestein Initiative*, 2006 (ISBN 978-90-411-2453-5).
59. Roger Blanpain, Frans Pennings & Nurhan Sural, *Flexibilisation and Modernisation of the Turkish Labour Market*, 2006 (ISBN 978-90-411-2490-X).

60. Roger Blanpain & Boel Flodgren, *Corporate and Employment Perspectives in a Global Business Environment*, 2006 (ISBN 978-90-411-2537-X).
61. Roger Blanpain, Shinya Ouchi & Takashi Araki, *Decentralizing Industrial Relations and The Role of Labor Unions and Employee Representatives*, 2007 (ISBN 978-90-411-2583-3).
62. Roger Blanpain, *European Framework Agreements and Telework: Law and Practice: A European and Comparative Study*, 2007 (ISBN 978-90-411-2560-4).
63. Roger Blanpain, Jim Kitay, Leanne Cutcher & Nick Wailes, *Globalization and Employment Relations in Retail Banking*, 2007 (ISBN 978-90-411-2620-1).
64. Roger Blanpain, Russell Lansbury, Jim Kitay, Nick Wailes & Anja Kirsch, *Globalization and Employment Relations in the Auto Assembly Industry: A Study of Seven Countries*, 2008 (ISBN 978-90-411-2698-6).
65. Roger Blanpain & Michele Tiraboschi, *The Global Labour Market: From Globalization to Flexicurity*, 2008 (ISBN 978-90-411-2722-8).
66. Roger Blanpain, Michele Colucci & Frank Hendrickx, *The Future of Sport in the European Union: Beyond the EU Reform Treaty and the White Paper*, 2008 (ISBN 978-90-411-2761-7).
67. Roger Blanpain, Linda Dickens, *Challenges in European Employment Relations: Employment Regulation, Trade Union Organization, Equality, Flexicurity, Training and New Approaches to Pay*, 2008 (ISBN 978-90-411-2771-6).
68. Roger Blanpain, Hiroya Nakakubo & Takashi Araki, *New Developments in Employment Discrimination Law, 2008* (ISBN 978-90-411-2782-2).
69. Roger Blanpain, Andrzej Marian wiątkowski, *The Laval and Viking Cases: Freedom of Services and Establishment v. Industrial Conflict in the European Economic Area and Russia*, 2009 (ISBN 978-90-411-2850-8).
70. Roger Blanpain, William Bromwich, Olga Rymkevich, Silvia Spattini, *The Modernization of Labour Law and Industrial Relations in a Comparative Perspective*, 2009 (ISBN 978-90-411-2865-2).
71. Roger Blanpain, Juan Pablo Landa & Brian Langille, *Employment Policies and Multilevel Governance*, 2009 (ISBN 978-90-411-2866-9).
72. Roger Blanpain, European Works Councils; *The European Directive 2009/ 38/EC of 6 May 2009, 2009* (ISBN 978-90-411-3208-6).
73. Roger Blanpain, William Bromwich, Olga Rymkevich & Silvia Spattini, *Labour Productivity, Investment in Human Capital and Youth Employment: Comparative Developments and Global Responses*, 2010 (ISBN 978-90-411-3249-9).
74. Greg J. Bamber & Philippe Pochet, *Regulating Employment Relations, Work and Labour Laws: International Comparisons between Key Countries*, 2010 (ISBN 978-90-411-3199-7). General Editor: Roger Blanpain.
75. Roger Blanpain, Desislava Nikolaeva Dimitrova, *Seafarers' Rights in the Globalized Maritime Industry*, 2010 (ISBN 978-90-411-3349-6).
76. Roger Blanpain, Hiroya Nakakubo & Takashi Araki, *Regulation of Fixed- Term Employment Contracts*, 2010 (ISBN 978-90-411-3356-4).

77. Roger Blanpain, William Bromwich, Olga Rymkevich & Iacopo Senatori, *Rethinking Corporate Governance*, 2011 (ISBN 978-90-411-3450-9).
78. Roger Blanpain & Frank Hendrickx, *Labour Law between Change and Tradition: Liber Amicorum Antoine Jacobs*, 2011 (ISBN 978-90-411-3424-0).
79. Roger Blanpain, Thomas Klebe, Marlene Schmidt & Bernd Waas, *Trade Union Rights at the Workplace*, 2012 (ISBN 978-90-411-3460-8).
80. Roger Blanpain, William Bromwich, Olga Rymkevich & Iacopo Senatori, *Labour Markets, Industrial Relations and Human Resources Management: From Recession to Recovery*, 2012 (ISBN 978-90-411-4004-3).
81. Roger Blanpain, Hiroya Nakakubo & Takashi Araki, *Systems of Employee Representation at the Enterprise: A Comparative Study*, 2012 (ISBN 978-90-411-4080-7).
82. Roger Blanpain & Frank Hendrickx, *Temporary Agency Work in the European Union and the United States*, 2013 (ISBN 978-90-411-4769-1).
83. Roger Blanpain, Toker Dereli, Y. Pınar Soykut-Sarıca & Aslı en-Tabaı, *Emerging Patterns of Work and Turkish Labour Market Challenges under Globalization: Readings on Labour and Employment Relations*, 2014 (ISBN 978-90-411-4983-1).
84. Roger Blanpain, Pablo Arellano Ortiz, Marius Olivier & Gijsbert Vonk, *Social Security and Migrant Workers: Selected Studies of Cross-border Social Security Mechanisms*, 2014 (ISBN 978-90-411-4770-7).
85. Roger Blanpain & Nikita Lyutov, *Workers' Representation in Central and Eastern Europe: Challenges and Opportunities for the Works Councils' System*, 2014 (ISBN 978-90-411-4746-2).
86. Roger Blanpain, Ulla Liukkunen & Chen Yifeng, *China and ILO Fundamental Principles and Rights at Works*, 2014 (ISBN 978-90-411-4984-8).
87. Roger Blanpain, *The Use of Languages and Employment Relations*, 2014 (ISBN 978-90-411-5606-8).
88. Roger Blanpain, Hiroya Nakakubo & Takashi Araki, *Protection of Employees' Personal Information and Privacy*, 2014 (ISBN 978-90-411-5608-2).
89. Roger Blanpain, Jan Wouters, Glenn Rayp, Laura Beke & Axel Marx, *Protecting Labour Rights in a Multi-polar Supply Chain and Mobile Global Economy*, 2015 (ISBN 978-90-411-5662-4).
90. Roger Blanpain & Stefania Marassi, *Globalization and Transnational Collective Labour Relations: International and European Framework Agreements at Company Level*, 2015 (ISBN 978-90-411-4748-6).
91. Roger Blanpain, Frank Hendrickx & Petra Herzfeld Olsson, *National Effects of the Implementation of EU Directives on Labour Migration from Third Countries*, 2016 (ISBN 978-90-411-6257-1).
92. Roger Blanpain, Frank Hendrickx & D'Arcy du Toit, *Labour Law and Social Progress: Holding the Line or Shifting the Boundaries?* 2016 (ISBN 978-90-411-6747-7).

93. Roger Blanpain & Frank Hendrickx, *Reasonable Accommodation in the Modern Workplace: Potential and Limits of the Integrative Logics of Labour Law*, 2016 (ISBN 978-90-411-6258-8).
94. Roger Blanpain, Frank Hendrickx & Bernd Waas, *New Forms of Employment in Europe*, 2016 (ISBN 978-90-411-6239-7).
95. Roger Blanpain, Frank Hendrickx, Hiroya Nakakubo & Takashi Araki, *The Notion of Employer in the Era of the Fissured Workplace: Should Labour Law Responsibilities Exceed the Boundary of the Legal Entity?*, 2017 (ISBN 978-90-411-8470-2).
96. Elena Sychenko, *Individual Labour Rights as Human Rights: The Contributions of the European Court of Human Rights to Worker's Rights Protection*, 2017 (ISBN 978-90-411-8629-4).
97. William Bromwich & Olga Rymkevich, *Improving Workplace Quality: New Perspectives and Challenges for Worker Well-Being*, 2017 (ISBN 978-90-411-8628-7).
98. Sarah De Groof, *Work-Life Balance in the Modern Workplace: Interdisciplinary Perspectives from Work-Family Research, Law and Policy*, 2017 (ISBN 978-90-411-8630-0).
99. Sylvaine Laulom, *Collective Bargaining Developments in Times of Crisis*, 2018 (ISBN 978-90-411-8999-8).
100. Frank Hendrickx & Valerio De Stefano, *Game Changers in Labour Law: Shaping the Future of Work*, 2018 (ISBN 978-90-411-9953-9).
101. Ivana Palinkaš, *The Legal and Institutional Framing of Collective Bargaining in CEE Countries: Between Europeanisation and Decentralisation*, 2018 (ISBN 978-90-411-9199-1).
102. Jeremy Waddington, *European Board-Level Employee Representation: National Variations in Influence and Power*, 2018 (ISBN 978-90-411-9202-8).
103. Jan Pichrt & Kristina Koldinská, *Labour Law and Social Protection in a Globalized World: Changing Realities in Selected Areas of Law and Policy*, 2018 (ISBN 978-94-035-0093-5).
104. Matthew W. Finkin, *American Labor and the Law: Dormant, Resurgent, and Emergent Problems*, 2019 (ISBN 978-94-035-0654-8).
105. Giuseppe Casale & Tiziano Treu, *Transformations of Work: Challenges for the Institutions and Social Actors*, 2019 (ISBN 978-94-035-0891-7).
106. Miguel De la Corte-Rodríguez, *EU Law on Maternity and Other Child-Related Leaves: Impact on Gender Equality*, 2019 (ISBN 978-94-035-1452-9).
107. Valeria Pulignano & Frank Hendrickx, *Employment Relations in the 21st Century: Challenges for Theory and Research in a Changing World of Work*, 2020 (ISBN 978-94-035-1764-3).
108. Matteo Bottero, *Posting of Workers in EU Law: Challenges of Equality, Solidarity and Fair Competition*, 2021 (ISBN 978-94-035-2860-1).
109. Bernd Waas & Christina Hießl, *Collective Bargaining for Self-Employed Workers in Europe: Approaches to Reconcile Competition Law and Labour Rights*, 2021 (ISBN 978-94-035-2373-6).

110. Mathias Wouters, *International Labour Standards and Platform Work: An Analysis of Digital Labour Platforms Based on the Instruments on Private Employment Agencies, Home Work and Domestic Work*, 2022 (ISBN 978-94-035-4024-5).
111. Luca Ratti, *In-Work Poverty in Europe: Vulnerable and Under-Represented Persons in a Comparative Perspective*, 2022 (ISBN 978-94-035-4996-5).
112. Silvia Rainone, *The Role of the Court of Justice in EU Labour Law: A Case Study on the Transfer of Undertakings Directive*, 2023 (ISBN 978-94-035-2896-0).
113. Frank Hendrickx, Elena Gramano & David Mangan, *Privacy@work: A European and Comparative Perspective*, 2023 (ISBN 978-94-035-3106-9).
114. Elena Sychenko & Adalberto Perulli, *Employment Law and the European Convention on Human Rights: The Research of the Recent Jurisprudence of the ECtHR Related to Employment Law (2017-2021)*, 2023 (ISBN 978-94-035-3556-2).
115. Ilda Durri, *Casual Work Arrangements and Platform-Based Work: The Casual Work Agenda as a Way to Enhance the Labour Protection of Platform Workers*, 2023 (ISBN 978-94-035-3107-6).
116. Charalampos Stylogiannis, *Collective Labour Rights for Self-Employed Workers: A Human Rights-Based Approach of Platform Work*, 2023 (ISBN 978-94-035-0667-8).
117. Heather Kurzbauer, *Employment Vulnerabilities in the World of Orchestral Musicians: Symphonic Metamorphoses*, 2023 (ISBN 978-94-035-2737-6).
118. Natalie Videbæk Munkholm, Vincenzo Pietrogiovanni & Karsten Engsig Sørensen, *Managers in European Law: Rights and Duties of Executive and Non-executive Managers in a European Perspective*, 2024 (ISBN 978-94-035-3286-8).

Made in United States
Orlando, FL
12 May 2026

81305751R30164